TRANSLATING WORLDS

Hau
BOOKS

www.haubooks.com

TRANSLATING WORLDS
THE EPISTEMOLOGICAL SPACE OF TRANSLATION

Special Issues in Ethnographic Theory Series

Edited by
William F. Hanks and Carlo Severi

Hau Books
Chicago

© 2015 Hau Books

Hau Special Issues in Ethnographic Theory Series (Volume 1)

The Hau Special Issues in Ethnographic Theory Series prints paperback versions of pathbreaking collections, previously published in Hau: Journal of Ethnographic Theory.

Cover and layout design: Sheehan Moore
Typesetting: Prepress Plus (www.prepressplus.in)

ISBN: 978-0-9861325-1-3
LCCN: 2015952083

Hau Books
Chicago Distribution Center
11030 S. Langley
Chicago, IL 60628
www.haubooks.com

Hau Books is marketed and distributed by The University of Chicago Press.
www.press.uchicago.edu

Printed in the United States of America on acid-free paper.

Contents

List of Contributors

Adam Yuet Chau (Ph.D. in Anthropology, 2001, Stanford University) teaches in the Department of East Asian Studies, University of Cambridge, and is a Fellow at St. John's College. He is the author of *Miraculous response: Doing popular religion in contemporary China* (Stanford University Press, 2006) and editor of *Religion in contemporary China: Revitalization and innovation* (Routledge, 2011). He is currently working on book projects investigating the idiom of hosting (*zuozhu*) and forms of powerful writing ("text acts") in Chinese political and religious culture.

Emmanuel de Vienne is Associate Professor at the University of Nanterre, France. He conducted fieldword among the Trumai in the Upper Xingu Region (Mato Grosso, Brasil). His topics of interest include shamanism, ritual, and joking relationships.

Carlos Fausto is Associate Professor of Anthropology at the Museu Nacional, Universidade Federal do Rio de Janeiro. He is the author of *Os Índios antes do Brasil* (2000), *Inimigos fiéis* (2001) and *Warfare and shamanism in Amazonia* (2012). He is the coeditor (with Michael J. Heckenberger) of *Time and memory in indigenous Amazonia* (2007) and (with Carlo Severi) *L'image rituelle* (2014).

William F. Hanks received the Joint Ph.D. in Linguistics and Anthropology from the University of Chicago in 1983 and currently teaches in the Department of Anthropology, University of California, Berkeley, where he is also Director of Social Science Matrix, a cross-disciplinary research institute. He investigates the relation between grammar and communicative practices, colonial history, and contemporary shamanism among the Maya of Yucatán, Mexico.

John Leavitt eaches in the anthropology department of the Université de Montréal, specializing in linguistic anthropology. He has conducted field research in the Central Himalayas of northern India and in Ireland and has published on comparative mythology, oral poetry, and the history of linguistic relativity.

Geoffrey E. R. Lloyd is Professor Emeritus of Ancient Philosophy and Science at the University of Cambridge and is now based at the Needham Research Institute. He has published twenty-six books, initially concentrating on ancient Greek philosophy and science and then embarking on detailed comparative studies with ancient Chinese thought. His three most recent books, which tackle the underlying philosophical problems of such comparisons and related issues in cognitive science, are: *Cognitive variations: Reflections on the unity and diversity of the human mind* (2007), *Disciplines in the making* (2009), *Being, humanity and understanding* (2012), and *The ideals of inquiry* (2014), all from Oxford University Press.

Bruce Mannheim is Professor of Anthropology at the University of Michigan and a leading scholar of Andean languages, cultures, and history. His works span from a linguistic history of the Quechua language since the sixteenth century— and its shifting social ecology (the language of the Inka since the European invasion); to narrative; to ritual practices around places; and to Quechua ontology. His current research project is a theory of cultural replication—the ways in which cultural forms are stabilized across time and spread across populations.

Alan Rumsey is a Professor of Anthropology in the College of Asia and the Pacific, Australian National University. His research fields are Highland Papua New Guinea and Aboriginal Australia, with a focus on speech genres and on relations among language, culture, and intersubjectivity

Carlo Severi is Professor (Directeur d'études) at the École des Hautes études en Sciences Sociales and Director of Research (Directeur de recherche) at CNRS. A member of the Laboratoire d'Anthropologie Sociale of the Collège de France since 1985, he has been a Getty Scholar at the Getty Institute for the History of Art and the Humanities in Los Angeles (1994–95), a Fellow of the Wissenschaftskolleg in Berlin (2002–2003), and a Visiting Fellow at Cambridge (1990, 2012). He is the author of *La memoria rituale* (La Nuova Italia, 1993), *Naven or the other self* (with Michael Houseman, Brill, 1998; French edition: CNRS Éditions, 1994), and *The chimera principle* (HAU Books, 2015; French edition: Rue d'Ulm-Musée du Quai Branly, 2007).

Rupert Stasch is a Lecturer in Social Anthropology at the University of Cambridge. He is the author of *Society of others: Kinship and mourning in a West Papuan place* (2009). Since 1995, he has carried out twenty-one months of fieldwork with Korowai speakers of Papua, Indonesia. He is currently writing a book about interactions between Korowai and international tourists.

Anne-Christine Taylor is a social anthropologist, specializing in the study of lowland South American indigenous groups. She is Directrice de Recherche Emeritus at the Centre National de la Recherche Scientifique (CNRS, France), and headed the Department of Research and Teaching at the Musée du Quai Branly from 2005 to 2014.

Translating worlds
The epistemological space of translation

WILLIAM F. HANKS and CARLO SEVERI

WHY TRANSLATION?

Translation has played an important but equivocal role in the history of anthropology and linguistics. Linguists perform multiple translations, usually starting from an acoustic image of speech, or a visual image of a sign, which is transcribed in more or less phonetic detail and subjected to morphological, syntactic, semantic, or pragmatic analysis, depending upon the empirical focus and theoretical framing of the work. In the course of analysis, the object language is translated into the formalism of linguistic description. Even when not explicitly comparative, all of linguistics is virtually comparative insofar as formalisms are assumed to be applicable to many or all languages (Benveniste 1974, 2012). This also implies translating object languages and their grammars into typological categories. The dynamic field of linguistic typology is an outgrowth of this, with much to teach us about translation. Contemporary social and cultural anthropology are of course less formal than linguistics, but no less engaged in translation and comparison. When field notes are recorded, social institutions and discourses are analyzed (such as kinship, residence patterns, exchange or ritual practices), and ethnographic descriptions are crafted, translation is present in every step. And even when not overtly comparative, social and cultural anthropology inevitably involve comparison, and this means translation into some set of terms and concepts that can mediate between the differences among societies and best capture their particular dynamics. The importance of translation is therefore that it is through its multiple varieties that both disciplines constitute their objects and formulate generalizations.

The equivocal status of translating has several sources. First, with the exception of well-known debates in British social anthropology in the 1960s and 1970s, relatively few anthropologists would describe their own craft as a kind of translation—although the issue is coming back to the fore in the recent literature: see Pym (2010), Asad (2010), and Viveiros de Castro's (2004) provocative argument that translation rests on a kind of "controlled equivocation." For a working linguist, very careful attention is paid to analysis, but this analysis is rarely understood as a form of translation. For both fields, cross-language glossing, say from Kuna or Maya into French or English, is a mere heuristic. The load-bearing evidence comes not from a gloss, but from the social or linguistic practices themselves, and it is relative to their own social contexts that utterances, actions, or events gain their meaning. For these reasons, the previous paragraph may appear contentious to some readers. It would seem that we translate from the original mostly in order to abandon the translation in favor of the original. We know in principle that any translation is selective, which implies loss of features from the original, and that any translation also adds in supplementary features absent from the original (Benjamin [1923] 2004; Berman 2008). Ironically, the process of successive failed translation may be our best tool in discerning what is specific to any object society or to any "original." In other words, it becomes a method, as we will show in the next section. Translation is both how we constitute our objects and how we make claims about them. This equivocal duality surely raises the risk of circularity or at least incorrigibility.

A second source of equivocation lies in the fact that fully accurate translation is exceedingly difficult, if not impossible, and yet translation is ubiquitous in social life. We do it all the time. Not only experts translate, but ordinary speakers do too, in the course of everyday activities. Bi-or multilingualism, code switching, blending, crossing, paraphrasing, reported speech, and giving accounts are all well-established sociolinguistic phenomena, and all may involve the same key elements as canonical translation. The fact that they are part of everyday practice, and not only of social science research, is a good reason to pay close attention to translation as a process endogenous to social life.

A related source of equivocation is that while we think of translation as op-erating across languages or social worlds, it is a robust feature of any individual social world, even in monolingual or monocultural societies (if such actually exist). There is a strong line of argument to the effect that understanding is itself a matter of translation: the object understood is translated into some variety of interpretant or representation on the part of the understander. Following Peirce (1955), this can be thought of as a mental representation, a corporeal response to the object, or a variety of other kinds of sign, but in each case, the interpretant can be said to translate its object into an understanding of it. We expand on this point in the light of American pragmatism in the next section. The key point for now is that in the passage of meaning from one language or society to another, translation does not come into play only after the translator has understood the original. It is not an ancillary rerendering or glossing, but is itself the basis for understanding. Translation in one or another variety is always already in play, long before the overt act of rerendering some social object into a foreign lan-guage. This is why we speak of an epistemological space of translation. At stake is what we can know, how we can know it, and how we can make it known.

Translation at a general level is too widespread and the concept is too pow-erful to let it run loose. Our aim in these papers is to relate the anthropologi-cal issues of commensurability, description, and understanding to the linguistic issues of determining and redescribing meaning, at whatever level. We start from the conviction that while different varieties of translation raise different questions, there are important commonalities. By combining, rather than isolat-ing, linguistic and social analysis, we can improve both and point the way to a better theory of translation at all levels. This, we believe, will open a horizon for research in both fields.

FROM RELATIVITY TO INDETERMINACY AND INCOMMENSURABILITY

At least since Saussure ([1916] 2006), Boas (1989), Whorf (1956) and Sapir (1985), languages have been seen as systems whose differences make precise translation exceedingly difficult, if not impossible. In fact, cross-linguistic dif-ferences of nearly equivalent expressions are Saussure's preferred evidence for his signal concept of arbitrariness. The pairing of sound with meaning is ar-bitrary in that it is conventional, and the best evidence of this conventionality is cross-linguistic differences. Given what is ostensibly the same statement translated into, say, French, English, and Kwakiutl, each language expresses it in a unique way, according to its own way of "cutting up reality" into linguistic elements.

For Boas, this function of categorization was central, and he argued convincingly that it has consequences for how speakers of different languages perceive the world. His argument was not that language limits perception, but that the routine expressive patterns of one's native language, especially the obligatory categories, render automatic or unreflective certain features of the worlds we describe. Marking of person, number, tense, deixis, noun classes, and phonology provide well-known examples in which the native speaker is induced to attend to the corresponding features of the scenes (s)he describes. The relativity effect is not about what a native actor can express or understand, but what (s)he usually does express or understand. This gave rise to what is known as classic linguistic relativity in the writings of Edward Sapir and Benjamin Lee Whorf. The former expanded the Boasian focus on categories to include the major grammatical systems of the language, drawing heavily on analogy, while the latter emphasized "habitual ways of speaking" in which languages are used. For both, as for Boas, the twin facts of cross-language difference and intralanguage norms of expression combine to guide or channel the perceptual and expressive habits of speakers. Although it has proven very difficult to demonstrate relativity effects conclusively, there has been a resurgence of research in the area over the last two decades (Hill and Mannheim 1992; Lucy 1992; Levinson 2003; Leavitt 2010; Enfield and Levinson 2006; Enfield and Sidnell 2012) as well as a large literature in cognitive and psychologically oriented linguistics (see, e.g., Gentner and Goldin-Meadow 2003). Like the translator, the relativity theorist must know at least two languages, contrasting them in order to better understand the specificity of each. Unlike translation, however, relativity theory, at least in it mainstream variants, has been based on the model of the monolingual speaker. When Whorf describes how Hopi speakers conceptualize time, or when Boas makes claims about Kwakiutl, they are imagining the native speaker caught in the grips of the native grammar. But what if the Hopi or Kwakiutl speaker is also a fluent English speaker? For a classical relativist, (s)he would be caught in a sort of parallax in which competing constraints vie for causal impact on her or his expressive and perceptual habits. Alternatively, the bilingual speaker might be subject to both systems and their respective habitual patterns of expression, with the dominant role at any moment played by whichever language the speaker is currently speaking. But this too is confounded by any variety of language mixture or blending in which single utterances may contain elements from two or more languages. The scope of relativity would become a pragmatic problem, not a semantic or grammatical one. And of course, bilingual speakers often translate, restate, and paraphrase both between and within their languages. As an analytic method then, translation underwrites relativity by providing evidence of cross-linguistic difference. As an endogenous social practice, though, it undercuts relativity by weakening the grip of any one language on the expressive habits of the bilingual speaker.

Another line of intersection between semantics, pragmatics, and translation emerges in the work of the analytic philosopher Willard Van Orman Quine. In his well-known book Word and object (1960), and in a series of related papers, Quine argued that reference is ultimately inscrutable and translation between languages is in principle indeterminate. Distinguishing observation sentences, like "this is a rabbit," from standing sentences, like "democracy is a social good," Quine shows that even the former are ultimately impossible to define with precision. The more general standing sentences are, by extension, also impossible to pin down. In his famous thought experiment, the "radical linguist" (not to be confused with an actual linguist) confronts an entirely unknown language, without the benefit of a mutually understood contact language. Trying to determine the precise meanings of words in this other language, Quine's "linguist" finds it impossible to determine through ostension alone what terms like "gavagai" mean (apparently "rabbit," but perhaps better rendered "undetached rabbit part," "rabbit phase," etc.). Quine presses this dilemma, and the critique of empiricism it implies, from the limits on intelligibility of an unknown foreign language all the way to limits on understanding our own language, at which point reference truly goes "inscrutable." Philosophers, linguists, and some anthropologists were quick to pick up on the significance of his argument, which has remained a major position in the field today.

Quine's thought experiment, and the very idea of radical translation, are explicitly distinguished from the actual practices of linguists and anthropologists in the field. Nevertheless, there are certain distortions that call for comment because they put in question the applicability of his conclusions to actual translation. First, Quine posits a monolingual native speaker who is evidently incapable of formulating meaning statements in his own language. That is, the native informant is never given the opportunity to state in his own language what the term "gavagai" means, nor is the radical linguistic given the opportunity to ask him, simply, "What does gavagai mean?" It is clear that for Quine metalinguistic questions and responses inherit the very same limitations as the term they would seek to define. The problem with this from a linguistic perspective is that it is empirically false: metalinguistic statement may be multiplied, covaried with variations in the object term, and used to establish an array of contrasting terms which, in the aggregate, severely constrain the possible semantic range of the object term. The result may be a range of possible translations, but surely not an indefinite range. In a sense, Quine's native speaks a language in which neither paradigmatic nor syntagmatic contrasts can be deployed in order to discern the semantic boundaries of a term. Yet these contrasts are part of what any human language provides, and they are central both empirically and theoretically.

Second, Quine stipulates that in order to overcome indeterminacy, the linguist must derive an exact meaning from ostensive reference alone, and, moreover, that choice among alternative possible translations will ultimately turn on the linguist's assessment of what is most "natural," in the sense of corresponding best to his own (alien) sense of naturalness. Thus the linguist is, as it were, at sea without an independent point of reference. Neither of these problems is insuperable in linguistic fieldwork. The linguist gathers a wide variety of evidence for meaning hypotheses, including usage, metalinguistic commentaries, the ways in which the target term combines with others terms in syntactic constructions, analysis of the internal structure of the form (including morphology, compounding, etc.), and grammatical evidence of oppositions between the form and other forms in the language. Similarly, it is not what appears natural in the linguist's native language that guides his or her choice among alternative translations, but rather all that is known of universals of language, and the possible arrays of distinctions that are encoded in lexical forms. Quine is very clear that radical translation is a philosophical thought experiment and not a description of empirical research, but the point is that the problems that arise in his thought experiment arise from a deeply distorted set of assumptions about both languages and how they are analyzed. A third critique from linguistics would observe that for many expressions, it is not the semantic boundaries of words that distinguish them, but their focal or most prototypical meaning (as in the extensive literature on color terms). The implication of this is that the apparent imprecision of some semantic boundaries is to be expected, and need not reflect inherent limitations on what the foreign linguist can discern. Finally, Quine shifts inconsistently between "the anthropologist" and the "radical linguist" in his experiment, yet the two disciplines have quite different views of language and their methodologies are correspondingly distinct. One of the main goals of this special issue is precisely to bring the two disciplines together.

Focusing on the difficulty of translating technical terms from ancient science into the language of modern science (and by extension between any two scientific paradigms separated by revolution), Thomas Kuhn (2000, 2012; Kuhn et al. 2000; see also Hallen and Sodipo 1997) famously developed the concept of incommensurability. Kuhn, a historian-philosopher, is more careful than Quine to acknowledge the relation between translation, language learning, bilingualism, and the actual practices of translators. Unlike Quine, Kuhn rejects the equation of meaning with reference, insisting on the importance of style, nuance, and the difference between translation and interpretation. In his later work, he puts translation—its limits, potentials, and unavoidability—at the center of his views, and he proposes to view scientific communities as speech communities (Kuhn 2000: 166) where many forms of translation are constantly carried on, despite the theoretical incommensurability of paradigms. Translation ceases to be defined as an abstract impossibility. The challenge posed by the constant confrontation of "incommensurable" (yet translated) paradigms becomes in itself, on the contrary, a field for ethnographical inquiry.

ETHNOGRAPHY AS TRANSLATION

For most field linguists and ethnographers, translation is of limited utility. The empirical evidence for a social or linguistic category or practice must always be from the native language, not from a translation. It is common sense that if you do not work in the language you are trying to describe, you are missing your object. Interlinear glosses, explanations, and such in a European metalanguage are heuristic devices for the reader to follow distinctions made in the object language (e.g., a description of Kuna [object] in French or Spanish [metalanguage of description]).

However, it is also clear that ethnography, from a theoretical point of view, is unimaginable without translation. As Conklin has remarked, "The problems of ethnography are in the largest sense those of translation" (1968: 12). This is true not only because almost any ethnographer faces the task of translating words and concepts from one language to another, but also because to "do ethnography" is to make descriptions, judgments, actions, and theories proper to a specific culture understood in the language of social anthropology (a scientific community in Kuhn's sense). Seen from this point of view, translation ceases to designate only a linguistic technique. It becomes the definition of the core strategy of social anthropology itself.

Clearly, translation is a multidimensional phenomenon. A first dimension naturally concerns language. Jakobson (1959) and Benveniste (1974), in dialogue with Peirce (1955), both distinguished standard linguistic translation from one language to another from intralinguistic translation (restatement, gloss in the same language), and eventually from cross-modal translation (e.g., words to gestures, or verbal description to pictorial blueprint, or vice versa). However, even in a relatively language-centric view of translation, there are massive questions regarding the criteria under which some expression may be considered a "translation" of some other. In the last fifty years of research, linguistic anthropologists have made enormous strides toward understanding speech practices, developing socially embedded pragmatics (in the Anglo-Saxon sense based heavily on Austin [1975] and Grice [1989]), the ethnography of speaking, the study of indexicality, metalanguage and reflexive language, metaphor, style, conversation analysis, and increasingly the study of multimodal relations between speech, gesture, and material setting. As ever more aspects of communicative situations have been shown to frame talk, the question of what a source text even means has only become more subtle, let alone which aspects of meaning should be conveyed (under what circumstances) in a valid translation. If the translation is into language, as opposed to some other medium, then it too has all these elements of meaning. The simple pairing of head terms in one language with translations in another, as in bilingual dictionaries, obscures the fact that even the simplest lexical translation is multidimensional. When we move to pragmatically enriched utterances, the task becomes astronomically difficult. Therefore we must ask which elements of a putative meaning (in the source text) need to be present in a valid translation (the target text). Once we have answered that, we must decide which aspects of the translation itself must carry the critical information. Thus we confront the irony that valid translation gets ever more difficult to conceive the more we know about languages.

What we can know as anthropologists, how we can know it, what counts as warrant for knowledge, how we can express it in the language of our discipline, the sources and limits of anthropological knowledge—all of these questions engage translation either in principle or as a matter of fact in the practice of anthropology. The problems of inscrutability, indeterminacy, and incommensurability raised by Quine and Kuhn, for instance, all presume that the problem lies in capturing in one language meanings expressed in another. But when we look at translation as a historical practice, as Hanks (2010) does for the translation of Catholic doctrine into colonial Maya, we find a very different set of factors. For one thing, the target language is altered in the process of translation, which is pervasively and systematically neologistic. For another, translation is one part of a much broader colonial process involving religious conversion, conversion from hieroglyphic to alphabetic writing, and the reorganization of the political geography. Here not only is translation required on our part to capture this social world, but translation in the colonial setting produces the objects of our historical knowledge.

An analogous problem arises when we consider intracultural translation between significantly different registers of the same language. For example, can the language of a shaman in performance, or a ritual performer more generally, be rendered accurately in the ordinary nonritual versions of the language? Can it be translated into ordinary talk? Or more broadly, can the nonspecialist, say the patient, understand what the shaman is doing, and at what level of understanding? In fact there are significant differences between what the shaman in his own terms is doing in performance, on the one hand, and what the patient thinks he is doing from an everyday frame of reference, on the other. The asymmetries in their respective knowledge of what is going on are great, but they do not cause breakdown in communication. Hanks (2006, forthcoming) argues that the asymmetry of knowledge between participants, and the constraints on translation between the esoteric language of shamanism and ordinary Maya, are actually resources for shaman-patient interaction, not impediments. This in turn suggests that meaningful and consequential interaction can proceed in the absence of mutual translatability, or perhaps even intelligibility.

TRANSLATING WORLDS: COGNITION, ONTOLOGY, AND THE SCIENCE OF TRANSLATION

All we have seen until now suggests that there is more to translation than language. In cultural practices, translation constantly goes beyond it, for at least two reasons. First, this is because the concept of translation implies all forms of "social traductions." It designates the exchange not only of words, but also of values, theories, and artifacts from one culture to another, for instance in such processes as religious conversion, cultural mimesis, or messianic movements (Severi 2002, 2004).

The second reason translation exceeds language is because nonlinguistic forms of translation are constantly present in cultural traditions (Severi 2012). Words are translated into images, music into words, and gestures into objects. Furthermore, even within a single culture, translation processes enable the passage from one *context* of communication to another. Virtually everywhere, such formal contexts of the expression of meaning as ritual action, play, and other forms of performance generate their specific "ontologies." Things, artifacts, and living beings may then crucially *change their nature*, as in the famous "qualitative analogy" which transforms a cucumber into an ox in Evans-Pritchard's analysis of the Nuer sacrifice (1940). In these cases, the interpretation of such formal contexts of cultural representation transforms translation into a way to translate "*worlds*" (defined as "oriented contexts for the apprehension of reality"), not just words, or other ways to express meaning.

Translation is still, most of the time (see, e.g., Sammons and Sherzer 2000; Rubel and Rosman 2003; Silverstein 2003), with few exceptions (e.g., Keesing 1985), discussed only in technical terms. As *an epistemological principle*, it seems almost absent from the contemporary epistemological debate in the discipline. Two dominant trends in particular, cognitivism and ontologism, *seem unable* to understand what an epistemology of translation could be. For many cognitive anthropologists, and particularly for those adopting what Levinson (2003) has called "simple nativism" (e.g., Sperber 1996; Bloch 1998; Baumard, Boyer, and Sperber, 2010), this lack of understanding is a consequence of their denial of the epistemological import of cultural variations. If cultural differences have no fundamental influence on human cognition, where concepts (such as "continuity, solidity, gravity and inertia" [Spelke et al., 1992]) already exist independently from language, then translation is merely an ability to express a preexisting mental representation in the "phonetic clothing" (Levinson 2003: 28) of a specific language. It has, in itself, no cognitive relevance. As, for instance, Pinker puts it, "Knowing a language . . . is knowing how to translate mentalese into strings of words and vice versa" (1994: 82). Levinson has recently pointed to the two main difficulties generated by this approach: "First it is impossible to reconcile with the facts of variation across languages. Second, it is a theory of innate (thus biological) endowment outside biology" (2003: 26).

Ontologism raises other questions. Descola ([2005] 2013), for instance, distinguishes animism, totemism, analogism, and naturalism as implying different ontologies—different ways of going beyond any simple construal of nature vs. culture vs. other. In perspectivism, as developed by Viveiros de Castro, translation emerges as a sort of "controlled equivocation." So if the Jaguar offers manioc beer and what you find before you is human blood, thick and frothy, you have a perspectivist difference on the world of objects (Viveiros 1998, 2004). But what about the grey zones between perspectives or between modes of existence? What of the blending or grading or switching between systems, which surely occurs over the history of colonialism in the Americas, for example? Any typological schema will face the question of blends, and if we use translation to name the process(es) that cross between types, then we will have to deal with blending, and the emergence of new types or varieties. How, then, shall we translate ontologies, given that they are emergent and not static, blended and not pure?

We think the proper starting point of a new theory is neither preemptive universalism (which is almost always Eurocentric) nor typological divisions (which bound off individual types of ontology, even as they pluralize their space), but instead the study of processes and principles of translation. Given the scope of translational practices and the history of our field, the epistemological stakes of this (late-)Kuhn-inspired approach are high.

We should consider the study of these *processes and principles* of translation not only as an important way to improve a number of key technical operations for the interpretation of ethnography, but also as a new way to reformulate the general epistemology of our discipline.

THE CONTRIBUTIONS

In this volume, we have gathered a number of papers where these questions are treated from different points of view. In his paper, William Hanks argues that *intracultural* translation plays a constitutive role in the social life of any human group, and not only in mediating between different groups and languages. This is evident in all varieties of reported speech, paraphrase, commentary, and exegesis. These share with translation two features that distinguish it from other kinds of interpretation: a translation both refers to and paraphrases its source text. Hanks argues that it is the target language into which one translates that ultimately constrains the process. An adequate target language must be functionally capable of self-interpretation through metalanguage. Cross-linguistic translation presupposes intralinguistic translation. Historical examples of languages changing through intertranslation abound in (post)colonial contexts in which authoritative texts in a dominant language are translated into a subordinated language. This process inevitably alters the semantics and pragmatics of the subordinate language. The direction, scope, and depth of change are historically variable. Examples are adduced from modern and colonial Yucatec Maya and Spanish.

Carlo Severi is concerned with the relationship between translation and thought processes. He argues that forms of thought, from what Lévi-Strauss called the "systematization [of] what is immediately presented to the senses" to the causal theories studied by Evans-Pritchard in witchcraft, have generally been interpreted as an expression of a specific language or "culture." In this paper, he discusses this way of defining thought. Three classic objections are examined: (1) Societies sharing the same "system of thought" may speak different languages, and vice versa. (2) If a relation between language and thought exists, it is an indirect and controversial one, and we should never take it for granted (or infer qualities of thought from language structures) without further investigation. (3) The languages that we use to qualify different kinds of thought are constantly translated. Through a discussion of the context of translation, Severi argues that instead of seeing the possibility of translation as a theoretical difficulty for defining thought, we could, on the contrary, consider the ethnography of translation as a chance to observe the dynamics and structure of thought processes, and to study how they operate in different cultural contexts. Using three Amazonian examples, Severi describes the kind of cognition involved in the form of translation that Jakobson calls *transmutation*. From this ethnographic analysis, we can derive not only a better (both wider and more precise) idea of some, rarely studied, cultural translation processes, but also draw from it a new way to define the concept of "cultural ontology," both for Amazonian cultures and in more general terms.

Rupert Stasch presents a case study in the historically common phenomenon of a contact community between persons lacking any common language, such that their linguistic interactions are focused on linguistic otherness as such, or are mediated by a miniscule number of translation specialists. Stasch first explores contrasts in how international tourists and Korowai of Papua each take up the other's difference of language as a figure around which to express primordial definitions of their relation. He then examines how mutual incomprehension is valued as a resource for staying separate. Finally, he analyzes how the role of tour guide, qua translator, embodies a political model of authoritative speak-erhood that is antipathetic to Korowai egalitarianism, but nonetheless fosters egalitarianism-oriented paths of engagement with the quite different political formation of tourists' home social orders.

Anne-Christine Taylor's paper analyzes a series of intra- and intercultural translations involved in the shamanic practices of the northern Jivaroan Achuar. First, it shows how certain states of suffering, experienced as an unwanted meta-morphosis of selfhood, are reframed in the course of shamanic healing rituals as the symptoms of an insidious process of disempowerment and "whitening" unleashed by other, enemy Jivaroans. The curing session conflates the victim's sickness and the history of interethnic relations, construed as a painful pro-cess of involuntary qualitative change. A further series of translations come into being when the cure fails and the patient abandons his Jivaroan identity and moves into a lowland Quichua identity; this involves mapping the implicit autobiography of a Jivaroan moving from illness toward recovered health and social agency onto Quichua narratives of their own history. However, owing to increasing closure of ethnic groups, Jivaroans nowadays have to deal directly with the spoken and written words of the Whites, and this involves new forms of translation evoked in the final part of the paper.

Alan Rumsey's paper deals with two kinds of translation among Ku Waru people in the New Guinea Highlands: (1) translation between the local lan-guage and the national lingua franca within everyday interactions between young children and their caregivers; (2) intercultural translation between the story world of a local genre of sung tales and the contemporary lived world of Highlands PNG as practiced by skilled composer-performers of the genre. Although these two kinds of translation take place on very different planes, they both operate in terms of a well-developed set of procedures establishing equivalence, between words and worlds, respectively. On both planes a key role is played by parallelism, suggesting a connection between equivalence in the ordinary sense of the word and in the specific sense of it that was developed by Jakobson with respect to parallelism—a connection which is significant for the understanding of translation in general.

In his paper, Adam Yuet Chau starts from a couple of questions: How would one translate the word "menu" (i.e., restaurant menu) into the native language of an (imaginary) tribal people (with no writing and no restaurants)? And how would you explain to them how ordering from the menu works? It quickly be-comes clear that translating the *word* "menu" entails translating not only the *world* of restaurant-going and ordering from the menu but also our (i.e., ideal-typically Western) very conceptual and social world, which is another way to say that what seems to be a humble piece of paper listing a certain number of dishes is itself made by the world in which it is found and in turn contributes in a significant way to making that world. In this paper, Chau examines the restaurant menu as a world-making social and translocutional/transinscriptional technology (the menu as menu-logic and cosmo-menu). As a kind of *text act* that is situated at but one of many "iterative/inscriptional stations" along an indeterminate and continuous chain of translocutions and transinscriptions, the menu highlights the *temporal* dimension of all kinds of translations (translingual, intralingual, transmodal, transcultural, etc.).

Bruce Mannheim's paper starts with an epistemological claim: there is a line of continuity from Quine's work on translation to the more recent theories on "core cognition" (Carey 2009) and "domain specificity" (Gelman and Williams 1998, Gelman 2003). It is therefore possible to recuperate Quine's notion of "radical translation" within a framework that is richer ethnographically, linguistically, and cognitively. In order to illustrate his claim, Mannheim works on some crucial Quechua notions, arguing that, in order to fully capture their meaning, the linguist-ethnographer has to follow two main requirements: (1) every translation requires an alignment to a specific, socially identifiable register of Quechua; (2) translation cannot be a mere matter of identifying denotational equivalences—that is, replacing one set of linguistic forms for a denotatum with another. Rather, ethnographic translation has to be seen as an updated version of Quine's "radical translation," grounded in evidence linguistic and cognitive, and embedded in the contexts of use, and lexical and indexical relationships.

In their paper, Emmanuel de Vienne and Carlos Fausto focus on a specific case of translation that was attempted in 2006 by a Kalapalo Indian (from Mato Grosso, Brazil). This man in his forties created a radically new liturgy and cosmology by combining elements borrowed from local shamanism and mythology, Christianity and TV shows, among other sources. He thus managed to convince entire villages to take part in spectacular healing ceremonies. Since one of these rituals was filmed by two Kuikuro filmmakers, it is possible to examine the precise mechanisms of this cultural innovation, and therefore address with fresh data and methodology the old issue of Amerindian prophetism. They propose the concept of *translating acts* as a means to describe this native practice of translation, which consists as much of gestures and ritual actions as of linguistic expressions, emphasizes practical effects more than the negotiation of semantic equivalences, and is subject to constant reorientations in the course of interaction.

In his contribution, John Leavitt argues that the idea of translating worlds depends on the possibility that there are worlds to translate between. This has not always been the case in translation theory. This paper traces out some key moments in the history of translation theory in the West, which has shown an oscillation between what have come to be called "domesticating" and "foreignizing" approaches. The former seeks to present the referential meaning of the original work in an easily recognized and absorbed form for the reader. The latter seeks to preserve elements of the original work, and by implication its world, forcing the reader to work to reorient him- or herself, to cross a boundary into what is potentially another world, initially another language-world. The paper concludes with some examples drawn from Central Himalayan oral traditions.

In the final chapter, G. E. R. Lloyd acknowledges that the issues of translation and of translatability are general and concern the possibility of mutual intelligibility in many registers, including within a single natural language. Both anthropologists and ancient historians are faced with such problems, where the historians are at a disadvantage in not being able to check their understandings with those whom they are seeking to understand. But faced with seemingly paradoxical statements, beliefs, or practices, we must and can avoid the apparent dilemma (*either* those statements must be rendered in or reduced to our terms or we must admit they are strictly incomprehensible) by insisting on the revisability of our existing conceptual framework, especially in relation to such key terms as personhood, agency, causation, and nature. Instead of insisting on the dichotomy of literal and metaphorical, we should allow that any term may exhibit what is here called semantic stretch. Moreover, if we accept that the phenomena described are multidimensional, then the goal of a single definitive translation is a mirage. The open-endedness of translation is no threat to mutual intelligibility, but its precondition.

CONCLUSION

As we have seen, social anthropology mobilizes translation at many levels, from ethnography to comparative analysis, to the formulation of general theories. The analysis of these different processes of translation of *means of expression* and *context of communication* can enable us to account for what both cognitivists and ontologists do not see: the essential *plurality* both of mental operations and of "ontologies" which always exist *within a culture*, as well as in different cultures. From this perspective, the foundations of social anthropology (and, more specifically, the ground for comparison between cultures) are no more to be found in "a" universal cognitive endowment, which would exist independently from any cultural phenomenon. Nor should we look for the foundations of our discipline in a number of ontological "modes of inference," which would define the essence of a group of cultures, separated from the others. Our proposal is that, in order to understand "cultures" (and the kind of mental operations that the representation of cultural knowledge imply), we should focus not only on "differences," but also on the constant *work of translation* of languages, nonlinguistic codes, contexts of communication, and different traditions, which constitutes the field of "cultural knowledge," both within a single tradition and in different societies.

The analysis of these processes can provide for a new way to define translation, not only as a key technique for understanding ethnography, but also as a general epistemological principle. Since Boas, Sapir, and Whorf, anthropologists have defended the idea that every language elaborates the world in its own way. In this perspective, translation has been considered, at best, as an artificial and difficult process, a way to struggle against the constitutive differences that distinguish each language from others. In this way, however, a general and important fact has passed unnoticed: every language and every culture are not only *different* from each other; they are also *translatable* into each other. No untranslatable language, or culture, has ever existed. This quality of *being translatable* is inherent in all forms of human communication, as well as in the generation of cultural differences.

The recognition of the *universality of translation* as a principle can provide for the basis of a new way to look at cultural cognition, which would no longer be founded on an ideal (postulated) unity of the human mind, but rather on the empirical study of the cognitive processes involved in the various forms of translation of languages, means of expression, and contexts of communication of cultural phenomena. In this way, we could pass from a conception of cognition founded on a sort of universal cognitive grammar of human culture (a kind of logical form, postulated in a Platonic-Chomskyan perspective, which prevails today in the field of social cognition) to a Wittgenstein-inspired (1958) universality of cognition, conceived as an epistemological *principle of translatability* of language games, nonlinguistic codes, contexts of communication, and different ontologies. The concept of ontology would no longer refer to "conceptions of the world" linked to different languages, but to a plural and unsystematic way of constantly activating different forms of thought.

In this new perspective, social anthropology would be defined not only as the study of cultural differences, but also and simultaneously as a science of translation: the study of the empirical processes and theoretical principles of cultural translation.

ACKNOWLEDGMENTS

This collective volume originates from the symposium on "Cognition and Cultural Translation" held at the Fyssen Foundation, Paris, March 20–21, 2014. We want to express our gratitude to the Foundation for its help and support. The editors thank Bruce Mannheim for his contribution, which was not part of the original conference or special issue of *HAU: Journal of Ethnographic Theory* but is newly added to this volume.

REFERENCES

Asad, Talal. 2010. "The concept of cultural translation in British anthropology." In *Writing culture: The poetics and politics of ethnography*, edited by James Clifford and George E. Marcus, 141–64. Berkeley: University of California Press.

Austin, J. L. 1975. *How to do things with words.* Oxford: Oxford University Press.

Baumard, Nicolas, Pascal Boyer, and Dan Sperber. 2010. "Evolution of fairness: Cultural variability." *Science* 329 (5990): 388.

Benjamin, Walter. (1923) 2004. "The task of the translator." Translated by Harry Zohn. In *The translation studies reader*, edited by Lawrence Venuti, 75–85. Second edition. London: Routledge.

Benveniste, Émile. 1974. *Problèmes de linguistique générale*, Vol. 2. Paris: Gallimard.

———. 2012. *Dernières lecons, Collège de France 1968–1969*. Edited by Jean-Claude Coquet and Irène Fenoglio. Paris: EHESS/Gallimard/Seuil.

Berman, Antoine. 2008. *L'âge de la traduction: "La tâche du traducteur" de Walter Benjamin, un commentaire*. Vincennes: Presse Universitaires de Vincennes.

Bloch, Maurice E. F. 1998. *How we think they think: Anthropological approaches to cognition, memory, and literacy.* Oxford: Westview Press.

Boas, Franz. 1989. *A Franz Boas reader: The shaping of American anthropology, 1883–1911.* Edited by George W. Stocking, Jr. Chicago: University of Chicago Press.

Carey, Susan D. 2009. *The origin of concepts.* New York: Oxford University Press.

Conklin, Harold. 1968. "Ethnography." *International Encyclopedia of the Social Sciences* 5: 115–208.

Descola, Philippe. (2005) 2013. *Beyond nature and culture.* Translated by Janet Lloyd. Chicago: University of Chicago Press.

Enfield, Nicholas J., and Stephen C. Levinson. 2006. *Roots of human sociality.* New York: Berg.

Enfield, Nicholas J., and Jack Sidnell. 2012. "Language diversity and social action." *Current Anthropology* 53 (3): 302–33.

Evans-Pritchard, E. E. 1940. *The Nuer.* Oxford: Clarendon Press.

Gelman, Rochel and Earl Williams. 1998. "Enabling constraints for cognitive development and learning: Domain specificity and epigenesis." In, *Cognition, perception and language. Vol. 2. Handbook of Child Psychology*, edited by D. Kuhn and R. S. Siegler, 575–630. New York: Wiley.

Gelman, Susan A. 2003. *The essential child.* New York: Oxford University Press.

Gentner, Dedre, and Susan Goldin-Meadow, eds. 2003. *Language in mind: Advances in the study of language and thought.* Cambridge, MA: MIT Press.

Grice, Paul. 1989. *Studies in the way of words.* Cambridge, MA: Harvard University Press.

Hallen, Barry, and J. Olubi Sodipo. 1997. Knowledge, *belief and witchcraft: Analytic experiments in African ethnography.* Stanford: Stanford University Press.

Hanks, William F. 2006. "Conviction and common ground in a ritual event." In *Roots of human sociality: Cognition, culture and interaction*, edited by Nicholas J. Enfield and Stephen C. Levinson, 299–328. Oxford: Berg.

———. 2010. *Converting words: Maya in the age of the cross.* Berkeley: University of California Press.

Hanks, William F. Forthcoming. "Counterparts: Co-presence and ritual intersubjectivity." Special issue "Intersubjectivity across cultures," edited by Eve Danziger and Alan Rumsey, *Language and Communication.*

Hill, Jane H., and Bruce Mannheim. 1992. "Language and world view." *Annual Review of Anthropology* 21: 381–406.

Jakobson, Roman. 1959. "On linguistic aspects of translation." *On Translation* 3: 30–39.

Keesing, Roger. 1985. "Conventional metaphors and anthropological metaphysics: The problematic of cultural translation." *Journal of Anthropological Research* 41 (2): 201–17.

Kuhn, Thomas S. 2000. *The road since Structure*. Edited by James Conant and John Haugeland. Chicago: University of Chicago Press.

———. 2012. *The structure of scientific revolutions*. Chicago: University of Chicago Press.

Kuhn, Thomas S., Aristides Baltas, Kostas Gavroglu, and Vassiliki Kindi. 2000. "A discussion with Thomas S. Kuhn." In *The road since Structure*. Edited by James Conant and John Haugeland, 255–323. Chicago: University of Chicago Press.

Leavitt, John. 2010. *Linguistic relativities: Language diversity and modern thought*. Cambridge: Cambridge University Press.

Levinson, Stephen C. 2003. "Language and mind: Let's get the issues straight!" In *Language and mind: Advances in the study of language and thought*, edited by Dedre Gentner and Susan Goldin-Meadow, 25–46. Cambridge, MA: MIT Press.

Lucy, John. A. 1992. *Language diversity and thought: A reformulation of the linguistic relativity hypothesis*. Cambridge: Cambridge University Press.

Peirce, Charles Sanders. 1955. *Philosophical writings of Peirce*. Edited by Justus Buchler. New York: Courier Dover Publications

Pinker, Steven. 1994. *The language instinct: The new science of language and mind*. Harmondsworth: Penguin.

Pym, Anthony. 2010. Exploring translation theories. New York: Routledge.

Quine, Willard Van Orman. 1960. *Word and object*. Cambridge, MA: MIT Press.

Rubel, Paula G., and Abraham, eds. 2003. Translating cultures: Perspectives on translation and anthropology. Oxford: Berg.

Sammons, Kay, and Joel Sherzer, eds. 2000. *Translating Native American verbal art*. Washington, DC: Smithsonian Institution Press.

Sapir, Edward. 1985. *Selected writings of Edward Sapir in language, culture and personality*. Berkeley: University of California Press.

Saussure, Ferdinand de. (1916) 2006. *Course in general linguistics*. Translated by Roy Harris. Chicago: Open Court.

Severi, Carlo. 2002. "Memory, reflexivity and belief: Reflections on the ritual use of language." *Social Anthropology* 10 (1): 23–40.

———. 2004. "Capturing imagination: A cognitive approach to cultural complexity." *Journal of the Royal Anthropological Institute* (N.S.) 10 (4): 815–38.

———. 2012. "The arts of memory: Anthropology of a mental artifact." *HAU: Journal of Ethnographic Theory* 2 (2): 451–85.

Silverstein, Michael. 2003. "Translation, transduction, transformation: Skating 'glossando' on thin semiotic ice." In *Translating cultures: Perspectives on translation and anthropology*, edited by Paula G. Rubel and Abraham Rosman, 75–109. Oxford: Berg.

Sperber, Dan. 1996. *Explaining culture: A naturalistic approach.* Oxford: Blackwell.

Spelke, Elisabeth., Karen Breinlinger, Janet Macomber, and Kristen. Jacobson. 1992. "Origins of knowledge." *Psychological Review* 99 (4): 605–32.

Viveiros de Castro, Eduardo. 1998. "Cosmological deixis and Amerindian perspectivism." *Journal of the Royal Anthropological Institute* (N.S.) 4 (3): 469–88.

———. 2004. "Perspectival anthropology and the method of controlled equivocation." *Tipití: Journal of the Society for the Anthropology of Lowland South America* 2 (1): 1–22.

Whorf, Benjamin Lee. 1956. *Language, thought, and reality: Selected writings*, Vol. 5. Edited by John B. Carroll. Cambridge, MA: MIT Press.

Wittgenstein, Ludwig. 1958. *Philosophical investigations.* Translated by G. E. M. Anscombe. Oxford: Blackwell.

CHAPTER ONE

The space of translation

WILLIAM F. HANKS

Among the perennial challenges facing anthropologists, the obdurate difficulty of cross-cultural translation occupies a special place. For an ethnographer attuned to the subtlety of native concepts, the task of translating into the language of anthropology can be daunting and seems inevitably distorting. British social anthropology in the 1960s and 1970s; structural, symbolic, and interpetive anthropology; the critique of ethnographic writing—all engage the inherent difficulty of translating native concepts into our writings. More recent works on comparative ontologies (Descola [2005] 2013), perspectivism, and translation itself have placed a renewed focus on cultural difference, and with it the severe challenges to translation. Vivieros da Castro's "controlled equivocation" represents one interesting response to this challenge (see Hanks and Severi, this volume).

Running parallel to anthropological approaches, there is a large literature bearing on translation in philosophy, linguistics, and semiotics. In these fields, the problem is usually approached through fine-grained, often technical analysis of language. Thought experiments, isolated example sentences, and typologies are standard fare. The use of formal notations is already a process of translation, and the sheer complexity of human speech in its semantic, pragmatic, and sociolinguistic aspects poses formidable problems for the would-be translator

(Hallen and Sodipo 1997). This literature has much to say to anthropology and a great deal to gain from it as well. It contributes much-needed distinctions and an unparalleled level of precision and explicitness. It shows, among other things, that translation is a constant and unavoidable part of any single culture, and not only a problem of comparison. As soon as we recognize that translation is a family of social practices, it becomes an object of study and not only a means to an anthropological end. As we try to understand a cultural world, what is the relation between our translations of "them" and "their" translations of themselves?

From social anthropology, analytic approaches can learn about actual social worlds (not only experimental ones, which are systematically less interesting). This implies a wholesale recasting of the typically oversimplified ideas of context invoked in analytic work. More pointedly, actual social formations differ and are alike in ways far beyond what linguists and philosophers typically recognize. Here the empirical commitments of social anthropology reveal orders of social and historical embedding that change how we think of the elements and levels of translational practice.

The goal of this paper is therefore to articulate linguistic and semiotic aspects of translation with social and historical aspects of it. It is a first attempt to chart a thick boundary between the two broad traditions and to highlight some of their convergences and divergences. Translation as method and as practice is both too broad and too fine-grained to be encompassed by either alone. The paper therefore explores the space of translation both in the broadly anthropological sense of cross-cultural description and in the more narrow sense of rendering in one language what is expressed in another. We distinguish translation as a method of revealing difference and similarity, present in anthropology at least since Boas, from related but distinct practices aimed at interpretation. Drawing on the semiotics of Roman Jakobson, C. S. Peirce, and Charles Morris, the paper argues that *intracultural* translation plays a constitutive role in the social life of any human group, and not only in mediating between different groups and languages. This is evident in all varieties of what Urban (2001) called metaculture, including reported speech, paraphrase, commentary, and exegesis. Such processes are a key part of meaning production and circulation, and are in this sense generative. The ones just listed share with translation two features that distinguish it from other kinds of interpretation and reproduction: a translation both refers to and paraphrases its source text. While source texts and signs may be more or less difficult to translate, therefore, *it is the target language into which one translates that ultimately constrains the process.* In order for a semiotic system to serve as a medium of translation, it must be functionally capable of self-interpetation through metalanguage. As a shorthand, we can say that cross-linguistic translation presupposes intralinguistic translation. Moreover, just as the latter generates novel meaning statements, the former is also generative. Historical examples of languages changing through intertranslation abound, but the clearest are found in colonial contexts in which authoritative texts in a dominant language are translated into a subordinated language, for this process inevitably alters the semantics and pragmatics of the subordinate language. The variety of translation this entails is what I will call commensuration, a neologis-tic process. Cross-linguistic translation is therefore a metalinguistic process that takes place in a space of asymmetric difference and produces change in either or both of the languages. The direction, scope, and depth of change are histori-cally variable. Examples are adduced from modern and colonial Yucatec Maya, Spanish, and English.

TRANSLATION AS METHOD

Translation has long been used as a method in both linguistics and anthropol-ogy, and is arguably in play in any comparison across cultures or languages. A classic example of this is Saussure's *Course in general linguistics* ([1916] 2006), a foundational text for modern linguistics and what would become structur-alism in anthropology. Saussure demonstrates that the link between signifier and signified, a perceptible sign form and its associated concept, is arbitrary in any language. He does so by juxtaposing translations of "the same" idea in two or more languages, as in French *mouton* as a translation of English "sheep," or "mutton." Saussure's point in such examples is that languages differ in how they pair meanings with forms, and from this it follows that the pairings in any one language are a matter of convention—not of natural necessity or similarity be-tween sign and object. The signifier, itself an "image acoustique," pairs not with a thing, but with a concept.[1] Ultimately, Saussure's translations demonstrate

---

1. Benveniste (1966, 1974) correctly critiques Saussure for equivocating in this demonstration between the idea associated with the signifier, and the referent to which the signifier–signified pair refers. He also points out that for the native speaker, the pairing of form and meaning does not appear as mere convention, but as natural. It is under the perspective of cross-linguistic translation that the arbitrariness of any single language becomes visible.

the near impossibility of accurate cross-language translation. A pessimist would conclude that translation is impossible.

Boas (1911) and Sapir (1949) make essentially the same use of translation as does Saussure, but they draw the stronger conclusion that cross-linguistic differences are both profound and consequential for the ways that speakers of different languages grasp the world around them. This would become the relativity thesis, which continues to generate debate in the linguistic and psycholinguistic literature. Certainly one motivation for their relativistic view was that Boas and Sapir did extensive research on native languages of the North America, which presented varieties of structure and meaning hitherto unprecedented in linguistics based on analysis of Indo-European languages. It was their position that the grammatical models inherited from European linguistics were simply inadequate to describe New World languages, which required description "in their own terms."[2] As is typical in modern linguistics, cross-linguistic translation is a heuristic indicator, but the load-bearing evidence for any analysis must come from the language itself.

Some of Boas' most striking comments on translation involve demonstratives like English "this, that," which in many North American Indian languages encode a distinction between visible and invisible (Boas 1940: 229), as in (1):

1. Visibility as a distinctive dimension in Kwakiutl; demonstratives
    T'e'semgya   "this stone (visible, near me)"
    T'e'semgya'   "this stone (invisible, near me)"

A similar point is made repeatedly in Boas (1911). His larger point is that demonstratives in many North American languages distinguish visibility of the referent to the speaker at the time and place of utterance, and that the speakers of such languages are in effect forced to attend to the visual access that they have

---

2. In critiques of the relativity hypothesis, it is sometimes assumed that if it were accurate, then it should be impossible to learn or even understand foreign languages. But this *reductio* is absurd and finds no basis in the writings of either Boas, Sapir, or Benjamin Lee Whorf, all of whom also argued that languages have universal properties. Boas and Sapir were polyglot and neither was naïve about the ability of speakers to learn even very different foreign languages, nor about the prevalence of bi- or multilingualism. The point is rather that through cross-linguistic translation, one can glimpse the uniqueness of structures and meanings in different languages, but it is only in relation to its own grammatical system that any expression can be ultimately analyzed.

to the objects they refer to. Speakers of European languages, which do not so clearly encode visibility in the demonstratives, are not so obliged.

Perceptual access to situated referents is widely attested in the world's languages. In order to translate the simple English forms "this" and "that" into the languages listed below, we are forced to pay attention to the perceptual features shown, since they correspond to different deictics in the target language. Conversely, if we translate a demonstrative expression from one of these languages into English, we are forced to annotate the English or lose the distinctions.

Perceptual access to referents: Visibility in North America (after Hanks 2011)

- *Quileute* has distinctive deictics for Visible vs. Invisible objects. The Visible category is split into Proximal vs. Medial vs. Distal.
- *Kwakwa'la* and *Chinook* have distinct deictic series for Visible vs. Invisible.
- *Crow* distal deictics are split into Visible vs. Invisible.
- *W. Greenlandic* has a special morpheme marking Invisible objects.
- *Ute* makes a three-way distinction between Proximal vs. Distal vs. Invisible.
- *Maya* (Yucatec) distinguishes Tactile, Visual, and Peripheral sensory access.

Such examples illustrate the peculiar status of translation as an instrument used ultimately to reveal not equivalence but difference-within-sameness between languages. As many would do after them, Boas and Saussure both use it more to contrast systems than to align them.

At a very different level of description, ethnographers have also used the method of translation as a way of revealing and making sense of difference, and, like Boas, the objective for anthropologists has usually been to make sense of the foreign language in its foreignness. For example, Evans-Pritchard ([1937] 1976: Appendix 1) is scrupulous to make his translations into English strictly accountable to the coherence of Azande concepts in their own cultural context, a strategy also pursued in his classic study of Nuer religion ([1956] 1970). As a result, the English glosses are purely heuristic. Talal Asad's (1987) well-known discussion of cultural translation in British social anthropology starts from a similar position, but introduces power asymmetry between the source languages and the (European) target languages. Asad is ultimately concerned not with cultural or linguistic differences as such, but with power relations between languages—reminding us that translatability is not only a question of interlinguistic relation, but also one of power, authority, and legitimacy. We will see in a moment some effects of power difference, although neither the original nor the target language is necessarily dominant.

We might say that any time an ethnographer or linguist attempts to explicate the coherence or meaning of a concept from a distant culture in the language of anthropology, translation is the mediating process. This is so even if word-for-word translations are abandoned, because analysis or comparison themselves translate. The intuition of this paper is that translation so understood is not merely a problem of redescribing a cultural form, but of understanding it in the first place. In other words, it has to do with our ability to gain knowledge of other cultures, a point made forcefully by Severi (this volume).

INTRALINGUAL TRANSLATION AND UNDERSTANDING

Whatever the problems and prospects of translation as a method of cross-cultural comparison, it is also a pervasive part of social life in any single language or culture. Speakers of any language routinely translate themselves and others in the same language. Rumsey (this volume) makes strong use of this in his comparison of bilingual interactions with *tom yaya kange* performers in Ku Waru. Both translate, even though the performers are speaking solely in Ku Waru. In general, any time a speaker reports the speech of another, paraphrases, glosses, overtly imitates, or renders in "prose" register a text in poetic register (verse or vice versa), translation is in play. Once we introduce the sociolinguistic truism that all languages have multiple registers, it becomes clear that intralingual translation is not only a fact of social life, but is, in effect, a design feature of language.

The classic statement of intralingual translation is Jakobson's ([1959] 2004) article on linguistic aspects of translation. Whereas the sometimes profound differences between languages have led some to suggest that accuracy is ultimately impossible, or at least vanishingly rare, Jakobson takes the opposite position: not only is translation a ubiquitous feature of ordinary monolingual speech, but the intralingual translation of an expression quite simply *is its meaning*. If this is so, then intralingual translation is incorrigible, because one cannot compare the target text to the meaning of an erstwhile independent source. Once we move from cross-linguistic to language-internal translation, this circularity becomes unavoidable. This is all the more striking if the interpretive process is institutionalized in such a way that some interpretations are considered authoritative, a fact common to textual traditions like Christianity (Durston 2007; Hanks 2010) and Islam (Messick 1996).

Jakobson makes a three-way distinction, between three varieties of translation: (1) traditional cross-language translation; (2) the intralingual translation that occurs every time one speaker paraphrases, reports, or even understands another; (3) the cross-modal translation of speech into gesture or vice versa. The third of these implicates a problem that has become increasingly focal in linguistic anthropology and is relevant to any anthropologist who examines the relations between multiple media. Jakobson treats all three as instances of what Peirce called the interpetants of a sign. Every sign or representamen consists of a perceptible sign vehicle, an object stood for in some respect, and an interpretant. As Peirce puts it, the sign "addresses somebody, that is, creates in the mind of that person an equivalent sign or perhaps a more developed sign. That sign which it creates I call the interpretant of the first sign" (1940: 99). In his extensive corpus of writings, Peirce discusses interpretance in many places, distinguishing among kinds of interpretants, and suggesting that different classes of signs call forth different types of interpretant. Of particular relevance in the present context is his distinction between immediate interpretants, which manifest in the correct understanding of the sign, and dynamical interpretants, which are the direct result of the sign. Thus if I said to you, "I smell smoke, something's burning," the immediate interpretant would be your grasping the meaning of the utterance, and the dynamical interpretant might be the alarm you feel at the prospect of a fire, the gesture of sniffing or looking for the source of smoke, or calling for help. Both kinds of interpretant can be multiple and give rise, themselves, to further interpretants.

It is clear that if translation is equated with the process of generating interpretants, then it is at the very heart of understanding, and we can see why Jakobson says that translation *is* the meaning: to understand is to produce an immediate interpretant. Thus it is a crucial part of all semiotic processes, and not only those in which the first sign and the interpretant are in different languages. This way of formulating the question makes it self-evident that there are epistemological stakes in translation. How I translate Maya into English, or Maya culture into the language of anthropology, what I chose to compare it to, and so forth—all of these involve translating, and if the translations are inaccurate or full of spurious projections, then so is the knowledge they express. At the same time, to simply collapse translation into interpretance is far too general. Peirce never requires that an interpretant bear a specific relation of similarity to the sign it interprets—any further propagation of signs will do. The interpretant need not even overlap in reference with the first sign, as in (2):

2. A telephone exchange
    A: "Hi. Is Ben home?"
    B: "You've got the wrong number"
    B': "He should be back in 5 minutes"

It seems to me unhelpful to say that B's response is a translation of A's question, but both B and B' are perfectly good interpretants of it. Similarly, if some third person C is with B when the call occurs, and interupts B's response, B can raise his hand, palm out, to signal "Please be quiet" or perhaps "Please stop." This gesture is a fine dynamical interpretant to C's interruption, but it is no translation of it. On the other hand, if in making the gesture B says "Please be quiet" or "Shh!" then the utterance and the gesture are arguably in a cross-modal translation relation.

Therefore only some interpretants are translations. We need constraints. In this paper I will follow Nelson Goodman (1978) in stipulating that one representation is a translation of another if (and only if) it both refers to and paraphrases the other. *The reference constraint* captures the fact that the translation stands for the source, which is its first object in the Peircean sense. Failing this, we may have two similar statements, but neither translates the other. *The paraphrase constraint* captures the fact that there must be some relation of similarity, analogy, or partial equivalence between source and target. This raises the key question of evaluation, which in turn requires that we be clear on the purpose of translation. It is one thing if the purpose is to capture truth-functional meaning, but quite another if one wants the translation to "paraphrase" style, tone, speech act force, and so forth.[3] It is only relative to a frame of reference that partial equivalence can be judged.

---

3. There is a large literature on the problem of translating style, much of it produced by Americanists grappling with the difficulties of translation Native American oral traditions into written English. For classic statements bearing on Mesoamerica and South America, see Tedlock (1983), Gossen (1985), Sherzer (1990), Urban (1991), and Sammons and Sherzer (2000), and compare Rafael (1993) on Spanish and Tagalog in the Philippines, Shieffelin (2007) on Kaluli (PNG), and Rumsey (2008) on Ku Waru (PNG).

LINGUISTIC RESOURCES FOR TRANSLATION

Any human language can be used as its own metalanguage. That is, one can define English words in English, French words in French, Maya words in Maya. Any competent speaker is capable of asking an addressee "What does that mean?" or its near equivalent. Similarly, anyone can in principle paraphrase their own speech in response to such a question. The monolingual dictionary or grammar is based on this, but the phenomenon is much more widespread in ordinary talk, regardless of whether the language is written. In the clearest cases, metalinguistic discourse refers to, and therefore objectifies, language, its parts, or its products in an utterance or text. The distinction between object language and metalanguage, and the recognition that one and the same language can function in both modes, has a considerable history in linguistic thought. In this paper, most relevant is the line of thought leading from Morris (1971), to Jakobson (1957, [1959] 2004), Silverstein (1976), myself (Hanks 1983, 1990, 1993), and Urban (2001). The first two were concerned with distinguishing "thing sentences" from metalinguistic sentences in order to rectify language as a medium of analysis. Unrecognized metalanguage resulted in "pseudo thing sentences," which, because they stipulate the meaning of the words in which they are stated, are marred by circularity. Drawing on Peirce, Jakobson integrated the distinction into his famous article "Shifters, verbal categories and the Russian verb" (1957), which was adapted by Silverstein in his "Shifters, verbal categories and cultural description" (1976). The term "shifter" refers to certain linguistic categories which have in common that one must attend to the utterance context in which they occur, in order to fix the reference. In Jakobson's (1957) terms, they illustrate "message referring to code" or "code referring to message." Thus "here, now, there, this, that" and all other deictics are shifters because their reference is strictly context-sensitive; they illustrate code referring to message. For both Jakobson and Silverstein, this obligatory anchoring of meaning in utterance context illustrates the "metalinguistic function" of language, a topic I have examined in depth elsewhere (Hanks 1983, 1990, 1993, 1996, 2011). Urban (2001) argues that metasemiosis, encompassing both kinds, is among the most potent forces for the circulation of cultural form.[4]

---

4. It is important to distinguish the functional capacity for reference to language from the social authority to exercise that capacity. All human languages are functionally designed to serve as their own metalanguage. The right to exercise that function, however, is far from universal; it is distributed over social persons and contexts.

This line of thought, then, distinguishes (1) metalinguistic function (as in deixis, where immediate interpretation of shifters requires reference to the utterance context in which the sign occurs: "I like it here") from (2) metalinguistic discourse (in which explicit reference is made to language, for the purpose of glossing, paraphrasing, etc.: "here" designates a place close to you when you say it) from (3) the general self-interpreting capacity of any human language ("We are a plurilingual nation," "You should be polite when speaking to someone older than you"), and from (4) canonical translation between two languages ("Here" *veut dire* "*ici*"). One insight of the pragmatist tradition is that these four are all intimatey related, and in effect, all three grow out of the first. Our ability to translate between languages is grounded in our ability to translate within our language, and this is in turn rooted in the metalinguistic function that underlies much of ordinary referring.

In "Language and human nature," Taylor (1985) identifies this self-interpreting capacity as a fundamental feature of any human society. Taylor notes that native expression and self-description have a constitutive role in the social realities they ostensibly describe. While it is clear that much of what he is referring to is not metalinguistic in any close sense, still it is reflexive in the sense suggested in point (3) above, and developed by Lucy (1993). The implication is that intralingual translation may be part of what actually shapes any language, just as self-description is part of what shapes any cultural order. This capacity to shape makes self-description consequential, even if it is distorting. According to Taylor, social description that is limited by the self-interpretations of native members thereby runs the risk of incorrigibility. The reason is clear: if the self-description helps define the facts, then the facts cannot be confronted with the description in order to refute it.

Any human language provides multiple resources that make possible this act of reflexive translation. These include, for example, the following:

1. The ability to mention or cite language forms, without actually using them. For instance "'Sign' is a four-letter word."
2. The ability to distinguish actual speech from hypothetical speech. For instance, "If you say 'I give you my word,' then you've made a promise," in which the if-clause is hypothetical and the then-clause is a metalinguistic claim by the speaker.
3. Various ways of reporting speech (as in "Ben said 'Go!'," "Ben said to go," "Ben told them to start," etc.). This points toward the lexicon of verbs of

speaking and the grammar of complements of speaking. Prosody, deixis, evidentials, and other features may shift systematically to maintain recoverability of the original speaker from the report.

4. Deictic shift: "I like it here" becomes "Bill said he liked it there."
5. Prosodic shifts to distinguish quotation, as in mocking repetition of a speaker's utterance.

Depending upon the language, there are numerous other resources for glossing, reporting, and commenting on speech in the same language. The main point is that languages are rich in these resources, which reflect the fact that intralingual translation is a design feature of human language.

This then opens up a second path to translation as method, because this reflexive capacity is a very powerful resource for any student of a language, whether a child native learner, a second-language learner, or a researcher. In my own work in Yucatec Maya, I conducted all of my fieldwork in Maya, and for this, the metalinguistic resources of the language were crucial.[5]

In addition to a wealth of evidence about how Maya speakers objectify their own speech practices, metalinguistic discussion revealed their common-sense assumptions about which uses are more typical than others. They even went so far as to reject as unacceptable expressions that they themselves used on other occasions (Hanks 1993, 1996). This underscores the point that native language translations do not always define the rigorously linguistic meaning of expressions—they may actually distort facts of observable usage. Evaluated as rigorous claims of meaning or descriptions of use, therefore, they can only give clues, since they are, as Boas (1911) put it, "secondary interpretations." Yet as testaments of native common sense, they are primary evidence. And what they tell us is how native speakers typify usage. Like Jakobson's ([1959] 2004) translations, they simply *are* the relevant meanings. But we can recognize this root circularity in common sense while retaining the ground to distinguish native typification from linguistic or anthropological analysis. The two refer to different orders of social fact and, in particular, they do so from different vantage points. One can retain the ability to evaluate the translation relative to its object for analytic

5. Like Evans-Pritchard ([1937] 1976, [1956] 1970) or indeed Boas (1911), my attitude as a researcher was for many years that glosses in Spanish or English from the Maya were purely heuristic and had no evidence value in my analyses. It was only after spending many years studying the colonial history of Maya language and culture that I came to see translation as a key topic for research.

purposes, while recognizing that the two are confounded if the frame of reference is native common sense.

METALANGUAGE AND TRANSLATION OF DEICTIC EXPRESSIONS

Boas' frequent observations on the salience of perceptual access in the meanings of deictics in North American languages foreshadowed what has become a major area of cross-linguistic research.[6] At first blush, expressions like "here" and "there" appear far removed from the concerns of most anthropologists, and they have been poorly analyzed by traditional linguistics. One reason for this is the apparent lack of meaning conveyed by such expressions, since "here" and "there" tell us little about the places or objects to which they refer when uttered. They seem to have none of the social importance one associates with more standard examples of categorization (like kinship terms) or interpersonal address forms (like honorifics and titles). Moreover, there is an obviousness to the notion of "here"—what is close to me when I say "here"—and this apparent transparency has shielded it from scrutiny. Over the last three decades of research however, it has become clear that these received assumptions are both false. In fact, deictic systems vary widely in unexpected ways (Hanks 2011), and this variation reveals a wealth of social information about how cultures organize interactive context. By studying kinship, ethnobotanical, or ethnomedical terminologies, for instance, one can learn a great deal about how different peoples construe the domains of human relatedness, plants, or the living body. By contrast, a lifetime studying demonstratives like English "this and that" reveals next to nothing about how people categorize the objects that such expressions denote when uttered. This is because indexical expressions differ fundamentally in the kinds of information they encode.

Whereas standard descriptive terms reveal properties of the object they designate, deictics, including demonstratives, are notoriously sparse on such information. They seem to be so abstract as to be mere representatives of richer categories. Compare "mother's brother's daughter" with "that one" or just "her." Yet what the indexicals precisely code is just what is missing in the kinship term: the relations

---

6.   In what follows, I will use the term "shifter," "deictics," and "deixis" as general terms to cover deictic adverbs (place, time), demonstratives (nominal deictics), and pronouns (participant deictics).

between the speaker and the addressee of the utterance, between addressee and referent, and between speaker and referent. It is precisely these interactive relations that are delicately coded in the structure and use of deictics. When one spells out the spatial deictics in any language, for instance, one taps into schemas not of the objects referred to, but of the interactional relations in which referring is performed, and the situated perspectives from which participants in talk have access to the objects, places, and persons to which they refer. Moreover, the corporeal field in which such elementary referring occurs is a key part of the meaning of deictics, whereas standard descriptive terms reveal little about the body unless corporeality is the designation. This basic difference is linked to the metalinguistic function of deixis and raises two questions for translation. First, what happens when speakers attempt to translate deictics into paraphrases? And second, under what conditions is it possible to translate deictics across languages?

In (3) I have asked Don Ponso, an adult monlingual Maya speaker, the meaning of *kó'oten té'ela,'* glossable as "Come (right) here." His response puts the form in a scenario in which the would-be speaker is sitting in his own house, and offers a seat to a visitor. In order to do this, the speaker stands up, and offers a chair that he has in hand, saying "Come (over) here." The gloss captures the pragmatic force of the utterance as an invitation, and cites a cross-modal translation relation between the words and the gesture of offering a seat. Given the functional density of the deictic, Don Ponso immediately glosses the expression by situating it as an utterance in context, thus engaging intralingual and cross-modal translation in a metapragmatic statement.

3. . . . *bey xan hú tz'ik tech umpʼée báʼal akutaleʼ,*
     . . . also he'll give you a thing to sit (on),

    kulíikʼleʼ, kyáaik techeʼ, kóʼoten téʼelaʼ. Eskeh umpʼée báʼal
    he gets up, he says to you, "Come here." It's that a thing

    umachk utzʼáa techeʼ. Ká kulakechi.
    he takes in hand to give you. For you to sit on it. [1.A.25]

(3) also suggests that the form *téʼelaʼ* is used in addressing an addressee who is already close at hand and face to face with the speaker. This condition, which turned out to be pretty accurate, was explicitly stated by Don Ponso less than a minute later, as shown in (4).

4. *kóoten téela', k'abéet nàatz' yàan techi'*
   "Come (right) here" he has to be close to you (already). [1.A.061]

So how would a Yucatec speaker call an addressee who is at some remove, such
as one on the other side of the market, in another part of the household, or out
of sight in the woods? The answer is: *kóoten waye,'* "Come here." The form *waye'*
is another kind of "here." It designates an egocentric space around the Speaker,
and to comply with this imperative, the Addressee need only follow the voice to
its source. Don Ponso has tersely translated into words an unstated pragmatic
constraint on typical usage of *téela'*: the interlocutors are already close, and, as
illustrated in (3), the Speaker shows the referent to the Addressee.

(5) shows another example in which Don Ponso makes explicit background
assumptions about context. I have asked him to comment on *héelóoba,'* "here
they are" (a presentative, predicative deictic similar to French *voici*).

5. *héelóoba', amachmah [. . .] wá má amachma e',*
   "Here they are," you've grabbed them [. . .] if you haven't grabbed them,

   hé' yàan héelo'.
   (you say) "There they are"   [19.B.094]

Native metalinguistic glosses like these are an invaluable part of fieldwork on
deixis in the language. By working in the native language, taking full advantage
of the metalinguistic capacity of the language and its speakers, we can create
a snowball effect whereby speakers' commentaries reveal other features of the
language, as well as translating into words their judgments of typical and proper
usage. When we explore speakers' typifications of usage, we are exploring their
common-sense pragmatic schemas. It is on the basis of these that they can
translate from pragmatic presuppositions to overt statements. We might say
that any native speaker of a language is an interpreter of her or his language.[7]

---

7.   This is a point on which Quine's justly famous experiment in "radical translation"
     positively distorts not only the fieldwork practices of linguists, but what it means to
     know a language. Quine (1960) stipulates that the imaginary linguist confronts a
     hitherto unknown language without the aid of an interpreter. But the monolingual
     native speaker is in fact always already an interpreter of her or his own language (see
     Hanks and Severi, this volume).

I propose that it is precisely this native capacity for self-translation in any human language that underlies the ability to engage in cross-linguistic translation. In order to translate into a second language, that language must be self-interpreting. Any sign or collection of signs can be translated, but not any language can translate in the strong sense. The same semiotic and linguistic resources that permit self-interpretation in Maya, English, or Spanish are what make it possible to translate between the three.

One corollary of this is that, if we found a semiotic code incapable of self-interpretation, we would have a code *into* which translation would be severely limited, if not impossible. An example of this might be the well-known signs produced by bees, which are remarkably precise in indexing the direction and distance of pollen sources. Such signs can be approximately glossed into a human language, but no human signs can be translated into the gestural signs of bees, for these are not self-interpreting.

It is therefore not so much the source text that places limits on translatability, although this might pose specific problems. It is the target language that must meet the baseline requirement of the metalinguistic function of self-interpretation. Failing this, one cannot translate into the language.

As both Peirce and Jakobson observed, this process of translation interpretance within human languages generates new signs, new distinctions, and new ways of evaluating speech. The interpretant was proposed by Peirce to explain how signs beget signs, and thus the study of interpretance was, for him, part of rhetoric. In other words, irrespective of its ultimate "accuracy," intralingual translation is productive and plays a crucial role in the social life of any language.

Does cross-language translation also generate new meaning and new usage, or is it merely a matter of accurately relaying meaning? History shows that it can be generative.

TRANSLATION AND MEANING PRODUCTION

Theories of translation differ in terms of the emphasis they place on the source text or the target text. Benjamin, for instance, judges the best translation to be the one that is most under the sway of the original (see Sammons and Sherzer 2000), while others have called for the transformation of the original according to the norms of expression in the target language. (Pym 2010 gives a useful discussion of both positions, and compare Mounin 1963.) The difference is essentially a matter of fixing the frame of reference for evaluation. From my perspective what is most important is that both ways of evaluating—privileging source over target or vice versa—assume a binary relation (source, target) and proceed by comparing the one to the other. The more different the two languages, the harder it is to balance fidelity to source with fidelity to target.

When we examine historical cases of translation, however, this picture shifts in a subtle but important way (Santamaría 1992; Durston 2007; Whalen 2003) . The target language may be altered in the process of translation. It may be incremented by neologisms, newly coined uses for existing forms, proper names, or portions of the source text left untranslated in the target. This is evident in all missionary translation as well as in literature like the usage manuals in products sold on the international market.

The importance of this fact is that the translation is no longer a simple binary relation between, say, Spanish and Maya. Rather, it becomes a three-part relation between Spanish, Maya, and the neologized version of Maya, which we can call Maya*. The neologized Maya* has elements of both languages, and serves as a medium of exchange between them (Burkhardt 1989; Bricker 2002).

The relation here is similar to a currency system into which value from incommensurable domains (say, labor and cattle, or Christianity and Post-Classic Maya religion) can be converted and hence compared. It was simply impossible to translate theologically freighted Spanish terms like "*bautismo*" directly into Maya, but it was entirely possible to create a medium of semantic exchange in which to commensurate between the two languages.

A simple illustration of this is provided by the translations of "baptism" into Maya by colonial missionaries in Yucatán. As with virtually all of the theologically loaded language of the missionaries, the idea of baptism had no equivalent in Maya:

6. From *Bocabulario de maya than* (Acuña 1993: 141)

baptism	**Baptismo**	caa put çihil	Twice birth
the sacrament of baptism	el sacramento del baptismo	u sacramentoil oc haa	Its sacrament enter water
to baptize	bapti[ç]ar	ocçah haa ti pol; caa put çihçah	Enter water to head Twice cause to be born

Note in (6) that there were two quite different translations of the Spanish *baptismo*, one focusing on the way the sacrament is performed (enter water) and the other on the sacramental effect (second birth). It is also worth noting that "*sacramento*" is untranslated—which disambiguates the Maya "enter water." The same phrase was used in ordinary Maya to describe "leaky," as in a leaky roof.[8]

Moreover the Maya "twice birth" renders explicit the theological backing of Catholic baptism, namely that the person is reborn in Christ. The same expression "twice birth" is used in Maya* for the resurrection of Christ. Thus a Maya speaker learning that "twice born" translates *bautismo* immediately knows something that a Spanish speaker will only learn through exegesis, namely that baptism is a form of resurrection. There are many scores of examples like this in the colonial corpus, where neologized Maya* essentially renders explicit elements of the conceptual or theological backing left implicit in the corresponding Spanish terms (for many more examples, see Hanks 1988; Laughlin and Haviland 1988; Smith-Stark 2007; Knowlton 2010).

Examples like (6) are the product of a special kind of translation, which I call *commensuration*. The heart of the process lies in redescribing in grammatically correct Maya the objects or concepts stood for by the corresponding Spanish. The result is a generalized medium of semantic exchange in which the conceptual backing of the Spanish is paired with existing or newly formed signifiers in the Maya. In both cases, the resulting sign is a neologism.

Commensuration is a practical solution to the existential problem of incommensurability. When two languages or systems make distinctions sufficiently different as to make it impossible to intertranslate directly, then one translates via neologism and periphrastic description. Ultimately in a case like Maya, the neologos would bloom into a register that would in turn spread into the official discourse of the Maya republics.[9] By the late colonial period, Maya* is in use in all genres of writing by native Maya writers (Hanks 2010).

---

8. The same phrase, *och ha*, occurs in Classic Maya hieroglyphic inscriptions, with the meaning "to die." It is uncertain whether the missionaries knew this, but it further amplifies the aptness of the gloss for baptism, which marks the end of one person and the rebirth of a new person.

9. I use the term "register" in the sense developed by Agha (2006): that is, a variety of the language that is recognizable as distinct, backed by a discourse, and in a determinate relation to the standard. There is a substantial literature in linguistics on the concept of "mixed languages," reopening questions raised in pidginization and creolistics. See Meyers-Scotten (2003) and papers in the same volume.

Commensuration relies on precisely the same metalinguistic capacity as we saw in Don Ponso's pithy translations of deictic utterances into descriptive statements. Don Ponso used Maya to refer to and paraphrase Maya. Four hundred years earlier, Franciscan missionaries and their Maya assistants used Maya* to refer to and paraphrase the Spanish of catechism and law. The difference is that in the colonial case, two cultural worlds are being commensurated for the purpose of exchanging meaning. The exchange was bidirectional, to be sure, but it was inevitably asymmetric, with power residing clearly in the European doctrine. As a result, it was Maya that underwent neologization under the pressure of Spanish, and not the other way around.

This may be a point on which Asad's plea for power really strikes home. In cases of commensuration like this one, it is the subordinate language that is altered by neologism.[10] By contrast, in ordinary intralingual metalanguage, speakers feel no need to create neologisms, because the gloss and what it glosses are in the same language and not divided by power asymmetry.

Under this account, what is special about commensuration is that it operates over incommensurable cultural worlds, and provides a "common denominator" by which to bring them into alignment. Ordinary intralingual glossing is more a matter of (partial) equivalence within a single lingua-cultural world. It renders as translation a process of interpretance already autochthonous to the language.

But if Spanish–Maya commensuration was improvisational, it was still highly constrained. The missionaries were translating sacred language that expressed Truth. Proper reference and Truth preservation were the sine qua non of adequate translation. Pernicious ambiguities or unwonted entailments in Maya* were a constant concern, and the translations were revised throughout the colonial period.

Judging by the entire colonial corpus, the missionaries were guided by five principles (or perhaps preferences):[11]

---

10. Though see Santamaría (1992) for ample evidence of how Mexican Spanish was also altered through its intermingling with indigenous languages.

11. I am summarizing a large body of evidence spelled out in Hanks (2010), where the concept of commensuration is first proposed. Compare Canger (1997), Thiemer-Sachse (1997), and Smith-Stark (2007).

1. *Interpretance* is the starting premise that for any expression in Spanish, it was in principle possible to find an adequate Maya interpretation.

2. *Economy* dictated that translators use the minimum number of Maya roots to express the maximum number of distinct Spanish concepts. This was important for the register of Maya* to be learnable.

3. *Transparency* dictated that translators craft Maya* neologisms whose morphosyntactic elements were clearly distinguishable and relatable to discrete aspects of the target meaning. "Enter water" for baptism is an example, as are "cast sin" for confession (sacrament of reconciliation), *chochkeban* "untie sin" for absolution, and so forth. Transparency required mastery of Maya grammar (especially verbal morphology, compounding, incorporation, transitivity in the verb, among others). Without such knowledge, economy would fail because different senses of the same root would be indistinguishable.

4. *Indexical grounding* is the process whereby newly minted neologisms were bound to their canonical referents. Part of this process was the binding of the expressions into prayers and other texts, so that their meaning would be anchored in the cotextual elements.

5. *Beauty* stipulates that, all other things being equal, an aesthetically pleasing translation was to be preferred because it would more effectively move the heart of the new Christians. The Franciscans displayed a preference for simplicity, directness, and "aptness" in translation. For instance, *chochkeban*, "untie sin," is a very apt translation of absolution, because in canonical terms, absolution is the action whereby the priest unties sin.

One of the most striking features of commensuration in the colonial Maya case is that it altered the semantics of Maya language far beyond the confines of the missions. Just as translation was an ongoing process under revision, this transformation of Maya was a protracted historical process. Maya* was picked up by Maya speakers and writers, and became effectively the standard variety of the language. By the middle of the nineteenth century, this variety, Maya*, would become the language of rebellion against the colonial order under which it was born. This process, which I believe has analogues in many historical circumstances, raises a number of very productive questions, of which I mention two.

First, how did this appropriation occur? In broad outline, it took place through the local Maya governments, all of which functioned in Maya, and whose documentary archives are saturated with Maya*. Alphabetic writing was taught in the missions, and the local scribes were chosen and trained there.[12] Maya* simply became the variety of Maya that was written in the colonial period. Being associated with the church and provincial governance, this variety also became the language of legitimacy and power. Catechism classes enforced verbatim repetition and regular prayer, thus further driving the neologos into the expressive habits of Mayas operating in the colonial world.[13]

The second question I want to raise is: What happens to a translation if the erstwhile source text is lost or otherwise "untied" from it? The missionaries always tied their labors back to the canonical texts, but for Christian Mayas, the Maya* versions of the prayers are effectively the originals. It is the Maya* version of the Our Father or the Credo that they repeated daily and from which lines were transposed into other genres. Regardless of the conditions under which the new variety was produced, as it became native, it ceased to be translation and became its own original. This process, which took about two centuries in Yucatán, signaled a veritable conversion of Maya language (Hanks 2013).

As a minor illustration of what was a pervasive spread of linguistic change, consider example (7), taken from one of the native histories known as Books of Chilam Balam. These books are usually taken to embody "classic" Maya, which may be true in some respects, but is thoroughly undercut by the ubiquitous presence of specifically Christian Maya* in the books (see Bricker 1989, 2002, 2007).[14]

Thus in (7), the references to *hunab ku canal talane*, "One God come from heaven" (7.1), to worship *tuhahil auolah*, "in the truth of your heart" (7.4), the monumental belief of *oces tauol*, literally, "cause it to enter your heart" (line 7.6), are all neologisms found in the catechism. There is not one single morpheme of Spanish in this passage, nor is it presented as a translation, but it is a recognizable commensuration in which the semantic backing is Spanish and the

---

12. Writing introduces a whole new order of questions regarding translation. See Benveniste (2012), which combines Peircean interpretance with Saussurian semiotics. And for fascinating case studies in Native America, see Tedlock (1983) and Sammons and Sherzer (2000). The Maya case makes a very productive comparison with Quechua as described in depth by Durston (2007).

13. For detailed study of an analogous process among Quechua people of Peru, see Durston (2007). For further background on the Yucatec case, see Restall (1997), Chuchiak (2000), Okoshi Harada (2006), and Hanks (2010).

14. Compare Edmonson (1970, 1973) and Knowlton's (2010) excellent study and translation of the creation myth portions of the Books of Chilam Balam.

linguistic forms are Maya*. It is the product of translation, but in which there is no reference to the source, and therefore illustrates the ongoing conversion of Maya into Maya*.

Observe that this passage also displays exacting metalanguage in which the prophet quotes his own speech, and then (in 7.7–7.8) refers to it and paraphrases it as "weeping speech" and "explanation." The term *tzol* was also (and still is) the term for cross-linguistic translation in Maya, thus introducing a highly apt ambiguity.

7. Quoted speech in Codice Perez, page 73, lines 22–30 (Miram and Miram 1988: 3:67)

7.1	La u chicul hunab ku canal talane	*BEHOLD THE SIGN OF ONE GOD COME FROM HEAVEN*
7.2	la akulteex ah itzaexe	*BEHOLD THE ONE YOU SHALL WORSHIP, ITZA!*
7.3	ca a kulte helelae u chicul ku likul canale	*WORSHIP TODAY THE SIGN OF GOD FROM THE SKY*
7.4	ca a kulte tu hahil auolah	*WORSHIP HIM IN THE TRUTH OF YOUR HEART*
7.5	ca a kulte hahal kue	*WORSHIP TRUE GOD!*
7.6	oces tauol uthan hunab ku tali canal ...	*BELIEVE THE WORD OF ONE GOD COME FROM SKY*
7.7	yoktuba inthan cen Chilam balam	*MY WORDS WEPT, I (WHO) AM CHILAM BALAM*
7.8	ca tin tzolah u than hahal ku	*WHEN I EXPLAINED THE WORD OF TRUE GOD*

Lines 7.1–7.5 are cognate with Book of Tizimin f. 20, l. 2-4, but in the first person plural. Examples are taken from Hanks (2010).

This one example is barely the tip of an iceberg, but will suffice to show that Maya language was fully capable of intralingual glossing, and Maya speakers deployed this functional capacity with astuteness. In the Classic Maya inscriptions studied by epigraphers, there is a great deal of metalanguage as well, showing that this capacity is in no way a product of colonization. Signs have been identified for "write, speak, tell," and "signs" of various kinds. Throughout the colonial period, the prevalence of translation combined with the specific practices of commensuration to transform both the language and the consciousness of its speakers.

CONCLUSION

In this brief paper I have sketched out a line of thinking in which translation is not only productive but at the heart of language as a social form, and society as the dynamic product of self-interpretation. From an anthropological perspective, the examples I have adduced may appear narrow in their linguistic detail, but the processes involved are anything but narrow. As a method of comparative anthropology, translation reveals difference as much as similarity. This is an advantage. The very difficulty of translating terms as apparently simple as demonstratives casts the ethnographer onto the shoals of difference and clarifies the task of understanding a culture or society in terms of its own values (see Laughlin and Haviland 1988). The point is not to fetishize difference, but to situate the analytic task in the tension between partial similarity and partial difference. This is arguably the most subtle and difficult task for ethnographic description, and one with a long history in our discipline. It raises questions of commensurability, incorrigibility, and relativity. How can we recognize the constitutive role of self-interpretation in social life while avoiding the pitfall of collapsing analysis into native self-description? Native actors, including ourselves, are neither unconscious of the conditions of their lives nor are those conditions transparently available to them. They are neither caught in the blindness of sheer relativity, nor able to disembed their experiences and consider them dispassionately from afar. Language is neither the final arbiter of these questions, nor is it the mere projection of linguists. What is called for is a balanced recognition of the large mid-range in which these questions become not absolutes but variably blended elements.

Sooner or later, any understanding of translation, however generalized, must come to grips with language, which happens to be among the most delicate and finely calibrated institutions in any human society. And while we may focus selectively on key terms or concepts, no language is a collection of words, and to treat it as such is to distort it beyond recognition. In its variation, its generativity, its reflexive capacity for self-objectification, its ubiquity in social life, and its plurifunctionality, language is among the central features of social life. Boas and the Americanists were surely correct in attempting to discern the specificities of language in relation to consciousness, but they surely overstated its uniqueness. The sheer frequency with which speakers gloss, paraphrase, report, and justify linguistic practices demonstrates the robustness of their awareness. It is a truism that native metalanguage is not to be confused with the results of full-scale linguistic analysis: to know a language is not to be able to push an analysis to its logical limits, any more than knowing how to ride a bike implies the ability to spell out the physics implied in doing so. But this observation is merely the first step toward pluralizing ways of knowing and the knowledge to which they give rise.

I have insisted that the basis of cross-linguistic or cross-cultural translation lies in the self-interpretation that inheres in being a native actor. It is true that certain forms of translation pose formidable challenges, such as religious concepts, basic premises like perspectivism among some Amazonian groups, or banal assumptions as to the relatedness of objects and events which appear, from outside, as unrelated. It is equally true that in occupying any social world, one is always in the business of translating, transposing perspectives, transforming the implicit into the explicit, commensurating over difference, and shifting the figure–ground relations to leave implicit what is elsewhere explicit. It is always possible to gloss, but almost never possible to produce exact equivalence. We should therefore conceive of a family of operations instead of a static or monolithic relation between the translation and that which it purports to translate. This family would include cross-linguistic translation under carefully reasoned criteria, explanation, interpretation, and description of one lingua-cultural formation in the terms of another. But we must not forget that these operations are at work *within* any culture, and it is for that reason that we can even conceive of their operation across cultures. When a native Maya speaker glosses an indexical expression into a description of the force, meaning, or consequences of uttering that expression, (s)he is performing a metalinguistic act of objectification and interpretation, of rendering explicit pragmatic schemas that are at play implicitly in all speech. It makes no difference that their claims can be shown to be partial or contingent. This explicitation is the great advantage of such glossing, and it goes on when children are taught to speak and adult speakers are called upon to justify or interpret utterances by themselves or others. It is the stuff of understanding, and it is part of what it means to be a native actor. This is all the more true in that most societies are multilingual, and issues of translation and commensuration are inseparable from the ability to act and interact. We need not rush to the exotic in order to see this problem; it is a matter of daily practice.

However formidable the challenges of translating between truly different, maybe even incommensurable realities, such as colonizing religions and the beliefs or practices of those subjected to them, history demonstrates that people do manage to commensurate, however skewed and partial the results. It is ironic that exact translation is virtually impossible, but varieties of practically serviceable translation are everywhere. Here arises the question of evaluative criteria, for the impossibility is judged relative to a set of criteria usually foreign to those of people who actually translate on a daily basis. (This problem is one of the main issues addressed in Sammons and Sherzer 2000.) One way to state the challenge is to say we need to disembed the practice of translation from the institutionally defined concept of the translator as expert and arbiter of equivalence. We need to resituate it in the ordinary practices of native actors. Sometimes, as in the colonial Maya case, commensuration gives rise to a new register in the target language (Maya in this case). In less dramatic cases, sociolinguistic differentiation, blending, and "code switching" are virtually inevitable results of social plurality. Translation ceases to be a binary relation between two languages, and becomes a triadic relation between two languages mediated by a neologistic register in one (or both) of the languages. A neologized register, like Maya *reducido* (refered to above as Maya*), emerges in the manner of a generalized medium of exchange between the two starting languages. It commensurates between disjoint spheres, the way a money system commensurates between disjoint spheres of value. This is a historical process with consequences far beyond the language as a semantic system. When such a register spreads and is adopted by the speakers of the "target" language, it cuts loose from the source languages, ceasing to be translation and emerging as its own original. Here it is justified to speak of linguistic conversion and to spotlight the generative consequences of translation, so long as we keep in mind that what is emerging is no mere linguistic system, but a universe of practices, ways of self-objectifying, and schemes of interpretation—in short, if not a new world, then new ways of being in the world.

REFERENCES

Acuña, René, ed. 1993. *Bocabulario de maya than: Codex Vindobonensis N. S. 3833: facsimil y transcripción critica anotada.* Mexico: Instituto Nacional Autónoma de México.

Agha, Asif. 2006. *Language and social relations*. Cambridge: Cambridge University Press.

Asad, Talal. 1987. "The concept of cultural translation in British anthropology." In *Writing culture: The poetics and politics of ethnography*, edited by James Clifford and George E. Marcus, 141–64. Berkeley: University of California Press.

Benveniste, Émile. 1966. Problèmes de linguistique générale. Paris: Gallimard.

———. 1974. Problèmes de Linguistique Générale II. Paris: Gallimard.

———. 2012. *Dernières leçons: Collège de France (1968–1969)*. Paris: Gallimard/Seuil/EHESS.

Boas, Frans. 1911. "Introduction." In *Handbook of American Indian languages*, Vol. 1, edited by Franz Boas, 1–83. Washington, DC: Smithsonian Institution.

———. 1940. *Race, language and culture*. Chicago: University of Chicago Press.

Bricker, Victoria R. 1989 . "The last gasp of Maya hieroglyphic writing in the Books of Chilam Balam of Chumayel and Chan Kan." In *Word and image in Maya culture: Explorations in language, writing, and representation*, edited by William F. Hanks and Don S. Rice, 39–50. Salt Lake City: University of Utah Press.

———. 2002. *An encounter of two worlds: The Book of Chilam Balam of Kaua*. Tulane, LA: Middle American Research Institute.

———. 2007. "Literary continuities across the transformation from Maya hieroglyphic to alphabetic writing." *Proceedings of the American Philosophical Society* 151 (1): 27–41.

Burkhart, Louise. 1989. *The slippery earth, Nahua–Christian moral dialogue in sixteenth-century Mexico*. Tucson: University of Arizona Press.

Canger, Una. 1997. "El arte de Horacio Caroche." In *La descripción de las Lenguas Amerindias en la época colonial*, edited by Klaus Zimmermann, 59–74. Frankfurt: Verfuert Verlag.

Chuchiak, John. 2000. "The Indian Inquisition and the extirpation of idolatry: The process of punishment in the Provisorato de Indios of the diocese of Yucatán, 1563–1812." Dissertation, Tulane University, UMI Dissertation Services, Ann Arbor, MI.

Descola, Philippe. (2005) 2013. *Beyond nature and culture*. Translated by Janet Lloyd. Chicago: University of Chicago Press.

Durston, Alan. 2007. *Pastoral Quechua: The history of Christian translation in colonial Peru, 1550–1650*. Notre Dame, IN: University of Notre Dame Press.

Edmonson, Munro S. 1970. "Metáfora maya en literatura y en arte." In *Verhandlungen des XXXVIII Internationalen Amerikanistenkongresses*, Vol. 2, 37–50. Stuttgart/Munich.

———. 1973. "Semantic universals and particulars in Quiche." in *Meaning in Mayan languages: Ethnolinguistic studies*, edited by by Munro S. Edmonson, 235–46. The Hague: Mouton.

Evans-Pritchard, E. E. (1937) 1976. *Witchcraft, oracles and magic among the Azande*. London: Clarendon Press.

———. (1956) 1970. *Nuer religion*. Oxford: Clarendon Press.

Goodman, Nelson. 1978. *Ways of worldmaking*. Indianapolis, IN: Hackett.

Gossen, Gary. 1985. "Tzotzil literature." In *Supplement to the handbook of Middle American Indians*, Vol. 3, edited by Munro S. Edmonson, 65–106. Austin: University of Texas Press.

Hallen, Barry, and J. Olubi Sodipo. 1997. *Knowledge, belief and witchcraft: Analytic experiments in African philosophy*. Stanford: Stanford University Press.

Hanks, William F. 1983. "Deixis and the organization of interactive context." Ph.D. dissertation, Department of Linguistics and Department of Anthropology, University of Chicago.

———. 1988. "Grammar style and meaning in a Maya manuscript." *International Journal of American Linguistics* 54 (3): 331–64.

———. 1990. *Referential practice, language and lived space among the Maya*. Chicago: University of Chicago Press.

———. 1993. "Metalanguage and pragmatics of deixis." In *Reflexive language: Reported speech and metapragmatics*, edited by John Lucy, 127–58. Cambridge: Cambridge University Press.

———. 1996. "Language form and communicative practices." In *Rethinking relativity*, edited by John J. Gumperz and Stephen C. Levinson, 232–70. Cambridge: Cambridge University Press.

———. 2010. *Converting words: Maya in the age of the cross*. Berkeley: University of California Press.

———. 2011. "Deixis and indexicality." In *Handbook of pragmatics*, Vol. 1, edited by Wolfram Bublitz and Neal R. Norrick, 313–46. Berlin: Mouton de Gruyter.

———. 2013. "Language in Christian conversion." In *A companion to the anthropology of religion*, edited by Janice Boddy and Michael Lambek, 387–406. Oxford: Wiley.

Jakobson, Roman. 1957. "Shifters, verbal categories and the Russian verb." Department of Slavic Languages and Literatures, Harvard University.

Jakobson, Roman. (1959) 2004. "On linguistic aspects of translation." In *The translation studies reader*, edited by Lawrence Venuti, 138–43. Second edition. London: Routledge.

Knowlton, Timothy W. 2010. *Maya creation myths: Words and worlds of the Chilam Balam*. Boulder: University Press of Colorado.

Laughlin, Robert M., and John B. Haviland. 1988. *The great Tzotzil dictionary of Santo Domingo Zinacantán, with grammatical analysis and historical commentary. Volume I: Tzotzil–English*. Washington, DC: Smithsonian Institution Press.

Lucy, John, ed. 1993. *Reflexive language: Reported speech and metapragmatics*. Cambridge: Cambridge University Press.

Messick, Brinkley. 1996. *The calligraphic state: Textual domination and history in a Muslim Society*. Berkeley: University of California Press.

Meyers-Scotton, Carol. 2003. "What lies beneath: Split (mixed) languages as contact phenomena." In *The mixed language debate: Theoretical and empirical advances*, edited by Yaron Matras and Peter Bakker, 73–106. Berlin: Mouton de Gruyter.

Miram, Helga-Maria, and Wolfgang Miram. 1988. *Konkordanz der Chilam Balames*, Vols. 1–6, Transcriptions Vols. 1–4. Hamburg: Toto-Verlag.

Morris, Charles. 1971. *Writings on the general theory of signs*. The Hague: Mouton.

Mounin, Georges. 1963. *Problèmes théoriques de la traduction*. Paris: Éditions Gallimard.

Okoshi Harada, Tsubasa. 2006 . "*Kax* (monte) y *luum* (tierra): La transformación de los espacios mayas en el siglo XVI." In *El mundo Maya: Miradas Japonesas*, edited by Kazuyasu Ochiai, 85–104. Mexico: Universidad Naciónal Autónoma de México.

Peirce, Charles Sanders. 1940. "Logic as semiotic." In *Philosophical writings of Peirce*. Edited by Justus Buchler, 98–119. New York: Dover.

Pym, Anthony. 2010. *Exploring theories of translation*. London: Routledge.

Quine, Willard Van Orman. 1960. *Word and object*. Cambridge, MA: MIT Press.

Rafael, Vicente L. 1993. *Contracting colonialism: Translation and Christian conversion in Tagalog society under early Spanish rule*. Durham, NC: Duke University Press.

Restall, Matthew. 1997. *The Maya world, Yucatec culture and society, 1550–1850*. Stanford: Stanford University Press.

Rumsey, Alan. 2008. "Confession, anger and cross-cultural articulation in Papua New Guinea." Special issue, "Anthropology and the opacity of other minds," edited by Alan Rumsey and Joel Robbins, *Anthropological Quarterly* 81 (2): 455–72.

Sammons, Kay, and Joel Sherzer. 2000. *Translating native Latin American verbal art: Ethnopoetics and ethnography of speaking.* Washington, DC: Smithsonian Institution Press.

Santamaría, Francisco. 1992. *Diccionario de Mejicanismos.* Fifth. Mexico: Editorial Porrua, SA.

Sapir, Edward. 1949. *Selected writings of Edward Sapir.* Edited by David G. Mandelbaum. Berkeley: University of California Press.

Saussure, Ferdinand de. (1916) 2006. *Course in general linguistics.* Translated by Roy Harris. Chicago: Open Court.

Schieffelin, Bambi B. 2007. "Found in translating: Reflexive language across time and texts in Bosavi, Papua New Guinea." In *Consequences of contact: Language ideologies and sociocultural transformations in Pacific Societies*, edited by Miki Makihara and Bambi B. Schieffelin, 140–65. New York: Oxford University Press.

Sherzer, Joel. 1990. *Verbal art in San Blas: Kuna culture through its discourse.* Cambridge: Cambridge University Press.

Silverstein, Michael. 1976. "Shifters, verbal categories and cultural description." In *Meaning in anthropology*, edited by Keith H. Basso and Henry A. Selby, 11–55. Albuquerque: University of New Mexico Press.

Smith-Stark, Thomas C. 2007. "Lexicography in New Spain (1492-1611)." In *Missionary linguistics IV/Lingüística misionera IV. Lexicography. Selected papers from the Fifth International Conference on Missionary Linguistics.* Mérida/Yucatán.

Taylor, Charles. 1985. "Language and human nature." In *Human agency and language: Philosophical papers*, Vol. 1, 215–47. Cambridge: Cambridge University Press..

Tedlock, Dennis. 1983. *The spoken word and the work of interpretation.* Philadelphia: University of Pennsylvania Press.

Thiemer-Sachse, Ursula. 1997 . "El vocabulario castellano-zapoteco y el arte en lengua zapoteca de Juan de Córdova–Intenciones y resultados (perspectiva antropológica)." In *La descripción de las lenguas Amerindias en la época colonial*, edited by Klaus Zimmerman, 147–74. Frankfurt: Vervuert Verlag

Urban, Greg. 1991. *A discourse-centered approach to culture: Native South American myths and rituals.* Austin: University of Texas Press.

———. 2001. *Metaculture: How culture moves through the world.* Minneapolis: University of Minnesota Press.

Whalen, Gretchen. 2003. "Annotated translation of a colonial Yucatec manuscript: On religious and cosmological topics by a native author." Final report to the Foundation for the Advancement of Mesoamerican Studies.

CHAPTER TWO

Transmutating beings
A proposal for an anthropology of thought

CARLO SEVERI

> *Ineluctable modality of the visible: at least that if no more:*
> *thought through my eyes*
> —Joyce, *Ulysses* [1922] 1972: 42

In his *Remarks on Frazer's Golden Bough*, Wittgenstein writes that a good theory of magic should "preserve its depth," not simply condemn it as a mistake from the point of view of rationality. This "cancelling of magic"—he adds immediately after—would "have the character of magic itself" (Wittgenstein [1967] 1979: 1). Wittgenstein captures here one of the more deeply rooted ambitions of social anthropology: to reach a rational understanding of the forms of thought that we find enacted in ethnography. Classically, these forms of thought, from what Lévi-Strauss called the "systematization [of] what is immediately presented to the senses" ([1962] 1966: 11), to the causal theories studied by Evans-Pritchard, for instance in Zande witchcraft and oracles (1937), have been interpreted, at least since Boas (1989), as an expression of a specific language or "culture." To use a more recent terminology, thought has been linked to "ontologies" associated with certain languages and societies. This is why we still commonly speak of "Chinese," "Greek," "African," or "Amazonian" thought.

From a theoretical point of view, this way of defining thought calls for an epistemological preliminary remark and for three objections. The preliminary remark concerns the definition of thought itself From Lévy-Bruhl's considerations on "pre-logical mentality" (1949), up to Sperber's arguments on apparently irrational beliefs (1982), a great part of the anthropological literature devoted to this topic does not really concern the study of thought as a general human activity. It concerns the opposition between rationality and irrationality. In this perspective, anthropologists usually compare an abstract definition of "rationality" with an empirical counterpart, mostly founded on the analysis of some forms of categorization and theories of causality. It is obvious, however, that there is much more to human thought than categorization, or propositional rationality. Ideas about perception and space, language and communication, right or wrong moral values, for instance, are constantly present in ethnography. It would be hard to qualify them as "rational" or "nonrational" (or even "symbolic"). As we know, at least since Austin (1975), concepts of this kind would be better qualified as "appropriate" or "inappropriate," "felicitous" or "infelicitous" in a certain context, than as rational or nonrational. In sum, when approaching the idea of an anthropology of thought, there is a preliminary choice to make. Either one chooses what we may call a Piagetian model of thought-as-rationality, seen in its various manifestations, but defined only through the opposition between rational or nonrational (e.g., Piaget [1923] 2001, [1926] 2007); or one refers to a more extensive, and more realistic, definition of thought. One of the classic authors who have worked in this direction (and whom we could, in this respect, oppose to Piaget) is Vygotsky, the great Russian psychologist (Vygotsky 1978). Not unaware of the problems posed by cultural differences, Vygotsky elaborated a multifaceted conception of the exercise of thought, which includes not only rational inference, but also metalinguistic, metacommunicational, aesthetic ("thought through our eyes," as Joyce defines it), and narrative thought. In this exploratory and speculative paper, I will take, as a starting point, this Vygotskian option, and try to develop it in a new direction. But let us first examine the three classic objections to the definition of thought, so common in our discipline, as directly linked to culture, language, and society.

The first objection is empirical and has been known at least since the works of Sapir (1985) on North American cultures. Societies sharing the same "system of thought" may speak different languages, and vice versa. Thus, we know of cases (consider, for example, the Quechua-speaking peoples of the Amazon—Gutierrez Choquelvica 2010, 2011) in which language is not necessarily a good key to understand culture.

The second objection has a more theoretical character. The idea that we can establish a direct relationship between thought and language has, in many ways, proven to be logically weak. In his classic essay about translation, Jakobson has an amusing episode illustrating this point. "In the first years of the Russian revolution there were fanatic visionaries who argued in Soviet periodicals for a radical revision of traditional language and particularly for the weeding out of such misleading expressions as 'sunrise' or 'sunset.' Yet we still use this Ptolemaic imagery without implying a rejection of Copernican doctrine" (Jakobson 1959: 234). Jakobson's conclusion is clear: if a relation between language and thought exists, it is an indirect and controversial one, and we should never take it for granted (or infer qualities of thought from language structures) without further investigation.

The third objection is that the languages that we use to qualify different kinds of thought are constantly translated. Despite all its difficulties, translation in all its various forms, from translation of different languages to "translation of different systems of thought" (as analyzed, for instance, by Kuhn [(1962) 2012] or Lloyd [1996, 2006, 2007]), is a cognitive task that the people we study are often and in many ways confronted with. As Jakobson again remarks: "Both the practice and the theory of translation abound in intricacies and from time to time attempts are made to sever the Gordian knot by proclaiming the dogma of untranslatability. . . . [However,] all cognitive experience and its classification is conceivable in any existing language" (1959: 232). One might think that in the classic debate that opposes relativists to universalists, Jakobson is here the taking side of universalism. However, his argument on translation is more nuanced that it may appear at first sight. His position relies on a distinction that both universalists and relativists rarely pay attention to. Jakobson remarks that since, as Boas (1938: 127) has observed, "the grammatical pattern of a language (as opposed to its lexical stock) determines those aspects of each experience that must be expressed in the given language," languages "differ essentially in what they *must* convey and not in what they *may* convey" (Jakobson 1959: 235–36). For instance, many North American Indian languages encode a distinction between visible and invisible, as in this Kwakiutl example:

T'e'semgya   "this stone (visible, near me)"
T'e'semgya'   "this stone (invisible, near me)"

Since these languages distinguish visibility of the referent to the speaker, the speakers of such languages are forced to attend to the visibility or invisibility of the objects they refer to. To designate a stone in Kwakiutl, one must mention whether it is visible and close to the speaker, or not. This does not mean that Kwakiutl, as a language, could not express the same "cognitive experiences" that are commonly expressed in languages, like European languages, which do not encode visibility in demonstratives (cf. Hanks, this volume). Despite a number of constraints concerning what they "must convey" (aspects of reality they "have to" express in words), all languages are translatable and constantly translated. From these considerations, one can draw the conclusion that universalists are right when they affirm that "all cognitive experience . . . is conveyable in any existing language" (Jakobson 1959: 234) and relativists are not entirely wrong when they underline that different languages obey different grammatical constraints "that determin[e] those aspects of each experience that must be expressed in the given language" (ibid.: 235–36).

Once these points are granted, however, one might still wonder whether the potential translatability of all languages is a good reason to stop minding, or (as some universalists would argue) even thinking about, the kind of cultural difference which is thus expressed by language use. It is true that one difficulty in accounting for these grammatical differences in theoretical terms lies in the fact that it is often hard to understand their raison d'être. They seem to obey no general rule. Differences in grammatical patterns might be episodic. Hence, they seem to have no general (theoretical) import. One can simply disregard them, or consider them curious but hardly relevant for an analysis of thought necessarily based on general principles.

To respond to this objection, one might use the distinction, currently used in logic, between the *power* (the possibility to account for a limited number of features valid for a great number of cases) and the *expressivity* (the possibility to account for a great number of features belonging to a limited number of cases) of symbolic systems (Mangione 1964: 52–53). Any case-centered inquiry (e.g., a fieldwork-based ethnography) needs to be in some measure expressive, while any comparative or statistical analysis needs to be reasonably powerful. With this distinction in mind, one could say that all human natural languages have potentially the same logical power, while they constantly differ in degrees of expressivity. This not only means that the grammatical differences between languages are specific forms of a general logical property of all symbolic systems ("degrees of expressivity"), not simply "episodic" or contingent phenomena; it also means that (as the indecisive results of the debate about linguistic relativism also indicate) the controversy between universalists and relativists, if still formulated in traditional terms, might well prove to be quite undecidable. Seen from this perspective, the problems posed by cultural translatability would not be solved by taking a universalistic attitude, trying to eliminate different degrees of expressivity that we find in different languages.Equally unproductive would be a relativistic theory that refused to admit any general property of human languages. In this paper I would like to show that a good account of the question, and a solution of the controversy, would rather lie not in the elimination of one of the two aspects of the question, but in the possibility of understanding the many ways in which logical power and expressivity, in different languages and in different semiotic codes, may relate with each other. In short, more theoretical and empirical work is needed not only to solve the problem of the translatability of cultures, but also to formulate it correctly.

I will argue that, instead of seeing the possibility of translation as a theoretical difficulty for defining thought, we could, on the contrary, consider the ethnography of translation as a chance to observe the dynamics of thought processes, and to study how they operate, both in adapting to constraints and in exploiting possibilities, in different cultural contexts. From this ethnographic perspective, the question of understanding the kind of cognition that might be involved by the use of "a" language (with its own specific degree of expressivity), or by the formulation of "a" specific ontology (or "system of thought"), ceases to be the only question we are confronted with. Another question, equally important, arises: How are we to describe the kind of cognition that is constantly mobilized *in the process of translating* languages (and in passing from one "ontology" to another)? To use Jakobson's terms, how is it possible to pass from what a language" (or any other symbolic system) *must* convey" to what it "*may* convey"?

Furthermore, the distinction between what a symbolic system "must" or "may" convey is not necessarily confined to semantic and grammatical questions, or to cultural differences. Ethnography constantly shows (and Jakobson also admits) that there is more to translation than language. Processes of "translation" (involving specific cognitive tasks) operate not only between different cultures (or languages), but also between different pragmatic contexts in the same language, and between linguistic and nonlinguistic ways of expression, even within single societies. Thus, a second series of questions related to the question of translatability arises: How can we describe these forms of cognition? Are they identical, comparable, or totally different from the cognition involved in linguistic translation processes? Does the logical distinction between what "has to" be conveyed and what "might be" conveyed also apply to this context-to-context or verbal-to-nonverbal form of translation?

Obviously, to try to give a full answer to all these general questions in a single paper would be unreasonable. I will, then, limit my argument to a single kind of translation, as it operates in a specific ethnographic area. Using three Amazonian examples, I will try to describe the kind of cognition involved in the form of translation that Jakobson calls *transmutation*. I will argue that from this ethnographic analysis, we can not only derive a better (both wider and more precise) idea of some, rarely studied, cultural translation processes, but also draw from it a new way to define the concept of "cultural ontology." The anthropology of the Amazon offers an ideal field for this kind of analysis. In the last twenty years, at least since the publication of Descola and Taylor's "La remontée de l'Amazone" (1993), the question of the relationship between iconographies, narrative structures, ritual chants, and, in general, the pragmatics of the transmission of knowledge has been intensely and productively debated in this area of study, The groundbreaking work of Rafael José de Meneses Bastos (1978, 1999, 2007) has shown how music performed in ritual action can function as a sort of lingua franca in the Upper Xingu, providing for a common ground of shared knowledge in a multilingual group of societies where a pidgin was never invented. A crucial corollary of this general conception is that the original source of music is not human, but essentially animal (e.g., Beaudet 1983, 1997; Brabec de Mori and Seeger 2013). Humans generally "learn" or "acquire" their music from nonhumans. This is why music is also used for communicating with spirits.

The group of researchers first gathered by Vidal, Pessis, and Guidon (2000), probably inspired by the fundamental work of Guss (1986, 1989), and subsequent work by Gow (1988, 1999), Barcelos Neto (2002, 2008, 2009, 2011, 2013), Taylor (2003), Velthem (2003, 2013), Lagrou (2007, 2009a, 2009b, 2011, 2013; Severi and Lagrou 2013), Belaunde (2009, 2013), Cesarino (2011), Fausto (2011a, 2011b, Langdon (2013), and Fausto and Penoni (2014), among many others, have shown that myths cannot be used as "captions" of iconographies, nor can images or artifacts be understood as illustrations of myths. A complementary relation exists in Amazonian iconographic practices, just like in other kind of Amerindian iconographies (Severi 2012), between myths, ritual chants, and the drawings, picture-writings, or body-decorations related to them. As a consequence, iconographies are no longer seen as redundant decorations. They are understood as "variations" of the same "conceptual imagination" that generates mythical narrations (Barcelos Neto 2013: 181; Severi and Fausto 2014). Eventually, as, for instance, Meneses Bastos (1978), Basso (1981), Beaudet (1997), Piedade (2004), Seeger (2004), Fausto, Franchetto, and Montagnani (2011), and Brabec de Mori and Seeger (2013)have also shown, synesthesia is everywhere in the Amazon. Not only do complex verbal compositions, like shamanistic chants, always presuppose the experience of vision (e.g., Luna 1992; Townsley 1993; Hill 1993, 1994, 2009; Severi [2007] 2015), but "what can be seen as an image" can always be perceived, by another subject and from another perspective (Viveiros de Castro 2004), as a sequence of sounds. This is why, as Barcelos Neto has recently shown, the image of a mythical anaconda can be interpreted, among the Wauja, simultaneously as a sequence of graphic themes and as a sequence of chants (Barcelos Neto 2013: 183).

How can we understand this situation of constant "synesthetic fusion" (ibid.: 187) where "what is seen" can be constantly translated into "what is heard," and vice versa? What happens when the same concept (often expressed by a proper noun) is "translated" from verbal expressions to images and from images to sounds?

FORMS OF TRANSLATION: DEFINITIONS

Let us get back to Jakobson. He has defined three forms of translation: intralinguistic, interlingual, and transmutation. According to him, "intralinguistic translation or "rewording" is an interpretation of verbal signs by means of other signs of the same language," "interlingual translation or *translation proper* is an interpretation of verbal signs by means of some other language," and "intersemiotic translation or *transmutation* is an interpretation of verbal signs by means of signs of nonverbal sign systems" (Jakobson 1959: 233). A very rich literature in linguistics and in anthropology has been devoted to the intricacies, both practical and theoretical, of the two first kinds of translation (and to the general question of linguistic relativism that they imply).[1] The third form has been, by far,

---

1. To give an account of this tradition of studies, one should refer at least to the classic question of linguistic relativity (from classic works by Boas, Sapir [1985] and Whorf [2012] to Kay 1978; Kay and Kempton 1984; and Gilbert et al. 2006; see also Lucy 1992 or Gumperz and Levinson 1996) and the recent debates on the nature of linguistic translation (see, e.g., Rubel and Rosman 2003). Both tasks are well beyond the scope of this paper.

less studied. In the paper I have just quoted, Jakobson tends to consider it only a theoretical possibility. He is far from being the only scholar who adopts this attitude. When approaching the subject, the great majority of authors—with few notable exceptions (among them Goodman [1976] and Baxandall [1993])—avoid any attempt at detailed analysis. Some authors simply confuse transmutation with its reverse: verbal comment on visual or acoustic images (see, e.g., McGaffey in Rubel and Rosman 2003: 257–58). Others affirm that this form of translation, because it relies upon heterogeneous codes of signs (verbal and nonverbal), can hardly generate a consistent way to represent knowledge. Others (among them Wittgenstein [(1914–16) 1974] and Bateson [1979]) think that since an iconic code is not a means of communication comparable to writing, no cultural tradition, or transmission of knowledge, can be built on it. As a result, transmutation is seen as either too arbitrary or too subjective to be really compared to linguistic translation.

We anthropologists cannot afford this attitude. The ethnography of "oral" traditions often confronts us not only with consistent, effective, and long-lasting systems of interpretation of verbal signs by means of images (like, for instance, Plains Indians picture-writings, the Andean khipus, or Nahuatl pictography—Severi 2013), but also with a fourth variety of translation, which we could call *transmutation proper*. In many Amerindian cultures, for instance, we find that the interpretation of signs belonging to a nonverbal system can also be realized by means of signs belonging to *another* nonverbal system. For instance, a statement or a notion usually expressed through words can be first "translated" into images, and then further "translated" (one should say "*transmutated*") into music or ritual gestures. My purpose is to show:

(a) that in these cultures, transmutation, far from being "arbitrary" or "subjective," has general technical (semiotic) properties that generate a specific logical form that we shall define as a multilayered four-term analogy; and

(b) that the analysis of cultural forms of transmutation can reveal a special kind of "cognition about ontology" that leads to the construction of interspecific beings.

I will take here the example of three Amerindian iconographic traditions from the Upper Orinoco region (Yekwana, Wayana, and Wayampi) where the process of transmutation of narrations into visual images, and then of visual images into sequences of sounds ("transmutation proper"), is developed in particularly interesting ways, both in iconographic and in musical traditions.[2] The Yekwana and the Wayana are Carib-speaking hunters and horticulturalists from the Upper Orinoco region of Venezuela and Brazil. The Wayampi, who speak a Tupi-Guarani language, are neighbors of the Wayana and belong to the same cultural group. I will use the first ethnographic case, Yekwana weavings, to identify some basic formal (or semiotic) features of transmutation as a nonarbitrary and non-subjective form of translation "from verbal signs to nonverbal signs." I will use the second and third cases, Wayana iconographies (which are an interesting and consistent development of the Yekwana visual tradition) and Wayampi music, not only to confirm the formal features of transmutation (and transmutation proper), but also to raise some new questions concerning the concept of ontology, and the kind of thought which is expressed through these iconographies.

YEKWANA WEAVINGS AND MYTHOLOGY: TWO FORMAL PROPERTIES OF TRANSMUTATION

Yekwana mythology (de Civrieux [1970] 1997; Guss 1989) is composed of a long cycle of tales describing the various bloody episodes of a conflict that is seen as governing the entire universe. The conflict is between Wanadi, a positive being associated with the sun, who presides over human material culture (agriculture, fishing, hunting and tool-making), and his twin brother, Odosha, who is a personification of evil, misfortune, illness, and death. This cosmic battle is not simply responsible for the creation of the universe, but has continued unabated since the beginning of time, and still affects everyday human existence, often with tragic consequences. According to the Yekwana, evil always triumphs over good, which is why their ally, Wanadi, lives in a distant part of the heavens and has limited contact with the human world below. In contrast, his evil twin, Odosha, who lives surrounded by demons (often represented as invisible animal and plant "masters"), is a constant, threatening presence. This explains why representations of Odosha include a wide range of different, maleficent creatures (howler monkeys, snakes, jaguars, and foreign cannibals), whereas Wanadi, the sole defender of humans, is holed up in his corner of the heavens. Indeed, the

---

2. I have written a first analysis of Yekwana and Wayana iconographies in a paper devoted to the nature of "chimerical" representations (Severi 2011). On the Yekwana pictographs as an example of the Amerindian "arts of memory," see Severi (2013).

Yekwana consider that all hunting or fishing or agricultural activities must be carried out against the will of a host of "invisible masters" of plants and animals. This world of potential enemies belongs to Odosha and his demons. This basic asymmetry between good and evil is coupled with an idea that the one constantly transforms into the other. For the Yekwana, all cultural achievements (weapons, weaving techniques, body-painting, etc.) are the result of a transformation of evil or of the creatures that rely on it. This means that all creatures and creations are necessarily ambiguous as everything that is useful or good contains a transformation of some evil being.

As David Guss (1989) has shown, the visual memory associated with this mythology is linked to a specific iconography, woven into twill-plaited basketry, which constitutes a sort of "catalogue" of the names of these creatures. Among the Yekwana, the skill of weaving baskets "measures the maturity and character of any developing male member of the society" (ibid.: 79). To weave baskets has, for Yekwana boys, a veritable initiatory role that can be understood as a cycle of ritual actions. A young man cannot become a husband without learning this technique and the knowledge of the graphic patterns that is associated with it. At his marriage, every young man must weave for his bride a series of baskets in a strict prescribed order. With each basket are associated symbols of rebirth, health, and purity, but also threats of death. Actually, depending on the design inscribed in it, a basket can feed a person, but it also can poison him or her. This is the reason why the choice of a graphic pattern for a basket has to be made with extreme care. To choose the decoration of a basket, the husband has to consult his father, who usually is the human "owner" of the design. The father will hand to him the right to weave a number of designs into the surface of the basket (ibid.: 81–82), and the young man will have to weave them for all his life. In this sense, writes Guss, a basket design might assume the importance of a family crest passed on from generation to generation, though its real function is, for the Yekwana, to define a couple's identity, representing in a durable way what has been until then an amorphous and transitional relation. As long as husband and wife remain together, the special images woven into the basket will be a clear statement of the strength and uniqueness of their bond (ibid.: 82).

Actually, the twill-plaited baskets, decorated with designs that every man has to weave to prepare for and confirm his marriage (and to accomplish his male initiation), are strictly connected with the ritual relations that humans entertain with nonhuman and mythical beings. The baskets incorporate a complex system of symbols that acts as an index and key to the rest of the culture. This point explains, as Guss also remarks, why "the most accomplished ritual singers and the most skillful basket makers are inevitably one" (ibid.: 85). Actually, baskets are generally said to be the property of nonhuman supernatural "masters." But this notion of property often becomes much stronger: baskets as artifacts are themselves said to be "embodiments" (ibid.: 102) of the mythical beings. Like the ancestral predators they incarnate, they are "living beings" that can attack humans. Their designs woven into their surface are the "body paints" that decorate the skin of the mythical predators (ibid.). "The identification of the baskets with the demonic forces of Odosha is reaffirmed in every story in which they appear," writes Guss. "When a Yekwana narrated the origin of the baskets to the French explorer Gheerbrant, the power he ascribed to them was that of Odosha himself. Baskets did not simply signify death, they actually caused it" (ibid.: 103). A myth quoted by Guss confirms this point very clearly. When the artifacts appear in the narration of the origin of the world, they are immediately shown to be living beings with decorated skins: "The baskets began to walk, and they entered the water [of a river]. They were caiman-alligators—you had only to look at their skins to see that" (Gheerbrant 1954, cited in ibid.: 103).

We will get back to the kind of agency, connected to ritual action, which is attributed here to the Yekwana artifacts. We will see that many other artifacts of this kind, in all our Guyana cases, are ritually endowed with life. Let us focus, for the moment, on the interpretation of the graphic patterns appearing on the baskets and related to the chants, "mostly composed of lists of names of mythical beings" (Guss 1989: 36), that accompany their weaving. It is remarkable that, rather than trying to represent a particular mythological event in a "realistic" way, Yekwana weaving organizes mythological knowledge at a more profound level: in the iconography, each being is graphically linked to its invisible side. Let us see how. As we have already noted the two central tenets of this mythological system are a constitutive opposition between two principal types of creatures (good and bad) and the idea that a process of continual transformation affects them. These metamorphoses take two forms. On the one hand, a multiple being such as Odosha may "take the form" of a whole series of other creatures—in which case we see a movement from an individual to a series. On the other hand, this process of constant metamorphosis (wherein good is necessarily a transformation of evil) gives rise to individual creatures possessed of an inherent ambiguity that makes them simultaneously positive and negative—in which case the movement is from a series of creatures to one complex being that synthesizes them.

Yekwana iconography proposes precise visual translations of these two organizational principles. Indeed, all visual themes representing spirit names are
derived from a single grapheme: a sort of inverted "T" that represents Odosha
(Figure 1). A few simple geometrical transformations allow all other mythical characters to be derived from this grapheme. This conveys the idea of the
creatures' singularity (as monkeys, serpents, toads, etc.) as derivations of an elementary pattern (Figure 2). In this way, the different characters are developed
out of a single basic form in a system that is capable of representing not only
specific characters, but also their possible relationships. These relationships (of
analogy, inclusion, and transformation) bespeak an internal organization clearly
predicated on a single criterion: the representation of the *potential plurality* of
all creatures. But this is not all. The visual technique outlined above implies the
interplay between forms (or between form and background) that allows for the
simultaneous representation of a specific creature and one of its potential metamorphoses. Several mythical characters (e.g., monkeys, bats, toads) can thus be
represented as potentially dual beings. An example of this "chimerical character"
of the being represented by this iconography is the graphic theme called *woroto
sakedi* ("jaguar mask," Figure 3), which simultaneously represents Odosha and
Awidi, one of his serpent avatars, depending on whether one focuses on the
form of the T, which functions here as a frame, or on one of its segments, which
represents, with its spiriform pattern, the enrolling of Awidi, the coral snake.
Let us briefly analyze now the formal properties which, in this case, preside
over the process of translation of narrations ("verbal signs," here represented
by proper nouns) into images. It is clear that in the Yekwana case the passage
from verbal to nonverbal code does not involve a simple equivalence between
code-units. Rather, this form of translation mobilizes two equivalent messages
in two different codes, language and conventional iconography. Each code is
organized following its own rules. In other words, there is indeed semiotic heterogeneity. Nonetheless, the relation between the two codes is not arbitrary, nor
episodic. The technique that enables the Yekwana weaver to realize the passage from verbal to nonverbal signs actually follows at least two basic features.
The first is *selectivity*. Not every sign belonging to a narration is "translated
into" images in the weavings—only the nouns of the mythological creatures
are translated. Verbs or adjectives, for instance, are never represented in visual
terms. The second feature is *visual redundancy*. The visual pattern woven into the
surface of a basket not only represents the name of the creatures of the myth;
it also reveals, in the case of the first series (Figure 2), their relationship to the

"elementary pattern" (Odosha/Wanadi) they all derive from. In the case of the "jaguar mask,"" the "chimerical" creature that associates Odosha and Awidi in a single image, the image is generated by the superposition of Odosha and the "coral snake" pattern (Figure 3). In both cases (the series and the "chimera"), the geometrical pattern on which the image is based is redundant, since it "gives hints" about the nature and mutual relationships of mythical creatures that are not present in their names.

Figure 1. Odosha (from Guss 1989: 172).

Figure 2. The Toad and (below) the Frog (from Guss 1989: 201).

Figure 3. Awidi, the snake, and Odosha, combined in the pattern known as "jaguar mask" (from Guss 1989: 182).

I have shown elsewhere (Severi 2013) that the two basic features of selection and redundancy play a constitutive role in American Indian picture-writing, and that they can generate more complex configurations. But even from this first example, we can conclude that "transmutation" in Amerindian iconographic traditions, even if it does not "follow rules" in the same way that the grammar of a language does, can be shown to be—quite unexpectedly—logically consistent and, in its own way, systematic. We can draw the conclusion that in the Yekwana iconography, the passage from verbal to nonverbal signs is neither arbitrary, nor subjective.

WAYANA ICONOGRAPHIES: LOGICAL FORM AND ONTOLOGY

Let us now turn to the Wayana. They share with the Yekwana the technique of weaving and a very similar notion of iconographic representation (and even particular graphic themes, such as that of the jaguar [Velthem 2003: 352–56]). For both groups, iconographic representation is an elaboration of simple geometrical forms such as triangles, squares, spirals, and intersecting or parallel lines, and for both groups, this type of representation concerns the commentary and memorization of myths, and has close connection with ritual action. For the Wayana too, weavings are potentially living beings, and can become active in specific situations. What distinguishes Wayana from Yekwana iconography is the complexity of the discourse surrounding visual representation. Four concepts play a central role in this context. The first is *wayaman*. For the Wayana, a geometric theme woven into the surface of a basket is not merely the sign or emblem of a mythological being; it is also the reflection of a specific form of knowledge known as *wayaman*, which is metaphorically situated in the pupil of the person who masters weaving techniques. *Wayaman* is an "inverted figure" of an anthropomorphic spirit present in the pupil of the basket-weaver, and it is the *wayaman*, not the person who made it, who is the object's true "author." The *wayaman* is conceived of as a type of "thought," but also as a reflection of this "other" who lives in the weaver's eyes and "guides his hand," and it is only truly revealed when the object is created in accordance with traditional rules. Once the form is completed, then the object will reveal its true nature and show itself to be "like a living creature," and the "property" and incarnation of an ancestral nonhuman being.

The second concept concerns what the Wayana call the "skin" of the image. Actually, in Wayana tradition, artifacts, humans, and nonhumans can, and sometimes must, be adorned in the same way. In these cases, they "adopt the same skin." This is a key notion because for the Wayana the skin, or rather the skin painted with a recognizable pattern, represents "that element that allows for the identification of a being's actual nature" (Velthem 2003: 129). Thus, if some ritual artifacts are thought of as "copies" or "imitations" of ancestral predator beings (such as anaconda, vulture, and jaguar), it is because they bear the same skin. Because of this "identity of design" (and of the *wayaman* they incarnate), artifacts (as in the Yekwana case) can "dance", "talk," and even "attack" like predators. To illustrate the complexity and flexibility of this notion of "skin," Velthem cites the example of the dances held in the men's ceremonial hut. The men's ceremonial hut is supposed to be "inhabited by certain fishes," who feature (alongside numerous other animals) on the central ceiling wheel of the great ceremonial hut (Figure 4). But the fishes are also represented as "bearing the skin of long-beaked hummingbirds," and so when masked men, during their dances, "act like fishes," they *also* become "long-beaked hummingbirds." To be more precise, they then *adopt the skin* of a series of beings: fishes, long-beaked hummingbirds, and young male human beings.

Figure 4. A central ceiling wheel of a Wayana ceremonial hut. (Geneva, Musée d'Ethnographie. Photo: J. Watts.)

The third concept related to Wayana iconography refers to a particular way to categorize "supernatural" beings. The idea of a potential and unceasing transformation of all beings is widespread throughout the Amazon. We have seen that among the Yekwana, this is expressed via the opposition between two enemy brothers, Wanadi and Odosha, who represent good and evil, respectively. The Wayana share this idea. However, for them, predators and nonpredators are not individual characters with distinct personalities. Where the Yekwana rely on paradigmatic personalities, the Wayana think in terms of classes. Instead of contrasting a Wanadi to an Odosha, they distinguish between different *modes of existence* that can be applied to all creatures, be they animal, vegetable, human, or artifact. Consider the anaconda, one of the classic predators. "Its acts of predation," Velthem notes, "are so paradigmatic that not only do they invariably evoke the wider supernatural dimension, but they can also refer to the acts of any other species." This notion of predator-as-paradigm is not limited to the anaconda. It is usually extended to other predators. "This conception", Velthem continues, "allows other creatures, such as caterpillars, centipedes, fishes, and birds, to display predatory instincts in a supernatural setting via their association with jaguars, vultures, or anacondas" (ibid.: 105). In such cases, the anaconda (or the jaguar or the vulture) will "bear the name, the *wayaman*, and the skin" of the animals in question.

This type of categorization is also present in language. Velthem remarks that "this coupling of creatures is linguistically signaled for instance, by the suffix *okoin,* which means 'qua anaconda' and is applied to a specific species" (ibid.: 105). So *kiap* (the toucan) becomes *koimë* or "toucan-qua-anaconda" and is represented by a long-beaked serpent whose skin is covered with feathers of different colors. A similar process also exists for the jaguar, whose presence is signaled by a different suffix (*kaikuxin*), which marks the transformation of animals like the rodent *quatipuru* into "rodent-qua-jaguar."

Sometimes, these complex definitions are interpreted as referring to "qualities," or "gradient of qualities," belonging to different species (Viveiros de Castro 1998; Lima 2000). However, qualities are *partial* properties attributed to a (logically preexisting) object. For instance, in a statement like "this butterfly is red," I suppose the potential existence of other properties, such as "light," "noisy," "flying," and so on. When I designate, as the Wayana do, "a toucan-qua-anaconda," I am using a *being,* not a property, to designate the mode of existence of another being. Instead of enumerating the properties of a single being, I am connecting in a single statement two different beings. The result of this connection is a plural creature, not a series of qualities belonging to a single being. Consider the example we have just mentioned of the dances held in the men's ceremonial hut. When masked men "act like fishes" and thus behave also "like long-beaked hummingbirds," they give birth to new, ritually generated complex creatures, not to an enumeration of the possible qualities of a preexisting being. The same is true for the twofold (or serial) characters of the Yekwana baskets and, as we will see later, for the "acoustic complex beings" of Wayampi music.

Actually, we should understand terms like "toucan-qua-anaconda" as "verbal chimeras" that describe composite and changing beings that belong to a common class by virtue of their suffix. The concept of a "series," which is also present in Yekwana iconography, here assumes a different aspect, for the Yekwana series are, so to speak, linear series of beings. In the Wayana series, beings are *embedded in* each other. Thus, in another kind of dance, linked to the initiation of young men, the initiate wears a series of masks that transform him into a composite being made up not only of different spirits (macaws, falcons, fish, sun, rainbow, etc.), but also of different forms of these spirits "qua" incarnations of different predators: jaguars, vultures, and anacondas (Velthem 2003: 212). In this double series of markings on the initiate's body, the concept of chimerical representation reaches unprecedented levels of complexity. The ritual becomes a site of transformation wherein masked young men progressively "assume the painted skin" (and the *wayaman*) of a whole series of animal, vegetable, and human spirits that are themselves subject to innumerable metamorphoses.[3]

Let us see some examples of this kind of representation in iconography. Wayana graphic themes are divided into three distinct categories: those that "belong" to anaconda body-decorations; those that are linked to the skin of the jaguar; and those that evoke the skin of "anthropomorphic monsters" (a category that includes enemies such as white people). Particular visual motifs that retain their specific referent are then used to identify groups or entire categories of creatures. For instance, writes Velthem, "one of the paradigmatic forms of predation is the act of 'wounding, stabbing or piercing'. The act that synthesizes such predation ('to pierce the skin with a projectile') is characteristic of an artifact (the arrow) as well as of several animals, including cobras, wasps, scorpions, and birds such as the maguari stork (*Florida caerulae*)" (ibid.: 322–23). This bird is recognized as the prototype of piercing creatures and is represented by a motif called the "maguari beak" (Figure 5), whose outline depicts the animal's "wary and attentive posture." "In fact, this graphic theme represents both the arrow as artifact and any predatory animal that can strike its prey like an arrow. The double arrow symbol, then, describes fairly indeterminately 'everything that pierces'" (ibid.: 183).

In other cases, we can find the same principle differently deployed. We have seen that the "maguari beak" is a single symbol that designates several beings. But "Wayana graphic patterns can be themselves composite" (ibid.: 313). In such cases, the image can be broken down into several parts, each with its own distinct referent. So, for instance, the theme "crab" (Figure 6) also contains the theme "tapir's eye." Interpretation then relies on what Velthem calls an "internal dialogue" of forms that takes place within the graphic theme itself.[4]

The fourth fundamental Wayana concept related to iconicity is the distinction between the *ukuktop* (or "perceptual image" of an animal that can be observed in the forested environs of a village, with its morphology, normal behavior,

---

3.   For Velthem, beings considered "qua-anacondas" are those capable of clasping and devouring humans; meanwhile those associated with caterpillars, themselves thought of "qua-jaguars," include beings capable of "biting [humans] from within," often almost imperceptibly, as in illnesses (ibid.: 320).

4.   We find startling echoes of these representations of a single "complex being" in the documents collected by Barcelos Neto (2002) among the Waura (Xingu), which include representations of supernatural anacondas comprising series of images each of which refers to a different animal.

Figure 5. The motif called "maguari beak" (Wayana) (from Velthem 2003: 322).

food preferences, etc.) and the *mirikut* (the graphic theme that represents the animal in traditional weaving). "Though all *mirikuts* are, of course, images . . . not all images are *mirikuts*" (ibid.: 317). The *mirikut* allows one to interpret (or "decipher from its painted skin") the "true nature" of an animal. The geometric theme does not (just) represent the (familiar and essentially harmless) animal, but also its "normally invisible and monstrous double" (ibid.). This is further evidence of the essentially serial nature of Wayana iconography: a creature or being can never be understood only in terms of its singularity. Its "painted skin" always defines it as a member of a class or of a sequence of possible "modes of existence."

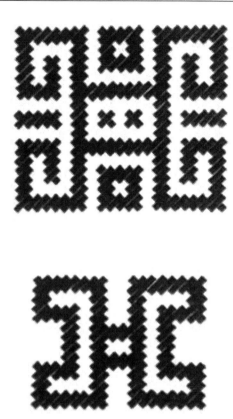

Figure 6. The theme "crab" combined with the theme "tapir's eye" (Wayana)
(from Velthem 2003: 312).

From a technical (semiotic) point of view, we can conclude that the Wayana technique of "transmutation" is, in its own way, selective and redundant. Wayana iconography is, like the Ye'kwana's, linked to the representation of lists of proper nouns—whether it represents specific entities or logical series. Furthermore, the Wayana have conceived a recursive principle that enables them to "embed" classes of beings in other "classes of beings." From the ontological point of view, both the Yekwana and the Wayana cases follow the same logic. The "invisible aspect" of nonhuman beings ("what really is there" in ontological terms—beyond their appearance) is shown through the construction of composite pictures, constituted either by individual "complex" figures such as Wanadi/Odosha among the Yekwana, or by serial beings, or even "classes of serial beings embedded in each other," as among the Wayana. It is also remarkable that images are, in both cases, always perceived as displaying their nature and power during ritual action (as in the case of Wayana dances of initiation), or in direct connection to it, as for the Yekwana weavings, which are also seen as living beings.

THE MUSIC OF THE WAYAMPI: AN EXAMPLE OF "TRANSMUTATION PROPER"

The underlying logic of this process of transmutation of concepts concerning "special beings" from names found in mythical narrations to nonverbal signs linked to ritual action can be taken yet further, to the passage from one non-verbal code to another. In the music of the Wayampi (who also have weavings, just the way the Yekwana and Wayana have music), we find a very similar way to represent the "real nature" of invisible predators as collective beings. The first point to mention is that Wayampi musicians perform names of spirits (currently used in mythological narratives) just in the same way that the Wayana and Yekwana represent them in visual terms. Actually, performing any music on an instrument, such as a flute or a clarinet, is, for the Wayampi, a precisely defined act of communication, primarily addressed to nonhuman beings. What we may call the pragmatics of ritual musical performances is, as a consequence, both complex and explicit. A Wayampi musician inherits the right to perform every single piece of music from a master or an elder member of his family. Every piece has a proper occasion in which it has to be performed, either by a soloist or by a group of performers, a link to a named place, and a relation to a specific nonhuman being (Beaudet 1997: 128). Furthermore, the music of the Wayampi is not only "addressed to" animals. It has, in itself, a nonhuman nature. To perform a piece of music, even the simplest melody, is to imitate the nonhuman "owner" (and inventor) of the music. In this sense, every musical performance, for the Wayampi, is a *call*. In its simplest form this "calling" involves a specific form of musical onomatopoeia, which selects a single acoustic trait (a melodic fragment, in musicological terms) to designate (and "call") a specific animal. The call is the musical incarnation of its name. In order to "call" a toucan, for instance, one "sings" or performs (e.g., on a flute) a theme called "toucan". Beaudet (ibid.), who gives beautiful examples of these calls, underlines that this "toucan theme" does not necessarily imitate only the "cry" of a toucan. Other aspects of the bird can be represented acoustically, like its elegance, its agility, the vividness of its colors, or the like. Such a theme can become, in other forms of daily-life compositions, the "signature" of a piece, also called "toucan," where this precisely identified group of sounds, performed by a soloist, can be repeated and subjected to different types of variations.

When music is ritually addressed to an invisible spirit, this relationship between the performed motif and the being it addresses (and imitates) becomes stronger. In that case, the invisible spirit is no longer "only imitated" by the music. It "is" the music. The music becomes the only index of its presence during the performance. "When the anaconda hear its music," Beaudet remarks, "he comes to listen to it" (ibid.: 137). This is the reason why performing ritual music can become dangerous. While playing, the performer knows that the spirit is there to check that "its" music is correctly performed. If the performance is wrong, the musician or even the whole village may be punished, or become ill (ibid.: 144–46). In Wayampi mythology (see, e.g., ibid.: 143), the knowledge of a certain piece of music (a song, an instrumental piece, or a long suite) is always presented as the result of a fragile agreement with the spirits, a sort of truce that rules out both sex relationships and aggression between them and human beings. Many myths narrate that animal spirits have given certain pieces of music to humans as a token of this agreement (ibid.: 156). Every performance reenacts the conditions of this agreement, and can consequently become dangerous. Not to remember correctly a piece of music, or the simple fact of performing it badly, is understood as a transgression, which might provoke a revenge, and the reactivation of a state of conflict between human and nonhuman beings.

Actually, the Wayampi distinguish between several kinds of musical "calls." In certain cases (mostly nonritual performances), a simple group of sounds, imitating its cry, can be sufficient to "call" a bird, or a monkey, and even to establish a dialogue with them. In other cases, when the being called for is an important spirit, the structure of the music (which acquires, in this case, strong "shamanistic connotations," ibid.: 172) becomes far more complex. Let us consider, for instance, the acoustic representation of a predator like the anaconda. To "make the anaconda present," one has to perform a particular musical suite of themes, made of a sequence of pieces, performed by a group of clarinets (and/or a group of dancers). The structure of this composition is based on the alternation of individual pieces, each of them characterized by a theme and performed by a soloist, with the repetitions/variations of another single theme. This theme, collectively performed by a group of musicians, and repeated after the performance of each solo piece, characterizes the entire suite, and gives to it its name.

Let us have a look at the suite, called Moyotule, which acoustically represents the anaconda. From a formal point of view, it follows the Wayampi traditional pattern. It is an alternation of several pieces, each characterized by its theme and played by a soloist, with another theme which characterizes the suite and is performed collectively. Performed by a group of clarinets, the "anaconda" theme is slowed down and iterated with minor variations after the performance of each solo piece. Following the rule of alternation that we have seen, a number of pieces belonging to *other beings* are then inserted into the "large and collective" version of the anaconda theme. In the list that Beaudet (1983) has recorded of the names of the pieces included (Beaudet 1997: 139), a number of animals appear. Among them the falcon, the monkey, several kinds of birds, insects, mammals, and fish are "called for," in order to construct an acoustic image (and to generate the indexical presence) of the invisible predator that "owns" this music. The "anaconda" theme collectively performed becomes thus (from the point of view of perception) a sort of musical background on which a series of themes—shorter and performed by a soloist—designating other animal species are embedded. The result of this process is a suite which "bears the name" (in Wayana terms, one could say that it "takes on the skin") of the anaconda, where a sequence of other beings "existing in the form of the predator" is made present. An acoustic image of a "complex invisible being" is thus generated.

The formal analogy of the Wayampi music with Ye'kwana–Wayana iconographies is, of course, striking. The Yekwana represent invisible beings (like Odosha and Wanadi) either as complex compositions, in which different beings are embedded, or as series of other beings, resulting from the variation of a single form. The Wayana have developed this model, inventing more complex forms of variations involving classes of beings existing as visible manifestations of invisible predators. In Wayampi instrumental music, we find sequences of visible (perceivable) beings as indexes of other invisible beings. The sequence of their "calls" (as they acquire saliency from the background) allows one to infer the actual presence of the anaconda (or of other mythical beings) during the ritual performance of "its" music. The Wayampi seem to play with music the same game that Wayana and Yekwana play with images.

TRANSMUTATION AND ANALOGY

We can now try to draw some conclusions from the analysis of these ethnographic cases. Let us consider first the definition of transmutation as a cultural form of translation, and then the kind of "cognition about ontology" that is mobilized by these musical and visual ways to define complex nonhuman beings.

We have already seen that, in the Yekwana and Wayana cultures, "simple" transmutation (involving the passage from verbal to nonverbal signs) is both selective and redundant. In the music of the Wayampi, we can recognize the same features. The music of a Wayampi suite is selective because its use of onomatopoeia for designating a being results from a selection from all the possible aspects belonging to it (the musical form of its cry, but also its elegance, rapidity, etc.), that music "transcribes" in sounds. As we have seen, a theme ("signature") of a piece always is a stylized portrait of a nonhuman being. But Wayampi music can also be redundant. The "anaconda" suite that we have briefly studied "tells" more about the nature of a predator than a simple name. It indicates that such an exceptional being as the spirit of the anaconda is described not by its acoustic appearance, but by a series of acoustic signals related to the different beings that indirectly designate its invisible presence. In both visual and acoustic images, the passage from verbal to iconic signs (or from one nonverbal code to another) mobilized by transmutation never limits itself to the description of the appearance of the beings it represents. On the contrary, the process of transmutation of words in images (be they visual or acoustic) makes the presence of supernatural beings indirectly perceivable through the appearances of *other* beings. To use again a Wayana notion, music and visual iconographies aim to construct *mirikut*, images of concepts and relationships, not *ukuktop*, imitations of appearances. Only through sequences of this kind does the nonhuman being represented (or made present) by music or graphic themes become perceptible, and thus imaginable, and even thinkable. The aim of transmutation proper is both to make relations between signs (be they technically interpreted as icons or as indexes) perceptible—and "supernatural" special beings imaginable as generated by relationships between them.

How is this realized? Can we describe a sort of method, a logical form presiding over these forms of transmutation, beyond the two basic operations of selection and redundancy that we have seen until now? Let us compare our three ethnographic cases and the cultural forms of transmutation they mobilize. In the Yekwana and the Wayana cases, iconographies woven into baskets tend to represent complex beings (designated by group of names, such as Odosha/Wanadi, Toad, Monkey, etc.) or whole categories of special beings through complex images. In the second form of transmutation (illustrated by the Wayana basketry comparison with Wayampi instrumental music), groups of sounds "translate" groups of visual themes into sequences of sounds. Music makes audible implicit relationships that collectively designate special (nonhuman and invisible) beings, which are thus "called for" and made ritually present.

It is remarkable that in all the cases we have seen, the passage from one code to another (language, iconography, music) is never direct. Never, as in the ancient and medieval theories of translation, is an "exact equivalent," a sort of cast of every word (or sign, image, or sound), searched for. The object of the translation always is *an intuitive relation* between concepts. Yekwana weavings "describe" the antagonism between Odosha and Wanadi using a specific *visual* means to express opposition, be that the combinations of different shapes in one, or even the contrast between shape and ground. In other cases, Yekwana designs may describe connections of other sorts (relationships deriving from the transformations of Odosha) using visual ways to express them: analogies of patterns, inclusion, parallelism, and so forth. When we pass from the comparison of Yekwana and Wayana basketry to the comparison between Wayana weavings and Wayampi music, we discover that ordered sequences of images are "transmuted" into ordered sequences of sounds in the same way. Again, the object of translation (transmutation) is never the individual image, word, or sound. It is always the intuitive relation, previously established, between groups of sounds, images, and words. Using a concept formulated by Saussure, we could describe this process as the progressive construction of a four-term analogy (Saussure [1913] 2006) between relationships previously established in each semiotic code involved. This complex form of analogy would operate at two levels (Figure 7). At the lower level we could represent the relationships identified (through selection and redundancy) within each semiotic (verbal, visual, musical) code. At the second level we could represent the relationship established between these groups of relationships. To this last (and more complex) relation, which establishes a logical link between groups of analogies, and only to it, we could then give the name of transmutation. At both levels of our four-term analogy, *only* relationships represent relationships. Relations between sounds in music represent relations between images in iconographies; relationships between images represent oppositions (and other forms of connection) expressed in words, and so forth. When a higher-level relationship is established between groups of relationships, a transmutation is generated. What is represented then are not individuals, or qualities, or single actions, but similarities, oppositions, inclusions, derivations, and so forth. In other words, transmutation thus overcomes precisely the difficulty that we have seen so many authors affirm: the heterogeneity of semiotic codes. The four-term analogy operates, in fact, as *a way to establish an order* in the assemblage of these heterogeneous codes. From an abstract point of view, it thus assembles entities possessing the same logical nature and the same intuitive apprehension. The stuff transmutation "is made of" is relationships. We might add to this theoretical model the hypothesis that the distinction Jakobson has drawn between what *must* be expressed and what *may* be expressed in language applies to each level of our diagram. We could conclude that selection and redundancy are the first steps in a process of ordering relationships that can be represented, in all the ethnographies that we have studied, by a complex form of four-term analogy, constituted by two logical levels.

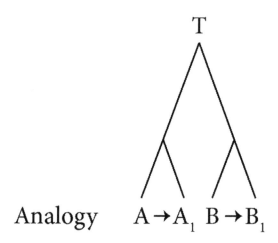

Figure 7. Transmutation and analogy.

Let us now turn to ontology, and to the consequences that our analysis of the transmutation processes might have for the definition of this concept.

TRANSMUTATION, COGNITION, AND ONTOLOGY

In a recent comment on Lloyd's book *Being, humanity, and understanding* (2012), I have argued (Severi 2013) that the concept of ontology, as it has been defined in Western philosophy, is not fully understood by anthropologists. Many of our colleagues tend to call "ontology" any discourse about the origins and nature of the world. However, since Parmenides, the term "ontology" does not refer to the various material constituents of the universe (fire, water, air, etc.) and their different ways of combining. The ontological argument is about "being itself." It aims to the construction of an "ontology" as a science of abstract principles (founded on the analysis of predicates of being such as necessity versus contingence, possibility versus impossibility, subsistence versus potentially, and the like) not as a discourse about the origins of what physically exists. Nor does Parmenides look for a classification of the different beings inhabiting the universe. He wants, on the contrary, to identify an abstract relationship between *nous* and *physis*, and looks for the conditions under which the world is thinkable. This is why a classification of the categories of different beings, following, for instance, the distinctions between animate/inanimate, human/animal, male/female (which is often understood as "ontological" by anthropologists), technically does not make for an "ontology." In the works of Aristotle, for instance, the study of these forms of knowledge belongs to the *Parva Naturalia*, not to the doctrine of Being, which is the object of metaphysics. Needless to say, Parmenides' approach to being-as-being has been fundamental for the history of Western philosophy, from Aristotle to Kant, and still is discussed in very similar terms in modern philosophy (see, e.g., the famous debate on Russell's "theory of descriptions" and its consequences for the relation between language and "what it is": Quine 1943, 1948; Russell 2005; Carnap 2009).

I have come to the conclusion that, if we do an epistemological analysis of this concept in Western philosophy, the kind of world-visions anthropologists usually study are precisely *not* ontologies but natural philosophies *without* ontologies. In short, the risk involved in ignoring the theoretical import of this concept is to mistake Melanesian or Amazonian "conceptions of the world," founded on "background commonly shared assumptions" about physical and social observable phenomena (Lloyd 2012: 67), for pseudo-Parmenidean ontologies. And, consequently, to understand them as coherent systems of thought: "unique, immobile, and unchanging" like the Parmenidean concept of Being.

I think that there are no empirical reasons to understand them as such. Only a wrong decision to view cosmologies as such may transform them into systematic ontology, or even (adopting an extreme Heideggerian idealism) into indigenous metaphysics. In this latter case, cosmologies would become no more than anthropological artifacts. In my view, what anthropologists tend to call "cosmologies" are de facto regularities in the establishment of a number of shared assumptions, very rarely expressed in the form of an explicit argument, and always related to specific practices, systems of relationships, and genres of discourse. They are linked to ritual, mythology, or daily-life contexts, and thus to the kind of semiotic means in which thoughts are formulated. These discourses might sometimes intersect, generating the appearance of a unitary "discourse on 'the nature of what it is.'" But what is particularly interesting about them is precisely their semiotic complexity and their unsystematic character, the fact that they always leave a space open for different strategies of thought.

In this paper, I have tried to give an example of this strategic plurality of thought that characterizes the cultures we study, and to show what kind of "blind spot" the use of an uncritical concept of "ontology" can generate in our understanding of ethnography. By analyzing three examples of transmutation in three Amazonian traditions, we have been able to show that the passage from words to images and to music that "transmutation" enables is meant to designate the existence of plural beings. Among the Yekwana, this class of inter-specific beings is represented by key individual plural figures that dominate the myth cycle. Among the Wayana, these chimerical individual figures develop into classes (and sometimes classes of classes) of hybrid entities embedded in each other. In Wayampi music, alternation of themes, linked to the identifica-tion of different animals, replaces the Wayana embedding, but still generates an analogous form of designating complex beings. In all three cases, as elsewhere in Amazonia, this kind of ritual representation of the invisible is linked to the representation of living beings whose defining traits never entirely overlap with those of recognized human, animal, and vegetable species.

This kind of ontological ordering of beings is in sharp contrast with the way Amazonian ontology has been described until now. In a number of influential papers (e.g., 1998, 2004), Viveiros de Castro has claimed that the conception of the relationship between souls and bodies that we find throughout Amazonia should be understood as an interconnection of the different "points of view" generated by the "perspectives" belonging to human and nonhuman beings. He refers to this set of ideas ("for simplicity's sake," as he says) "as though it was a cosmology." "This cosmology," he writes,

> imagines a universe peopled by different types of subjective agencies, human as well as nonhuman, each endowed with the same generic type of soul, that is, the same set of cognitive and volitional capacities. The possession of a similar soul implies possession of similar concepts, which determine that all subjects

see things in the same way. In particular, individuals of the same species see each other (and each other only) as humans see themselves, that is, as being endowed with the human figures and habits, seeing their bodily and behavioral aspects in the form of human culture. (Viveiros de Castro 2004: 6)

According to Viveiros de Castro, this strategic position of human culture in the relationship with nonhumans (the animals being here "the paradigmatic Other") should generate a new epistemological paradigm. We should pass from the traditional idea of multiculturalism (where one single nature faces different cultures) to the idea of a "multinaturalism," where many natural appearances are understood as sharing the same culture.[5] As is well known, this theoretical approach, which invites the redefinition of "subjects" as "points of view" (ibid.), has been both influential and controversial. It is obviously impossible to discuss it here in full detail, but it is undeniable that Viveiros de Castro's approach (as well as the work of Descola on this point) has transformed the somewhat immobile traditional distinction between Nature and Culture into a distributed system of differences, where both natural and cultural features or properties are interpenetrated. I would like to focus here on only one aspect of this theory: the kind of categorization which is implied by this system of differences. The central point, in this respect, is the role played by "corporeal differences" (Viveiros de Castro 1998: 470).[6] In a system where there is only one culture (the human's culture), Viveiros de Castro underlines several times that the difference between subjects, in this cosmology dominated by a "spiritual unity," is given by the "specificities of the bodies" (ibid.: 470, 478).

---

5. "What changes when passing from one species of subject to another," writes Viveiros de Castro, "is the 'objective correlative,' the referent of these concepts: what Jaguars see as 'manioc beer' (the proper drink of people, Jaguar-type or otherwise), humans see as 'blood.' Where we [humans] see a muddy salt-lick on a riverbank, tapirs see their big ceremonial house, and so on. Such difference of perspective— not a plurality of views of a single world, but a single view of different worlds— cannot derive from the soul, since the latter is the common original ground of being. Rather, such difference is located in the bodily differences between species, for the body and its affectations . . . is the site and instrument of ontological differentiation and referential disjunction" (ibid.: 6).

6. In Amazonian cosmologies, "the body appears to be the great differentiator, that is as that, which unites beings of the same type, to the extent that it differentiates them from other beings" (ibid.: 479).

In Viveiros de Castro's argument, the concept of "corporeal diversity" has two different meanings. The first refers to the morphology of organisms. "The body of every species is unique," writes Viveiros de Castro (ibid.: 478), for instance, a statement that, while suppressing individual differences within each species, supposes an identity between the concept of "body" and the notion of "species." However, he attributes to the concept of the "body as differentiator" also a second meaning, which refers to "an intermediate plane" situated between "the formal subjectivities of souls" and "the substantial materiality of organisms." "What I call body is not a synonym for distinctive substance or fixed shape; it is an assemblage of affects or ways of being that constitute a habitus" (ibid.). Viveiros de Castro here curiously uses this notion (originally introduced by Bourdieu [(1972) 1977]) to designate not only what a body looks like, but also "what a body eats, how it communicates, where it lives, whether it is gregarious or solitary, and so on" (Viveiros de Castro 1998: 478).[7] However, when the concept of difference becomes crucial in his argument, species (both as "sets of habits or processes" [ibid.: 480] and as bodies that are morphologically different) are constantly referred to.[8] In substance, as far as categorization of differences is concerned, Amazonian ontology is described as composed by classes of "beings," typically humans versus nonhumans, mostly predators or the like, which define each other through their "bodily" differences. These binary oppositions critically (though, sometimes, tacitly) coincide with the appearance and typical behavior of species. This is why, in this cosmology, we constantly see human beings opposed to various forms of nonhumans, be they animals, plants, stones, or artifacts.

As is well known, the focus of this approach, and the paradigm of its epistemology, is myth. As Viveiros de Castro writes, myth is "the vanishing point where the differences between points of view are at the same time annulated and exacerbated." This is why, for perspectivism, "myths takes on the character

---

7.   The use of this notion to designate the "true origin of perspective" (ibid.) is surprisingly ambiguous. Needless to say, Bourdieu used it to define any process which leads to the constitution of a *cultural* tradition.

8.   Among the many passages where this notion is invoked, see, for instance: "the notion of animals as people is always associated with the idea that the manifest form of each species is just an envelope" (ibid.: 470); "we would have a distinction between an anthropomorphic essence of a spiritual type . . . and a variable body appearance, characteristic of each individual species. . . . Such difference of perspective . . . is located in the bodily differences between species" (ibid.: 471).

of an absolute discourse" (ibid.: 483). The study of our three Amazonian cases shows that, if we focus on iconographies linked to ritual action and the specific processes of transmutation that mobilize them, a radically different kind of ontological "way of ordering beings" emerges. The classes represented by Yekwana and Wayana iconographies, as well as the Wayampi "acoustic creatures," do not coincide with species, to be opposed to one another. Quite the contrary, these images designate classes of special beings, where members of different species are associated in sequences. In all these cases of transmutation, a logic focused on the construction of composite beings possessing an invisible presence emerges. Instead of binary oppositions of "bodily" classes defined through relevant "natural" differences, we find the generation of inter-specific beings. The analysis of the forms of thought implied by transmutation leads to the conclusion that another form of "ontology," based on very different principles, exists in the same area where perspectivism allegedly rules every cultural expression of meaning. We might call it a plural ontology for transmutating beings, linked to ritual action and visual thinking.

TRANSLATION AND THE ANTHROPOLOGY OF THOUGHT

This conclusion can help us in giving a more precise definition of what might become the horizon of a new anthropological theory of thought. Our analyses have shown that the crucial distinction that Jakobson has formulated between what must and what may be expressed in a language does not concern only linguistic (grammatical) patterns in interlinguistic translation, but it also applies to many other forms of translation, as the intersemiotic transmutation, and the visual and analogical thinking that it mobilizes. With this conclusion in mind, we could go a step further, and formulate the hypothesis that Jakobson's logical distinction characterizes not only "language" and nonlinguistic codes, but also the exercise of thought itself. In this way, we could pass from an abstract opposition between "thought" (defined as rationality and categorization) and "language" (essentially defined as grammatical patterns) to the study of a set of multiple relations between forms of cognition (related, for instance, to ritual action and visual thinking) and intralinguistic, interlinguistic, and intersemiotic forms of translation. As we have seen, these forms of translation do not exist only between different languages, but also between different codes, and different pragmatic contexts, within a single culture. In this new perspective, variations in the use of codes and variations in the establishment of pragmatic contexts (not only variations between cultures and languages) would become *sources* for the variation of thought processes, and for the subsequent definition of "states of the world," or of ontologies.

The essential plurality of "ontological" thought, of which we have seen an example in this paper, would thus find its general theoretical principle. "Worlds" vary when not only the abstract structure of a grammar but also many practices of language use (of which intersemiotic transmutation is an example) generate forms of thought where what must be conveyed joins, at a different level, what may be expressed. The consequence would be that if a general concept of ontology could be formulated for understanding cultures, it would refer not to "conceptions of the world" linked to different languages, but to a plural and unsystematic way of constantly activating different forms of thought. In short, it would designate not a single system, but a form of life where different systems constantly combine. To look at the relationship between language, thought, and culture in this perspective could be a way, as Wittgenstein wrote of magic in his *Notes on Frazer's Golden Bough*, to fully "preserve its depth."

REFERENCES

Austin, J. L. 1975. *How to do things with words*. Oxford: Oxford University Press.

Barcelos Neto, Aristóteles. 2002. *A arte dos sonhos: Uma iconografia ameríndia*. Lisbon: Assírio & Alvim.

———. 2008. *Apapaatai: Rituais de máscaras no Alto Xingu*. São Paulo: Editora da Universidade de São Paulo.

———. 2009. The (de)animalization of objects: Food offerings and the subjectivization of masks and flutes among the Wauja of Southern Amazonia. In *The occult life of things: Native Amazonian theories of materiality and personhood*, edited by Fernando Santos-Granero, 128–53. Tucson: University of Arizona Press.

———. 2011. "Le réveil des grands masques du Haut-Xingu: Iconographie et transformation." In *Masques des hommes, visages des dieux*, edited by Jean-Pierre Goulard and Dimitri Karadimas, 27–52. Paris: éditions CNRS.

———. 2013 " O trançado, a musica e as serpentes da transformaçâo no Alto Xingu", in *Quimeras en diálogo: Grafismo e figuração na arte indígena*, edited by Carlo Severi and Els Lagrou, 181–97. Rio de Janeiro: Viveiros de Castro Editora.

Basso, Ellen B. 1981. "A musical view of the universe: Kalapalo myth and ritual as religious performance." *Journal of American Folklore* 94 (373): 273–91.

Baxandall, Michael. 1993. "Pictorially enforced signification: St. Antonius, Fra Angelico and the Annunciation." In *Hülle und* Fülle*: Festschrift für T. Buddensieg*, edited by Andreas Beyer, Vittorio Lampugnani, and Gunther Schweikhart, 31–39. Alfter: VDG Verlag.

Bateson, Gregory. 1979. *Mind and nature: A necessary unity.* New York: Dutton.

Beaudet, Jean-Michel. 1983. "Les orchestres de clarinettes tule des Wayãpi du Haut-Oyapock." Doctoral dissertation, Université Paris Ouest Nanterre La Défense.

———. 1997. *Souffles d'Amazonie: Les orchestres tule des Wayãpi*, Vol. 3. Nanterre: Société d'Ethnologie.

Belaunde, Luisa Elvira. 2009. *Kené: Arte, ciencia y tradición en diseño.* Lima: Instituto Nacional de Cultura.

———. 2013. "Movimento e profundidade no kene shipibo-conhibo da Amazônia peruana." In *Quimeras en diálogo: Grafismo e figuracão na arte indígena*, edited by Carlo Severi and Els Lagrou, 199–223. Rio de Janeiro: Viveiros de Castro Editora.

Boas, Franz. 1938. "Language." In *General anthropology*, 127–55. Boston: D. C. Heath.

———. 1989. *A Franz Boas reader: The shaping of American anthropology, 1883–1911.* Chicago: University of Chicago Press.

Bourdieu, Pierre. (1972) 1977. *Outline of a theory of practice.* Translated by Richard Nice. Cambridge: Cambridge University Press.

Brabec de Mori, Berndt, and Anthony Seeger. 2013. Introduction: Considering music, humans, and non-humans. *Ethnomusicology Forum* 22 (3): 269–86.

Carnap, Rudolph. 1991. Empiricism, semantics, and ontology. In *The philosophy of science: An historical anthology*, edited by Timothy McGrew, Marc Alspector-Kelly, and Fritz Alhoff, 356–65. Oxford: Wiley-Blackwell.

Cesarino, Pedro de Niemeyer. 2011. *Oniska, poética do xamanismo na Amazônia.* São Paulo: Editora Perspectiva.

de Civrieux, Marc. (1970) 1997. *Watunna: An Orinoco creation cycle.* Translated by David M. Guss. Austin: University of Texas Press.

Descola, Philippe, and Anne-Christine Taylor, eds. 1993. "La remontée de l'Amazone." Special issue, *L'Homme* 33 (2–4).

Evans-Pritchard, Edward. 1937. *Magic, witchcraft and oracles among the Azande.* Oxford: Oxford University Press.

Fausto, Carlos. 2011a. "Masques et trophées: De la visibilité des êtres invisibles en Amazonie." In *Masques des homes, visages des dieux*, edited by Jean-Pierre Goulard and Dimitri Karadimas, 229–54. Paris: CNRS Éditions.

———. 2011b, "Les masque de l'animiste: Chimères et poupées russes en Amérique indigene." Special issue, "Pièges à voir, pièges à penser," edited by Carlo Severi, *Gradhiva* 13: 48–68.

Fausto, Carlos, Bruna Franchetto, and Tommaso Montagnani. 2011a. "Les formes de la mémoire: Art verbal et musique chez les Kuikuro du Haut-Xingu (Brésil)." *L'Homme* 197: 41–69.

Fausto, Carlos, and Isabel Penoni. 2014. "Les effigies rituelles: La figuration de l'humain dans le Haut-Xingu." In *L'image rituelle*, edited by Carlo Severi and Carlo Fausto, 14–38. Paris: L'Herne.

Gheerbrant, Adrian. 1954. *Journey to the far Amazon.* New York: Simon & Schuster.

Gilbert, Aubrey L., Terry Regier, Paul Kay, and Richard B. Ivry. 2006. "Whorf hypothesis is supported in the right visual field but not the left." *Proceedings of the National Academy of Sciences of the United States of America* 103 (2): 489–94.

Goodman, Nelson. 1976. *Languages of art: An approach to a theory of symbols.* Cambridge, MA: Hackett.

Gow, Peter. 1989. "Visual compulsion: Design and image in Western Amazonian art." *Revindi: Revista Indigenista Americana* 2: 19–32.

———. 1999 "Piro designs: Painting as meaningful action in the Amazonian lived world." *Journal of the Royal Anthropological Institute* (N.S.) 5: 229–46.

Gumperz, John. J. and Stephen C. Levinson, eds. 1996. *Rethinking linguistic relativity.* Cambridge: Cambridge University Press.

Guss, David. M. 1986. Keeping it oral: A Yekwana ethnology. *American Ethnologist* 13 (3): 413–29.

———. 1989, *To weave and sing: Art, symbol, and narrative in the South American rain forest.* Berkeley: University of California Press.

Gutierrez Choquevilca, Andrea-Luz. 2010. "Imaginaire acoustique et apprentissage d'une ontologie animiste: Le cas des Quechua d'Amazonie péruvienne." *Ateliers du LESC* 34. http://ateliers.revues.org/8553 ; DOI : 10.4000/ateliers.8553.

————. 2011. "Sisyawaytii tarawaytii: Sifflements serpentins et autres voix d'esprits dans le chamanisme quechua du haut Pastaza (Amazonie péruvienne)." *Journal de la Société des Américanistes* 97 (1): 179–221.

Hill, Jonathan D. 1993. *Keepers of the sacred chants: The poetics of ritual power in an Amazonian society.* Tucson: University of Arizona Press.

————. 1994. 'Musicalizing the other: Shamanistic approaches to ethnic-class competition in the Upper Rio Negro region." In *Religiosidad y resistencia indígenas hacia el fin del milenio,* edited by Alicia Barabas, 105–28. Quito: Abya-Yala.

————. 2009. *Made-from-bone: Trickster myths, music, and history from the Amazon.* Urbana: University of Illinois Press.

Jakobson, Roman. 1959. "On linguistic aspects of translation." *On Translation* 3: 232–39.

Joyce, James. (1922) 1972. *Ulysses.* London: Penguin Books/Bodley Head.

Kay, Paul, and Chad K.McDaniel 1978. "The linguistic significance of the meanings of basic color terms." *Language* 54: 610–46.

Kay, Paul, and Willett Kempton. 1984. "What is the Sapir–Whorf hypothesis?" *American Anthropologist* 86 (1): 65–79.

Kuhn, Thomas. S. (1962) 2012. *The structure of scientific revolutions.* Fiftieth anniversary edition. Chicago: University of Chicago Press.

Lagrou, Els. 2007. *A fluidez da forma: Arte, alteridade e agência em uma sociedade amazônica (Kaxinawa, Acre).* Rio de Janeiro: Topbooks.

————. 2009a. *Arte indígena no Brasil: Agência, alteridade e relação.* Belo Horizonte: Editora C/Arte.

————. 2009b. "The crystallized memory of artifacts: A reflection on agency and alterity in Cashinahua image-making." In *The occult life of things: Native Amazonian theories of materiality and personhood,* edited by Fernando Santos-Granero, 192–213. Tucson: University of Arizona Press.

————. 2011. "Le graphisme sur les corps amérindiens: Des chimères abstraites?" Special issue, "Pièges à voir, pièges à penser," edited by Carlo Severi, *Gradhiva* 13: 69–93.

————. 2013, "O grafismo nos corpos ameríndios, quimeras abstratas?" In *Quimeras en diálogo: Grafismo e figuração na arte indígena,* edited by Carlo Severi and Els Lagrou, 38–66. Rio de Janeiro: Viveiros de Castro Editora.

Langdon, Esther Jean. 2013. "Perspectiva xamanica: Relaçoes entre rito, narrativa e arte grafica." In *Quimeras en diálogo: Grafismo e figuração na arte indígena*, edited by Carlo Severi and Els Lagrou, 111–39. Rio de Janeiro: Viveiros de Castro Editora.

Lévi-Strauss, Claude. (1962) 1966. *The savage mind.* Chicago: University of Chicago Press.

Lévy-Bruhl, Lucien. 1949. *Les carnets.* Paris: Presses Universitaires de France.

Lima, Tânia Stolze. 2000. "Towards an ethnographic theory of the nature/culture distinction in Juruna cosmology. ". *Revista Brasileira de Ciências Sociais* 15 (99): 43–52.

Lloyd, Geoffrey E. R. 1996. *Adversaries and authorities: Investigations into ancient Greek and Chinese science*, Vol. 42. Cambridge: Cambridge University Press.

———. 2006. *Principles and practices in ancient Greek and Chinese science*, Vol. 849. Farnham, UK: Ashgate.

———. 2007. *Cognitive variations: Reflections on the unity and diversity of the human mind.* Oxford: Clarendon Press.

———. 2012. *Being, humanity, and understanding: Studies in ancient and modern societies.* Oxford: Oxford University Press.

Lucy, John A. 1992. *Language diversity and thought: A reformulation of the linguistic relativity hypothesis.* Cambridge: Cambridge University Press.

Luna, Luis Eduardo, 1992. "Icaros: Magic melodies among the Mestizo shamans of the Peruvian Amazon." In *Portals of power: Shamanism in South America*, edited by E. Jean Matteson Langdon and Gerhard Bauer, 231–53. Albuquerque: University of New Mexico Press.

Mangione, Corrado. 1964. *Elementi di logica matematica.* Turin: Boringhieri.

Meneses Bastos, Rafael José de. 1978. *Etnomusicologica Kamayura.* Universidade Federal, Santa Catarina, Florianopolis.

———. 1999. "Apùap world hearing: On the Kamayurá phono-auditory system and the anthropological concept of culture." *The World of Music* 41 (1): 85–96.

———. 2007. "Música nas sociedades indígenas das terras baixas da América do Sul: Estado da arte. " *Mana* 13 (2) : 293–316.

Piaget, Jean. (1923) 2001. *The language and thought of the child.* Translated by Marjorie and Ruth Gabain. London: Routledge.

———. (1926) 2007. *The child's conception of the world.* Translated by Joan and Andrew Tomlinson. Lanham, MD : Rowman & Littlefield.

Piedade, Acácio Tadeu de Camargo. 2004. "O canto do Kawoká: Música, cosmologia e filosofia entre os Wauja do Alto Xingu." Ph.D. dissertation, Universidad Federal de Santa Catarina.

Quine, Willard Van Orman. 1943. "Notes on existence and necessity." *Journal of Philosophy* 40 (5): 113–27.

————. 1948. *On what there is.* Washington, DC: Catholic University of America, Philosophy Education Society.

Rubel, Paula G., and Abraham Rosman. 2003. *Translating cultures: Perspectives on translation and anthropology.* New York: Berg.

Russell, Bertrand. 2005. *Collected papers of Bertrand Russell,* Vol. 29. Hove: Psychology Press.

Sapir, Edward. 1985. *Selected writings of Edward Sapir in language, culture and personality,* Vol. 342. Berkeley: University of California Press.

Saussure, Ferdinand de. (1913) 2006. *Course in general linguistics.* Translated by Roy Harris. Chicago: Open Court.

Seeger, Anthony. 2004. *Why Suyá sing: A musical anthropology of an Amazonian people.* Evanston: University of Illinois Press.

Severi Carlo. (2007) 2015. *The chimera principle: An anthropology of memory and imagination.* Translated by Janet Lloyd. Chicago: Hau Books.

————. 2011. "L'espace chimérique: Perception et projection dans les actes de regard." Special issue, "Pièges à voir, pièges à penser," edited by Carlo Severi, *Gradhiva* 13: 5–163.

————. 2012. "The arts of memory: Comparative perspectives on a mental artifact." *HAU: Journal of Ethnographic Theory* 2 (2): 451–85.

————. 2013 "Philosophies without ontologies." *HAU: Journal of Ethnographic Theory* 3 (1): 192–96.

Severi, Carlo, and Carlos Fausto, eds. 2014. *L'image rituelle.* Paris: L'Herne.s

Severi, Carlo, and Els Lagrou, eds. 2013. *Quimeras en diálogo: Grafismo e figuração na arte indígena.* Rio de Janeiro: Viveiros de Castro Editora.

Sperber, Dan. 1982. "Apparently irrational beliefs." In *Rationality and relativism,* edited by Martin Hollis and Steven Lukes, 149–80. Cambridge, MA: MIT Press.

Taylor, Anne-Christine. 2003 "Les masques de la mémoire: Essai sur la fonction des meintures corporelles Jivaro." In Special issue, "Anthropologie et image," edited by Carlo Severi, *L'Homme* 165: 223–48.

Townsley, Graham. 1993. "Song paths: The ways and means of Yaminahua shamanic knowledge." Special issue, "La remontée de l'Amazone," edited by Philippe Descola and Anne-Christine Taylor, *L'Homme* 33 (2–4): 449–68.

Velthem, Lucia von. 2003. *O belo e a fera*. Universidade de São Paulo.

———. 2013. "Homens, guaribas, mandiocas e artefactos." In *Quimeras en diálogo: Grafismo e figuração na arte indígena*, edited by Carlo Severi and Els Lagrou, 139–63. Rio de Janeiro: Viveiros de Castro Editora.

Vidal, Lux Boelitz, Anne-Marie Pessis, and Niéde Guidon. 2000. *Grafismo indígena: Estudos de antropologia estética*. São Paulo: Studio Nobel..

Vygotsky, Lev S. 1978. *Mind in society*. Cambridge MA, Harvard University Press.

Viveiros de Castro, Eduardo. 1998. "Cosmological deixis and Amerindian perspectivism." *Journal of the Royal Anthropological Institute* (N.S.) 4: 469–88.

———. 2004. "Perspectival anthropology and the method of controlled equivocation." *Tipití: Journal of the Society for the Anthropology of Lowland South America* 2 (1): 3–22.

Whorf, Benjamin Lee. 2012. *Language, thought, and reality: Selected writings of Benjamin Lee Whorf*. Cambridge, MA: MIT Press.

Wittgenstein, Ludwig N. (1914–16) 1974. *Notebooks 1914–1916*. Translated by G. E. M. Anscombe. Chicago: University of Chicago Press.

———. (1953) 2010. *Philosophical investigations*. Translated by G. E. M. Anscombe. London: John Wiley & Sons.

———. (1967) 1979. *Remarks on Frazer's Golden Bough*. Translated by A. C. Miles, edited by Rush Rhees. Atlantic Highlands, NJ: Humanities Press.

CHAPTER THREE

Powers of incomprehension
Linguistic otherness, translators, and political structure in New Guinea tourism encounters

RUPERT STASCH

In their Introduction to this volume, Hanks and Severi draw on Kuhn (2000) to distinguish translation as an actual linguistic activity from the commensurability of concepts of the different communities whose discourse is translated. The idea that interacting people might be oriented by noncommensurate concepts does not stand or fall with the possibility that they can communicate through translation. Rather, "the challenge of constant confrontation of 'incommensurable' (yet translated) paradigms becomes in itself . . . a field for ethnographical inquiry" (Hanks and Severi, p. 7, this volume). Distinguishing translation and incommensurateness, Hanks and Severi are also setting them into active relation. Translation practices come into focus as a site where larger structures of noncommensurateness are probed, transformed, dissolved, renewed, masked, or otherwise mediated. This turn of reasoning can also be taken to imply that processes of commensuration are likely to be multilayered and partial rather than singular and absolute. Translation practices create points of commonality and coordination across different participants' conceptual frameworks, even as these translation practices are integral with the persistence or rise of further levels of noncoordination and mutual obliviousness.

In the European historical field, the most prototypic image of human interaction across noncommensurate understandings is early New World and Pacific encounters. The name "New World" itself expressed this central idea of noncommensurateness of life, as noted by Pagden (1993: 3), elaborating on a passage from explorer Antonio de Ulloa. The mythic resonance of scenes of "first contact" flows from the understanding that such a scene dramatizes the otherness of embodied understandings and concepts held by the previously separate people. "Primitivist tourism," in which metropolitan travelers visit communities that are figured as archaic in time, is one of the many different cultural forms around the globe today that is organized as a repetition of this mythic idea (Stasch 2014d).

Korowai of Papua have for two decades been a world-famous destination for this kind of tourism. In this article, I examine linguistic dimensions of encounters between tourists and Korowai. A theoretical concern with "commensurability" might seem to align primarily with issues of language as a denotational medium, such as whether or not different people are expressing the same semantic categories through their speech. But I understand Hanks and Severi's Kuhn-influenced charter for actual "ethnographical inquiry" into the relations between translation and commensurability to be concerned with the full range of sociocultural levels to what is being *done* by language users, not just what is being *denoted* by them. Such a widening is unavoidable in study of contact communities of mutual incomprehension, which are common in history but which defy academic scholars' axiomatic association of language with transmission of denoted meanings (see, e.g., Taylor 1992). As we will see, the most notable facts about translation in the Korowai tourism contact community are how little of it occurs, and how heavily the translation which does occur is freighted with extrasemantic meanings about the social relation between the mutually incomprehending participants.

In light of primitivist tourism participants' great reflexive attention to human otherness in their approaches to the encounters, one ethnographic concern of this article will be to trace how translation and linguistic difference work for all parties as figures in a broader drama of inquiry into cultural difference, and into the condition of living culturally and historically as such. In particular, I will trace ways that around linguistic otherness, tourists and Korowai express specific forms of socially valuing the other, and specific visions of how their mutual social obligations might be created or limited. Alongside tracing patterns of tourist and Korowai *modeling* of the noncommensurateness and emergent commensuration of their social communities, I will also put forward my own provisional *analytic* generalizations about structures of noncommensurateness and emergent commensuration that I see as running through these ethnographic patterns. Broadly, I will describe the encounters as a process of creating coordination between the noncommensurate sociocultural formations of primitivist ideology and market-structured social relations on tourists' part, and a political ethos of egalitarianism and exchange-constituted kinship on Korowai people's part. Significantly, there seems to be a close link between cross-linguistic performance in this contact community, and questions of different participants' value and authority. While the relative value of persons is probably a primordial question of all social relations, there is a particularly raw character to how social relations across gulfs of historical and cultural separation unfold as dramas of asymmetry. I look in special detail at how, for Korowai, the figure of the tourism translator—known as a "head"—has emerged as a new kind of authoritative speaking role, taking hold in the interstices between historical Korowai egalitarian logics of speech and the global institutional order of market-mediated social bonds.

LANGUAGE AND TRANSLATION IN THE TOURISM CONTACT COMMUNITY

About four thousand Korowai live dispersed across five hundred square miles of forest in the southern lowlands of Papua, the Indonesian-controlled western half of the island of New Guinea. Tourists started visiting around 1990, as an innovation on other primitivist itineraries in Papua, then called "Irian Jaya." The imagery motivating tourists' visits is focused on the special appeal of Korowai people's "treehouse" architecture, as well as the broader idea that Korowai are a "Stone Age" people living in harmony with their surrounding environment and in isolation from global consumer culture. The costliness of transport to the area and the special visual appeal of treehouses have meant that a large fraction of visitors are film crews. Most nonmedia tourists are salaried professionals such as engineers, investment bankers, doctors, scientists, information technology workers, small business owners, and educators. Tourists have included citizens of almost every European country and most settler colonies. German and US nationals accounted for half of travelers in the 1990s, but in the 2000s US tourists dropped away and citizens of ex-Soviet bloc countries became prominent. There have also been film crews from several East and Southeast Asian countries. Most tour groups are accompanied by a professional Papuan or Indonesian tour guide from the coastal city of Jayapura. The groups arrive by chartered airplane or longboat at gateway villages that were initially created in the 1980s at the initiative of a Dutch missionary organization then active at the southwest edge of the Korowai area (Stasch 2013). From these new settlements, tour groups trek to the forested territories of specific local patriclans, where they see treehouses and are able to meet and photograph Korowai in traditional dress.

A main feature of relations between tourists and Korowai is that they share no common language. Tourists speak English as their lingua franca of travel, while Korowai speak their vernacular and in some cases also a local dialect of Indonesian. Most communication of spoken meanings that does take place is mediated by the professional tour guides, who are bilingual in Indonesian and English, and by certain Korowai who speak Indonesian exceptionally well, and who translate between Indonesian and their vernacular (Figure 1). Apart from this bottleneck of limited chain translation between tourists and Korowai via the guide and his Korowai partners, the overall situation is one of Korowai conversing densely with each other in their language, tourists conversing densely in their home-country language, considerable English speech between guides and tourists that is not translated into Indonesian, and considerable Indonesian speech between guides and Korowai that is not translated into English. This plays into the wider organization of tourism as close social involvement between actors with very different understandings of their relation, each side circulating among themselves elaborate bodies of exoticizing stereotypes about the other which the other knows little about.

A good illustration of the incomprehension that regularly obtains under these linguistic conditions occurred in September 2006, when Australian news personality Naomi Robson traveled to Papua with her television crew to film their intended rescue of a Korowai orphan said to be in danger of being killed as a witch. The boy's plight had been brought to Robson's attention by a magazine writer who had visited Korowai a few months earlier, accompanied by personnel of a competing tabloid news show. Indonesian officials expelled Robson's group before they visited Korowai, and a media firestorm ensued in the Australian press surrounding the two programs' mutual recriminations, the immorality of their cannibalism-focused sensationalism, and disagreement among

Figure 1. Chain translation during production of a reality TV show, July 2011. The two Danes at center-left ask questions in English of the monolingual Korowai man being filmed. The Papuan tour guide at far left translates between English and Indonesian, while his Korowai partner at far right translates between Indonesian and Korowai.

commentators over whether the boy was actually likely to be in danger. I visited Korowai a few months after these events, and there was a predictably wide gulf between the representations that had circulated in the international media and the boy's actual history as understood by his kin and co-villagers (who had no awareness of the media coverage). Almost all persons I spoke with said that the exclusive reason the first film crew's guide had been approached by villagers about taking the orphan to town was so that he would go to school, become literate in Indonesian, and return as a teacher, nurse, or government official. These numerous persons matter-of-factly denied my suggestions that the boy had been rumored to be a witch, or had been in danger of being killed.[1]

1.   Only the boy's uncle (and main caregiver) said there had been talk that the boy was a witch and might someday be in danger of being killed, though this man was not able to tell me concrete persons speaking in these terms. The uncle also said another main reason for sending the boy to town was wanting him to go to school. The uncle seemed to mix the witchcraft threat into the picture out of a perception that this

A full account of these events would be a study of its own, but what I want to highlight are the multiple social links of incomprehension and distortion extending between the boy at one end and the Australian media public at the other. Contrary to press reports, the boy and his caregivers were speakers of Kombai rather than Korowai. But several Korowai known as tourism "heads" were important in the affair, because they were the main local partners of the Indonesian tour guide. These Korowai mediators, together with the boy's Kombai uncle, spoke with the Indonesian tour guide; the guide spoke with the Australian magazine writer; the magazine writer spoke with Robson and her producers; and the producers broadcast stories to their Australian audiences. Much as in the children's game in which a message is whispered from one person to the next down a line, from one end of this chain to the other, the idea of sending the boy to town for schooling turned into the idea that he was about to be cannibalized for witchcraft (see Voorhoeve 1979). Korowai tourism encounters at large are characterized by parallel levels of elaborate miscomprehension between persons who are right next to each other.

The social role of "guide," or literally "head" (Kor. *xabian*), is a new category in Korowai discourse that is applied both to the Indonesian-speaking professional tour guides who visit Korowai transiently, and to new tourism specialists within the Korowai community who partner with these outsiders. To Korowai, linguistic translation is the defining activity of the "head" role. I return later to these "heads," whose importance is paralleled by numerous other polyglot mediators in earlier histories of cross-societal encounter worldwide (see Karttunen 1994; Metcalf 2005). Yet while most actual translation passes through these specialists, all tourists and Korowai have experiences of linguistic incomprehension and ideas about linguistic otherness. Having introduced the broad language situation of tourism meetings, I now look at some specific Korowai and tourist practices of relating to the foreignness of the other's language, which are important aspects of the overall fabric of language-focused figuration of cultural difference in the tourism encounters.

---

would make the request more urgent to the guide, and out of personal anxiety about the boy's future colored by the trauma of another much older relative's recent killing for adultery and witchcraft. Well after Robson had been sent home, her Indonesian tour guide in fact brought the boy to the coastal city of Jayapura, and he now lives in Sumatra.

IDEAS ABOUT KNOWING THE OTHER'S LANGUAGE

Korowai and tourists each enact a diverse range of ideologies and practices about linguistic otherness. Here I will set out two juxtapositions that suggest certain broad lines of contrast between the two groups' orientations, though of course the generalizations I develop are provisional and heuristic in character.

A first juxtaposition concerns each side's ideological assumptions about the most primordial linguistic act. Like other people in regions characterized by extreme linguistic diversity, Korowai have had ample experience of linguistic otherness even prior to their involvement with speakers of a colonial or national lingua franca (which for Korowai dates to the last few decades). Persons whose land was located near the fringes of the Korowai area were particularly likely to be multilingual, due to regular interaction with speakers of neighboring languages. From the complexities of this deep history of engagement across linguistic boundaries, I will focus here on just one detail of metalinguistic discourse, namely that the epithet by which Korowai describe someone (including oneself) as a disfluent speaker of a second language is "only sago and water" (*xo-mail-lanux*). Sago is the regional food staple. This idiom compactly expresses an understanding that the primordial linguistic act is to request or give food and drink, typically in a scene of a guest having entered other people's house at some distance from his or her own home.

This Korowai ideology contrasts with the tourist view that the first things to know in a foreign language are how to say "hello," "thank you," and "goodbye." This tourist view is reflected in the rise of the Korowai term *manop*, "good," as a one-word pidgin of tourism encounters. Virtually all tourists learn this word, whether they are taught it by tour guides when they ask how to greet Korowai, or learn it directly from Korowai who say it to them. This single word is thus an exception to my statement that Korowai and tourists lack any shared language. Guides, tourists, and Korowau use *manop* (or the phrase *manop telobo*, "it's good") hundreds of times across a visit, to complement arrivals, departures, handshakes, acts of giving or physical help, smiles, or just ongoing copresence. To Korowai and tourists alike, the utterance is a verbal equivalent of a handshake or joint laugh, indexing mutuality of pleasure in each other's presence.

Among themselves, Korowai do not use *manop* as a greeting or valediction, and there are no other ritual expressions for entering or leaving one another's interactional presence (Stasch 2009: 52). When guests enter a house, for example, everyone generally stays silent. The house owners busy themselves preparing food, and let the guests eventually speak first, about whatever topic they see fit. The newness of people's presence to each other, and the question of why guests have come or what standing they have among their hosts, are too sensitive to comment on through autonomy-violating remarks directly signifying that newness in language. The problem of transitions in copresence is more aptly addressed through other sensory and bodily media, in keeping with wider New Guinean patterns of the ideological privileging of material gifts over words (Robbins 2007; Merlan and Rumsey 1991). There are also no conventional Korowai expressions that verbally ritualize departure or an affect of gratitude. The word *manop*, "good," occurs frequently in people's running commentaries on day-to-day social interaction, but such use has been tremendously expanded and reconventionalized in the tourism context. This has occurred as a direct reflection of tourists' expectation that an expression of greeting and thanks is the first and most important linguistic form to learn in a foreign language. The word *manop* is emblematic for tourists of an idea of meeting Korowai on their own terms, since the linguistic form is marked as Korowai. Yet the usage is actually a pragmatic calque of a speech form and its supporting understandings from the tourists' home communities. Korowai coproduce this new convention with tourists and guides, and all participants share a loosely aligned understanding of what the convention expresses and what it can be used for.

This contrast between models of the primordial linguistic act respectively held by Korowai and tourists suggests a broader contrast between an idea of language as intertwined with material economies of care, and an idea of language as preeminently an instrument for expressing interior affect. A Korowai sense that questions of comprehending a language are one and the same with questions of exchange obligations to its speakers was also reflected in an event recounted to me by an elderly monolingual woman in 2011. When I asked this woman, named Xau, whether she had any experience with tourists, she recalled a time when a helicopter flew overhead. She said that when she heard it, she jumped out of her house and ran through the underbrush into the forest. I asked her why she had been afraid, and I expected her to emphasize something fearful about the aircraft as a technological form, or feelings of bodily danger and perceptual shock. But instead Xau answered that she had feared that the helicopter would land and people in it would ask her questions in their language, which she would not be able to speak.

Xau's fear of being addressed in a language she did not know reflects how central linguistic incomprehension is to Korowai experience of tourism. Yet her imagined scene illustrates a wider Korowai emphasis on responsibility to the other, and to the relation with that other, that is basic to how people think about language. Even with somebody who has dropped out of the sky, there is an imperative to understand them and to reply. The same scene of transactional crisis is a frequent point of worry for monolingual Korowai in relation to village space. Indonesian is being widely learned across the entire Korowai region today, but the language continues to be strongly associated with the new settlement form of "villages" in contrast with traditional "forest" space, and it is spoken by a greater proportion of men than women (Stasch 2007, 2013). Monolingual Korowai women who live in villages frequently describe themselves as avoiding other parts of the village where non-Korowai speakers live, out of fear of being unable to answer queries put to them in Indonesian. Such women also report their husbands urging them to learn Indonesian, in anticipation of an imagined scene of an Indonesian speaker walking up to the house while the man is away, and the woman needing to answer what the visitor says.

We could see these Korowai sensitivities as running parallel to tourists' feeling of the importance of knowing a term of greeting in encountered people's language, rather than awkwardly being in their presence but having no common speech. But the linguistic imperatives felt by Korowai seem to extend to giving other people information they are seeking, rather than only giving greetings. And the imagined scenes seem to imply a greater level of intrinsic social obligation and social crisis in the encounter with linguistic others than obtains for tourists.

A second juxtaposition I will offer is between tourist and Korowai practices of adopting the other's linguistic forms as emblematic of the encounter and the exocultural relation. On tourists' side, *manop* is already a case of this. Besides using *manop* in speech toward Korowai, tourists also take it up as iconic of their trips in general. For example, a Swedish tourist who traveled to the Korowai area as part of a large group in 2007 later circulated to his cotravelers a film about their trip titled *Manop Torobo*. The helicopter that scared Xau was carrying cameramen for a 2008 episode of the reality TV show *Rendez-vous en terre inconnue* in which a pop singer lived for a time with a Korowai family. The episode culminates in a nighttime scene of this artist playing her guitar for Korowai and extemporizing sung lyrics consisting of the word *manop* and the names of two of her Korowai hosts. The word *manop* and its all-purpose uses are almost universally discussed in tourist blogs. Tour group members also commonly start using *manop* jokingly with each other. All these usages involve an idea that fellow feeling across cultural divides is the very image of the trip. They also involve a focus on the linguistic otherness of a specific Korowai form, and the tourist's ability to assimilate that form, as likewise a basic image of the trip's logic.

Parallel processes unfold in relation to Indonesian-language forms among the small minority of tourists who speak some Indonesian and do not rely on a professional English-speaking guide. For example, a private travelogue produced by members of a German tour group is titled on its front cover *Tidak bisa: Awimbon–Senggo 2002*, where the Indonesian expression *tidak bisa* means "You can't do it" and Awimbon and Senggo are names of the endpoints of the trip. The book's next page features in large, colorful, nonrectilinear type the same phrase *tidak bisa*, along with other Indonesian expressions meaning "We're afraid" and "We're not ready," over their German glosses. The travelogue quotes many instances of Korowai saying these phrases, typically in relation to the tourists' efforts to determine how or when they can get to their next destination. The paratextual prominence of these expressions at the front of the document reflects how these communicative patterns became, for the tourists, humorously iconic of their overall relations with Korowai.

A related pattern is tourist interest in language documentation, within the larger modeling of trips as exercises in anthropological and scientific observation. Individual tourists may occasionally interact linguistically in a sustained way with individual Korowai without a tour guide's mediation. Typically in these contexts the tourists will seek to exchange knowledge of personal names, but they may also try to elicit body-part words and other words for immediately visible objects. A Spaniard who visited in 2007 posted a series of her images of Korowai subjects to a photo-sharing website. Under one photo depicting a Korowai woman climbing a treehouse ladder against an orange-purple sunset, she placed a caption mentioning that while falling asleep each night near Korowai who talk on endlessly, "you have the feeling that all the time they are saying the same sentence."[2] But below another photo, she recalled:

> I communicated with them through an ex-Korowai named Pai, who was half-civilized by Dutch missionaries twenty years ago. Now he devotes himself to

---

2. The sunset photo and caption were formerly viewable at http://fc-foto.es/17830377. At the time of this article's publication, the caption can be found here: http://www.alphaspain.es/forums/forum.php?paramurl=dG9waWWMzODQzOC5odG1s.

organizing groups of porters from Yaniruma, a village of about forty houses in which dwell ex-Korowais most of whom moved from the jungle when they were orphaned or sick, and that was created by the Dutch missionaries and then later abandoned by them because they could not convert the Korowais. Pai speaks Indonesian and I am escorted by a Moluccan guide, Toni, with whom I converse in English. So the communication was as follows: from Korowai to Indonesia, from Indonesian to English, and then by me from English to Spanish for my partner. Now I translate some of the most common words, written as they sound phonetically in Castilian:

laki laki – senior man, big man.
bizard –- big, long, huge
mandi – swim, bathe, get wet
linta – leech
parau – canoe
babi – pig/boar
yalan – come on, come on, now
yantan – exclamation at something surprising
quenapa – because
macan – eat, food, hunger
ini – this, that[3]

Here documentary recording of token translation equivalences is iconic of a larger situation of collecting cross-cultural knowledge and experience. These vocabulary notes are also unwittingly illustrative of the communicative constraints under which tourists operate. The words the author learned are Indonesian rather than Korowai, and Pai is not a Korowai speaker but a Western Dani man who moved to the area as an airstrip worker. He does work occasionally in tourism alongside Korowai, but he is not a leader in organizing treks. The idea that anyone would be "ex-Korowai" also makes little sense in local ethnolinguistic reasoning, but reflects ideas of loss and deculturation central to tourists'

---

3. This caption was formerly posted at http://www.fotocommunity.es/pc/pc/cat/16110/display/17830436. At the time of this article's publication, the caption can be viewed at http://www.sonystas.com/foro/fotografia-social/korowais-el-viaje-de-mi-vida-parte-ii/ and at http://www.alphaspain.es/forums/forum.php?pa ramurl=dG9waWMzODQzOC5odG1s. I thank Raquel Pacheco for translation assistance.

primitivist model. Tourists lack resources to grasp local social heterogeneity, and they reason about Korowai in highly stereotype-driven forms, as Korowai do about them. For example, monolingual Korowai routinely make inferences similar to this woman's misunderstanding: they assume that Indonesian speech they uncomprehendingly hear is the native language of tourists.

However, the main Korowai pattern I want to juxtapose to the above-sketched tourist engagements with Korowai linguistic otherness is the naming of children after tour guides. A major desire of tourists in their visits is to form relations of deep mutual emotional involvement with Korowai, but in reality tourists usually remain very generic figures even to Korowai persons whom they encounter face-to-face. Ironically, it is instead the tourists' paid guides who come into focus for Korowai as differentiated individuals and as friends or kin. Many different Papuan or Indonesian tour guides have brought tourists to the Korowai area, but two dozen of the most experienced guides account for about three-quarters of groups. In contrast with most tourists, these guides visit repeatedly, they speak Indonesian, they engage extensively in practices of payment and exchange, and they negotiate directly with Korowai over the logistics and politics of the tourists' presence. Many guides also act toward Korowai in ways that Korowai find quite culturally recognizable, or are even pulled into intra-Korowai social conventions and political processes. Reflecting this salience of guides in Korowai eyes, there are now about a hundred Korowai children who have been named after them. As one woman narrated her choice of a name for her son, for example, "There's the tourist head Kalfin, and he himself is Kalfin. I saw the tourist head Kalfin from afar, and later I named my son Kalfin." This pattern follows a broader fashion of attraction to Indonesian-language names today. But no other category of outsider has such prominence as namesakes. Korowai are motivated in these naming practices by a sense that guides are good, valuable, or beautiful persons whom people desire to have bonds with. Often parents name their children after guides specifically out of admiration for the guides' possession of money and consumer goods. Children are themselves figures of intense value and desire, and the guides' names aptly match how other people feel about the children, or what they want for the children in life.

There is a vast range of other phenomena of language contact in which Korowai learn speech forms associated with tourists and adopt them into their own repertoires. For example, in the 1990s Korowai borrowed the word *tulis* into their language from Indonesian *turis*, "tourist," as an overall ethnic designation for the foreign visitors. Likewise, even monolingual Korowai speakers know the borrowed word *asli*, which in standard Indonesian means "authentic, original, indigenous, primitive," but to Korowai means "naked, wearing traditional dress rather than imported clothing," since this is what tourists and guides most directly are talking about when they actually use the term around Korowai. But continuing the characterization I outlined with reference to ideas about the primordial linguistic act, I would like to take the example of guide names specifically as highlighting a contrast between what might be termed tourists' and Korowai people's respectively spectatorial versus transactional ideologies of linguistic difference. Once again, there is some overlap between tourist and Korowai actions: each catches hold of token linguistic forms associated with the other, and makes use of those forms in their own lives in a quotational mode. But naming one's own children after radical foreigners is a striking act of taking something alien and making it very intimate. It puts visitors and visited in the same sociopolitical field, even if the outsiders continue to be marked as strange. By comparison, the para-ethnographic recording of foreign vocabulary, or humorous iconization of specific pragmatic expressions of politeness or frustration as linguistic emblems of the intercultural relation, seem to involve ongoing assertion of a fundamental difference of relational status.

If this is an accurate inference from the small sample of ethnographic materials I have presented, the generalization harmonizes with parallels and contrasts in the more global models of the other's difference that orient tourist and Korowai approaches to each other. I cannot discuss in depth here the primitivist framework motivating tourists' travel, involving as it does a Manichaean opposition between a human condition of archaic purity and another of modern corruption (see Stasch 2011, 2014a, 2014d). It is probably fair to say, though, that while tourists oriented by this framework value Korowai and draw on their meetings with them to reflect critically on their own lives' domination by market-mediated social relations, the model involves strong commitment to the ultimate political and transactional separateness of the encountering people.

Korowai have similarly exoticized tourists as radical others, often grounded in stereotypic likening of tourists (along with all other new strangers) to a category of malignant monsters humans become after they die, called *laleo* ("demons") and resembling a walking corpse. For Korowai historically, death was the most pronounced context of close mental involvement with extreme otherness of being. It made obvious sense to apply understandings of the otherness of the dead to the new problem of the strangers who began intruding in the 1980s. Korowai think of the dead in strongly ethnoterritorial and ethnographic terms, as they now do of tourists as well. But as I have detailed elsewhere (Stasch 2007, 2009: 69–71, 215–23), even in the elements of deformity, fear, and repulsion that are prominent in Korowai thought about the demonic dead and the new foreigners, there is a strong sense that the relation of radical otherness is also a relation of unavoidable mutual involvement and obligation—much as Xau imagined herself owing something socially and communicatively to visitors who might descend in a helicopter.

"WE DIDN'T TELL HIM *MANOP* MEANS 'FUCK YOU' IN FRENCH"

While we have seen some ways that Korowai and tourists positively value knowing token elements of the other's language, another aspect of the "bottleneck" ecology is that participants often actively value and exploit each other's lack of cross-linguistic comprehension. In passive ways, linguistic incomprehension facilitates the smoothness of tourism as an overall structure of "working misunderstanding" (Dorward 1974; also, e.g., Gershon and Raj 2000 and Leite forthcoming, among many others). It is common for Korowai to labor away in a photogenic scene before a tour group's cameras, while talking animatedly about plans for buying store-bought commodities, rumors of government-sponsored village housing projects, money the tour group will hopefully give, and other topics at odds with tourists' idea of Korowai as living in isolation from global consumer culture. Linguistic incomprehension also facilitates processes of Korowai or guides staging appearances to match tourists' expectations. In a 2010 film called *Path to the Stone Age*, the French cameraman and his Danish wife are at one point interested in whether Korowai they visit have previously met white people. Their Dani tour guide asks a Korowai interviewee in Indonesian, *Bapak lihat orang putih? Orang putih? Sudah lihat, kah?* and this utterance is aptly translated in English subtitles as "Have you ever seen white men?" The Korowai partner of this Dani guide is expected to translate the question into Korowai. While the translator's Korowai utterance is subtitled as "He's asking you if you ever saw white men," what he actually says is a series of directives: "Say 'No, none.' Say 'None at all.' Say 'I have not seen white-skinned people, this is the first time'" (*Mafem, dim. Afe mafem-e dim. Nu xal-xeyo anop nu bimbaleda, xəniləxa ifip dim*). The interviewee indeed responds by narrating a history of not having met whites, then hearing about them, and now finally meeting them for the first time.

So too, while a dominant emotional strand of tourism encounters is mutual goodwill and enthusiasm, participants on all sides also frequently joke about each other or comment negatively on each other's characteristics, under the assumption that the other does not understand what is being said. They also stand up in various ways for their interactional separateness from the others. In August 2011, I was with members of a German tour group who were watching Korowai men construct a large fish trap, when one tourist asked what the family relation was between two of the men. The question was translated by the tour guide and his Korowai partner, and one of the men working on the trap gave a brief answer, but then after a long pause added, "Why is she asking?" For Korowai, such "why?" constructions have a conventional rhetorical force of expressing the speaker's objection to the action in question. To this man, the exhibitionary performance in its visual and bodily aspects was a comfortable enough convention to occupy, while the spoken inquiry about his social relations was a slight breach of that comfortable distance.

On an earlier occasion, in 2007, I was similarly following the activities of a Francophone Swiss group, when its members at one point exchanged repetitive utterances of the phatic term *manop* with a specific Korowai man, and then one of the foreigners said to me in English, in an offhanded aside, "We didn't tell him *manop* means 'fuck you' in French." The exchange of *manop* had followed a material negotiation, which is a context when tourists might experience more antagonistic feelings toward Korowai than in other contexts of their visits, during which feelings of affection generally predominate. But the Swiss man's joke to me depends on a broader idea of ongoing indeterminacy behind even the minimal one-word "shared" language of *manop* that appears to bridge the tourism divide. The joke invokes tourists' own exclusive relation of belonging in relation to their home language, as amounting to a bedrock of their private possession of their own intended meanings and ongoing social difference.

Drawing on Hanks' work on Maya shamanism, Hanks and Severi note that "asymmetry of knowledge between participants, and the constraints on translation between the esoteric language of shamanism and ordinary Maya, are actually resources for shaman–patient interaction, not impediments. This in turn suggests that meaningful and consequential interaction can proceed in the absence of mutual translatability, or perhaps even intelligibility" (p. 9, this volume). Tourism encounters in the Korowai area are also a case in which non-commensurateness of interacting persons' ideas of who they are and what they are mutually doing is crucial to how well they coordinate socially. For example, a major orientation of Korowai to tourism is that they hope through it to become in effect more like tourists, in the sense of gaining access to money, consumer goods, the town-centered educational and occupational system, and so forth; while the tourists who visit them desire Korowai exactly for being *unlike* the tourists and their home socieconomic conditions. Linguistic incomprehension is part of what makes it possible for Korowai and tourists to serve each other's goals in such highly coordinated ways, while not realizing how contradictory their respective goals actually are.

Many tourists are subtly reflexive about what they do not understand about visited people's lives, and they express strong regret about the linguistic barriers between themselves and Korowai. But overall, there is a synergy between linguistic incomprehension and the primitivist model. As has been often claimed about tourism and related historical complexes in European modernity (e.g., Urry 1990; Bennett 1988), foreigners who visit Korowai are focused on a spectatorial organization of *vision* as a path of knowledge, and on Korowai people's bodies, facial expressions, physical skills, and material articles as the locus of who they are. This is evident in the intensified attention that tourists give to Korowai in traditional dress when they first encounter them after having seen many other Korowai in imported clothes, and in how tourists read lack of clothing as the direct embodiment of Korowai people's state of purity outside the global market order (Stasch 2014b). A related pattern is the expansion of material culture, especially the visible aspects of Korowai making their livelihood from their surrounding environment, as a focus of tourists' sense of the utopian character of the visited people's world. Lack of linguistic channels of communication is consonant with the reproduction of a vision-based experience of Korowai as walking avatars of a universal primitive type. In this sense, in some tourists' experience the idea of the primitive may be not just an archaic condition outside of markets, but a condition of bodily being and social fellowship that is beneath the difficulties of language.

TRANSLATORS AS "HEADS": TOURISM MEDIATION AND A NEW POLITICAL ORDER

To this point, my discussion has dealt with ways that tourists and Korowai express stances about their mutual linguistic otherness at a metalinguistic and tokenistic level, while in reality not communicating very much and staying largely separate as discursive communities. I now turn to the "bottleneck" itself, the so-cial position of the specialist tour guides who mediate the discourse that actually is translated. I will discuss Korowai perspectives on the translator role, but these perspectives highlight a more generally relevant point that translators' knowledge across cultural and linguistic lines draws to the fore questions of authority and asymmetry in people's value. To the extent that tourists deemphasize language as an aspect of their encounters with Korowai, while nonetheless experiencing the encounters as events of chronotope-crossing true encounter with a human condition of primitive purity radically different from their own being, the market logic of guiding is a main instrument by which tourists are able to elide language but still coordinate socially with their chosen others. The specialist role of "guide" helps make problems of language disappear through the guide's abilities as a bi-lingual intermediary who can relate alternately both to his clients and to Korowai to bring into existence an order of social relating between both encountering groups. Tourists are able to experience this order of social relating relatively inde-pendently of the actual linguistic processes that have gone into its constitution.

As I noted earlier, to Korowai the new category of tourist "head" is centrally defined by the activity of translation. "Head," "guide," and "translator" are all one concept. For example, Korowai sort out who among themselves belongs to the new occupational subgroup of tourist "heads" mainly using the criteria of whether the individual under discussion speaks Indonesian and ever works as a translator for tour groups. Many individuals have moved in and out of this tourism specialization at different times, but about a dozen Korowai men are best known as tourism "heads." Most of them are residents of one of the main gateway villages by which tourists first arrive in the area. For example, the most experienced Korowai head, Fenelun Malonggai, lives in the airstrip village that was throughout the 1990s the main point of entry for tourists (Figure 2). Fenelun's tourism work started shortly after the end of his time as the primary linguistic consultant of two mission-affiliated foreigners who lived in his village in the 1980s (see van Enk and de Vries 1997).

What I think is most worth analytic attention around the "head" phenom-enon is the mingling of heads' status as translators with their status as a speaker role embodying a new understanding of political community. To develop this point, I need to fill in two background patterns. The first is a basic Korowai un-derstanding that speech is a primordial site of questions of subordination in so-cial relations, and the second is a broader semantic innovation that has unfolded around the Korowai word "head" in its uses even beyond tourism.

Figure 2. Korowai "head" Fenelun Malonggai (right) with Indonesian "head" Herman Sihotang, 2007.

I suggested above that Korowai tend to understand entry into linguistic coin-volvement as tantamount to entry into transactional relations of exchange, care, and obligation. A stronger statement of this point is that Korowai see speech as foundationally associated with political subordination. Korowai are intensely egalitarian in their political ethos. For example, they historically lacked any named roles of political leadership, and in the present as in the past they are quick to rebuke any person who tries to tell others what to do. Their egalitarian ethos is also reflected physically in past and ongoing practices of living spread out thinly across the landscape, which they explicitly link to a desire to make their livelihoods and raise their families according to their own wills (*xul-melun*, lit. "thoughts") rather than being impinged on by desires and demands of others. Yet absence of stable roles of political authority is not the same as absence of social subordination as such. On the contrary, Korowai have a clear idea of the possibility of subordination in social life. They often marvel approvingly at it when it occurs, as a realization of values of relatedness and coordination. They express the idea of subordination by saying that one person "listens" to another person, or literally "hears the speech/voice" of that person (*aup dai-*). The same idea is expressed also by the slightly more politically direct phrase "fulfill the speech/voice" (*aup kümo-*). For example, a woman explained to me that when certain persons organize a formal performance troupe to travel to a feast, they do not do so "according to their own thoughts," but rather "they fulfill the talk from the jaws of the feast owners" (*gil anop bongol aup kükümomate*). The question of whether someone "listens" to another is often particularly posed of a son-in-law with respect to his mother-in-law, or a wife in relation to her husband, but it comes up in countless other kinds of relational situations as well. In this model of "listening" as a basic political form, there is still generally much emphasis on autonomy. It is an egalitarian choice of one person to agree with what another person says and act upon it (Stasch 2008). Significantly, the model also extends to expressing the question of adherence to sociocultural order at large as residing in whether one "fulfills speech" of others. People routinely explain their whole life practice, for example, by saying, "I am fulfilling the talk of my parents," or "fulfilling the talk" of a world-creating demiurge. Adherence to norms of how to reside on the land, how to hold feasts, how to organize kinship relations, and the like, is recognized as ultimately a form of "talk" or "discourse" (*aup*).

Coincidentally, the main metalinguistic expression by which Korowai speak of knowing a language is the same collocation *aup dai-*, "hear speech," as in the expression *laleo-aup dai-*, "know Indonesian [lit. 'hear Indonesian']." In this construction, *dai-*, "hear," is used in the sense of "comprehend" rather than "agree with and act upon." Yet this identity of a main expression for political subordination and the main expression for speaking a language again aptly reflects a broad Korowai understanding that to know a language is one and the same with entering into a dialectics of listening to the expressed subjectivity of others and answering to their calls of whether one might align one's subjectivity with theirs.

These egalitarian dynamics have also been at play in the new Korowai uses of the word for "head." Hanks and Severi note that one issue arising when we "look at translation as a historical practice" is that translation *creates* languages and linguistic communities, such as when "the target language is altered in the process of translation" (p. 9, this volume). Older Korowai speakers consistently report that until recent times, the Korowai word for "head" was used only to refer to anatomical heads of bodies, or to parts of inanimate physical objects analogized to a head. Today, though, "head" (*xabian*) is also used to refer to stable social roles of authority. This usage grew initially from Korowai exposure to outsiders' routine use of the Indonesian word *kepala*, "head," to refer to leadership roles. In the 1980s, the first cohorts of men in certain parts of the Korowai landscape began learning Indonesian and traveling to faraway administrative centers, where they met government-appointed "village heads" (*kepala desa*) or salaried "heads of administrative offices" (*kepala kantor*). By the 1990s, a few centralized settlements in the Korowai area began to have "village heads" of their own, in local iterations of official Indonesian government structures. In the early 2000s, there occurred a further meteoric rise in use of the Korowai word *xabian*, "head," to mean in effect "boss." This new usage of "head" as a term for all manner of roles of political authority took hold across the entire Korowai region. The change happened not only because more Korowai became familiar with the Indonesian word *kepala* and its uses, but also because vertical relations of wealth and power came to stand out to Korowai as *the* signature social form of the distant urban-centered society they were growing increasingly connected to.

Urban society is generically portrayed by Korowai as a space of "head" relations, in which persons of authority live from food and wealth that is "just there" rather than being produced by their own labor, and live by dispensing wealth to others who do their bidding (Stasch 2014c). The new "heads" whom Korowai regularly talk about include faraway district administrators and provincial government officials, business owners, and salaried government or church employees such as civil servants, schoolteachers, health nurses, police, soldiers, and church ministers. A main Korowai image of their own possible future advancement is that if they send their sons to school in towns, these boys will become "heads" themselves, bringing salaries and knowledge back to kin who supported their schooling (see also Stasch forthcoming). This is the idea that was being pursued by Kombai and Korowai participants in the earlier-described affair of the Australian television personality and the Kombai orphan.

The late 1990s and early 2000s were also when Korowai routinized use of the word *xabian*, "head," to refer to exogenous tour guides and the Korowai translators who partner with them. International tourists have been a more concrete interactional presence than government officials or traders for many Korowai, because the tourists come directly to Korowai lands. Yet there is also a broad conflation of tourists' and guides' home lives with the overall image of urban space as a social order of "head" relations and amazing consumer wealth. In Korowai interpretations of what makes someone a tourism "head," the feature of exercising authority through speech is closely merged with the core feature of being a translator. Innovative application of "head" to guides was motivated by the new category's fascinating spotlighting of structures of social subordination, which also stood out to Korowai as a fundamental characteristic of tourism relations.

The way that lexicalization of "guide" as "head" was informed by the authority dimension of the "head" idea is underlined, for example, by a pattern in how most Korowai initially understood the sociology of tour groups. When tourism started in the 1990s, most Korowai had little sense of the groups' internal differentiation. Once the idea of a group being composed of "tourists" and a guide or "head" came into focus, this understanding was widely seized upon. Consistently at different times and places, though, persons who are newly developing knowledge of tourism have inferred that it is tourism clients who are the political subordinates of guides, rather than the reverse. Korowai see the tourists as coming to the Korowai area in the first place because the guides tell them to do so, and as doing what the guides tell them to do while there.

Korowai themselves are also addressees of guides' authoritative speech. The exogenous and Korowai "heads" alike tell Korowai to build shelters, organize exhibitionary performances of emblematic cultural activities, observe rules of spatial segregation, carry baggage, and so on. From many Korowai persons' points of view, tourism's moral bargain consists in doing whatever "heads" tell them to do, in exchange for expected payments and gifts. Concerning the pattern of naming children after Indonesian and Papuan tour guides, I already noted that these exogenous guides are a focus of Korowai admiration and desire, based on association with material wealth. In a similar way, Korowai "heads" tend to be regarded very positively. Far from resenting these heads' disproportionate access to material benefits from tourism (as is a frequent Korowai egalitarian response to wealth inequality), most persons appreciate the heads' privileged positions as a transactional asset to themselves (see also Stasch 2014e). In general, Korowai have a highly developed sense of their lack of any foothold in tourists' social systems, and their inability to arrange tourist visits. Heads stand out as persons whom other Korowai can actually communicate with, yet who have the ability to bring about desired tourist visits to specific places on the landscape.

Writing about another New Guinea location, Handman (2014) has examined in detail how Guhu-Samane speakers have taken creation of vernacular translations of Bible passages as iconic and indexical of larger processes of spiritual and historical transformation. She also shows that "language in the era of Christianity, which is often characterized as the era after wars ended, has nevertheless become the power to create division, animosity, and fighting" (ibid.: 26).

This is because Christian social organization and wide Guhu-Samane involvement in translation and interpretation of sacred texts dramatically expanded
"licensed speakerhood," by comparison to the centralized restriction of authoritative speaking positions in the past institution of the men's house. In a parallel
way, the guide and translator is for Korowai an exemplary figure within a wider
reorganization of political order. Amidst this wider reorganization, the act of
verbally ordering people around has a strikingly ambiguous status. It is bizarrely
novel in Korowai political culture, but also very recognizable. While the new
use of "head" is a linguistic calque of Indonesian *kepala* and a cultural calque of
market and state hierarchy, it is also an elaboration of ideas of "listening" already
latent in Korowai political thought. Korowai adhere to an egalitarian political
ethos that means rejecting hierarchical structures of leadership, somewhat in the
image of a "society against the state" as modeled by Clastres ([1974] 1977). Yet
we have seen that this involves *sensitivity to* political subordination rather than
simply absence of it. Living by an egalitarian ethos can entail clearsightedness
about how irreducible such subordination is as an aspect of social relating. It can
even entail attraction to subordination, as impressively productive of desirable
social outcomes, if it can somehow exist without triggering a feeling that values
of autonomy and equality have been violated.

A small example of how Korowai have molded their uptake of the anti-Ko-
rowai social category of "head" in forms aligned with their own political values
is the frequent tendency for it to be construed as overtly relational, and even
reciprocal. About a newly arrived group of tourists, a speaker will ask, "Who is
their head?" A specific exogenous tour guide is the "head" of a specific Korowai
partner, and that Korowai partner is the "head" of the exogenous guide. And in
a revealing interpretation of my own activities in tourism-colored terms, many
people in conversation with me routinely refer to my closest Korowai friend
as "your head," meaning "your tour guide," in consideration of his work as my
research assistant and social mediator, while also speaking of me as his "head."
In English and other languages, categories like "boss" or "supervisor" are also
intrinsically relational, as can be foregrounded through genitive constructions
parallel to the Korowai ones. But in the Korowai case, these common genitive
usages ("their head," "his head," "your head") echo ubiquitous use of possessively
prefixed kinship terms as the single most frequent type of person-referring noun
phrase in discourse. I have argued elsewhere that Korowai often represent persons or roles as metonymies of relationships, more strongly than seeing a relationship as the sum of two or more independent persons (Stasch 2009: 73–104).

The idea of stable vertical social relations like patron–client ties is broadly new to Korowai, and yet the relational aspect of this tie is immediately familiar.

There may also be a political metaphor in using "head" for anatomical referents, even before there is an anatomical metaphor in using it for political referents. For example, there is at least a single weak exception to my generalization that "head" was historically not used to designate social roles prior to the era of contact with the Indonesian language. The expression *xabian milo-*, "go first at the head," has long existed as a set phrase for describing someone as walking at the front of a column of other people, such as in a procession traveling to a feast, analogizing the column of walkers to an anatomical body. Even in this connection, though, the word and role "head" seems never to have been separated out on its own from the concrete activity and verb "walk first in a column" (*milo-*). But there is a slight sense of political hierarchy to just the temporally bounded action of being at the front of a procession, even in a conceptual system concerned with containing and dampening such hierarchy.

So, too, the elaboration of a speaking role of telling others what to do has made sense to Korowai because of their characteristically New Guinean orientation to material objects and exchange as the truth of relations. As long as tourism can lead to satisfying exchange outcomes, doing what tour guides say is a satisfactory relation of subordination, even from the point of view of egalitarian political values. The "head" category is a linguistic innovation that crystallizes a complex interaction between endogenous Korowai political principles and the whole social history of new interactions with an exogenous state- and market-grounded social formation. The social system surrounding guide-translators is a new institutional organization of talk's relation to wealth and the ability to make events happen that nonetheless elaborates on selective areas of "equivocal compatibility" (Pina-Cabral 2010) between Korowai people's heritage order and the order of state- and market-organized populations they are interacting with through tourism.

CONCLUSION: POWERS OF INCOMPREHENSION

The ethnographic topic of Korowai understandings of the role of tourism "heads" makes particularly overt a sense of connection between cross-linguistic speaking and the power dimension of social relations, since in these understandings, to translate is to be a boss. Yet in sampling a few other levels of Korowai and tourist engagement with otherness of language in the midst of their encounters, I have sought to describe these areas of practice also in ways that bring into focus how the question of a speaking voice, as it arises in relation to boundaries of incomprehension and otherness of code, bears foundational links to questions of the distribution of value, obligation, and authority in the full social relation between the people encountering each other across that linguistic divide. We have glimpsed a diversity of ways that linguistic otherness is a figure around which participants try to set terms of what each owes the other, what is good or bad about each party and their relation, and whose frames of meaning will structure or interpret the course of interaction. It is particularly striking how much of this work of signification is carried by foreignness and incomprehension as such, on top of the limited denotational content that is shuttled across the linguistic boundaries.

Speech and mutually foreign linguistic codes play a major role in mediating the practical intersection between two much larger noncommensurate sociocultural formations, which I have rudimentarily characterized here as a formation of primitivist ideology and market-grounded life on tourists' side, and a political ethos of egalitarianism and exchange-constituted kinship on the side of Korowai. Language's role in the forging of new articulations and partial commensurabilities between these formations unfolds at the level of social complexes surrounding an act of cross-language action: being an authoritative voice by dint of positionality and skill as a translation specialist, celebrating the other's worth or likening oneself to the other's foreign identity through the catching of a foreign speech form, keeping distance by overtly exploiting the other's incomprehension, and so on. Otherness of language has indexical and iconic values within these complexes that are main sources of language's efficacy in mediating the larger commensuration process. Denotation is crucially present, but quite miniscule in proportion to the full traffic of "meaning" actually in play.

There is much existing scholarly work on language-crossing processes in which forms of linguistic otherness—sometimes, fully incomprehensible otherness—are made into figures of the larger relation between categories of people. To mention just one kind of example, authors such as Graham (2002, 2011, 2013) and Richland (2008) have richly charted the indexical and iconic significance of alternate codes in contexts of long-term settler colonization, and in contexts of the shifting circulation of "indigenous"-marked voices in the mass media and formal state institutions. I have sought here to extend that inquiry toward contact communities of the most incipient or transient kind, in which incomprehension is a proportionally even more dominant feature of all that goes on between people in speech. The note of wonder on which I would like to close is just how fluently these incipient communities seem to be able to come together around forms of linguistic otherness. They rapidly converge in making those forms, even in their incomprehensibleness, into markers in would-be construals of the political and evaluative structure of the unstable new relation.

ACKNOWLEDGMENTS

I am extremely grateful to Carlo Severi, Bill Hanks, Alan Rumsey, and Nick Evans for invitations that led to the writing of this essay, and I am similarly grateful to all audience members at my presentations in Australian National University's Coombs Building in September 2011 and the Fyssen Foundation offices in March 2014. I am also in great debt to the *Hau* editorial team and peer reviewers for their work and patient suggestions.

REFERENCES

Bennett, Tony. 1988. "The exhibitionary complex." *New Formations* 4: 73–102.

Clastres, Pierre. (1974) 1977. *Society against the state*. Translated by Robert Hurley and Abe Stein. New York: Urizen Books.

Dorward, David C. 1974. "Ethnography and administration: A study of Anglo-Tiv 'Working Misunderstanding.'" *Journal of African History* 15 (3): 457–77.

Gershon, Ilana, and Dhooleka Sarhadi Raj. 2000. "Introduction: The symbolic capital of ignorance." *Social Analysis* 44 (2): 3–14.

Graham, Laura. 2002. "How should an Indian speak? Brazilian Indians and the symbolic politics of language choice in the international public sphere." In *Indigenous movements, self-representation, and the state in Latin America*, edited by Jean Jackson and Kay Warren, 181–228. Austin: University of Texas Press.

———. 2011. "Quoting Mario Juruna: Linguistic imagery and the transformation of indigenous voice in the Brazilian print press." *American Ethnologist* 38 (1): 164–83.

———. 2013. "From 'ugh' to 'Babel' and beyond: Linguistic images of Native Amazonians in cinema." Paper presented at the American Anthropological Association Annual Meeting, Chicago, November 23.

Handman, Courtney. 2014. *Critical Christianity: Translation and denominational conflict in Papua New Guinea*. Berkeley: University of California Press.

Karttunen, Frances E. 1994. *Between worlds: Interpreters, guides, and survivors*. New Brunswick, NJ: Rutgers University Press.

Kuhn, Thomas S. 2000. *The road since structure: Philosophical essays, 1970–1993*. Edited by James Conant and John Haugeland. Chicago: University of Chicago Press.

Leite, Naomi. Forthcoming. *Global affinities: Portuguese Marranos and the alchemy of ethnic kinship*. Berkeley: University of California Press.

Merlan, Francesca, and Alan Rumsey. 1991. *Ku Waru: Language and segmentary politics in the western Nebilyer Valley, Papua New Guinea*. Cambridge: Cambridge University Press.

Metcalf, Alida. 2005. *Go-betweens and the colonization of Brazil, 1500–1600*. Austin: University of Texas Press.

Pagden, Anthony. 1993. *European encounters with the New World: From Renaissance to Romanticism*. New Haven, CT: Yale University Press.

Pina-Cabral, João de. 2010. "The dynamism of plurals: An essay on equivocal compatibility." *Social Anthropology* 18 (2): 176–90.

Richland, Justin B. 2008. *Arguing with tradition: The language of law in Hopi tribal court*. Chicago: University of Chicago Press.

Robbins, Joel. 2007. "You can't talk behind the Holy Spirit's back: Christianity and changing language ideologies in a Papua New Guinea Society." In *Consequences of contact: Language ideologies and sociocultural transformations in Pacific societies*, edited by Miki Makihara and Bambi Schieffelin, 125–39. Oxford: Oxford University Press.

Stasch, Rupert. 2007. "Demon language: The otherness of Indonesian in a Papuan community." In *Consequences of contact: Language ideologies and sociocultural transformations in Pacific societies*, edited by Miki Makihara and Bambi Schieffelin, 96–124. Oxford: Oxford University Press.

———. 2008. "Knowing minds is a matter of authority: Political dimensions of opacity statements in Korowai moral psychology." *Anthropological Quarterly* 81 (2): 443–53.

———. 2009. *Society of others: Kinship and mourning in a West Papuan place*. Berkeley: University of California Press.

————. 2011. "Textual iconicity and the primitivist cosmos: Chronotopes of desire in travel writing about Korowai of West Papua." *Journal of Linguistic Anthropology* 21 (1): 1–21.

————. 2013. "The poetics of village space when villages are new: Settlement form as history-making in West Papua." *American Ethnologist* 40 (3): 555–70.

————. 2014a. "Primitivist tourism and romantic individualism: On the values in exotic stereotypy about cultural others." *Anthropological Theory* 14 (3): 191–214.

————. 2014b. "Toward symmetric treatment of imaginaries: Nudity and payment in tourism to Papua's 'treehouse people.'" In *Tourism imaginaries: Anthropological approaches*, edited by Noel B. Salazar and Nelson H. Graburn, 31–56. Oxford: Berghahn.

————. 2014c. "Singapore, big village of the dead: Cities as figures of desire, domination, and rupture among Korowai of West Papua." Manuscript under review.

————. 2014d. "Introduction: Double signs and intrasocietal heterogeneity in primitivist tourism encounters." *Ethnos* 80 (4). http://dx.doi.org/10.1080/0 0141844.2014.940989.

————. 2014e. "How an egalitarian society structures tourism and restructures itself around it." *Ethnos* 80 (4). http://dx.doi.org/10.1080/00141844.2014. 942226.

————. Forthcoming. "From primitive other to Papuan self: Korowai engagement with ideologies of unequal human worth in encounters with tourists, state officials, and education." In *From "Stone-Age" to "real-time": Exploring Papuan mobilities, temporalities, and religiosities*, edited by Martin Slama and Jenny Munro. Canberra: ANU Press.

Taylor, Talbot. 1992. *Mutual misunderstanding: Scepticism and the theorizing of language and interpretation*. Durham, NC: Duke University Press.

Urry, John. 1990. *The tourist gaze: Leisure and travel in contemporary societies*. London: Sage.

van Enk, Gerrit, and Lourens de Vries. 1997. *The Korowai of Irian Jaya: Their language in its cultural context*. Oxford: Oxford University Press.

Voorhoeve, Bert. 1979. "Turning the talk: A case of chain-interpreting in Papua New Guinea." In *New Guinea and neighboring areas: A sociolinguistic laboratory*, edited by Stephen Wurm, 177–206. The Hague: Mouton.

CHAPTER FOUR

Healing translations
Moving between worlds in Achuar shamanism

ANNE-CHRISTINE TAYLOR

In their introduction to this volume, Hanks and Severi argue that translation, understood as the move not only between languages but more broadly from one context or register of communication to another, is a pervasive feature of the production of culture, at the level of a single group as well as between different societies and between registers of expression. Insofar as meaning and meaningful action are generated by inferential processes drawing on analogic extension from one domain of experience to another, processes that depend in turn on the reflexivity that is an intrinsic feature of communicative behavior, the work of translation in this sense is the very stuff that constitutes culture, and therefore should be the true object of anthropological inquiry. The aim of this paper[1] is to contribute to the discussion of this view of cultural processes (and of the science devoted to studying them) by evoking some of the operations of translation involved in Upper Amazonian shamanic practices. The ethnographic material this contribution is based on is drawn from fieldwork conducted mainly between

---

1. This contribution draws on, and sometimes repeats, several previous publications (notably Taylor 1997 and 2007).

1978 and 1981 among the northern Achuar, one of the several "tribes" that make up the large Jivaroan ensemble spread over the lowlands of southeast Ecuador and northeast Peru.[2]

The notion that shamanic therapeutic practice is in some way analogous to translating is anything but novel. The point has been made frequently by various lowland specialists, though usually the analogy is offered in a loose way, precisely as a means of "translating" an enigmatic indigenous form of action and discourse for the benefit of a Western audience. The parallel between shamanism and translation rests on a series of features widely reported in the ethnographic literature pertaining to this region: the cosmopolitism of shamans—they have usually traveled outside of their tribal territory, have undergone apprenticeship with nonlocal shamans, claim to speak foreign languages, and above all have established close links with invisible nonhuman beings—the fact that their curing chants are generally couched in some form of more or less hermetic "other" language that presumably implies operations of translation on the part of both the practicing shaman and his audience, and, finally, the fact that indigenous shamanism "works" in transcultural contexts, as it caters increasingly to non-indigenous patients, thus involving further processes of cultural translation. Carneiro da Cunha (1999) has taken up the issue of shamanism as a mode of translation in more precise way, arguing that shamans are translators in the Benjaminian sense of the term (Benjamin [1923] 1968) insofar as their goal is to establish "harmonies" or "resonances" between worlds or planes seen from different perspectives: in particular, they seek to articulate local and global perspectives—global meaning in this case an overarching view of the larger regional economic and political dynamics that shape the lived world of both Indians and mestizo Amazonian populations. Though Carneiro da Cunha does not develop this point, her argument presupposes that the misfortune shamans are called to deal with is somehow connected with the manner in which these ever-changing dynamics are experienced at the local level. This is the issue I want to take up here: how illness is transmuted through shamanic practice into a condition that is readable in terms of the history of interethnic relations, a process involving

---

2. Besides the Achuar, the Jivaroan ensemble includes the Shuar proper, located primarily in Ecuador, the Awajun and Wampis of the Maranon basin, and the Shiwiar of the middle Pastaza valley, closely connected to the Achuar. Though their language seems only remotely related to the Jivaroan family, the Candoan groups (Kanduash and Shapra) of the lower Pastaza region clearly belong in all other respects to the Jivaroan cultural set.

an ordered sequence and combination of "trans-lations" (i.e., shifts from one plane to another and the "harmonic" effects thus created) that I will try briefly to describe, as it occurs among and between the northern Jivaroan Achuar and the Quichua-speaking forest groups that have developed in post-conquest times in their neighborhood. I will argue that the healing techniques of these people are grounded in a series of moves between three nested fields of reference. The first is language use: during the cure, shamans perform their ability as translators of the discourse of spirits with which they interact, though there is actually very little reported speech in their "translations." The second is intracultural and centers on the weaving of correspondences between certain forms of suffering and the history of relations to dominant White[3] outsiders as it is locally conceptualized. The third is intercultural and revolves around the move between two neighboring indigenous cultures and their respective regimes of historicity. I will try to show that overall these practices reveal a paradoxical mode of translation that aims at maintaining rather than suppressing the difference between the "texts" involved.

'WARRIOR' AND SHAMANIC STATES OF SELFHOOD

Since I will concentrate here on indigenous understandings of states of unwellness and the means of overcoming them, let me begin by describing the two states of selfhood that Achuar men consider desirable and strive to achieve. My focus on masculine forms of subjectivity throughout this contribution is due in part to limitations of space, but it also reflects the Jivaroan perspective on ethnic identity. It is assumed that women are less marked than men in terms of tribal identity because, while sharing the martial values that orient much of Jivaroan behavior, women do not have the means of embodying them: they lack the high level of "heat" or "anger" that fuels men's capacity to confront and kill.[4] Being an exemplary Jivaroan—as opposed to merely living in a Jivaroan group—is thus

---

3. I use the term "White" as a shorthand label for all nonindigenous people regardless of the color of their skin, in accordance with Achuar and Shuar usage: they call all such people *apach'*.

4. Brown observed similar attitudes among the Awajun (2014: 222). He tentatively attributes the shockingly high rate of suicide among Awajun women and young men to their difficulty in living up to the demands of the assertive form of male individualism that orients traditional values.

a male prerogative, as only men's bodies fully incarnate the dispositions that are held to be paradigmatically Jivaroan. Since my interest lies in analyzing what is implied in the indigenous understanding of "being a Jivaroan" as well as the link between the waxing and waning of ethnic identities and local understandings of relationships to non-Jivaroans, I believe my emphasis on masculine forms of selfhood is justified in the context of this article, though it evidently results in a highly skewed picture of Jivaroan lifeways.[5] As I have argued elsewhere (Taylor 1996, 2007), male Jivaroan identity is predicated on the strong linkage set up between "normal" states of healthy selfhood and the disposition to engage in antagonistic relationships. To be a proper adult male Jivaroan is to live in a predatory stance vis-à-vis Others (primarily other tribal Jivaroans) and to be therefore capable of making and defending a "family": that is to say, a more or less extensive collective of congeners or conspecifics defined as *winia shuar*, "my people," an expression that, according to context, may refer to a person's nuclear family, household group, extended bilateral kin web, or tribe as a whole.[6] This type of selfhood is shaped by engagement, from a very early age on, in a series of ritualized agonistic interactions with same-sex humans (in ceremonial discourse, war-related rituals, encounters with Whites in institutional contexts, etc.) as well as with spiritual beings (in vision quests, in dreams, in hunting expeditions, etc.), and relations of seduction and taming with female and/or junior Others (potential spouses or lovers, young animals, adopted or procreated children). These gradually fostered interactions, particularly the frightening, drug-induced encounters with powerful spirits called *arutam*—the ghosts of dead prominent Jivaroans, normally of the same tribe as the vision seeker—lead to the kind of magnified selfhood that in principle allows men to occupy the high ground in any dual relationship and to influence others' aims and dispositions—in short to become *kakaram*, that is, powerful/eminent individuals.[7] This form of subjectivity is in turn linked to the ability to narrate autobiographical histories centering on intratribal feuding and intertribal (but endo-Jivaroan) warfare. This kind of historiography is notable for the glaring absence in it of

---

5.   For a view of gender relations among the Jivaro, see especially Bant (1994); Bianchi (1980); Kelekna (1981); Seymour-Smith (1991); Maader (1999); Taylor (2000, 2008); Perruchon (2003).

6.   On the logic underlying the indigenous use of ethnonyms, see Taylor (1985).

7.   On *arutam* quests, see Karsten (1935); Harner (1972); Descola ([1993] 1998); Maader (1999); Taylor (2000, 2003); Rubenstein (2012).

any mention of, or reference to, the centuries-long, highly conflictive relations between Jivaroans and representatives of the colonial and neocolonial Republican dominant society. The autobiography of Tukup', a famous Shuar *kakaram* or *uunt* ("old/big one"), collected in 1982 and analyzed by Hendricks (1993), offers an illustration of this point: while the oral memory of the Macabeos—the mestizo population of the frontier town of Macas settled in Shuar territory—is full of dramatic accounts of the *kakaram*'s much-feared visits to the settlement, Tukup' barely alludes to his repeated performances of confrontation with the town's authorities. The Achuar male autobiographies collected by us during our fieldwork, some of which are partially transcribed in Descola's *The spears of twilight* ([1993] 1998), are identical to Tukup's narrative in their narrow focus on vengeance-driven intra- and intertribal conflicts to the exclusion of interethnic strife, or even of evocations of the narrator's life-course outside of his involvement in feuds—in particular of his experiences of travel outside Jivaro land and encounters with non-Jivaroans. In this respect Achuar historiographical accounts stand in sharp contrast both to the ritualized *jawosi* fixed-form songs analyzed by Oakdale (2007), in which Tupian Kayabi men evoke their travels as well as their war experiences, and to the Kalapalo narratives of encounters with Whites described by Basso (1993). Among the Achuar, unless solicited by visitors such as anthropologists, men did not at the time of our main fieldwork produce detailed accounts of their interactions with outsiders, and these did not belong, as is the case for warrior autobiographies, to a stabilized and distinctive discursive genre. I will return to this point further on.

The belligerent stance expected of Achuar men and the kind of selfhood it is associated with—call it the "warrior stance" for convenience's sake—is shared to some extent by shamans, but the latter elaborate their identity through a mode of subjectivation distinct from that of warriors. Instead of engaging directly in antagonistic rivalry with human and nonhuman Others, shamans cultivate ongoing "amicable" (usually kin-based, more precisely affinal) relations with specific classes of Others, in this case with the entities responsible for afflicting humans with illness, misfortune, and mortality and spirits that control game animals—often the same class of beings. Shamans thus develop a kind of Janus-like dual identity, predicated on their affiliation to two distinct species or groups, that of their own kin-based local group and that of their supernatural affinal relatives—typically, aquatic animals such as otters that present themselves to lone hunters as beautiful young women and draw them into their underwater world, pictured as an urban habitat of cement houses, cars, bars, and police or military garrisons.[8] The fact that Jivaroan shamans, as well as those of the neighboring Quichua-speaking tribes, do not engage in overt, face-to-face warfare and homicide, and usually abstain from hunting, does not mean that shamans are "peace oriented." To the contrary, they are in a state of constant warfare with other rival shamans intent on gaining control over their opponent's helper spirits[9] and magic darts (*tsentsak*, the material instruments for inflicting and curing illness) and on harming whichever group of humans the latter may be affiliated to. To this extent, shamans actively participate in the feuding complex central to the existence of the Achuar, not least by orienting the focus of hostility toward more or less clearly defined enemies, in tandem with the local *kakaram* they usually pair with. Nonetheless, shamans and warriors have distinctive ways of framing identities, based on different ways of relating to Otherness.

The relation that lies at the heart of Jivaroan warriorhood (the default state of adult men) is defined by a permanent tension between Ego and an Alter defined as "Enemy,"[10] that is to say, as maximally different from Self. The axiomatic difference between the terms of the relation is both presupposed and reproduced by exacerbated antagonism. In abstract terms, "antagonism" is a process of anti-identification that blocks the incorporation or assimilation of one term by the other: while the polarity of the relation is reversible—"killer" can become "prey" and vice versa—a transformation indeed central to many Amazonian rituals—neither of its terms can be subsumed by the other, short of canceling the relation. This is precisely the relational form designated by the concept of predation, as it has been defined by Viveiros de Castro ([1986]

---

8. On the "otherwordly" travels and encounters that are the source of shamanic skills, see Pellizzaro (1978) and Rubenstein (2002) for the Shuar, Brown (1986) and Greene (2009) for the Awajun; for the lowland Quichua, see especially Whitten (1976) and Kohn (2007, 2013).

9. Helper spirits, called either *pasuk* or *tunchi* among the Achuar, are usually figured as invisible animals (often birds, because of their song and ability to fly) that act both as the shaman's "eyes" and as guides or leaders of the magical darts. In the context of healing sessions, they are often referred to by shamans as their "children." However, the *pasuk*, the magical darts they command, and indeed the shaman himself tend to merge or be interchangeable in shamanic discourse.

10. The Achuar have two words to refer to enemies: *nemas*, feuding adversaries of the same tribe as the locutor, and *shiwiar*, a modulation of the word *shuar*, "person," the default autodenomination of most Jivaroan groups. *Shiwiar* specifically designates other tribal Jivaroan enemies.

1992, 1993; Viveiros de Castro and Fausto 1993), and further refined by Fausto ([2001] 2012) through his exploration of the means whereby alterity is transmuted into sociality through the taming process he calls "familiarization." In shamanic multiple selfhood, by contrast, the relation between Ego and Alter is built on a process of identification rather than on one of differentiating antagonism. In such a process of identification, each term of the constitutive relation is poised to subsume the other, instead of being opposed to it. "Self" can thus slide into an "Alter" fragmented into a multiplicity of instantiations (animals, other humans, spirits, etc.) and become a congeries of "I"s, since it is no longer dependent, to exist, on its continued predatory stance vis-à-vis a unified "Other" (the Enemy). The polarity of a process of identification is, however, just as reversible as in a process of differentiation: Self can either subsume, or be subsumed by, Alter; it may, in other words, become irrevocably "animal" or more generally "Other," just as it may pull "animality" or 'Otherness' into itself.[11]

BECOMING SICK AND BEING CURED

As it is easy to imagine, being a Jivaroan male is a highly demanding vocation; and while Jivaroan culture as a whole is extremely resilient, the state of being defined as paradigmatically Jivaro is fragile. As in any highly competitive mode of sociality, the relative hierarchy of individuals is unstable and constantly shifting. Jivaroan selfhood is thus highly vulnerable to the erosion of the web of relations that constitute it. Feelings of social and physical weakness, continued lack of fortune at hunting, repeated bouts of illness in the nuclear family, symptoms of discomfort or pain that have no visible physical cause and that can't be rapidly cured by traditional pharmacopeia or Western medicine (when available) are soon interpreted as the manifestation of a shamanic aggression. Such states

---

11. Interestingly, the contrast between these two modes of subjectivation translates at the iconographic level into distinctive kinds of figuration: the "warrior" configuration is materialized by the shrunken-head trophies (tsantsa, also ritually called misha, "profile"), central protagonists in Shuar war-related ceremonies that articulate the opposed perspectives of Self and Enemy, whereas shamanic selfhood is expressed by the image of the Jurijri, a being conceived by the Achuar, and often portrayed by Quichua potters, as a two-sided creature, with a smiling human face at its front and a monstrous, predatory face at its back hidden under itse hair.

often lead to prostration and an abrupt disengagement from ongoing social relations and practices: the ill person retires to his bed and communicates only minimally with his kin, if at all. This condition, particularly if it is lasting, invariably calls for shamanic therapy.

Schematically, an Achuar shamanic cure develops along the following lines.[12] Faced with a patient in a state of paralyzed agency, usually accompanied by one or several relatives, the officiating shaman or *uwishin* begins by absorbing *natem* (commonly known as *ayahuasca*, a decoction of scrapings of lianas of the *banisteriopsis* genus) and modifying the felt environment within which the session is taking place (the light, the flow of air, the smell- and soundscape, etc.). While scrutinizing the patient's body, he[13] begins to whistle and hum, and then starts to sing, first softly then loudly, to summon and communicate with his helper spirits and the stock of magic darts he keeps in his saliva or phlegm, figured as an inner pond (*kucha* or *cocha*, Quichua for "lake"). There are innumerable classes of *tsentsak*, each with a generic name, distinctive color and texture, and presumed mode of action (e.g., spider monkey *tsentsak*, wasp *tsentsak*, corral snake *tsentsak*, black *tsentsak*, etc.). The *uwishin* must counter the darts afflicting his patient with his own stock of corresponding *tsentsak*; thus, shamans try to acquire from other *uwishin* as many varieties of *tsentsak* as they can. Animated and guided by the shaman's singing, his darts couple in the patient's body with those sent by the opposing shaman's. The aggressive darts "hooked" by the healer's *tsentsak* are then sucked back into the curing shaman's body, "tamed" and converted by him so that they will fly back and attack the enemy shaman responsible for the patient's illness.[14] The cure ends, or, if the session is lengthy, is interrupted with

---

12. For a fuller description of Jivaroan shamanic sessions, see especially Pellizzaro (1978); Greene (1998, 2009); and Rubenstein (2002).

13. Female shamans are not unheard of among the Achuar, but the general feeling is that women, particularly if they are of childbearing age, cannot cope with the double life imposed by a shamanic vocation and lack the power needed to confront enemy shamans. Women shamans seems to be more common among the Shuar (Rubenstein 2002; Perruchon 2003).

14. *Tsentsak* are supposed to hunger constantly for fresh "meat," and they are therefore difficult to control; shamans are always suspect of losing their hold over their stock of darts and thereby endangering their kin. Hence the ambivalent feelings aroused by the presence within a local group of a recognized shaman, who can easily slip from the position of protector into that of hidden aggressor. As one of Perruchon's informants pithily expresses it, "There are bad *uwishin* and good *uwishin*, but they are all bad" (Perruchon 2003: 226).

phases of "ordinary" conversation between the shaman and the patient or his accompanying relatives. In this register the *uwishin* delivers allusive and elliptic accounts of what he is seeing as he or his *pasuk* (helper spirits) travel over distant places, and offers advice on the dietary and behavioral precautions the afflicted person should observe to hasten his or her recovery.

Throughout the session, the curing shaman interacts with a rival shaman intent on killing or—to use the term favored by the Achuar—"eating" the patient. The predatory aggression is carried out by the enemy shaman's invisible allies, who under his orders attack the victim as a hunter would pursue a prey. This action implies a form of identification of the attacking shaman to his spirit helpers, but also and primarily a process of differentiation between them (the shaman and his helpers) and the victim, viewed simply as meat, an eatable non-congener. The curing shaman's task is to reverse the polarity of this process. To achieve this, he also sets up an identification with his spiritual allies by stressing his bond with them and his familiarity with their language, but instead of leading them to see the patient as prey, he presents the victim to his helper spirits as a fellow "human" (i.e., a conspecific) rather than as meat. As the shaman insists in his sung discourse, the victim's body is "transparent" to him, he sees into it, thereby implying that he, like a spirit, sees the victim's inner being as a "human" rather than his "clothes" as a being of another species. He thus draws the patient into an affiliation to a nonhuman collective (the one the shaman is connected to) and, by implication, into an identification with him, the officiating shaman. As the healer fosters recognition of the patient as a congener by his spiritual allies, he also deals at the same time with the patient's (real) human side, by engaging the victim and his relatives in conversation and drawing them into the context of the cure. Thus the patient, like the shaman, becomes dual, with the difference that, unlike the shaman's, his or her human identity is weak and vacillating. Meanwhile, the curing shaman is working to reverse the polarity of the predator/prey relation within which the patient is trapped by the enemy shaman, such that the latter falls prey himself to a predatory attack by his "turned" darts and, it is hoped, succumbs to their onslaught. As I have suggested, Jivaroan shamanism is enmeshed in the predational scheme governing the system of relations with "Other" collectives. This means that the switch in the polarity of the predator/prey relation effected by the shaman has powerful social effects. By setting up a process of identification between the patient and the invisible entities that afflict humans, the shaman simultaneously strengthens the patient's affiliation to his human (Shuar) kin group by reinstating and fueling the agonistic stance that feeds his identity; and the more precise is the shaman's identification of the enemy, the more this effect is heightened. Intensification of hostility through focalization and intensification of solidarity are mutually implicating.

In summary, the cure revolves around the shaman's ability to shift an afflicted person from a condition of weakened or paralyzed agency (the patient is trapped in a double process of "desubjectivation," by spirits acting at the behest of an enemy, and by his own kin group, from which he or she is cut off by the collapse of his status as an active interlocutor and proper kinsperson) to a situation allowing for the "jump-starting" and bolstering of the mechanisms feeding healthy magnified selfhood, through a kind of transfusion of condensed, properly oriented relationality.

THE WORLD OF WHITES IN SHAMANIC DISCOURSE

On the face of it, Jivaroan shamanic curing rituals are thus firmly grounded in the dynamics underlying the production of "warrior" selfhood and their continued reproduction, a mode of being closely associated, as I mentioned earlier, with a kind of historical discourse carefully insulated from reference to the outside, White-dominated world. Yet the healing songs elaborated to reactivate the warrior mode of being as well as "informal" shamanic discourse are replete with allusions to the very world excluded from traditional Jivaroan autobiographical narratives. In these utterances, as well as in the myths on the origins of shamanic power, objects and icons indexing relations to powerful foreigners are insistently foregrounded. Typically, an Achuar shaman will describe himself as located in some markedly White location (towns, military garrisons, air control towers, etc.), he or his *pasuk* dressed in elements of foreign attire (boots, uniforms, helmets, etc.) and manipulating the most significant objects of their environment (pens, motors, books, swords, tanks, etc.). Tsakimp, the Shuar shaman whose life-story Rubenstein recorded and analyzed, describes his *natem* visions in the following terms: "It was like I was in a plane, above everything, . . . I saw many people . . . figures passed back and forth: clowns, monkeys, a beautiful woman . . . thousands of beautiful women and a temple, a big structure passed by" (Rubenstein 2002: 159). In the same vein, the myths relating to the aquatic spirits named *tsunki*, who are the ultimate source of shamanic abilities and with whom the *uwishin* explicitly identifies, describe them as living in underwater cities full of machines and seated on turtles seen as cars (Pellizzaro 1978). Above all, the shaman repeatedly alludes to his mastery of foreign languages, either through direct metalinguistic assertions ("I speak the language of . . . I call my *pasuk/tunchi* in the language of . . .") or through frequent recourse to diglossia, particularly the use of Quichua words and sentences, Quichua being viewed as a kind of generic foreign language—as indeed it was in the context of the network of *reducciones* conforming the huge Jesuit Mainas mission established in the Upper Amazon between 1638 and 1768. By way of illustration, here are excerpts from a song performed in 1979 by Dumink, an Achuar shaman settled close to Canelos Quichua territory, to cure a young man suffering from chronic stomach pain.[15]

About twenty minutes after absorbing a cup of *natem*, Dumink begins to shake a leaf bundle over the patient's body while whistling and humming; after a while he starts singing:

> . . . I, I, I, I . . .
> Being a *tsunki* person . . .
> I am resting on my stool . . .
> I rest in a cement house . . .
> Being a *tsunki* person
> *Ari ri ri ri ari ri ri ri* . . . (*ari* is Quichua for "come here")
> My darkening *tsentsak* flock to me . . .
> Eagerly they come they come . . .
> Being a Napo shaman . . .
> My *pasuk* dons his metal helmet . . .
> They stand all in shiny armor around me . . .
> Eagerly my armadillo *tsentsak* come to me . . .
> Eagerly and smelling of perfumed soap
> My white paper *tsentsak* come running . . .
> With their pistols with their motors they fly over there
> Being a Napo shaman I rest here, I rest in my *cocha*

---

15. . Collated from author's field notes, April 17–20. The audience included the patient's wife and mother-in-law as well as two anthropologists. The singing went on for over two hours, with interruptions for "normal" conversation, whistling, sucking and spitting, and loud sighing.

In my cement house I, I, I, I . . .
Ari ri ri ri ri, ari ri ri . . .

The language of Achuar shamanic chants is not, as such things go, particularly difficult for noninitiates to understand, contrary to the situation prevailing among, for example, the Panoan Yaminahua as described by Townsley (1993), or the Kuna, whose shamanic ritual discourse is notoriously esoteric (Lévi-Strauss 1963; Severi 1987; Fortis 2012). While there is some distortion of language (syllabic repetition, use of foreign words, etc.), most of the vocabulary and syntax is familiar to an Achuar audience. Further, the songs are neither elaborate nor fixed in their content and transmitted verbatim from initiate to novice; indeed, some *uwishin* assert that the words count less than the song-sound and only hum or whistle during their performance (see also Maader 1999; Perruchon 2003), claiming that this is how they hear and speak to their *pasuk*. In Achuar shamanic sung discourse, the constant shifts in deictic markers make it difficult to disentangle the enunciator(s) standing behind the "I" used by the singer, as well as the time(s) and place(s) he/they is or are located in any given episode of the chant.[16] Nonetheless, the script of the actions performed by the enunciator(s) is relatively easy to follow. In the healing sessions we recorded, shamanic discourse alternated between, on the one hand, evocations of the magical darts' attitudes and behavior in regard both to the patient's body and to the healer's body from which they emerge, and, on the other hand, allusions to what the shaman and/or his *pasuk* see as they travel over "foreign" landscapes studded with icons of White power such as towns, hydroelectric dams, markets, churches, and motorized vehicles. The shaman thus weaves threads of correspondence between the patient's experience of suffering, which is given shape and concreteness through the healer's description of what he sees in the victim's body, and elements of an "other" world marked by symbols of foreign might. Though the patient and his or her attending relatives may not (and indeed are not meant to) grasp all the metaphors and allusions spun by the shaman, they catch enough of these linkages to build a representation both of the sick person's condition and of the shaman's practice and perspective.

---

16. On "multiple enunciatiors" in ritual discourse and the ways shamans distribute their various "I"s, thereby bridging different places, times, and planes of reality, see especially Oakdale (2007) and Severi ([2007] 2015, 2009).

The world shamans build up through their healing songs is thus a strange, dream-like space mixing elements of different times, places, and types of outsiders, above all Whites. This is of course a feature of shamanic practice that has often been noted. Given shamans' position as brokers of alterity, the proliferation in their ritual chants of indices of their familiarity with the Whiteman's world has often been interpreted as the symptom of a discourse of resistance to domination and cultural dissolution, through the mimetic appropriation of White power (see, e.g., Chevalier 1982; Taussig 1993; Santos Granero 2002).[17] However, this understanding does not address the question of why this type of discourse is developed solely or primarily in the context of a therapeutic intervention, in the face of states of existential woe; nor does it resolve the paradox generated by the contrast between the aims and dynamics of the cure—the activation in a ritual context of the mechanisms underlying the build-up of magnified, Jivaro-centered warrior subjecthood— and the means of achieving this goal—the evocation in song of a world full of Whitemen's past and present acts, objects, and images.

ILLNESS AS 'ORPHANHOOD'

The answer, I believe, needs to be looked for in the indigenous conceptualization of states of unwellness. Among the Jivaro, as in many lowland groups, suffering is not viewed as the secondary symptom of an underlying physiological cause; rather, it constitutes in itself the illness. This is particularly true of the kind of ill-being—internal pain, feelings of depression, anxiety, and weakness—that is rapidly interpreted as the result of a shamanic aggression. This condition constitutes a negative mirror image of the changes in self-perception

---

17. *Contra* this view, Gow (1994) has argued that the *ayahuasca* shamanism common to many Indian groups of the Upper Amazon and to large sectors of the non-Indian local population actually originated among urban mestizos, as a metaphor of the historical and economic processes inherent in their own "ethnogenesis," and then spread to the Indians during the late nineteenth and early twentieth centuries. I remain skeptical of this historical hypothesis—colonial documents attest to the existence of *ayahuasca* shamanism long before this, at least among the Jivaroans— but I think Gow is right in assuming that the wide, transethnic diffusion of this kind of shamanism can be explained at least in part by it capacity to figuratively represent the basic processes underlying the political economy of Western Amazonia, in particular the regional system of debt-driven labor known as *habilitacion*.

associated with a successful quest for *arutam* encounters, as described by the Achuar: a sudden increment in clarity of purpose, a feeling of physical and social power, intensified "anger" against the ever-present Enemy and the urge to destroy him, coupled with a heightened sense of care for one's spouses and children and the ability to produce proper kin relationships. *Arutam* encounters, in short, bring about a positive metamorphosis of the self, attributed to the incorporation of the spirit as a kind of internal "voice" or guiding consciousness. The "hyper-I" produced by this internalized dialogic configuration linking a live and a dead Jivaroan stands in sharp contrast to the debilitated, purposeless "I" of the suffering individual. Nonetheless, there is a commonality of pattern in the form of the changes involved in vision quests and sickness which leads people to interpret this kind of unwellness as the outcome of an unwanted metamorphosis, caused by an internalized malevolent agent—as opposed to the desirable transformation induced by the incorporation of an *arutam* spirit.

The positive and negative forms of metamorphosis that are implicitly paired feed into distinct experiences of temporality. While *arutam* vision quests endow men with the ability to make and to narrate history in the Jivaroan warrior mode, and thus to give shape and direction to the flow of time, the unwanted conversion induced by shamanic attacks traps the victim in an elongated, directionless temporality of pain that confers a particular saliency to the experience of negative change. When describing this condition, the Achuar liken it to a state of orphanhood, an assimilation that makes sense in light of the social isolation entailed by the victim's prostration. In keeping with the widespread Amazonian view of bodies as sites where relations to others are created, transformed, or terminated (Conklin 2001; Vilaça 2007), the sickening of the victim's body makes him or her remote from his or her family, cut off from it by the inability to act in and communicate with it; and the victim's kinspeople respond by talking about and around—rather than with—him or her, a situation akin to that of parentless children, at least during the period before they are fully integrated into the household of a relative. Further, illness is a reversion to a childlike state of vulnerability and inability to cope with asymmetric, threatening, or challenging relationships. But the allusion to orphanhood has yet another dimension: loss of parents carried with it the very real threat of becoming the life-long slave of a White person, insofar as parentless children were, until the mid-twentieth century, the persons most exposed to being traded to White or mestizo *patrones* (bosses), who usually adopted and raised them as household domestics, later to be used as indentured *peones* on the boss' landholdings. Even when they did not experience it directly, this was a condition familiar to the northern Achuar through their close relations with neighboring Quichua families, few of which escaped debt peonage at the hands of mestizo traders and landholders throughout the late nineteenth and early twentieth centuries.[18] Beyond this, most Achuar men in their late seventies had spent some months or years as young men working for White bosses, usually itinerant traders (locally known as *regatones*) who traveled through indigenous territories exchanging hugely overpriced manufactured goods against forest products such as dried meat, pelts, various kinds of fibers and resins, and low-grade rubber latex. Such experiences were undergone "to learn," according to the Achuar, and by this they meant to gain familiarity with the geography of power evoked in shamanic discourse; by the same token, the voyages alluded to by shamans in their songs resonate with the experiences of distant travel and servitude experienced by most adult Achuar men (see also Kohn 2007). This is one of the reasons, I surmise, why Achuar men do not tell stories about these episodes of their life: narrating them would be tantamount to claiming shamanic knowledge and ability.

In short, while the Achuar managed throughout the heyday of the rubber boom and the subsequent tropical hacienda system to preserve their autonomy and their control over their labor force, they were well acquainted with the extreme forms of exploitation that framed relations between Indians and Whites in lowland Ecuador and Peru until the last decades of the twentieth century. The condition of illness provoked by an invisible aggression and calling for urgent shamanic intervention thus involves the experience of an involuntary and painful process of induced change, assimilated to the exit from a Jivaroan identity into a child-like subservient position in the White-dominated world as an anonymous laborer—what the Achuar call a "person for nothing" (*nankami aents*) or "tame parrot." This is why the curing shaman foregrounds allusions to the White world in his singing: if sickness is an insidious process of disempowerment at the hands ultimately of dominant Whites, the identifications and

---

18. Taussig (1987) presents a compelling view of the "cosmography" generated by the debt-peonage system as it developed in Western Amazonia during and in the wake of the rubber boom. For a fuller description of the workings of this system among the Ecuadorian lowland Quichua, see especially Whitten (1976, 1985); Muratorio (1987); Kohn (2007, 2013).

differentiations elaborated by the shaman necessarily involve the major symbols of foreigners' power.

BEING 'WHITENED' AND APPROPRIATING WHITE POWER

As I have mentioned, the history of relations between Jivaroans and Whites is not encompassed in traditional autobiographical narratives, nor is collective tribal history recorded in features of the landscape, as is the case among, for example, the Yanesha (Santos Granero 1998) and the Eastern Tukanoan and Arawak tribes (e.g., Hill & Wright 1988), or encoded in the jungle environment, as it is among the Napo Quichua (Kohn 2007, 2013). Jivaroan history is emphatically in the first person and rarely refers to a plural "we," except in a narrow sense to designate a group of men directly participating in the events described by the narrator. This view of history accords with the Jivaroans' emphasis on the achievement of enhanced individuality and with their "presentist" or, more accurately, forward-looking stance. The Jivaro see themselves not as a "society" endowed with a durable identity or tradition, but as a collection of like but unique persons striving each to forge an exemplary life-course. Accomplishing this aim depends on men's ability to magnify their selves by confronting enemies and by absorbing lesser kinsmen's subjectivities into their own personhood through the social influence they wield. The capacity to be fully Jivaroan hinges in turn on encounters with *arutam*, forgotten, singular dead Indians, precisely the kind of spirit they will become posthumously, thus ensuring the transmission of new potentialities of making history in the Jivaroan manner.

But why are interactions with Whites, including successful feats of arms against them, excluded from these narratives? My hypothesis is that such interactions cannot be encompassed by the causal logic of vengeance that fuels autobiographical historiography (Carneiro da Cunha and Viveiros de Castro 1985). While the presence of Whites constitutes a permanent threat because of the forces of dispossession that accompany it, Whites themselves are too ubiquitous, come under too many guises, and engage with Indians in too many and different ways to be subsumed under the category of *shiwiar*, "Enemy." In this sense, they—and what they bring into the universe—are more like an environment than a fixed category or species of person, something that is built into the texture of experience, a dimension of the lived world that flows from Whitemen's singular ability to externalize their presence not only in buildings, objects, and institutions but also in the forces that determine the movements of persons and things throughout the region.[19] This is not a freakish view of the way foreigners with Western values unleash economic forces while naturalizing them and distancing themselves from the consequences wrought by these forces. Denying indigenous people control over their lifeways, destroying their habitat, and pillaging forest resources are not as such willed acts: they are, according to prevailing ideology, the unintended effect of the march of Progress, History, or the Market. This, I suggest, is why the history of involvement with the dominant society is construed by the Jivaroans as an ongoing process of defense against the pressure of unwanted change, rather than a linear chain of chronologically ordered events. In sum, contacts between Jivaroans and Whitemen are viewed as a prolonged and painful process of transformation, analogous to the shifting sense of self and the feeling of disempowerment brought on by illness.

Given these Indians' preoccupation with the quality of selfhood and its manifestation through bodily states, and with the threat of others' power to modify it by crippling a person's agency through an attack on his or her body, the conceptual conflation of interethnic history and sickness is understandable: both modes of being are negative experiences of transformation. In contrast to Amazonian groups such as the Kayabi or the Wari (Oakdale 2007; Vilaça 2007), Jivaroans strongly resist the "whitening" of their bodies; maintaining Jivaroan corporality is a condition for holding fast to their identity.[20] History is for them the memory of repeated attempts at global conversion[21] —and not only in the religious sense—just as illness is the perception of an untrameling of the tissue of relations underpinning healthy selfhood. In both cases, these

---

19. On indigenous perceptions of capitalist forces in the Upper Amazon, see Santos Granero and Barclay (2010); for a wider comparative view, see Bashkow (2006).

20. This does not mean that Jivaroans do not try to incorporate elements of White bodily power, such as that transmitted by Western medication or foods; but such efforts are seen as a Jivaroan metabolization of foreign physiology rather than a "whitening" of Jivaroan bodies.

21. Unlike the "fickle" Tupi, whose apparent receptivity to Christianization so gratified early missionaries (see Viveiros de Castro 1993; Fausto [2007] 2012), the Jivaro were and are notoriously resistant to religious conversion. From the sixteenth century on, missionaries sent among them never ceased to complain of the Indians' "crass materialism" and "'Voltairean' skepticism"; they roundly declared the Jivaro to be "the most difficult mission in the world." (On missionaries' view of the Jivaro, see Taylor 1983.)

shifts of subjectivity are the consequence of an indeterminate malevolence mediated in such a way that no one assumes responsibility for it. Enemy shamans and Whites wreak their havoc in the same insidious way. For this reason, and because relations with Whites have to do with qualitative, continuous processes of change rather than discontinuous events, interethnic history lies outside the scope of the kind of narrative developed in warrior autobiographies, which emphatically stress individual agency and the consequences of intentional acts. Social memory of interethnic history is instead encapsulated in the images generated by the shamans' ritual chanting.

The framing during the cure of the patient's illness as an invisible process of predation somehow connected to the dynamics of the Whites' world also implies a parallel reframing both of the shamanic aggression and of the curing process. Thus, when the healing shaman describes his invisible nonhuman allies (and therefore himself, insofar as he identifies with them) as a collective that has "seen" and mastered the most significant aspects of the White world, the identification he sets up between the patient and himself as a member of his supernatural family—and by implication between the patient and these nonhumans who have successfully incorporated White power—does not mean that he is acting as a proxy for Whites, nor that he is he engaged in "whitening" his patient; rather, he is drawing a sick, "proletarianized" Jivaro into a position that reverses the polarity of the relationship he or she is caught in by making him or her into a White-absorbing dominant subject—just as he, the shaman, is himself. Or rather as he purports to be: needless to say, the shaman's position is in fact highly ambiguous and the orientation of his loyalties is open to suspicion: is he truly an "über-White," that is to say, a Jivaroan who has appropriated and mastered the tools of White power, or is he the fifth column of the encroaching army of outsiders? The ambiguity of the relation between the shaman and the foreigners whose world he summons in his chant helps to account for the outbreaks of "witch-hunting" that occasionally sweep through Jivaroan territory and lead to the simultaneous killing of a number of recognized or suspected practitioners of shamanism—a phenomenon that, by recent accounts, is becoming ever more frequent and widespread as the threats to Jivaroan lifeways proliferate. The same ambiguity, it should be added, attaches to the patient who has undergone the cure, insofar as he or she has in effect been made into a quasi-shaman, or has at least taken the first step leading to a shamanic career, namely that of being recognized as a kinsperson, that is, a human, by a collective of Others. Normally, this shamanization is limited to the context of the cure, and the possibility of it lasting beyond it is counterbalanced by the patient's ostensible engagement in practices normally avoided by shamans: hunting, eventually joining in feuding expeditions, and above all talking about the experience of the cure as he or she understands it. Active shamans never talk about their nonhuman family and their interactions with them, because otherwise they would lose their connections with it and their supernatural allies would turn against them.

SHIFTING IDENTITIES, CONNECTING HISTORIES

What happens if the cure fails, or if the patient decides to prolong and develop his or her state as a quasi-shaman? As I stressed, the aggressor shaman responsible for the victim's suffering is presumed to be another Jivaroan, or at least to be acting at the behest of other Jivaroans, given that the relation of permanent hostility that shapes the Jivaroan social world is largely confined to the ethnic group. The Enemy is, axiomatically, a fellow Jivaroan and his or her kin group. But these adversaries work in fact as agents of "dejivaroization," since the outcome of their attacks is to destroy the scaffolding that upholds the kind of identity held to be paradigmatically Jivaro, and ultimately to reduce their victim to a condition of anonymous servitude within a world governed by the impersonal relations of exploitation of a capitalist political economy. The sufferer is thus trapped in an impossible relation: he is being "eaten" by enemy Jivaroans but is deprived of the means to assume the warrior-stance that such an aggression normally calls forth. This may be why chronic or prolonged illness of the kind we have been dealing with used to entail exiting from a Jivaroan identity for some period of time—sometimes for good—and adopting a Runa (forest Quichua) identity. While boundaries between Jivaroan tribes are strongly emphasized, those between Jivaroans and their Quichua neighbors have been from the outset far more porous; indeed, there is good historical evidence that the Canelos Quichua bordering northern Achuar territory came into being during the late seventeenth and early eighteenth centuries by absorbing former Shuar and Achuar people escaping from epidemics, attacks by colonists settled in the upper Upano valley, and heavily militarized, Jesuit-led missionary expeditions. Throughout the nineteenth century and during a good part of the twentieth century, Canelos Quichua communities continued to incorporate a steady trickle of Achuar fleeing real or imagined threats to their lives, or attracted by the Quichua's proximity to the sources of Western goods and their reputation as powerful shamans.[22]

In the case of ill persons, the process of transculturation came about gradually, as the victimized Jivaroan person sought out distant shamans presumed to be more powerful, and drifted ever closer to the powerhouses of shamanic ability located in neighboring Quichua territory (often near or in significant White settlements or establishments such as military bases, hospitals, or mission posts). Quichua shamanic healing sessions usually develop over a long period of time; consequently, the patient would often move into the curing shaman's household, or settle close by. Not infrequently, he would use the opportunity either to enter into apprenticeship with the Quichua *yachaj* and start a career as a shaman or to marry into the Quichua shaman's kin group. Entering into this state implied a new series of "trans-lations": at the most obvious level, it meant adopting a new language and ethos, a new style of behavior and interaction. This may seem like a huge step. Actually it is no such thing: although Jivaro-Quichua bilingualism is neither formally transmitted from parents to children nor indeed publicly claimed among the northern Achuar—as if each person had to gain for him or herself the experience of "converting" to Quichua culture—the Quichua language was in fact familiar to most people (among men at least), as was the style of interaction characteristic of Quichua persons. Both Quichua and Jivaroans imitate each other's "typical" behavior for fun—Achuar ceremonial dialoguing and agonistic attitudes among the Quichua, brawling and indiscriminate eating among the Achuar—and their mimicry is flawless. In short, contrary to appearances, there was little translation (in the ordinary sense of the term) involved in these processes of transculturation. Rather, such identity shifts implied highlighting different aspects of what was in reality a largely shared cultural background in terms of everyday practices and representations.

However, there is one kind of knowledge, more accurately one expression of knowledge, that is specific to the Quichua and did require a real process of translation: namely, learning to reframe both collective and individual experience of

---

22. Reeve (1993–94) makes the important point that, according to the Curaray Quichua she worked with, the reason why people from other tribes chose to become Runa was to escape from illness, victimization, and the threat of extinction. For a synthetic view of the historical dynamics shaping ethnic identities and relations in the northern Upper Amazon, see Taylor (1999, 2007); for a fuller account of the ethnogenesis of the Quichua Canelos, see Whitten (1976).

relations with Whites in terms of the kind of historical "narrative"[23] specific to the lowland forest Quichua cultures.[24] This mode of history elaborates a linear sequence of "times" (*ura*) involving a series of collective transformations. The first "Time" is conceived as a precontact "wild" state characterized by unmediated relation to the forest environment (hunting, collecting, no horticulture, no sedentary settlements, etc.), social isolation, intense internal warfare, and ignorance of the outside world. Then came "times of slavery" (or "time of the bosses"—the labels given to this stage of Quichua history vary from one lowland group to another), paradoxically typified as a positive though painfully oppressive phase of "learning" essential knowledge about the White world though firsthand experience of a relation of subservience, and finally the "present times" of political emancipation and mastery over the proper combination of White and Sacha Runa (forest people) knowledge and practice. This kind of historical narrative clearly refers to the ethnogenesis of the Quichua groups out of the remnants of distinct tribal groups decimated between the early seventeenth and nineteenth centuries by contact with Whites, within the framework of some form of oppressive articulation to mestizo or missionary settlements. However, from an Achuar point of view, learning to understand and master this kind of history does not require the acquisition of new substantive knowledge—all indigenous people in this region share the same memories of demographic collapse due to epidemics, debt slavery at the hands of rubber bosses, tropical *hacendados* or rapacious traders, forced evangelization, and so on—but for Jivaroans it does imply a reorganization of this shared memory, since among them the history of interethnic relations is not elaborated in a stabilized, linear form of collective narrative.

At the same time as it accounts for the coming into being of a collective identity and way of relating to Self and Others that is specific to the Quichua groups, this kind of historical narrative constitutes an idiom for generating a representation of a trajectory of transculturation. It maps onto implicit autobiographies of illness and recovered healthy selfhood, via a "time of wildness" that evokes both Jivaroan sociality as seen by the Quichua and the condition of

---

23. I place the term "narrative" in inverted commas because this brand of history in not exclusively discursive: it is coded in landscape, ritual, and ceramic iconography.

24. On lowland Quichua regimes of historicity, see especially Whitten (1976, 1985); Muratorio (1987); Reeve (1988, 1993–94); and Kohn (2007, 2013); see also Gow (1991).

"orphanhood" constitutive of illness as seen by the Achuar, through oppressive shamanic learning of a proper perspective on the White world at the hands of a dominant, boss-like Quichua master-shaman and/or father-in-law, and on to a state of recovered health marked by the capacity to face Whites in an empowered position. At this point, the healed person may either revert to his initial ethnic identity and resume his engagement in the behaviors and practices central to his culture of origin, or decide to remain a Runa, having in the meantime absorbed a conceptualization of history that is a central feature of forest Quichua identity.

It is noteworthy that until recently (in the case of men at least—that of women is somewhat different), transculturation almost never led to permanent exit from the indigenous world and adoption of a mestizo identity. Though increasingly involved in the economy and politics of the Ecuadorian and Peruvian nation, Jivaroan persons remain to this day firmly attached to their identity as non-White forest people. But over the past twenty years it has become more and more difficult for them to sustain it: while they are adept at finding new niches (indigenous political organizations, armed conflicts between states, etc.) within which to deploy the adversarial relationships that underpin male magnified selfhood, the practices that used to sustain these relations (feuding, war-related rituals, ceremonial dialogues, etc.) are losing ground or becoming neutered through cultural patrimonialization. At the same time, the threat to the land and autonomy of all Jivaroan tribes is growing, as oil and lumber companies, agro-industrial and tourist enterprises, as well as state agencies, vie to move into their territory and intervene in their community affairs.

As the fear of a generalized process of "whitening" intensifies, and as the possibility of switching to a Runa identity steadily diminishes in the wake of the (uni)cultural ethnic politics now pervasive in Andean nations, shamanism is gaining ground among all Jivaroan groups, both as a defensive resource and as a ubiquitous threat. Because of their ambiguous position as brokers of White power, shamans are suspect of fostering or hastening the process of "dejivaroization," not least by adopting the tools of White "shamanism," namely the kind of popular sorcery described in the penny literature sold in the markets for poor people (Perruchon 2003). A troubling outcome of the growing fascination for these "how to" manuals of witchcraft is the suspicion that attaches to the possession and circulation of written material of any sort, particularly among the young, feared because of their knowledge of reading and writing in Spanish and therefore open to accusations of having secretly converted to White-inspired black magic[25]—again, other Jivaroans acting as proxies for outside, clearly White, agents. At the same time, shamans are the only ones who can "see" what is going on and have the means of countering the effects of sorcery. Thus, Jivaroan people nowadays are constantly oscillating between the need for shamanic therapy and the urge to expunge from their communities—sometimes by outright lynching— all and every real or suspected agent of "whitening," including young adolescents and even children.

CONCLUSION

This contribution focuses on a series of intra- and intercultural transpositions or linkages of domains of experience effectuated by and around shamanic practices. I have tried to show how certain states of suffering implying sociological deprivation and weakened agency, subsumed under the label of "orphanhood" and experienced as an unwanted metamorphosis mirroring in a negative way the process of enhancement of Self resulting from *arutam* encounters, are reframed in the course of shamanic healing rituals as the symptoms of an insidious process of disempowerment, more accurately of "going peon" in the White-dominated world, unleashed by other enemy Jivaroans. This "B version" of the patient's illness emerges from the conflation operated in and by the shaman's healing chants between the victim's sickness and the history of relations with powerful foreigners, construed as a painful process of involuntary qualitative change.

The linkage of the experience of illness with an experience of history and attempted conversion (and vice versa) runs parallel to another process of "translation," involving in this case a series of shifts between the language of the spirits heard and spoken by the shaman and the language of the patient and the audience. The metadiscourse of translation elaborated by the healer articulates the two worlds in which the shaman acts as a "human," that of his supernatural allies and that of his (real) human kin group, and is oriented toward the conversion of his invisible servants (his helper spirits and magic darts) into kinspeople

---

25. These developments are being documented by Gregory Deshouillères among the Shuar and Simone Garra among the Awajun and Wampis, both of them currently finishing their Ph.D. dissertation. I thank them both for sharing their knowledge with me.

of the patient instead of predators. Through this affiliation the patient is both
identified with the healing shaman and lifted out of his position of vulnerability, reinstated as a subject capable of absorbing and mastering White power. At
the same time, by focusing the patient's and his relatives' hostility against the
enemy shaman and by heightening thereby the kin group's solidarity, the healer
reconnects the victim to his social environment and to a purposeful existence
as a warrior.[26]

At the horizon of these dual processes of connecting different domains of
experience, which themselves reverberate many other ongoing changes of registers and contexts not explored here, lies a further series of shifts which are
activated when the cure fails and the patient abandons his Jivaroan identity and
moves into a Runa identity. The primary trans-lation involved in this process of
transculturation is not so much the expected translation of one language and
more generally of knowledge of culturally appropriate behavior into another;
rather, it is the conflation of Runa narratives of their history and the implicit
autobiography of a Jivaroan moving from illness and disempowerment toward
recovered health and social agency. Since this way of dealing with states of "dejivaroization" has become largely unavailable to the Achuar, owing to increasing
closure of ethnic groups under pressure to become clearly bounded tribal entities each "possessing" a specific culture, the relation between Jivaro and Whites
is nowadays far less mediated—and actually far more violent, though on the
surface less overtly conflictive—than it used to be. Presently all Jivaroans deal
permanently and directly with the spoken and written words of the Whites, and
this involves new forms of translation. The illness of "whitening" henceforth affects everybody, and not just some individuals suffering from temporary states
of existential malaise; also 'healthy' Jivaroans have in effect become part White.
Thus, the current attempts to master the power of Whites through a shamanic
appropriation of their own witchcraft increasingly pit Jivaroans against their
own selves as well as against their fellow kinspeople, always suspect of acting as
proxies for White masters, even when—and particularly when—they are acting
as proper Jivaroans.

The processes I have discussed may seem far removed from what is usually
understood as translation, that is, the transporting into another language of the

---

26. In concrete terms, if circumstances are favorable to a precise identification of the
    person(s) responsible for the patient's misfortune, chances are he or his relatives will
    be in short order the target of a killing expedition.

semantic content of a source speech. Yet if we take translation in a broader sense, as the work carried out to bridge and bring into resonance different spheres of practice and contexts of communication in order to open avenues for the imaginative production of meaning, particularly in areas that are of core concern for a given culture, I believe the processes I have described can be usefully analyzed as strategies of translation, even though a noteworthy feature of Achuar shamanism is the strong resistance it evinces to the idea and possibility of translation in the ordinary sense. The Jivaroan case illustrates a mode of translation as "resonating juxtaposition" that emphasizes the heterogeneity of the fields of experience involved and maintains the differences in perspective that are brought into play, rather than seeking to resorb them in a new language. In other words, while the possibility of translation is constantly evoked in shamanic discourse, it is never actually carried out: the shaman repeatedly claims to speak "foreign" languages, and to be communicating with his spirits in these idioms, but his statements are never direct quotations of the utterances of spirits—except when he is humming or singing without words. . . . Thus, the *uwishin* foregrounds his capacity as a translator—he knows the language of Others—but he does not in fact speak for these Others, as their spokesperson: he only speaks *to* them. Indeed, he enhances this position of "nontranslating translator" through the mediation of his *pasuk*, whom he addresses, who relay his calls to the *tsentsak* and report back to the performing shaman; but this embedded translator does not give voice to the *tsentsak* and ultimately to the spirits any more than does the shaman, who describes the effects of the *pasuk*'s vocal herding but does not present it as reported speech. Likewise, the *uwishin*'s audience do not ask him what the spirits are saying; instead, they insistently ask him what he or his *pasuk* see rather than hear, despite the fact that shamanic discourse stresses the communicative aspects of the shaman's performance. These facts are entirely consistent with the transversal dimension of Amazonian shamanism underscored by Viveiros de Castro ([2009] 2014): the aim of shamanic performance is to exhibit the dual nature of shamans and the coexistence and hence possible articulation of perspectives it allows, rather than to transmute or strictly translate diverging points of view. By contrast, the process of transculturation that leads ailing Achuar to adopt a Runa identity does seem to involve a full-scale operation of translation, since the point of such a move is to exit from a Jivaroan mode of being and communicating and switch to a different repertoire of attitudes, behaviors, and codes, a move that by definition requires multiple forms of translation. No "nontranslating translator" here: you are either a Jivaroan or a Runa.

Yet even this configuration carries strong echoes of shamanic dual "citizenship." To begin with, Runa identity is itself dual, predicated as it is on the ability to be simultaneously a "docile" Christian person connected to the White world and an autonomous forest person, to combine Alli Runa and Sacha Runa being, as shown by Whitten (1976) in his classic monograph. Further, claims to submerged, originally non-Quichua identities play a strong part in Runa ethnicity (see Reeve 1993–94); in some cases these backgrounded identities reemerge to fuel the ethnogenesis of new ethnic groups—most famously in that of the Ecuadorian Zaparo, who until the 1990s seemed to have been entirely absorbed into the Quichua lowland population but have since reappeared as a distinct, territorialized, and officially recognized tribe. Thus, at both a collective and an individual level, the juxtaposition of different indigenous identities—and of the social knowledge they carry—is a structural feature of Runa culture. To this extent, all Runa persons share a shamanic mode of selfhood; and by the same token, they share the Jivaroan *uwishin's* stance as performers of heterogeneous perspectives—as mediators or diplomats rather than as translators.

REFERENCES

Bant, Astrid. 1994. "Parentesco, matrimonio e intereses de genero en una sociedad amazonica: El caso aguaruna." *Amazonia Peruana* 12 (24): 77–103.

Bashkow, Ira. 2006. *The meaning of Whitemen: Race and modernity in the Orokaiva cultural world.* Chicago: University of Chicago Press.

Basso, Ellen. 1993. "A Kalapalo testimonial." *L'Homme* 126–28: 379–407.

Benjamin, Walter. (1923) 1968. "The task of the translator." In *Illuminations.* Edited by Hannah Arendt, 253–63. New York: Harcourt Brace Jovanovich.

Bianchi, Cesare. 1980. *Hombre y mujer en la sociedad shuar.* Mundo Shuar B (16). Sucúa: Centro de Documentación, Investigación y Publicaciones.

Brown, Michael.1986. *Tsewa's gift: Magic and meaning in an Amazonian society.* Washington, DC: Smithsonian Institution Press.

———. 1988. "Shamanism and its discontents." *Medical Anthropology Quarterly* 2: 102–20.

———. 2014. *Upriver: The turbulent life and times of an Amazonian people.* Cambridge, MA: Harvard University Press.

Carneiro da Cunha, Manuela. 1999."Xamanismo e traduçao." In *A outra margem do Occidente*, edited by Adauto Novaes, 223–26. São Paulo: MINC-FUNARTE/Companhia das Letras.

Carneiro da Cuhna, Manuela, and Eduardo Viveiros de Castro. 1985. "Vingança e temporalidade: Os Tupinamba." *Journal de la Société des Américanistes* 71: 191–208.

Chevalier, Jacques. 1982. *Civilization and the stolen gift: Capital, kin and cult in Eastern Peru*. Toronto: University of Toronto Press.

Conklin, Beth. 2001. *Consuming grief: Compassionate cannibalism in an Amazonian society*. Austin: University of Texas Press.

Descola, Philippe. (1993) 1998. *The spears of twilight: Life and death in the Amazon jungle*. Translated by Janet Lloyd. New York: New Press.

Fausto, Carlos. (2001) 2012. *War and shamanism in Amazonia*. Cambridge: Cambridge University Press.

Fortis, Paulo. 2012. *Kuna art and shamanism*. Austin: University of Taxas Press.

Gow, Peter. 1991. *Of mixed blood: Kinship and history in Peruvain Amazonia*. Oxford: Oxford University Press.

———. 1994. "River people shamanism and history in Western Amazonia." In *Shamanism, history, and the state*, edited by Nicholas Thomas and Caroline Humphrey, 91–113. Cambridge: Cambridge University Press.

Greene, Shane. 1998. "The shaman's needle: Development, shamanic agency and intermedicality in Aguaruna Lands, Peru." *American Ethnologist* 25: 181–201.

———. 2009. *Customizing indigeneity: Paths to a visionary politics in Peru*. Stanford: Stanford University Press

Harner, Michael. 1972. *The Jivaro: People of the sacred waterfalls*. Berkeley: University of California Press.

Hendricks, Janet. 1993. *To drink of death: The narrative of a Shuar warrior*. Tucson: University of Arizona Press.

Hill, Jonathan, and Robin Wright. 1988. "Time, narrative and ritual: Historical interpretations form an Amazonian society." In *Rethinking history and myth: Indigenous South American perspectives on the past*, edited by Jonathan Hill and Robin Wright, 78–105. Urbana: University of Illinois Press.

Karsten, Rafael. 1935. *Head hunters of Western Amazonas: The life and culture of the Jibaro Indians of Eastern Ecuador and Peru*. Commentationes Humanorum Litterarum, Vol. 7. Helsingfors: Societates Scientiarum Fennica.

Kelekna, Pita. 1981. "Sex asymmetry in Jivaroan Achuar society: A cultural mechanism promoting belligerence." Ph.D. dissertation, University of New Mexico.

Kohn, Eduardo. 2007. "Animal masters and the ecological embedding of history among the Ávila Runa of Ecuador." In *Time and Memory in indigenous Amazonia: Anthropological perspectives*, Carlos Fausto and Michael Heckenberger, 106–31. Gainesville: University Press of Florida.

———. 2013. *How forests think: Toward an anthropology beyond the human.* Berkeley: University of California Press.

Lévi-Strauss, Claude, 1963. "The effectiveness of symbols." In *Structural anthropology*. Translated by Claire Jacobson and Brooke Grunfest Schoepf, 186–205. New York: Anchor.

Maader, Elke. 1999. *Metamorfosis del poder: Persona, mito y vision en la sociedad Shuar y Achuar.* Quito: Abya-Yala;

Muratorio, Blanca. 1987. *Rucuyaya Alonso y la historia social y economica del Alto Napo 1850–1950.* Quito: Abya-Yala.

Oakdale, Suzanne. 2007. *I foresee my life: The ritual performance of autobiography in an Amazonian community.* Lincoln: University of Nebraska Press.

Pellizzaro, Siro. 1978. *El uwishin: Mitos, ritos y cantos para propiciar los espiritus.* Quito: Abya-Yala

Perruchon, Marie. 2003. *I am Tsunki: Gender and shamanism among the Shuar of Western Amazonia.* Uppsala: Uppsala University Press

Reeve, Mary-Elizabeth. 1988. "Cauchu uras: Lowland Quichua histories of the Amazon river boom." In *Rethinking history and myth: Indigenous South American perspectives on the past*, edited by Jonathan Hill and Robin Wright, 19–34. Urbana: University of Illinois Press.

———. 1993–94. "Narratives of catastrophe: The Zaparoan experience in Amazonian Ecuador." *Bulletin de la Société Suisse des Américanistes* 57–58: 17–24.

Rubenstein, Steven L. 2002. *Alejandro Tsakimp: A Shuar healer in the margins of history.* Lincoln: University of Nebraska Press.

———. 2012, "On the importance of visions among the Amazonian Shuar." *Current Anthropology* 53 (1): 39–79.

Santos Granero, Fernando. 1998. "Writing history into the landscape: Space, myth and ritual in contemporary Amazonia." *American Ethnologist* 25 (2): 128–48.

———. 2002. "St. Christopher in the Amazon: Child sorcery, colonialism and violence among the southern Arawak." *Ethnohistory* 49 (3): 507–43.

Santos Granero, Fernando, and Frederica Barclay. 2010. "Bundles, stampers and flying gringos: Native perceptions of capitalist violence in Peruvian Amazonia." *Journal of Latin American and Caribbean Anthropology* 16 (1): 143–67.

Severi, Carlo. 1987. "The invisible path: Ritual representation of suffering in Cuna traditional thought." *Res: Anthropology and Aesthetics* 14: 66-85.

———. (2007) 2015. *The chimera principle: An anthropology of memory and imagination.* Translated by Janet Lloyd. Chicago: Hau Books.

———. 2009. "La parole prêtée: comment parlent les images." In *La parole en acte*, edited by Carlo Severi and Julien Bonhomme, 11–42. Cahiers d'Anthropologie Sociale 5. Paris: Éditions de l'Herne.

Seymour-Smith, Charlotte. 1991. "Women have no affines and men no kin: The politics of the Jivaroan gender relation." *Man* (N.S.) 26: 629–49.

Taussig, Michael. 1987. *Shamanism, colonialism and the wild man: A study in terror and healing.* Chicago: University of Chicago Press.

———. 1993. *Mimesis and alterity: A particular history of the senses.* New York: Routledge.

Taylor, Anne-Christine. 1983. "'Cette atroce république de la forêt: les origines du paradigme jivaro." *Gradhiva* 3: 3–10.

———. 1985. "L'art de la réduction: les mécanismes de la différenciation tribale dans l'ensemble Jivaro." *Journal de la Société des Américanistes* 71: 159–89.

———. 1996. "The soul's body and its states: An Amazonian perspective on the nature of being human." *Journal of the Royal Anthropological Institute* (N.S.) 2 (2): 201–15.

———. 1997. "L'oubli des morts et la mémoire des meurtres: expériences de l'histoire chez les Jivaro." *Terrain* 29 : 119–24.

———. 1999. "The western margins of Amazonia from the early sixteenth to the early nineteenth century." In *The Cambridge history of native peoples of South America*, edited by Frank Salomon and Stuart Schwartz, 188–256. Cambridge: Cambridge University Press.

———. 2000. "Le sexe de la proie: représentations jivaro du lien de parenté." *L'Homme* 154–55: 309–34.

———. 2003, "Les masques de la mémoire." *L'Homme* 165: 223–48.

———. 2007. "Sick of history: Contrasting regimes of historicity in the Upper Amazon." In *Time and memory in indigenous Amazonia: Anthropological perspectives*, edited by Carlos Fausto and Michael Heckenberger, 133–68. Gainesville: University Press of Florida.

———. 2008. "Corps, sexe et parenté: une perspective amazonienne." In *Ce que le corps fait à la personne*, edited by Irène Théry and Pascale Bonnemère, 91–107. Paris: Éditions de l'EHESS, coll. Enquête.

Townsley, Graham. 1993. "Song paths: The ways and means of Yaminahua shamanic knowledge." *L'Homme* 126–28: 449–68.

Vilaça, Aparecida. 2007. "Cultural change as body metamorphosis." In *Time and memory in indigenous Amazonia: Anthropological perspectives*, edited by Carlos Fausto and Michael Heckenberger, 169–93. Gainesville: University Press of Florida.

Viveiros de Castro, Eduardo B. (1986) 1992. *From the enemy's point of view: Humanity and divinity in an Amazonian society*. Translated by Catherine V. Howard. Chicago: University of Chicago Press.

———. 1993. "Le marbre et le myrte: de l'inconstance de l'âme sauvage." In *Mémoire de la tradition*, edited by Aurore Becquelin and Antoinette Molinié, 365–431. Nanterre: Société d'Ethnographie.

———. (2009) 2014. *Cannibal metaphysics*. Edited and translated by Peter Skafish. Minneapolis: Univocal.

Viveiros de Castro, Eduardo B., and Carlos Fausto. 1993. "La puissance et l'acte: la parenté dans les basses terres d'Amérique du sud." *L'Homme* 126–28): 141–70.

Whitten, Norman E., Jr. 1976. *Sacha Runa: Ethnicity and adaptation of Ecuadorian jungle Quichua*. Urbana: University of Illinois Press.

———. 1985. *Sicuanga Runa: The other side of development in Amazonian Ecuador*. Urbana: University of Illinois Press.

CHAPTER FIVE

Bilingual language learning and the translation of worlds in the New Guinea Highlands and beyond

ALAN RUMSEY

In their introduction to this volume, Hanks and Severi argue that best starting point for a new theory of translation is "neither pre-emptive universalism . . . nor typological divisions . . . but instead the study of processes and principles of translation"—or, in other words, a focus on "the constant *work of translation* of languages, nonlinguistic codes, contexts of communication, and different traditions, which constitutes the field of 'cultural knowledge,' both within a single tradition and in different societies" (p. 16, this volume). In line with that proposal, in this article I develop an ethnographically based account of everyday practices of translation among the Ku Waru people in Highland Papua New Guinea. Examining two such practices which are otherwise quite different from each other, I show that they both operate in terms of a well-developed set of procedures for establishing *equivalence*, between words and worlds, respectively. On both of those planes a key role is played by *parallelism*, suggesting a connection between equivalence in the ordinary sense of the word and in the specific sense of it that was developed by Roman Jakobson (1961) a connection which I suggest is significant for the understanding of translation in general.

As also pointed out by Hanks and Severi, translation occurs in many different forms: "It designates the exchange not only of words, but also of values, theories, and artifacts from one culture to another" (p. 9, this volume). I would add that there is also wide variation in the extent to which the "languages" between which one translates (whether of words, values, artifacts, etc.) can be seen as comprising stable systems. At or near one end of the continuum in that respect are languages in the ordinary sense of the word. These are of course far less homogeneous or stable than they are often imagined to be, but they do have a degree of robustness such that, for example, there would be general agreement among French/Russian bilinguals as to which if either of those languages is being spoken at a given time. At or near the other end of the continuum would be the discourse patterns and interpersonal alignments that get established across the course of a single conversation (as discussed in, e.g., Goodwin and Goodwin 1992; Silverstein 2004). Somewhere between these two on the scale of stable systematicity would be the various "speech genres" (Bakhtin 1986) that are found within every language, and the more or less sedimented texts or "entextualizations"[1] (Bauman and Briggs 1990) that are associated with them.

In this article I will be concerned mainly with translation at the maximal level of stable systematicity referred to above, that is, translation across languages in the ordinary sense of the word, and at the intermediate level of speech genres and texts. Focusing in detail on interactions between bilingual Ku Waru children and their parents, I will examine the pattern of alternation between the two languages they speak, and the role played by translation in their language learning. I will then briefly consider one of the genres of verbal art that is practiced by adults in the same area, examine a kind of translation across "worlds" that takes place within it, and compare that to the kind of translation that takes place between the parents and children. But, first, why the main focus on bilingualism and on children?

Any attempt to understand processes of translation in cross-cultural and historical perspective must take into account the fact that much more of the world is bilingual or multilingual than monolingual (Grossjean 1982), and is likely to have been even more so for perhaps 99.9 percent of the human past

---

1. In a widely cited, seminal discussion of this topic, Bauman and Briggs (1990:73) define entextualization as "the process of rendering discourse extractable, of making a stretch of linguistic production into a unit—a *text*— that can be lifted out of its interactional setting."

(Evans 2010: 9–16). The very notion of interlanguage translation of course presupposes the existence of bilingual people to do the translating. Conversely, the process of becoming a bi- or multilingual person presupposes acts of translation by which such people develop a practical sense of equivalence in some respect between words and utterances in one language and those in another. In this article I discuss the way these processes work among the Ku Waru people of Highland Papua New Guinea, where nearly everyone speaks at least two languages, minimally including Ku Waru and Tok Pisin, the main national lingua franca. Moving toward the other end of the stability continuum, I will then discuss some examples of emergent discourse patterns in a genre of sung narrative that is practiced among Ku Waru people. Comparing these with the results regarding bilingual language acquisition, I will offer some general conclusions about the nature of the processes involved, and what can be learned from them about translation and its relation to other aspects of language and culture.

ETHNOGRAPHIC AND SOCIOLINGUISTIC BACKGROUND

Ku Waru means "cliff" (literally "steep stone"), and is used to designate a loosely bounded dialect and ethnic region of the Western New Guinea Highlands, named after the prominent limestone cliffs abutting it along the eastern slopes of the Tambul Range, near Mount Hagen.[2] The highlands are by far the most densely populated region of New Guinea, and the last to be contacted by Europeans, which didn't happen until the 1930s. Among Ku Waru people who are living in their rural homeland, the local economy is still largely a subsistence one, based on intensive cultivation of sweet potatoes, taro, and a wide range of other crops, raising of pigs, and use of locally obtained timber, cane, thatch, and other materials for building their houses and agricultural infrastructure. But although Ku Waru people are on that basis still largely self-sufficient for their everyday subsistence needs, there is now also intensive engagement with the cash economy, based largely on their growing of coffee for the world market and vegetables for sale to town dwellers in the provincial capital of Mount Hagen

---

2.   For a map and details concerning the dialect continuum to which Ku Waru belongs, and methodological justification for treating Ku Waru as a "language," see Rumsey (2010).

and more distant markets in coastal cities such as Lae (the main seaport for the highlands) and Port Moresby (the nation's capital and largest city).

Since Francesca Merlan and I first began fieldwork in the area in 1981, Ku Waru people have become much more mobile, many of them traveling regularly to Mount Hagen via commercially operated small buses and trucks that can get them there in about one hour, and, less frequently but for longer sojourns, to Port Moresby, which from the highlands can only be reached by plane. Correspondingly, there has been a steady increase in the rate of marriage to people from outside the region, and in the distance from which those people come. Since 2007, this increased mobility has been accompanied by greatly increased and accelerated interconnectivity due to the availability of mobile phones and network coverage across most of the Ku Waru region and the rest of Papua New Guinea and the wider world.

Associated with these changes over the past thirty to forty years, there have been considerable shifts in the language ecology of the Ku Waru region. Unlike in the town area in and around Mount Hagen to the east, all children in the Ku Waru region continue to learn the local language (Ku Waru) from the earliest stages of language acquisition, and everyone who has grown up in the region speaks it natively. But Tok Pisin has also made considerable inroads into the region. When Francesca Merlan and I first settled there in 1981, almost the only fluent Tok Pisin speakers were men under the age of about forty-five, adolescent boys, and children of age six and above.[3] Now it is spoken fluently by all but the most elderly men, by middle-aged and younger women, and by almost all children of age three and above. Nonetheless, except in certain restricted settings, Ku Waru remains the main or only language used in everyday interactions among Ku Waru people of all ages.

One setting where this is not the case is in the local school. Since 1973 there has been a community school in Kailge, near the center of the Ku Waru region. Until 2009 it included only preschool and grades 1–6; grades 7 and 8 have now been added. As is the case throughout PNG, the main language of the school

---

3. It may be the case that more adolescent girls and young women were able to speak Tok Pisin than was evident to us at the time, for two reasons: (1) in order to be able to communicate directly with as many Ku Waru people as possible by learning Ku Waru, we encouraged people to speak it with us and instruct us in it rather than in Tok Pisin; (2) the speaking of Tok Pisin by women at that time was somewhat stigmatized as it was associated with town life, a more peripatetic lifestyle than was considered appropriate for women, and in particular with prostitution.

and the language of all the texts used there is English,[4] although attempts were made between 1997 and 2012 to facilitate the learning of it through the officially sanctioned use of a model of "transition bilingual education."[5]. Though this model is no longer in use in Kailge, classroom interaction still takes place in various combinations of English, Tok Pisin, and Ku Waru, or related, mutually intelligible, dialects if known by the teacher. For various reasons that are beyond the scope of this article, English-language proficiency seems to have actually declined among graduates of the school over the past twenty years. The small number of graduates who do become proficient in it and go on to pass high school and university entrance exams do not generally return to live in the Ku Waru region, but do usually remain in contact with family and friends there and serve as highly valued links to the world beyond.

---

4. There have been considerable changes over the past thirty years in the extent to which this has been taken to preclude the use of other languages in school. When we first settled in Kailge in 1981 there was a large sign in the school showing a list of rules of conduct which the pupils were regularly called upon to recite out loud. Rule number one was "Don't speak language" (i.e., don't speak in the local language). The second rule was "Don't speak Tok Pisin." This confirmed what we had been told by an officer in the Education Department in Mount Hagen when we offered to help develop teaching materials in the local language. He said that he would like to accept our offer because he personally was very much in favor of using such materials, but that it was forbidden by Education Department policy, which called for the use of English only in schools. This changed dramatically a decade later, as described in note 5.

5. This is a model whereby literacy is first introduced in the local language in preschool ("Prep") and first grade, followed by a gradual shift to English over the next few years (Devette-Chee 2012, 2013). It was brought in at the national level beginning in the early 1990s (ibid.) and at the Kailge School in 1997 (John Onga, personal communication). In 2013 it was phased out there. In a discussion I had with the headmaster at the time, he said that was because the model was not working: children were failing to make a successful transition to English. He also told me that the abandonment of bilingual education had been mandated at the national level by a recent policy shift away from it by the PNG Education Department. Having later been unable to find any reference to such a shift on the internet, in May 2014 I interviewed the Superintendent of Operations at the Education Department Office in Mount Hagen, William Awa. He told me that there has been confusion about what had actually happened in that respect. He said that the only official change was that English had been reintroduced as a subject of study in Prep and grade 1. The option to use local language as a medium for teaching it still remained in place. He said that there had been discussion lately of the possible introduction of an "English only" policy (to which he himself was strongly opposed), but that the issue was still under consideration and that no such policy was yet in place.

The other settings in which languages other than Ku Waru are regularly used in the region are church services. The denominations in the area include Roman Catholic, Lutheran, Seventh Day Adventist, the PNG Bible Church, the Holy Spirit Revival Church, and the New Covenant Church. All of them make use of a complete Tok Pisin translation of the Bible that has been available since 1989, and most also make at least some use of various English translations. The services are generally conducted in a combination of Tok Pisin and Ku Waru with extensive *viva voce* translation and exegesis across those two languages, and of English-language scripture in each.[6]

LANGUAGE SOCIALIZATION AND BILINGUALISM AMONG KU WARU CHILDREN

Since 2013, in collaboration with Francesca Merlan, I have been engaged in a major research project on "Children's language learning and the development of intersubjectivity." The project will eventually include comparative studies from diverse languages and cultures, but for now its main substantive focus is on Ku Waru. The study builds on language acquisition data that I and two Ku Waru-speaking field assistants have been recording on a smaller scale since 2004.[7] Beginning in mid-2013, our new data have consisted of audio and video recordings of four Ku Waru children of various ages—Philip, Jakelin, Sylvia, and Ken—each of whom is being recorded in interactions with their parents and other caregivers for approximately one hour at monthly intervals. The recorded interactions are being transcribed in their entirety, and the transcripts computerized for analysis along many different dimensions.

One of the most striking developments that has become evident from the new data is a recent decrease in age of the youngest Tok Pisin speakers, and in

---

6.   The current Catholic priest in the region is a Papua New Guinean from another part of the country (the Sepik) who does not speak or understand Ku Waru. He conducts the services in Tok Pisin, interspersed with occasional rounds of translation into Ku Waru by his local assistants. As far as I know from my occasional attendance of the other local churches, all the current ministers speak Ku Waru and/or related mutually intelligible dialects, and use a combination of them and Tok Pisin in their services.

7.   For some of the results of that early work, see Rumsey (2013) and Rumsey, San Roque, and Schieffelin (2013).

the age of the children when the parents begin speaking Tok Pisin to them. In all of the transcript data that were recorded between 2004 and 2011,[8] there are almost no instances of Tok Pisin being used either by the parents or by the children, and most of the few instances of it are short, isolated utterances of one or two words only (*yu go* "You go!" *yu kam* "You come!," etc.). In the new data that were recorded in 2013, as exemplified and tabulated below, Ku Waru is still the most frequently used language, but there are also sizable numbers of utterances in Tok Pisin from three of the four children, and they are the youngest three (Philip, Jakelin, and Sylvia).

As we learned from our conversations with Ku Waru parents, this shift was not a random or entirely unconscious one. Rather, we found that there was a new trend among the parents in favor of deliberately exposing their children to Tok Pisin from an early age. The reason they gave us for this was that they believed it would give the children a head start in school. This is no doubt related to the recent abandonment within the Kailge school of the transition bilingual model (see note 5) and increased emphasis on the use of Tok Pisin rather than Ku Waru as the operative interlanguage. Whatever the reasons for that change, the Ku Waru parents with whom we discussed the matter took it as an endorsement of the efficacy of Tok Pisin over Ku Waru as a bridge to learning of English, which all of them valued highly on their children's behalf (perhaps all the more so as few are themselves fluent in English). That, they say, is what lay behind their increased use of Tok Pisin to their children. But all of them also thought it important that their children should continue to learn Ku Waru.

A certain tension between those two desires is evident from the three sets of transcripts in which Tok Pisin is used to any appreciable degree (i.e., those involving Philip, Jakelyn, and Sylvia). Evidence for that can be seen in Table 1, which shows patterns of language alternation vs. language consistency across conversational turns involving a parent or other caregiver as the first speaker and child as the second, responding one. For present purposes there are two things to notice about the figures shown in the table. One is that Ku Waru is the main language used between the children and their parents in all of the interactions, with Sylvia and her parents using the most Tok Pisin and Ken and his using almost none. The other relevant pattern is that, as shown by the figures in

---

8.   This comprises approximately seventy hours of recorded interaction involving children, which has been transcribed by hand onto approximately 13,000 A4 pages and is currently being computerized as part of our new project.

Table 1. Incidence of Tok Pisin vs. Ku Waru in interactions involving four children.

Child and age	Ku Waru > Ku Waru	Ku Waru > Tok Pisin	Tok Pisin > Tok Pisin	Tok Pisin > Ku Waru	Ku Waru / Tok Pisin mix
Philip 2;04.01	249 (94%)	11 (4%)	0	0	5 (2%)
Philip 2;05.02	236 (94%)	7 (3%)	1 (<1%)	1 (<1%)	7 (3%)
Philip 2;06.05	171 (94%)	9 (5%)	0	0	2 (1%)
Jakelin 2;10.29	298 (72%)	93 (23%)	13 (3%)	1 (<1%)	7 (2%)
Jakelin 2;11.27	105 (68%)	34 (22%)	9 (6%)	1 (<1%)	7 (4%)
Jakelin 3;00.27	136 (84%)	21 (13%)	1 (<1%)	0	4 (2%)
Sylvia 3;02.22	225 (75%)	20 (7%)	44 (15%)	0	10 (3%)
Sylvia 3;03.12	252 (67%)	8 (2%)	110 (30%)	1 (<1%)	4 (1%)
Sylvia 3;04.21	407 (76%)	12 (2%)	115 (21%)	0	2 (<1%)
Sylvia 3;05.21	340 (91%)	26 (7%)	5 (1%)	0	4 (1%)
Ken 3;08.11	441 (>99%)	1 (<1%)	0	0	0
Ken 3;09.26	421 (>99%)	1 (<1%)	0	0	0
Ken 3;10.27	420 (100%)	0	0	0	0
Ken 3;11.23	564 (99%)	3 (1%)	0	0	0

Key: Children's ages are shown in years;months.days For example 2;04.01 designates two years, four months, and one day. In the top row of the table, "Ku Waru > Ku Waru" indicates a pair of conversational turns in which the child was addressed in Ku Waru and responded in Ku Waru, "Ku Waru > Tok Pisin" one in which the child was addressed in Ku Waru and responded in Tok Pisin, and so on.

columns 3 and 5, in cases where the children initiate a switch from one language to the other, the direction of the switch is far more often from Ku Waru into Tok Pisin than vice versa. Based on this and other evidence,[9] it seems that the shift to Ku Waru/Tok Pisin bilingual language acquisition is actually being driven by the children to a greater extent than their parents seem to realize or take into account when discussing their own role in the process. As will be exemplified below, the parents seem to acknowledge that role at least implicitly in another way, by sometimes explicitly enjoining the children, after Tok Pisin has been spoken for several turns, to shift back to Ku Waru.

Let us now look at some examples of interlanguage alternation and interaction in the transcripts. In all three sets of interactions where Tok Pisin is used to any extent, it is often used in acts of more-or-less direct translation, both by the parents and by the children. An example can be seen in 1 below. The age of the child Philip at the time (shown in the format used in language acquisition studies) was 2;04.01 (two years, four months, and one day). He and his father Gabren are sitting on the floor of their house beside the fireplace in the middle of the main room. Positioned about one meter in front of them is the small digital audio recorder on which they are being recorded. With its two thimble-sized microphones protruding at ear-like angles from the top and small leg-like tripod on which it rests, it apparently looks to Philip like a little animal of some kind. While Gabren is talking to him about something else, Philip abruptly turns away from him toward the recorder, stands up, and makes shooing gestures at it as if it were a stray dog or other beastly intruder, and says <u>ko</u>, which is his baby talk version of the Tok Pisin word *go*, "Go." Gabren is at first taken aback, but then quickly realizes what Philip is up to and joins in the game. As can be seen, the interaction then proceeds as a series of alternations between Tok Pisin and Ku Waru. In this and all subsequent examples, Ku Waru words are shown in italic typeface and Tok Pisin ones in boldface. Words which are in the baby talk versions of those languages are underlined.[10]

---

9. For a fully adequate investigation of this question it would be necessary to tabulate all two-part turn sequences in which the child is the first speaker and the parent the second. While I have not done that, I have done a survey of representative portions of the transcripts and found that across all the interactions the incidence of Ku Waru > Tok Pisin shifts is far lower for child–parent sequences than for parent–child ones.

10. Some words in the transcripts below are impossible to assign exclusively to either Tok Pisin or Ku Waru. These are words that have been borrowed into Ku Waru

(1) a. Philip [to the recorder]: **ko**
go
Go away!

   b. Father: **ko** *meglayl pa*
go   thing   go
Go away, thing, go!

   c. Philip: **ko**
Go away!

   d. Father: *pa*
Go away!

   e. Philip: **ko**
Go away!

   f. Father: *melayl pa*
thing   go
Thing, go away!

   g. Philip: **ko**
Go away!

   h. Father: *pa*
Go away!

   i. Philip: *pa*
Go away!

Throughout this stretch of interaction, rather than directly addressing each other, Philip and his father Gabren are both addressing the recorder, but each

from Tok Pisin but are used in both languages, for example *tarasis* "trousers," *tok pisin* "Tok Pisin." When such words occur in lines that are otherwise in Tok Pisin, I show them in boldface like other Tok Pisin words. When they occur in lines that are otherwise in Ku Waru, they are shown without either boldface or italics.

with the other as what Erving Goffman (1981) would have called a "targeted overhearer." On that basis the entire exchange constitutes what is in effect an extended translation drill. After Philip's first utterance to the recorder in line a, which is in Baby Tok Pisin (BTP), as mentioned above, Gabren in line b echoes Philip by repeating his BTP form **ko**. He follows this up with a Ku Waru word *melayl*, "the thing," referring to the recorder. He then adds the Ku Waru word *pa*, which is the imperative form of the Ku Waru word for "go." This is a direct translation of Philip's BTP form **ko**, which he has first repeated before translating it. In the next two lines (c and d), Philip repeats his BTP form and Gabren his Ku Waru translation of it. The same thing happens again in lines e and f—with Gabren again adding *melayl* "thing" in line f—and again in lines g and h. In line i, Philip then finally in effect accepts Gabren's lead by repeating the Ku Waru word *pa* instead of sticking with **ko** as in lines c, e, and g.

Further below I will be discussing the question of whether and to what extent the acts of translation in this stretch of interaction involve the translation of "worlds" as well as of words. What I want to draw attention to here is the way in which the sequence of turns between the two speakers sets up an implicit relation of *equivalence* between **ko** and *pa* for certain purposes—namely, in this case for shooing something out of the house (or pretending to).

The next example (2) is also taken from a conversation between Philip and his father Gabren, this time with Philip at age 2;05.02. At this point Philip is just beginning to move beyond the stage of language acquisition where most of his utterances consist of a single word, as in 1, to one in which he is learning to use two or more of them in combination. In this conversation Philip and Gabren are again sitting in their house. Gabren has been picking up objects from the ones lying around them and asking Philip what they are. He picks up a used Coca Cola bottle with water in it and the conversation proceeds as in 2.

(2) a. Father: *ilyi   nabolka*
                this   what
                What's this?

   b. Philip: walam
               [???]

c. Father: *no* **lo** **mi**[11]

water belonging to me

My water.

d. Philip: wa **lo** **mi**

[???] belonging to me

e. Father: *no* **lo** **mi** *nu* *no*

water belonging to me you drink

My water, you drink it!

Note that in the transcript, walam in line b is identified neither as Tok Pisin (with boldface) nor as Ku Waru (with italics). This is because it does not belong to the established lexicon of either language, whether in baby talk or not. Rather, it is Philip's own creation, which Gabren responds to in such a way as to assimilate it to Baby Tok Pisin (BTP), while translating what he takes to be the first word of it into Ku Waru. In other words, he interprets the wa (or perhaps the wala) of walam as **wala**, the BTP form corresponding to the Adult Tok Pisin (TP) word **wara**, "water," for which in his response in line c he substitutes the Ku Waru word *no* (the core sense of which is "water," but which is also used more generally in reference to liquids). For the portion of Gabren's utterance that corresponds to the rest of Philip's **walam**, he uses a combination of the BTP word **lo**, "belonging to" (= TP bilong), and the TP word **mi**, "me." In line d Philip responds to this with an utterance in which the last two words repeat Gabren's last two, and in which Gabren's first word *no* with is replaced by wa. Although I have put question marks under that word to show that it does not belong to any of the local established lexicons, Philip has in effect treated it as equivalent to the Ku Waru word *no* by using it in place of that word in his follow-up to what Gabren has said in line d. In line e Gabren in effect confirms this equivalence by making the opposite move to Philip's, repeating his line exactly except for the first word, which he again replaces with the Ku Waru word *no*, which he then tells Philip to drink.

---

11. Here and in line e Gabren's **mi** refers not to himself but to Philip, from whose transposed perspective he is voicing his utterance. For discussion of this frequently used way of addressing children in Ku Waru and elsewhere in Melanesia, see below.

Notice that in example 2 as in 1 the translation process proceeds through the construction of what I have called "equivalence" across conversational turns. In 1 the equivalence pertained to utterances of single worlds, each of which comprised a whole turn at talk, and the equivalence was established through the identical pragmatic function that they were understood to be serving, namely to shoo something away (or pretend to). In 2 the equivalence is also in part a pragmatic one, namely the understood reference to a single object across all five lines: the bottle of water that Gabren was holding in his hand and directing Philip's attention to. But in 2 there is also another kind of "equivalence" that is established across the turns, namely that which is constructed through patterns of the kind that were brilliantly theorized by Roman Jakobson (1960) under the rubric of parallelism.

Building on the work of earlier theorists, including Robert Lowth and Gerard Manley Hopkins, Jakobson treated parallelism as an ordered interplay of difference and repetition, whereby partial repetition across metrical units such as lines of poetry or turns at talk sets up an implicit framework in which the nonrepeated elements stand out as linked to each other, in a relationship of the kind that Jakobson, after Lowth (1778), called "equivalence." What Jakobson meant by that term in this context was not that the "equivalent" terms are identical to each other, but that they are highlighted in such a way as to posit or call attention to some significant relationship between them. In the processes that we call "translation" in the strict sense, the relevant relationship is generally of the form "expression x is to language A as expression y is to language B." In 2 this process is managed by the father Gabren in a creative way which in effect treats Philip's wa as if it had an analogous place in *some* language (the partially idiosyncratic one being spoken by Philip) to that of *no* in Ku Waru.[12]

Besides parallelism, another way in which cross-linguistic equivalence (in the more ordinary rather than specifically Jakobsonian sense of the word) can be established is through metalinguistic expressions that explicitly characterize particular words or expressions of one language in relation to those of another: "*homme* is the French word for man," and so on. In the approximately two thousand pages of the 2013 Ku Waru child language transcript material that I have worked through so far, I haven't come across any examples of that kind (even though there are ways of saying such a thing in Ku Waru and in Tok Pisin).

---

12. For other uses of parallelism in child language socialization, see de León (2007) and Duranti and Black (2012).

The interlocutors do, however, sometimes refer in a general way to the fact that someone has been speaking Tok Pisin or Ku Waru, or should do so. An example is 3, from a conversation between Sylvia (age 3;02.22) and her mother Ani.

(3) a. Sylvia: **yu go lo aus**
              you go to house
              You go home.

     b. Mother: *ws*   **noken tok pisin mipela tok**
              [expression of disgust] don't   talk Pisin we   say/said
              Come on now, as we[13] said, don't speak Tok Pisin.

     c. Sylvia: **mi mi lai to pisin**
              I   I   like talk Pisin
              I like to speak Tok Pisin.

     d. Mother: *ws*   tok pisin *nun tek   moglun moglun*
              [disgust]   Tok Pisin you   doing stay   stay
              olyo pumulu tekemul
              we   will go are doing
              All right then, you can keep speaking Tok Pisin but we are leaving.

Apart from the these general characterizations of stretches of discourse as being in one language or another, the main metalinguistic expression that gets used in the transcripts is the verb *nyi-* "say."[14] Before exemplifying its use in Ku Waru child-directed speech, it is relevant to note that, in common with the

---

13. The Tok Pisin pronoun **mipela** actually means "I and others not including you the addressee." In this case the mother Ani is also presumably including within its reference Sylvia's father James and a family friend Kuin, both of whom are present and have also told Sylvia not to speak Tok Pisin.

14. The same is true other kinds of discourse in Ku Waru. In a transcript of 1850 lines of speeches that were given at a Ku Waru ceremonial exchange event, the most frequently found verb in the whole transcript was *nyi-* "say" (Merlan and Rumsey 1991: 119).

Kaluli[15] (Schieffelin 1990) and many other people around the world,[16] one of the main strategies that Ku Waru caregivers use when talking to children is to model appropriate speech for them by telling them what to say—sometimes in quotations explicitly framed by the imperative verb *nya* "say!," and sometimes just with the projected quotations, which the child comes to understand are being presented for him/her to repeat in his/her own voice (as in lines 2c and 2e above). Examples of the former kind may be found in 4, which comes from an interaction between Jakelin at age 2;10.29 and her mother Saina.

(4) a. Mother: *wapi*   *gai*   *bo*   *lyim-o*
                   [woman's name] sweet potato cutting got
                   nya
                   say (imperative)
                   Say "Wapi went to get sweet potato cuttings [to plant]."

     b. Jakelin: *api kai ki lip o*
                   [Jakelin's approximation of the above]

     c. Mother: *uj*   *sugla*   *meba*
                   wood split   will bring
                   She will split firewood and bring it.

     d. Jakelin: *us suk*
                   [Jakelin's approximation of the above]

     e. Mother: *ep*   *gai*   *kagluba*   *tekim-o*   *nya* (imperative)
                   now   sweet potato will cook is doing say
                   Say "Now she is about to cook sweet potatoes."

---

15. The Kaluli live outside of the highland region, on the Papuan Plateau, approximately 150 kilometers to the west/southwest of Ku Waru. Their culture is in many ways very different from Ku Waru (see, e.g., Rumsey 2001: 215–19), but their ways of interacting with children are similar in many ways (see, e.g., Rumsey, San Roque, and Schieffelin 2013: 179–80).

16. For examples, see Demuth (1986), Moore (2012: 212–14), and references cited therein.

f. Jakelin: **em   lak   kukim   kaka**
               He/she   like   cook   sweet potatoes
               She wants to cook sweet potatoes.

This stretch of interaction contains two instances of the imperative verb *nya* "say!," at the end of lines a and e. In each of those lines the mother Saina presents an utterance for Jakelin and tells her to say it. In line b Jakelin does as she is told, repeating after Saina in her own simplified version of the utterance that Saina has modeled for her. Notably, Jakelin does the same thing in line d, repeating what Saina has said in line c, even though in this case there is no imperative verb of saying to make it explicit that Saina's utterance is being presented as one for Jakelin to repeat. This is typical of interactions between Ku Waru parents and children, in that the modeled-speech routine between them is so common that the explicit framing of the parent's prompt with the verb "say" is unnecessary in order for the child to recognize that he/she is being prompted to repeat it. Be that as it may, in line e of this interaction the mother Saina does include the framing "say" verb *nya* again. What she gets in response from Jakelyn this time, in line f, is not the Ku Waru utterance that has been modeled for her, but an utterance in Tok Pisin which is nearly equivalent to it in its sense.

The same thing happened a few minutes later in the same interaction between Jakelin and Saina with an even closer semantic match between the lines as shown in 5.

(5) a. Mother: *na   nunga   lku   udo   nya*
                  I   your   house   came   say (imperative)
                  Say "I came to your house."

     b. Jakelin: **mi kam lo   as   po   yu**
                  He/she   to   house   belonging to   you
                  "I came to your house."

The main point I want to draw from examples 4 and 5 (which is also evident from 2) is that within the context of interactions between young Ku Waru children and their caregivers there is a well-established "prompting" or "speech modeling" routine whereby children are presented with utterances by the caregivers which are voiced from the child's viewpoint (as in 2c and 2e), which the child is meant to repeat in his or her own voice. I suggest that the frequent use of this routine socializes Ku Waru children from an early age into an understanding that some utterances (i.e., the ones with which they respond to the prompts) can count as equivalent to others (the ones with which they have been prompted). In relation to my present focus on bilingual language learning and the role of translation within it, it is fascinating to note that among all three of Ku Waru children in the sample who use Tok Pisin to any appreciable extent (Philip, Jakelin, and Sylvia, as shown in Table 1), the transcripts include examples of them using Tok Pisin in responses to prompts that have been put to them in Ku Waru, as in 4 and 5 (see also 1, lines e and g). Furthermore, as in those examples, the responses generally take the form of a translation.

In the discussion so far, I have been focusing on textual examples involving the three children who make the most frequent use of Tok Pisin. These are the youngest three children of the four in the study: Philip, Jakelin, and Sylvia. There is less to say about language switching or translation with respect to the other, eldest child, Ken, because there are so few instances in it of any other language than Ku Waru. As can be seen from Table 1, there are only five of them in total, across four sessions totaling approximately four hours. But the very fact of their scarcity in some ways makes their distribution all the more interesting. Of particular interest in this respect is the placement of the only utterance by Ken within the entire four hours that comprises a multiword utterance in Tok Pisin and shows that he has a productive knowledge of its grammar (albeit in a Baby form).[17] The utterance in question occurs in 6, from a conversation between Ken (at age 3;11.23) and his classificatory grandfather John Onga.

(6) a. Grandfather: *ep   nunga* tarasis   *kolsi   lelym mola mol*
             now   your   trousers a little be   or   not
             Now do you have some trousers or not?

     b. Ken: tarasis *puluyl lelym*
             trousers many   be
             I have a lot of trousers.

---

17. The other instances of Tok Pisin spoken by Ken are either single word utterances (e.g., **Go!**) or single Tok Pisin words used within utterances the rest of which are in Ku Waru (e.g., *lopa me* **wanpela** *ti pelym*, "There is one cat," where the Tok Pisin word **wanpela** "one" was used in addition to the Ku Waru word ti, which also means "one").

c. Grandfather: *puluyl lelym i*
many be eh?
So you have a lot, eh?

nai-n baim *tijirim*
who-AGENT buy did for you
Who bought them for you?

d. Ken: <u>na</u> dedi-<u>na</u>
me daddy-AGENT
My daddy.

e. Grandfather: *apa,* dedi *gol turum aduwa*
Oh! daddy lie did that
Oh, he lied about that.

f. Ken: *kani i*
this eh?
About this one?

g. Grandfather: *im*
Yes.

h. Ken: *kanuna gol naa turing*
about that lie not did
He didn't lie about that.

i. Grandfather: *im*
Yes.
Yes he did.

j. Ken: *we* <u>si</u> <u>si</u> *nim*
nothing true true told
No, he told the truth.

k. Grandfather: dedi   tarasis   *tena   baim   tirim*
                 daddy   trousers where   buy   did
                 Where did daddy buy the trousers?

l. Ken: **im   ko   aken**
                 he   go   Mount Hagen
                 He went to Mount Hagen.

This exchange takes place after approximately fifty-six minutes in which only Ku Waru had been used in connected speech. Indeed, as noted above, there had been no connected speech in Tok Pisin in any of the other three one-hour sessions recorded with Ken over the previous three months, as shown in Table 1 (and explained in note 17), our assistants' transcripts of which run to some six hundred pages. Since these were the first four sessions that had been recorded with Ken, and I had barely made his acquaintance at the time I first reviewed those four transcripts, I had been unaware that he could speak Tok Pisin at all. Under those conditions, the last line of 6 came as a real surprise to me. Why did Ken's breakthrough into a connected, conversationally appropriate utterance in Tok Pisin occur just at that point in the conversation? On reflection it seems to me highly unlikely that was a matter of pure happenstance. For it comes at a point in the conversation where Ken has been put on his mettle to show that his confidence in his father's truthfulness about the trousers is not misplaced.[18] In this context it seems likely that the nature of the topic being discussed, involving a trip to town—the main setting in which Ku Waru people speak Tok Pisin—was a major conditioning factor for Ken's switch to that language. If so, then it may exemplify a tendency for older Ku Waru children's use of Tok Pisin to become increasingly domain-specific, as opposed to the more frequent and random switches in and out of Tok Pisin by the younger children in the sample.

---

18. Elsewhere (Rumsey 2013) I show that the possibility of deceit is major theme in interaction between Ku Waru children and adults (as elsewhere in Ku Waru social life and as widely reported from other Melanesian locales). Across a sample of approximately seventeen hours of such interaction involving Ku Waru children between two and four year of age, and comparison with available transcripts of interaction between US parents and children of similar ages, I show that references to deceit in the Ku Waru transcripts are approximately twenty-nine times as frequent overall, and that such references by the Ku Waru children themselves are approximately sixty-two times as frequent.

FROM TRANSLATING WORDS TO TRANSLATING WORLDS

In the discussion so far I have been dealing with processes of translation at what may seem like a very low level of epistemological or ontological traction. I have treated the relevant languages—Ku Waru and Tok Pisin—as discrete systems between which translation is relatively unproblematic. Before shifting the discussion to another level where the processes of translation apply more evidently to "worlds," there are two points of qualification that I would like to raise about the kinds of translation that I have been dealing with above. One is that, notwithstanding the fact that many Tok Pisin words derive ultimately from English, which may give it a look of familiarity to English speakers, its grammar and semantics are in many important respects closer to those of languages of New Guinea and and the Southwest Pacific (Keesing 1988, Evans and Greenhill 2014). So to the extent that degrees of difference between languages make for corresponding degrees of difference in ease of translation, the process of translation between Ku Waru and Tok Pisin may in some respects be a more straightforward one than translation between Ku Waru and English. The other, even more important point in this connection is that, as should be clear from the discussion above, Ku Waru speakers themselves operate in terms of a well-developed set of procedures for establishing relations of cross-linguistic equivalence between expressions and utterances. The resulting presumptive equivalences might not always be enough to satisfy philosophers, logicians, or ontologically minded anthropologists, but they generally suffice for the conduct of everyday life among Ku Waru people.

That said, the question still remains, in what sense if any do such practices entail translation between *worlds*? That of course depends on how you define them. For present purposes I will accept the lead that has been generously provided by Hanks and Severi (this volume), who define "worlds" in a marvelously concise and suggestive way as "oriented contexts for the apprehension of reality" (p. 10, this volume). On that basis, let us now turn to some examples from my previous work on Ku Waru verbal art, and in particular on a genre of sung narrative known as *tom yaya kange*.

Tom yaya kange is one of a wide range of sung narrative genres found across three contiguous provinces of Highland Papua New Guinea.[19] *Tom yaya kange*

---

19. For detailed coverage of six of the regional genres from multiple disciplinary viewpoints, see Rumsey and Niles (2011).

are sung to fixed, bipartite melodies, each half-melody comprising an equal number of lines of text. The precise textual realization of any given tale varies across performances even within the work of a single performer, making creative use of parallelism and of formulaic expressions that fit the metrical requirements of the line.[20] The plots of *tom yaya kange* are various, but cluster around a canonical one in which a young man sets out from his home to court a young woman he has heard about in a far-away place, undertakes a long and arduous journey to her home, wins her hand, but then encounters various obstacles in his attempt to bring her back to his home and marry her, sometimes succeeding and sometimes not.

While the *tom yaya kange* genre dates from before the first arrival of Europeans in the region in the 1930s, nowadays its standard plots and imagery are sometimes used for presenting narratives with noncanonical, distinctly contemporary plots and themes.[21] For example, one of the most highly regarded *tom yaya* exponents, Paulus Konts, has composed and performed a tale about a trip to the coast to buy betel nut to bring back to the highlands for sale. The story casts himself in the leading role, but has him traveling not on foot, but by bus to Lae, then on a boat to the port at Finschhafen. There he buys a thousand kina's worth of betel nuts and takes them back with him, beyond the Nebilyer Valley where he lives, to Wabag, the capital of Enga Province to the west. When he discovers that there is already an ample supply of betel nut in the Wabag markets, he continues on through the mountains to Porgera—a much more remote locale, where prices are higher, and there is more cash on hand because of the mining operations there. He sells his betel nuts there at a huge profit and returns triumphantly home to Ambukl.

Notwithstanding its distinctly contemporary subject matter, this story was cast by Konts in classic *tom yaya* form, using the same rhythm and melody and many of the same standard *kange* thematic motifs as in other performances. For example, when preparing for his trip, Konts washes himself in a river, and dresses himself splendidly in a woven belt and bark belt hung with cordyline leaves, both standard motifs in the tales of courtship. When traveling on the bus to Wabag, he carries with him a long *dagla* spear and a pronged *timbun* spear, described in parallel lines, just as in the more standard narratives of quest and courtship.

---

20. For details, see Rumsey (2001, 2007).

21. For other examples besides the one discussed below, see Rumsey (2001, 2006).

In addition to *tom yaya kange* motifs such as these, which Konts uses in standard form in his tale of the betel nut trade, there are others which he artfully adapts to fit with contemporary subject matter. An example is the following passage, which was spoken by the hero to the betel nut wholesalers in Finschhafen.

na buai lyibu ud a	"I've come to get betel," he said.
eni lyi naa lyibu e	"I haven't come to get you."
eni a molai nyirim e	"You all can stay," he said.
nanga buai kenginsai nyirim a	"Just bring me my bags of betel."

To an audience familiar with *tom yaya kange*, those lines are thematically reminiscent of a saying which is commonly used by hosts when welcoming first-time visitors from afar, namely:

kung koily kiulu lelym e	We've an oven for roasting pigs.
yabu koily kiulu naa lelym e	We've no oven for roasting people.

In other words, "Relax, we are not cannibals who intend to eat you, but friends who intend to feed you." Within the canonical *tom yaya* narrative of courtship, the point at which this remark typically occurs is when the hero has completed his long journey and arrived at the home of the young lady whom he has gone to court. Her place and its people are beyond the ken of his own, and therefore, like everyone at the edge of the known social universe, suspected of being cannibals (see Rumsey 1999).

The same remark is sometimes also made by the hero to his hosts, to put them at ease about the prospects for their daughter among his own people. For example, in one of Konts' performances it was said by the young heroine Tangapa to her suitor Tagla just after he arrives at her place, and then, as they are about to leave for his place, he says the same thing to her, followed immediately by the lines:

na nu lyibu ui naa udiyl	I haven't come to get you.
nunga laikiyl nyikin akiyl-ya	You're doing what you've chosen to do.

In his betel nut story, by having the hero say "I haven't come to get you" at an analogous point at the outer end of his journey, Konts is both creating an implicit parallel to the more standard plot involving courtship, and playing humorously upon coastal people's stereotype of highlanders as more savage than themselves, and perhaps even inclined to cannibalism.

In conclusion regarding *tom yaya kange*, the artful adaptations of composer/performers such as Paulus Konts clearly serve to translate between worlds, in Hanks and Severi's sense of "oriented contexts for the apprehension of reality." One is the story world of canonical *tom yaya kange*, which Ku Waru people think of as a blend of fantasy and of how things actually were in the past before the arrival of Europeans in the 1930s and the colonial order that they instituted (leading up to independence in 1975). The other world is the contemporary one. The translation between them works in both directions at once. For example, when the theme of exogamous courtship is used as a figure for long-range market transaction, this in effect invites the audience not only to imagine that newer activity in terms of exogamous courtship and the widening of exchange ties, but also to reimagine those older activities in terms of the newer one.[22]

CONCLUSIONS

How does the translation process that is at play in Paulus Konts' *tom yaya kange* compare with the one I have discussed above in connection with bilingual language learning? At first blush they may seem so different as to raise the question: Why try to bring them together under the same rubric of "translation"? Konts' translation is one across "worlds" but within the same language in the strict sense (since Ku Waru is the only one used), whereas the translations in the parent–child interaction are across languages, but within what may seem to be a single "world." Again my responses to that apparent quandary are twofold. First, it remains an open question whether the latter processes do indeed take place within a single "world" in Hanks and Severi's sense. I will return to that question below. Secondly, there is an intriguing similarity in the nature of the processes themselves. In both cases they involve the construction or attribution of equivalence, and in both cases parallelism plays a central part in that process. In the language-learning cases that I have discussed, the parallelism was found

---

22. For further discussion of the ways in which the world of narrated events in various genres of highlands sung narrative is related to the here-and-now world in which the performance takes place, see Rumsey (2005).

at the micro level of adjacent conversational turns. In the case of the *tom yaye kange* it is was found at the macro level of plot organization across extended narratives,[23] whereby, for example, travel through a series of named places to the coast for betel nut is to successful commerce as travel through a series of named places to a distant mountain is to successful exogamous courtship.

Now how about the question of distinct "worlds" associated with Ku Waru and Tok Pisin in adult–child interaction? This is a question that has a long history in connection with studies of bilingualism (Grossjean 1982; Romaine 1989; Pavlenko 2011). While the very existence of bilingualism (and multilingualism) might seem to present a challenge to the idea of each of the languages being associated with distinct worlds, in the relevant literature much has been made to hang on the question of possible functional differentiation of the languages in their use by bilinguals. If "worlds" are thought of as kinds of "oriented context" (as per Hanks and Severi), then to the extent that it can be shown that bilinguals restrict the use of each of their languages to certain kinds of contexts, they may perhaps be thought of as moving between different "worlds" as they switch languages. There is no doubt a tendency for such domain-specificity to develop among older Ku Waru children, depending on the subject matter under discussion, as shown by the case of Ken Lep (example 6). It is also highly likely that the choice of language, and the switches between them, are conditioned to some extent by the nature of the relation between speaker and addressee, and the tenor of the interaction between them at any given time. There is, for example, a tendency for Tok Pisin to be used to issue brusque commands, as illustrated in examples 1 and 3 above, and in Rumsey (2014: 414–15).

All these matters call for further study based on the more extended longitudinal samples that will be recorded from the four children discussed here over the next two years. On the other hand, a notable feature of much of the language switching by the younger Ku Waru children in our sample—as exemplified above—is that it does *not* seem to be conditioned by any apparent contextual factors. Rather, the children seem to delight in making what appear to be random, unexpected switches from one language to the other (albeit more often from Ku Waru to Tok Pisin than vice versa), often in acts of translation,

---

23. This is not to say that parallelism occurs *only* at a macro level within *tom yaya kange*. On the contrary, it is a pervasive feature across the full range of levels (for details see Rumsey 2007). The point is rather that the patterns of parallelism that figure in the particular instance of intercultural translation I have discussed here are ones that operate at a macro level, within and across plots.

as we have seen. This has the effect of simultaneously highlighting both the difference between the languages as such and the potential equivalence of things that can be said in them.

Similar considerations apply to the translation of worlds that is practiced by *tom yaya kange* performers such as Paulus Konts. As I have said, the translation works in both directions at once, in effect inviting the audience both to reimagine the contemporary world in terms of the story world and vice versa. But it also entails an equally important tropic movement in the opposite direction, whereby the inclusion of what are in experiential terms incongruous touches, such as the betel-nut buyer wearing cordyline leaves and carrying battle spears with him on his bus trip to the coast, serves to highlight the differences between the story world of canonical *tom yaya kange* and the here-and-now world to which it is being juxtaposed—a separation which is a necessary condition for the metaphorical or "translational" use of one in relation to the other.[24]

There is, I think, a lesson to be drawn from the practice both of Ku Waru children and of Paulus Konts in this respect. It is that translation plays an equally important role both in allowing for communication between distinct worlds and in constituting them as distinct worlds in the first place. In that respect my findings from the Ku Waru cases treated here are consistent with Hanks and Severi's claim that the quality of being translatable is inherent not only in human communication as such, but also to in "the generation of cultural differences" (p. 16, this volume) across which it can take place.

ACKNOWLEDGMENTS

Many thanks to Bill Hanks and Carlo Severi for inviting me to write this paper for the "Translating Worlds" conference, and to Bill for presenting it there in my absence. For their helpful comments on various drafts, thanks to Darja Hoenigman, Don Kulick, Francesca Merlan, Lila San Roque, five anonymous referees, and participants at the 2014 Annual Conference of the Linguistic Society of

---

24. One of my referees comments as follows: "The 'plotting across narratives'/spaces & times in the poems is very thought provoking. One question arises: is this also—like the parent–child conversations—a switching that does not depend on context? Elucidating the lack of resort to 'context' (that is, as an indigenous epistemological framing) holds much general theoretical promise for anthropological practices of description." I heartily agree and thank the referee for this observation.

Papua New Guinea, where it was also presented. Special thanks to all the Ku Waru-speaking children and their parents who are named in the article, to the Ku Waru bard Paulus Konts, and to our field assistants John Onga and Andrew Noma, without whose hard and steady work this study would not have been possible. For funding the research I gratefully acknowledge the support of the Australian Research Council and the Research School of Asia and the Pacific at Australian National University.

REFERENCES

Bakhtin, Mikhail. 1986. *Speech genres and other late essays.* Translated by Vern W. McGee. Austin: University of Texas Press.

Bauman, Richard, and Charles L. Briggs. 1990. "Poetics and performance as critical perspectives on language and social life." *Annual Review of Anthropology* 19: 59–88.

de León, Lourdes. 2007. "Parallelism, metalinguistic play and the interactive emergence of Zinacantec Mayan siblings' culture." *Research on Language and Social Interaction* 40: 405–36.

Demuth, Katherine. 1986. "Prompting routines in the language socialization of Basotho children." In *Language socialization across cultures*, edited by Bambi Schieffelin and Elinor Ochs, 51–79. Cambridge: Cambridge University Press.

Devett-Chee, Kilala. 2012. "The impact of Tok Pisin and local vernaculars on children's learning in Papua New Guinea." *Language and Linguistics in Melanesia* 30: 47–59.

———. 2013. "Key findings on the use of Tok Pisin and vernacular languages in Papua New Guinea primary schools." *Language and Linguistics in Melanesia* 31: 90–120.

Duranti, Alessandro, and Steven P. Black. 2012. "Language socialization and verbal improvisation." In *The handbook of language socialization*, edited by Alessandro Duranti, Elinor Ochs, and Bambi B. Schieffelin, 433–63. Malden, MA: Wiley-Blackwell.

Evans, Nicholas. 2010. *Dying words: Endangered languages and what they have to tell us.* Malden, MA: Wiley-Blackwell.

Evans, Nicholas, and Simon Greenhill. 2014. "Using pronominal syncretisms as a tool for diagnosing phylogeny in Papuan Languages." Unpublished presentation given at Workshop on the Languages of Papua III, held at Manokwari, Papua, Indonesia, January 23.

Goffman, Erving. 1981. *Forms of talk.* Philadelphia: University of Pennsylvania Press.

Goodwin, Charles, and Marjorie Harkness Goodwin. 1992. "Assessments and the construction of context." In *Rethinking context: Language as an interactive phenomenon,* edited by Alessandro Duranti and Charles Goodwin, 147–89. Cambridge: Cambridge University Press.

Grossjean, François. 1982. *Life with two languages.* Cambridge, MA: Harvard University Press.

Jakobson, Roman. 1960. "Closing statement: Linguistics and poetics." in *Style in language,* edited by Thomas Sebeok, 350–77. Cambridge, MA: MIT Press.

Keesing, Roger. 1988. *Melanesian pidgin and the Oceanic substrate.* Stanford: Stanford University Press.

Lowth, Robert. 1778. *Isaiah: A new translation with a preliminary dissertation.* Boston.

Merlan, Francesca, and Alan Rumsey 1991. *Ku Waru: language and segmentary politics in the Western Nebilyer Valley.* Cambridge: Cambridge University Press.

Moore, Leslie. 2012. "Language socialization and repetition." In *The handbook of language socialization,* edited by Alessandro Duranti, Elinor Ochs, and Bambi B. Schieffelin, 208–26. Malden, MA: Wiley-Blackwell.

Pavlenko, Aneta, ed. 2011. *Thinking and speaking in two languages.* Bristol: Multilingual Matters.

Romaine, Susan, ed. 1989. *Bilingualism.* Oxford: Blackwell.

Rumsey, Alan. 1999. "The white man as cannibal in the New Guinea Highlands." In *The anthropology of cannibalism,* edited by Laurence Goldman, 105–21. Westport, CT: Bergin & Garvey.

———. 2001. "*Tom yaya kange*: A metrical narrative genre from the New Guinea Highlands." *Journal of Linguistic Anthropology* 11: 193–239.

———. 2005. Chanted tales in the New Guinea Highlands of today: A comparative study. In *Expressive genres and historical change: Indonesia, Papua New Guinea and Taiwan,* edited by Pamela J. Stewart and Andrew Strathern, 41–81. Aldershot: Ashgate.

———. 2006. The articulation of indigenous and exogenous orders in Highland New Guinea and beyond. *The Australian Journal of Anthropology* 17: 47–69.

————. 2007. "Musical, poetic and linguistic form in *tom yaya* sung narratives from Papua New Guinea." *Anthropological Linguistics* 49: 237–82.

————. 2010. "Lingual and cultural wholes and fields." In *Theory and practice in anthropology: The holistic perspective*, edited by Ton Otto and Nils Bubant, 127–49. Malden, MA: Wiley-Blackwell.

————. 2013. "Intersubjectivity, deception and the 'opacity of other minds': Perspectives from Highland New Guinea and beyond." *Language and Communication* 33: 326–43.

————. 2014. "Language and human sociality." In *The Cambridge handbook of linguistic anthropology*, edited by N. J. Enfield, Paul Kockelman and Jack Sidnell, 391–410. Cambridge: Cambridge University Press.

Rumsey, Alan, and Don Niles, eds. 2011. *Sung tales from the Papua New Guinea Highlands: Studies in form, meaning, and sociocultural context.* Canberra: ANU E Press.

Rumsey, Alan, Lila San Roque, and Bambi B. Schieffelin. 2013. "The acquisition of ergative marking in Kaluli, Ku Waru and Duna (Trans New Guinea)." In *The acquisition of ergativity*, edited by Edith Bavin and Sabine Stoll, 133–82. Amsterdam: John Benjamins.

Schieffelin, Bambi B. 1990. *The give and take of everyday life: Language socialization of Kaluli children.* Cambridge: Cambridge University Press

Silverstein, Michael 2004. "'Cultural' concepts and the language–culture nexus." *Current Anthropology* 45: 621–52.

CHAPTER SIX

Culinary subjectification
The translated world of menus and orders

ADAM YUET CHAU

TRANSLATING WORDS AND WORLDS

Perhaps we can start with a thought exercise: How would you translate the word "menu" (i.e., restaurant menu) into the native language of an (imaginary) tribal people (with no writing and no restaurants)? And how would you explain to them how ordering from the menu works?

Can we merely translate the restaurant menu into the native language as "a written list of dishes from which diners choose while dining in a restaurant"? It is my contention that we cannot explain the restaurant menu to these "prerestaurant" and "premenu" tribal people without explaining our whole conceptual and social world to them: What is a restaurant? What is eating out? What is a meal? What is dinner (or lunch)? Why would you need to make a reservation or queue in line for a table? What is a table? What is "getting seated"? Why is the eating area separate from the cooking area? What is a waiter? What is a cook? Why entrust a stranger to cook for you? Why trust food that you have not raised, grown, hunted, or caught yourself? Why are you eating with strangers sitting next to and around you? What is a course (appetizer, main course, dessert)? Why can't we eat everything altogether? What is a portion? What is ordering and taking an order? Why can't one order everything on the menu? What is choice? Why can you only eat food from the dish placed in front of you? Why are people eating in a group nevertheless eating different food? Why drink certain kinds of drink with certain kinds of dishes? Why do people talk while eating? Why is the restaurant so dark? Why is there a lit candle on the table? What is writing? What is a list? What is a price? What is money? What is a bill (or check)? Why do you have to pay for the food? What is a tip? What is a credit card? What is a receipt? Why are some dishes more expensive than others? Why can't we sleep in the restaurant? To this list we might also add: What is a take-away? What is a take-away menu? What is a children's menu? What is a vegetarian menu?, And so on.

Clearly, translating the *word* "menu" entails not only translating the *world* of restaurant-going and ordering from the menu but our very conceptual and social world (i.e., ideal-typically Western or Western-style), which is another way of saying that what seems to be a humble piece of paper listing a certain number of dishes is itself made by the world in which it is found and in turn contributes in a significant way to making that world. In this article I shall examine the restaurant menu as a world-making social and translocutional/transinscriptional technology.

The article is divided into several sections. I begin by explaining what a menu is and briefly tracing its history before examining, in the second section, the role of the menu in terms of social practices that it entails in the worlds of restaurant cooking and dining. In the following section I explain how the menu embodies (culinary) choice as an ideology. The menu is then examined as a translocutional/transinscriptional technology, and ordering from the menu is considered as a process of translating along a multitude of "iterative/inscriptive stations." In the fifth section, I look at menu planning as a process of translating from the chef's professional culinary language to the customers' language, and how both are constantly being transformed because of these incessant acts of translation. I then propose the term "culinary subjectification" to examine how customers resonate their culinary world with that which is embodied in the menu. This is further explicated through two common practices: the seeking of the culinary Other (mediated by the "textographic Other" which is the menu proffering exotic-sounding dishes and even written in exotic scripts) and abandoning the menu altogether and surrendering oneself to the dictates of the chef. In the penultimate section I examine the waiter's order slip as a specimen of "text acts," which call forth and actualize the dishes ordered and the meal composed by the customer. Using the Daoist talisman as an analogy, I argue that the waiter's order slip can be understood as a "potency tender." In the conclusion I explore briefly the implications of this investigation, especially in relation to the intersemiotic connection between orality and the written in processes of translation (between different culinary languages, along iterative/inscriptive stations, etc.). Ultimately this article is an investigation of how *worlds* get translated (and made and transformed) as *words* get uttered, negotiated, inscribed, transcribed, translated, transmuted, acted upon, and even transsubstantiated (e.g., when an item printed on the menu magically materializes into an actual dish).

If this largely theoretical essay lacks a specific "ethnographic context," it is because I have presumed the cultural competence and complicity of the reader in order for the arguments of this essay to work. If you can provide adequate answers to all the questions evoked above (e.g., What is a restaurant? What is eating out? What is a menu? etc.), you will have been already equipped with the necessary "ethnographic" cultural backgrounds to "picture" the different scenes in subsequent sections (e.g., you will have plenty of your own "menu stories"). There are of course an enormous variety of restaurants, menus, and practices of ordering from the menu. For the purpose of this article I evoke what might be called a "model restaurant" (indeed, even a "modal restaurant," in the statistical sense), a "model menu," a "model diner," and a "model menu-ordering experience" (see Eco [1979] 1984 on the "model reader").

WHAT IS A MENU?

There are three main usages of the word "menu" in modern social life.[1] In the English language, a menu (the equivalent of *la carte* in French and *die Speisekarte*

---

1. One of the reviewers objected to my "insouciant use of the word 'modern'" owing to its "tacit deictic" meanings, and suggested that I "be more precise about the social range that [I am] attributing to this word." Here I can only resort to the same "escape clause" mentioned in the previous section that invokes the images of the "model restaurant," the "model menu," etc., and so on, and plea for the complicity of the reader of this essay to bring their cultural/ideological upbringing and "prejudices" to bear. In my defense, I do not believe that the word "modern" is necessarily any more guilty of carrying with it "tacit deictic" meanings than are many other words used in this essay.

in German) is a list of itemized dishes from which diners choose for their meals, usually in a restaurant. A second, less common, usage of "menu" is a detailed listing of the dishes the diners will get in the course of a meal, especially at banquets and other formal dining occasions. For example, high-table dinners in Oxbridge colleges always have this kind of menu printed on cards, which are displayed on the dining table for the diners to consult—importantly, these menus also list, alongside the various courses, the accompanying wines. The expression "So what's on the menu?" refers to this usage, inquiring about what is to be served for a meal. (It seems that "bill of fare" used to be the equivalent of "menu," "fare" referring to "food and drinks.") A third usage of "menu" is its pervasive application as a metaphor, usually in a menu-like list of services from which customers can select, in contexts such as course offerings in an academic degree program, different services in a hair or nail salon, "bundled" offers from an internet provider or mobile phone company, or "apps" on a smartphone (but also as in "a menu of disasters"). This article will be primarily examining the first sense of the menu, that is, the restaurant menu, a list of itemized dishes from which diners choose in order to "compose" their meals.

Food historians have not ascertained when the restaurant menu was invented or where, but there are written testimonies to the existence of restaurant menus in the Song Dynasty (960–1279) in China about one thousand years ago.[2] Apparently the menu did not appear in the West until quite recently, say

---

2.   The following passage describes ordering from menus in the Song Dynasty (Northern Song with Kaifeng as capital and Southern Song with Hangzhou as capital):

Wine and tea houses in both Kaifeng and Hangchow [Hangzhou] lured customers with such luxuries as paintings by famous artists, flowers, miniature trees, cups and utensils of silver or of porcelain, and of course, with fine food. . . . A Southern Sung source gives a "casual list" of two hundred and thirty-four famous dishes that such places served, a list from the Northern Sung has fifty-one. Dinners probably started with a soup or broth like "hundred-flavors" soup, which heads both lists. They could then choose from dishes made from almost any variety of flesh, fowl, or seafood—milk-steamed lamb, onion-strewn hare, fried clams or crabs. Several kinds of "variety meats," lungs, heart, kidneys, or caul, were cooked in various manners. . . . Ordering was done in approximately the same way in Kaifeng and in Hangchow, where all restaurants had menus. "The men of Kaifeng were extravagant and indulgent. They would shout their orders by the hundreds: some wanted items booked and some chilled, some heated and some prepared, some iced or delicate or fat; each person ordered differently. The waiter then went to get the orders, which he repeated and carried in his head, so that when he got into the kitchen he repeated them. These men were called 'gong heads' or 'callers.' In an instant, the waiter would

as late as the eighteenth century, when eating out and restaurants became in-stitutionalized (e.g., MacDonogh 1987: 111; Pembroke 2013: 134–35; but see Carlin 2008).[3] Prior to the appearance of the restaurant menu, people of course also ate outside of their homes (e.g., when they traveled), but they would have to be content with whatever the inn or tavern owner had prepared for that day rather than ordering from a list of possible dishes.[4] When the rich (e.g., aristo-crats) traveled in the past, they would stay at the estates of other rich people and dine in, and sometimes they would bring their own cooks and kitchen staff; they did not eat in public (mixing with commoners or within their sight). The rise of the menu (and restaurants) resulted largely from the rise of the bourgeoisie in European history, when dining out among strangers in anonymous spaces became acceptable, and more and more prestige was attached to the pursuit of fine food, culinary diversity, mixed sociality, and the establishment of one's taste or culinary distinction in a public manner (see Bourdieu [1979] 1984).

WHAT DOES THE MENU DO? THE MENU AS A SOCIAL TECHNOLOGY

Just as the map is not the territory, the recipe is not the dish, and the blueprint is not the building, the menu is certainly not the meal. A menu facilitates the composition and production of meals. The menu is an inscribed space from which spring a great many possible meals through permutation. Even a mod-est menu with just a few items can potentially allow a very great number of possible meals, thanks to the structure of modular (see Ledderose 2001) and phased serving of dishes[5]. The menu interpellates the diners, spurs them into

---

be back carrying three dishes forked in his left hand, while on his right arm from hand to shoulder he carried about twenty bowls doubled up, and he distributed them precisely as everyone had ordered without an omission or mistake. If there were, the customers would tell the 'head man' who would scold and abuse the waiter and sometimes dock his salary, so severe was the punishment. (Freeman 1977: 160–61; containing a passage in quotation marks translated from Chinese)

3.   Since the main content of this article is not on the history of the menu, I beg readers' forgiveness for my cursory treatment regarding this aspect.

4.   This is the second sense of the menu as mentioned above, which has retained its use in restaurants as "dishes of the day" ("le menu" in French, as opposed to "à la carte").

5.   See Kaufman (2002) for a historical account of how the modern form of sequenced serving of courses was introduced (called *service à la russe*).

action, activates their culinary habitus and subjectivity, fires up their fantasy and appetite, and initiates a chain of actions—translocutional and transinscriptional, among others—that will eventually result in the ordered dishes appearing in front of the diners (more on this below).

But the menu does not only interpellate forward. Even before the diners enter the restaurant, sit down and read it, the menu has already interpellated "backward" all the actions necessary to produce and present all the dishes that it promises. These actions include the hiring and training of the chefs and other personnel (including kitchen assistants, the wait staff, etc.), the procurement of all the necessary ingredients, the fitting of the cooking equipment (stoves, ovens, grills, cooking utensils, etc.), the fitting of the dining room (including tables and chairs, tableware, stemware, cutlery, tablecloths, decorations, etc.), and of course the design and printing of the menu itself. All restaurateurs know that the success and failure of one's restaurant largely rests on the menu, and it is usually the chefs who have a decisive voice in its final range and shape.

The menu also orchestrates the meal. When people dine in a group, they invariably order their dishes in implicit coordination with one another so that everyone orders the same combination and sequence of courses and eats in a more or less coordinated manner in order to avoid the awkward situation of some eating while others are not. Indeed, knowing how to order in such a situation is very much part of the "civilizing process" (Elias [1939] 1994). Proper table manners begin not with the arrival of the first dish but with the act of ordering the meal.

THE MENU, CHOICE, AND "LIBERALITY"

Being able to choose one's own dishes and compose one's own meal is one of the most important features and attractions of the menu. And this "choice," though seemingly banal, is laden with ideological significance. It seems that this spirit of free choice based on a large number of possible dishes reached its zenith already in the nineteenth century in the United States of America, true to its image of the "land of the plentiful" (see Freedman 2011; Haley 2012). However, such boastful display of "liberality" sometimes drew amused comments and sharp criticisms. Below are some examples (italics added by this author for emphasis).

The first comes from a British visitor to the United States in the late nineteenth century:

> I shall never forget my feelings when a waiter bluntly placed before me for the first time *a list of the food provided for breakfast—I cannot call it a menu*—at one of the great hotels in New York, and asked what I would take. Being of an experimental turn of mind, *and doubting, moreover, whether all these various dishes could exist any where but in the "catalogue,"* I used to amuse myself by testing the capabilities of the kitchen, but it never failed. (Cited in Hawkins and Fanning 1893: 206)

US General Rush Christopher Hawkins, in the same period, reports on ordering from the menu as follows:

> To arrive at the third objective point involved a rest for one night at the most populous and popular resort in our whole country. For that purpose we selected the most "swell" and "quiet" hotel of the place, where the late dinner and breakfast proved to be quite the worst, as to quality, of the whole season. *The dinner menu must have contained about one hundred and ten items, and the one for breakfast at least seventy-five.* We were tempted to taste a certain "fancy dish," entree in other words, which purported to have been made of capon and truffles. It proved to be a sort of a cold pressed hash of veal and beef tongue, with not a particle of capon or even chicken in it, while the truffles were a composition of a shining black substance of the texture of isinglass. . . .
>
> The general aim seems to be to hoodwink patrons with *a show of great liberality—hence the dinner bill of fare with from eighty to one hundred and twenty-five items upon it, and the breakfast menu with from forty to seventy-five.* Such a *spread of printer's ink* looks large, panders to national vanity and convinces the native that he is not being swindled. . . .
>
> It is quite unnecessary to write that *not one in ten of those products of the kitchen named in the bill of fare are properly prepared or decently served.* The vegetables are usually cold and soggy, often slopped with a nasty-looking and worse-tasting sauce; the joints are usually tough and cold; *the flesh made dishes [entries], with high sounding French names, neither taste nor smell like anything we have ever seen before*; the sweets are often the better part of the dinner; but the fruits, in the

majority of instances, are the cheapest and poorest that can be found. . . . When asked why the hotels in America do not adopt *the Continental* table d'hote *dinner*, the answer always is: *"Americans won't have it that way; they want more liberality."* . . .

The American landlord applies the enforced theory of Colonel Sellers to the everyday actualities of hotel keeping. He has convinced himself that his guests do not need really palatable food; they only want the illusion, i.e., *to see a certain liberal display of items with high-sounding names on the bill of fare, and dishes filled with some sort of a beyond-understanding substance, to correspond with a certain name, which can be supplied when ordered.* No matter whether or not it is actual food fit to eat, *it represents an item printed, and fulfils one part of the contract existing between the landlord and the guest.* (Hawkins and Fanning 1893: 198, 200, 201)

It seems reasonable that when the "liberality" of ostentatious menu display is not matched by cooking of reasonable quality, the restaurants should draw ridicule. And it should not surprise us that the menu increasingly resembled a "catalogue" (as derided in the above quotes) as the shopping catalogue itself was just becoming fashionable amidst the booming shopping paradise in late-nineteenth-century urban Europe and the United States. Nevertheless, the display of plenitude and the existence of real choice underlie the modern institution of the restaurant menu. As Hawkins pointed out in the above passage, the menu is like a contract between the restaurant and the diner. Once the diner walks into the restaurant, the restaurant has to, in theory at least, abide by what the menu promises. And once the diner has placed the order, the kitchen is supposed to deliver the dishes ordered. Of course, sometimes the kitchen runs out of certain ingredients and therefore the chefs can't produce certain dishes, but this kind of situation should not happen too often or to too many dishes or else the menu would become a travesty. I will discuss the "high-sounding French names" of dishes below.

One interesting episode in the 2010 film *Never Let Me Go* (based on a novel of the same title by Kazuo Ishiguro) is very revealing of not only the necessity of learning how to order from a menu but more importantly the connection between the ability to freely choose one's dishes and one's ontological status and fate. The three protagonists, Kathy, Ruth, and Tommy, have grown up in a boarding school called Hailsham. All Hailsham students are clones whose destiny is to donate their organs until they eventually "complete," that is, die, despite rumors of being able to apply to opt out of the compulsory organ donor scheme. School life is very regimented and food is always served collectively, with everyone receiving the same meals. When Kathy, Ruth, and Tommy become teenagers they are transferred to a farm, still living a collective and quite regimented life. One day the threesome are brought to a restaurant. When they are presented with the menu, not knowing how to order, they all panic. To get out of the awkward and embarrassing situation, they all follow their more senior and experienced housemate and quickly order the same dish. Same dish, same destiny.

FROM MENU TO ORDER TO DISHES TO CHECK: THE MENU AS A TRANSLOCUTIONAL/TRANSINSCRIPTIONAL TECHNOLOGY

The notions of translation and cultural translation interest me the most in their ability to evoke a family of senses relating to words such as transfer, traversal, transit, transfusion, transaction, transliteration, transmutation, transport, transpose, transcript, trajectory, trespassing, and so on. All these words of course suggest a gap between two points (mostly on a spatial plane), the bridging of this gap somehow, a sense of directionality in this bridging via the movement of objects (be they physical objects or concepts, etc.), and a sense of transformation in the process of this bridging. In studies of translations between languages or cultural translations between "cultures," the spatial (real or metaphorical) gap and its bridging are usually emphasized. But it seems that the temporal dimension of linguistic and cultural translation has not received adequate attention. By temporal dimension I mean the mechanisms and processes of *sustained* articulation traversing the gap(s) between two or more "iterative/inscriptional stations" ("stations" since there is never any "terminal" or "final destination" for these continuous traversals), which are in turn defined as relatively stable (or momentarily "frozen" or "congealed") synchronic configurations of a collection of thus-traversed objects (physical or conceptual). If such a temporal focus of translation were something new, I believe it would have very interesting implications for our understanding of all kinds of translations (translingual, intralingual, transmodal, transcultural, etc.). I will use the rest of this article to illustrate this approach with sociocognitive practices surrounding the restaurant menu.

Let us first trace the trajectory of the multiple forms of iteration and inscription that the dishes on the menu traverse:

- ideas of dishes in the chef's head (including consultation of other restaurants' menus and deciding which would be the chef's so-called "signature dishes" [note the inscriptional metaphor]) →
- draft menu (called "menu planning")[6] →
- finalized menu →
- designing the menu (i.e., how it will look on the dining table [paper? with lamination? cardboard? with or without pictures? which typeface? etc.]) →
- printed menu (on the dining tables as well as outside the main entrance or stuck against the glass door) →
- the construction of the daily "today's specials" or "plats du jour" as an addition to the regular menu (to evoke the availability of freshly acquired ingredients or to suggest that there will always be something new at this restaurant) →
- diners' reading of the menu →
- diners' asking for the waiter's recommendations or explanations of various dishes →
- the waiter's recommending some dishes and explaining some others (e.g., difficult dishes such as "canard étouffé" or "Buddha jumps over the wall") →
- diners' selections of dishes (verbalized) →
- the waiter's jotting down of the orders (usually in some kind of shorthand) →
- the waiter's relaying of the order to the kitchen (e.g., by pinning the order onto a board in front of the chef) →
- the production of the actual dishes by the chef and his/her assistants (again often involving the verbalization of the names of the dishes) →
- the delivery of the dishes to the table (often accompanied by the waiter's shouting out the dishes' names to identify the right diners) →
- the diners consuming the dishes (the sequence from delivery of the dish to eating it repeated according to the number of dishes ordered) →
- the waiter's bringing the check (with the names of the dishes inscribed, now as a computer printout rather than handwritten like the order) →
- the diners' paying for the meal (the whole process repeated dozens of times depending on the total number of groups of diners) →

---

6. There are in fact specialized companies that help restaurants and restaurant chains with menu design (in senses broader than the one relating only to appearance). See, for example, the company called Menuology (http://www.menuology.com/).

- foodie bloggers or food critics' writing-up of their dining experience with the dishes and the restaurant, and so on.[7]

A great many instances of iteration and inscription take place during the course of such a menu-facilitated "culinary enactment," not to mention the many social agents and "agents of iteration/inscription" involved. We can also see the multiple and intimate relationships *between orality and writing*. These verbal and inscriptional relays are acts of translation (intralinguistic, interlinguistic, and intersemiotic), not across different languages but across/between different "iterative/inscriptional stations" with a strong overarching forward temporal drive. Spatial gaps are traversed as well (from dinner table to kitchen, from kitchen to dinner table, etc.), but it is the temporal forward motion that best characterizes the overall "menu-logic." In the next few sections I will examine a little more closely three of the key translocutional/transinscriptional processes mentioned above and how they exemplify important theoretical concepts: (1) menu planning; (2) ordering from the menu; and (3) the writing of the waiter's order slip.

MENU PLANNING

As can be seen in the above-mentioned schematic flow chart, constructing the menu for a particular restaurant is a complex process. The owner might have a vision for his restaurant, and this vision will reflect on what kind of head chef he is looking for (if he is not in fact himself the head chef). But ultimately it is usually the head chef who populates the empty template of the menu with names of dishes that he thinks he and his team in the kitchen can produce. The head chef brings to this menu-planning task an enormous background knowledge, training (from cooking schools, being a chef in previous restaurants), and a repertoire of management and cooking skills. He needs to reconcile the anticipated expectations of the customers with the availability of resources (personnel, ingredients, utensils, etc.), the calculation of cost-effectiveness and profitability (the restaurant has to make money), his own repertoire of dishes, and the identity

---

7. I thank one of the Paris Fyssen workshop participants for alluding to "stations of the cross" in connection to "iterative/inscriptional stations." For both kinds of stations, the temporal dimension is crucial.

he wishes to project to the world both for himself as the head chef and for the restaurant. But most importantly, the chef needs to translate the language of his profession (based on, among other things, recipes and professional understandings of culinary practices) into a menu language that the customers can understand and work with. When this process involves rephrasing, simplifying, and glossing in the same language, it is Jakobson's *intralingual translation*. When it involves explicating in a different language (e.g., when an English gloss appears underneath a dish in French or transliterated Chinese or Thai), it is Jakobson's *interlingual translation* (or translation proper).

In his article for this volume, William Hanks proposes to look at Spanish-colonial translation efforts through five principles or ideals (based on his study on the translation from Spanish into Maya during the colonial period and producing a new language, Maya*, in the process): interpretance, economy, transparency, indexical grounding, and beauty. I suggest that we can look at the chef's construction of the menu through a similar set of five principles:

1. *Interpretance*: any dish in principle can be expressed by a name that is understandable by the customer.
2. *Economy*: the name of the dish should be concise rather than a mouthful; this facilitates not only the learning of the dishes by the customers but the handling of the orders by the waiters as well.
3. *Transparency*: any menu neologism used to convey a culinary concept should have "morphosyntactic elements [that are] clearly distinguishable and relatable to discrete aspects of the target meaning" (Hanks, p. 39, this volume).
4. *Indexical grounding*: "newly minted neologisms [are to be] bound to their canonical referents . . .so that their meaning [is] anchored in the cotextual elements" (Hanks, p. 39, this volume); this is particularly important for so-called "ethnic-fusion" menus, where there are a proliferation of fanciful and playful made-up dish names (the equivalent of neologisms).
5. *Beauty*: dish names on the menu should achieve some kind of formal coherence and consistency (e.g., all dish names should be of a similar length) or even be poetic (many traditional Chinese dishes have poetic and evocative names).

However, to the extent that the chef's professional culinary language is a prestige language, it becomes inevitable that many features of this language will be introduced into the menu to assert superiority, authority, the mark of haute cuisine, and exoticism. The effect of such "difficult" menu language upon prospective customers is often anticipated and results from careful calculation; it should be challenging and thrilling but not overly challenging lest the customers lose face when they find themselves not being able to handle it at all or it necessitates an inordinate amount of intervention and explanation from the waiter, thus interrupting the smooth flow along the "iterative/inscriptional stations."

CULINARY SUBJECTIFICATION, MENU LITERACY, AND MENU MANEUVERS AS INTERSEMIOTIC NEGOTIATIONS

While the head chef and his team of cooks are bringing their professional culinary language to bear upon the menu, each one of the diners is also bringing his or her culinary knowledge and experience into the restaurant. The totality of one's culinary exposure, which is of course constantly shifting (often perceived as "improving" or "expanding"), functions as a powerful force of what might be called "culinary subjectification."[8] In fact, we can paraphrase Mikhail Bakhtin and understand culinary subjectification as a process of *individuals populating the culinary universe with their own intentions*. Below I have included the relevant Bakhtin quote with the language-related words struck out (with a strikethrough) and the cuisine-related words added (in square brackets):

> As a living, socio-ideological concrete thing, as heteroglot opinion [culinary construct], ~~language~~ [cuisine], for the individual consciousness, lies on the borderline between oneself and the other. The ~~word in language~~ [dish in cuisine] is half someone else's. It becomes "one's own" only when the ~~speaker~~ [diner] populates it with his own intention, his own accent, when he appropriates the ~~word~~ [dish], adapting it to his own ~~semantic~~ [culinary] and expressive intention. Prior to this moment of appropriation, the ~~word~~ [dish] does not exist in a neutral and impersonal ~~language~~ [culinary world] (it is not, after all, out of a ~~dictionary~~ [cookbook] that the speaker gets his words [dishes]!) but rather it exists ~~in other people's mouths~~ [in other people's kitchens, on other people's tables], in other people's contexts, serving other people's intentions: it is from there that one must take the ~~word~~ [dish], and make it one's own. (Bakhtin 1981: 293–94)

---

8. See Chau (2013) for an elaboration on the concept of "religious subjectification."

Going to restaurants is for many one of the most crucial sites where one's culinary subjectivity is formed (in addition to one's family cooking traditions, watching cooking shows on TV, reading cook books and restaurant reviews, etc.). One acquires one's own repertoire of culinary expertise, skills in "composing" an excellent meal in a carefully chosen restaurant, and, better still, a more-than-casual acquaintance with the chef (so that he comes out of the kitchen and sits down at one's table for a chat).

At the base of one's culinary subjectivity is menu literacy (see Rice 2011[9]), which is much more than just the ability to understand the individual words on the menu. One should not underestimate the cognitive skills and the learning process involved in ordering dishes from a restaurant menu. First of all, one needs to be quite literate (and know culinary French in the case of more "pretentious" restaurants) in order to feel at ease ordering food in a restaurant. In his entertaining memoir-cum-restaurant-history *Growing in restaurants*, the publisher James Pembroke relates how exhilarated and empowered he felt when he realized that he knew much better than his posher classmates how to order from the menu—he "grew up in restaurants" thanks to the fact that his mother hated cooking and his parents managed to claim all their family expenses, restaurant meals and the children's school fees included, as business expenses (with perhaps a certain degree of exaggeration):

> Until my fifteenth birthday, when my parents took three friends and me out for dinner, I had no idea that my precocious menu knowledge was unusual for someone of my age. My three mates were from posher backgrounds than my own, but their parents had not managed to have their prep school fees tax deductible, so their menu knowledge was kindergarten standard. They had only ever eaten out in hotels on special occasions or at a Wimpy for a treat. *All seventies menus were still in French* due to a subservience to the Master Race of the Kitchen and the belief that the language of Shakespeare lacked the sophistication of the French, who gave us words like serviette, dessert and toilet. *So, I translated virtually every line for them: crêpes Florentine, boeuf bourguignon, etc.* It was the first time I realised I had been spoilt. And, God, did I rejoice in it. (Pembroke 2013: 8, italics added for emphasis)

---

9.   I am grateful to Jeff Rice for kindly sending me a copy of his essay on menu literacy.

Among anthropologists, it was of course Jack Goody (1977, 1986, 1987) who first examined the broader sociocognitive impact of writing and literacy in a systematic manner. In his study on the corpus of writing by Ansumana Sonie, a man of the Vai people in West Africa, Goody suggests the interesting concept of "grapho-linguistic ability" in characterizing this man's literacy and ability to produce certain kinds of writing (e.g., membership lists, membership due payment lists, organizational regulations, etc.). He notes that Sonie had been a cook before becoming the chairman of his Muslim brotherhood organization, and it was his role as a cook that gave him the opportunity to acquire basic literacy such as making a grocery list.

Grapho-linguistic ability (or call it menu literacy) is certainly required of all diners ordering food from the menu (if they do not want to embarrass themselves by pointing to a neighboring table and saying, "I will have what she is having"). Indeed, the menu congeals a highly specialized vocabulary and has many unusual formal qualities, all of which takes some effort to get familiarized with and to master.[10]

Being menu-literate or restaurant savvy also means that one has to master the structure of the menu in relation to the structure of the meal (see Douglas [1972] 1999). Typically, children or people unfamiliar with dining out are (cognitively) overwhelmed by the amount of choices in each section of the menu. This is one of the reasons why some restaurants have a "children's menu," often accompanied by pictures of the actual dishes, as much to provide smaller portions as to delimit the number of choices and degree of complexity/sophistication for these culinary "savages."[11] One may also spend too much time pondering the menu, order either too little or too much, or be overly subversive with one's orders (e.g., ordering chicken salad but *sans* chicken). In other words, ordering from the menu calls for not only cognitive skills but social skills as well (or let's call them "sociocognitive skills").

---

10. One of the funniest scenes in cinema history concerns a lowly Japanese company employee who puts his stuffy bosses to shame by demonstrating his menu literacy at a fancy French restaurant where the menu is entirely in French. The film is *Tampopo*, a slapstick food-related comedy directed by Juzo Itami (released in 1985). The restaurant scene can be viewed on YouTube at http://www.youtube.com/watch?v=RRVLqUpHDJE (in Japanese with English subtitles).

11. In fact, for the longest time, restaurants were the exclusive domain of adults. So-called "family-friendly" restaurants were a quite recent twentieth-century invention.

The overall ensemble of sociocognitive practices around the menu can be called "menu maneuvers," which includes menu planning, menu reading, and ordering from the menu involving interactions with the waiter—these potentially complex interactions are the major site at which the culinary worlds (and languages) of the chefs and the customers collide with, construct, and transform, one another. These practices are in fact complex intersemiotic negotiations and translations, resulting in the constant transformation of the culinary universes of both the chefs and the customers. One may go as far as to say that the menu and all its associated sociocognitive practices (i.e., the "menu maneuvers") interpellate and *produce* the chefs, the waiters, as well as the diners. And we haven't even discussed the diners' (and of course also the cooks' and the waiters') "memories of past dishes" (a nod to Proust) (also complexly inscribed and constantly undergoing processes of translation).

IN SEARCH OF THE CULINARY OTHER AND DOING WITHOUT THE MENU

The formal standardization of the menu as a genre of text and the menu maneuvers as an ensemble of sociocognitive practices also encourage more adventurous diners to venture out of their comfort zone (though still armed with the reassurance of the familiar formal qualities of the menu, as a sort of Latourian "immutable mobile" [Latour 1986]) to seek the thrills of the exotic culinary Other.

When people venture into culinarily unfamiliar territories, such as so-called "ethnic" restaurants (I heuristically include French and Italian restaurants in this category), they frequently encounter challenges of a "grapho-linguistic" nature. In fact, one may even say that many bourgeois diners deliberately seek out these grapho-linguistic challenges for the thrill of *grapho-culinary* adventure. In these situations, intralinguistic and translinguistic translations occur to an intense degree, and the waiter's status is elevated to that of a Cuna shaman! But here it is not a difficult birth that the shaman is trying to ease or cure (see Lévi-Strauss [1958] 1963) but potentially interrupted iterative/transcriptional production. If the waiter can't satisfactorily "channel" "canard étouffé" or "General Tso's Chicken," we might have a problem, that is, an interrupted coproduction of the meal. This is why I believe the menu is also "iconographic" (and is therefore a "chimera-object") in the sense Carlo Severi proposes in the context of highlighting the importance of nonwritten but graphic modes of representation in their capacity to ground memories and enact narratives (Severi [2007] 2015).

Occasionally, however, the grapho-linguistic challenge proves too much to bear for the culinary adventurer and voyeur. Calvin Trillin, an American writer and frequent contributor to *The New Yorker*, relates his discomfort (to put it mildly) when confronted with Chinese menus scribbled on restaurant walls intended only for those who can read Chinese: "The walls were covered with signs in Chinese writing—signs whose Chinatown equivalents drive me mad, since they feed my suspicion that Chinese customers are getting succulent dishes I don't even know about" (2004: 111–12, cited in Rice 2011: 123). But perhaps it is precisely this grapho-linguistic and culinary handicap (and hence challenge) that is drawing Trillin and other culinary thrill-seekers back again and again to these maddening Chinese, and other ethnic, restaurants.[12]

Some other culinary adventures take the form of completely abandoning oneself to culinary chance encounters and doing without the menu (thus socio-cognitively returning oneself to a state of [culinary] infancy). The ethnomusicologist Steve Jones, who plays the violin in an early-music orchestral ensemble, relates (via a private email communication) the competitive bravado resulting from these culinary adventures:

> In the world of orchestral tours we have a kind of dream, an ideal, a spiel. As we split into various groups to look for a good restaurant, on our return we try to outdo the others with our report. It begins "Lovely little family-run place, very cheap, home-made wine . . ." and in its extreme form will involve "no sign outside at all, looks like a hovel," and "no menu, the cook just gave us what they were having," "old lady treading the grapes as we ate," "they wouldn't take any money," "they invited us to their daughter's wedding tomorrow, there are gonna be three family bands of launeddas players," etc., etc.

As if to reassure me that these "(no-)menu stories" are not fantasies, Steve finished off his message to me with his own personal experience: "I did find a great restaurant in Rome once with no sign outside. In the hills near Verona I

---

12. To help the linguistically perplexed and to heighten their culinary and grapho-linguistic joy, the University of Chicago linguist James D. McCawley even wrote *The eater's guide to Chinese characters* (1984), replete with specimen menus from various kinds of restaurants. I thank one of the reviewers for bringing this book to my attention.

had an amazing lunch where the cook did indeed just tell us what he would be bringing us."

Similarly, diners in certain nouvelle-cuisine restaurants would also not have any menus, surrendering instead to the whims and expertise of the chef:

> These [dining] experiences induce a state of surrender. We cannot validate the existence of anything but the stream of improbable perceptions. Judgment is inoperative, as it has nothing to rely on. In such trance-like states, we are held, led, entrusting our experience to the chef's expertise. That is why, I believe, some avant-garde restaurants (such as El Bulli) do not have any menus for us to choose from. That is also why we are sometimes instructed, like children being taught for the first time, how to eat our food. We succumb to the experience of being a newborn again, able to see only blurred spots and shades. We never know what this food is or where it came from. We just sit there, helpless and trustful as babes in arms, waiting for the impressions to flow through our senses. (Dudek 2008: 54)

Living in a world with a seemingly excessive degree of culinary "free choice" and "menu liberality," not exercising choice, and thus temporarily excusing oneself from the interpellation of the menu and its related sociocognitive practices, becomes strangely liberating.[13]

THE WAITER'S ORDER SLIP AS "TEXT ACT" AND "POTENCY TENDER"

One of the most curious and significant steps along the many menu-related iterative/transcriptive stations is how the waiter's order slip, when brought from the diners' table to the kitchen, will eventually yield the actual dishes. Clearly

---

13. One of the reviewers also relates his/her experience of some restaurants deliberately not working with the printed menu: "In many trendy restaurants I've been to of late, waiters make a big deal about orally performing the menu, both during the moment of ordering (especially reciting elaborate daily specials that are not written on the menu) and again when the dish is brought out, reviewing all the exotic ingredients brought together on the plate. Indeed, it is often disruptive of conversation around the dinner table." This practice obviously adds more dimensions to the orality–written iterative/transcriptive relays.

it is a case of Jakobson's intersemiotic translation, or what Severi (this volume) calls "transmutation proper," where translation takes place between and across entirely different existential modes. I have mentioned that the menu can be understood as a contract between the chef/restaurant and the diner; the restaurant has to honor the spread of choices promised in the menu. On the part of the diners, they also have to honor the choices they have made after they have composed their meals; they cannot change their mind once the order has been placed. What's more, they must pay for the choices they have made![14]

Inspired by speech-act theories (see Austin 1962), I propose to understand the menu as a "text act" (see Chau 2006: 92–98; 2008). A text act is an instance of writing that exerts its power more through its form (e.g., size, materiality, legibility, etc.) and performative context (e.g., placement, the source of enunciation, felicitous conditions, etc.) than through its referential meaning. Classic examples of text acts include Daoist talismans (with magical writing that is intended for the deities rather than humans), Maoist revolutionary slogan murals (usually immense in size), Qur'anic inscriptions around mosques (rarely for one to read), and so on. The "audience" (not so much readers) of these text acts are supposed to feel their power and act accordingly (e.g. to submit in awe, to respond with fervor, etc.). The fancier the restaurant, the more text-act qualities the menu takes on. Far from being simply a list of dishes, an haute-cuisine restaurant menu (together with the décor, the uniformed wait staff, and the often unusually long wine list, etc.) performs as an instrument of intimidation and culinary subjugation.

The waiter's order slip, inscribed with the dishes chosen by the diner, is a particular kind of text act, which is very similar in nature to the Daoist talisman in Chinese religious culture. Simply put, Daoist talismans (usually pieces of paper inscribed with magical signs by a Daoist priest) are symbolic weapons employed in magical actions commanding or combating invisible forces such as deities or demons.[15] As opposed to the most common form

---

14. Numeracy is indeed an important skill in the act of ordering dishes in a restaurant, as the diner is not simply ordering dishes that he or she likes but also mentally calculating if he or she can afford the eventual total cost of the meal thus composed.

15. Implicit in the use of talismans is a particular view on the sources of danger or misfortune. Unlike many societies where misfortune is perceived as originating from human agents (e.g., sorcerers), the Daoist talismanic world assumes an innocent human world and an unseen world full of evil spirits and baleful forces, and that humans are constantly in need of divine assistance to ward off evil spirits

of symbolic weapon found in almost all cultures, that is, incantations and curses, talismans are unique in their combination of material presence (e.g., paper, ink), visual representational form (the talismanic form), and the message contained in the talisman (e.g., "Demons be quelled!").[16] Talismans are often characterized as being tallies, whereby two halves of something are brought together to affirm authority. The etymology of the character *fu* (符) for talisman is indeed tallies. Yet the most common forms of talismans do not work as tallies at all; rather, they are more like a "potency tender" (the symbolic equivalent of legal tender, e.g., a money note) to effect some kind of divine interference in human affairs. To the extent that the waiter's order slip can magically command the cooks to yield the dishes ordered by the customers, it, too, is a potency tender.

---

and noxious miasmas. Daoist priests are specialists whose training has endowed them with the ability to command divine help in expelling evil forces. And the talismans are their weapon of choice. Most importantly, people have come to *recognize* the power of the talismans as efficacious. Talismans come in a wide variety of forms and materials, but the most common form is some combination of graphic elements and writing written in red (vermillion) ink on one side of a thin piece of rectangular-shaped yellow paper. The dimensions vary widely as well, though usually talismans are about one foot in length and four or five inches in width. Talismans have a long history in the Daoist tradition. There are over three thousand basic talismans that have been preserved in the Daoist Canon (Daozang), an authoritative collection of Daoist scriptures and manuals. The use of talismans is still very popular in contemporary Chinese societies (mainland China, Taiwan, Hong Kong, and Chinese communities in Southeast Asia and other parts of the world).

16. There are many parallels between Chinese talisman practices and Islamic and other "magical" practices, especially in the mixed use of incantation and writing. The anthropologist Michael Lambek describes Mayotte sorcery technique:

You tell the spirit what you want done and you give it a gift of food. If it accepts the food, then you know it will do your bidding. You write your name, the name of the person to be attacked, and the *wafaku* (a spell in a grid diagram that indicates how you want the victim to be affected) on a piece of paper. Then you fold the paper and put it around the neck of a chicken like a *hiriz* (amulet), whispering over and over again the name of the person you wish to harm. You slaughter the chicken, drenching the *sairy* and the written message in its blood. The spirit comes to eat the blood, reads the message, and immediately rushes off in search of the victim. (Lambek 1993: 243–44)

CONCLUSIONS: TRANSLOCUTIONAL/TRANSINSCRIPTIONAL PROCESSES

Traditionally, anthropology tended to emphasize the spoken and orality, and treated texts mostly as dormant documents (or at best as "text-artifacts" that are mostly transcriptions and reproductions/recreations of once oral utterances; see Silverstein and Urban 1996), because most anthropologists studied nonliterate societies. In these societies, where the introduction of writing was recent and literacy not widespread, religious and political authorities were still most often anchored and expressed through oratory and the mastery of forms of utterance. In anthropology, the emphasis on orality is closely linked to the disciplinary desire to directly represent the natives' voices. Verbal utterances denote immediacy, and verbatim transcriptions of verbal utterances denote faithfulness to the original. The highly sophisticated subdiscipline of linguistic anthropology deals with the oral almost exclusively (as evidenced, for example, by articles in linguistic anthropology journals). Because of its capacity to call forth multiple waves of iteration and inscription along "iterative/inscriptional stations," the menu allows us to think more critically and creatively about the relationship between orality and the written, and how the written (i.e., inscriptions) can be incorporated more prominently into studies on linguistic and cultural translation (see, e.g., Hanks 2010 and this volume).

More than merely a piece of paper (or cardboard), the menu is at once a *parole* (though the broader menu universe carries *langue* qualities), a cultural logic (or menu-logic?), a sociocognitive tool, a generative and structuring principle, a narrative, an organizational device (conceptual, taxonomic, as well as social), a civilizing machine, a conduit of (culinary) governmentality,[17] an ideological vehicle (e.g., about choice, freedom, taste, culturedness, civility, cosmopolitanism, social class, etc.), an ideological state apparatus in the Althusserian sense, a textographic fetish or text act (Chau 2006, 2008), and so on. Each menu is a cosmo-menu (which is why in order to explain the menu to our imaginary premenu, prerestaurant tribal natives, we have to explain our whole world). But above all, and more specific to the theme of this volume on "translating worlds," the menu is one of many "iterative/inscriptional stations" in the ensemble of acts of translation, or, more precisely, translocution and transinscription.

---

17. See Coveney, Begley, and Gallegos (2012) for a discussion on "savoir fare" (i.e., food savvy) as a form of governmentality.

ACKNOWLEDGMENTS

I thank Carlo Severi and William Hanks for their kind invitation to participate in the Hau–Fyssen workshop on "Translating Worlds," which took place at the Fyssen Foundation in Paris on March 20–21, 2014. I am particular grateful to the four Hau reviewers of the first submitted version of this article for their critical and useful comments and suggestions (two of these reviewers made additional, stimulating comments and suggestions on the revised version). Thanks also to Carlo Severi, Geoffrey Lloyd, Giovanni da Col, Steve Jones, Roel Sterckx, Philippe Descola, Hideko Mitsui, the other Hau–Fyssen workshop participants, and many others who have recommended useful sources, shared "menu stories," commented on earlier drafts, and discussed ideas with me. Justin Dyer at Hau improved this article's readability with his expert copyediting. The title of the article had input from Giovanni da Col and Joel Robbins.

REFERENCES

Austin, John L. 1962. *How to do things with words*. Cambridge, MA: Harvard University Press.

Bakhtin, Mikhail M. 1981. *The dialogic imagination: Four essays*. Edited by Michael Holquist. Translated by Caryl Emerson and Michael Holquist. Austin: University of Texas Press.

Bourdieu, Pierre. (1979) 1984. *Distinction: A social critique of the judgement of taste*. Translated by Richard Nice. Cambridge, MA: Harvard University Press.

Carlin, Martha. 2008. "'What say you to a piece of beef and mustard?': The evolution of public dining in medieval and Tudor London." *Huntington Library Quarterly* 71 (1): 199–217.

Chau, Adam Yuet. 2006. *Miraculous response: Doing popular religion in contemporary China*. Stanford: Stanford University Press.

———. 2008. "An awful mark: Symbolic violence and urban renewal in reform-era China," *Visual Studies* 23 (3): 195–210.

———. 2013. "Religious subjectification: The practice of cherishing written characters and being a Ciji (Tzu Chi) person." In *Chinese popular religion: Linking fieldwork and theory*, edited by Chang Hsun, 75–113. Taipei: Academia Sinica.

Coveney, John, Andrea Begley, and Daniella Gallegos. 2012. "'Savoir fare': Are cooking skills a new morality?" *Australian Journal of Adult Learning* 52 (3): 617–42.

Douglas, Mary. (1972) 1999. "Deciphering a meal." In *Implicit meanings: Selected essays in anthropology*, 231–51. London: Routledge.

Dudek, Nir. 2008. "Reading a plate." *Gastronomica: The Journal of Food and Culture* 8 (2): 51–54.

Eco, Umberto. (1979) 1984. *The role of the reader: Explorations in the semiotics of texts*. Indianapolis: Indiana University Press.

Elias, Norbert. (1939) 1994. *The civilizing process*. Translated by Edmund Jephcott. Oxford: Blackwell.

Freedman, Paul. 2011. "American restaurants and cuisine in the mid-nineteenth century." *The New England Quarterly* 84 (1): 5–59.

Freeman, Michael. 1977. "Sung." In *Food in Chinese culture: Anthropological and historical perspectives*, edited by Kwang-chih Chang, 141–76. New Haven, CT: Yale University Press.

Goody, Jack. 1977. *The domestication of the savage mind*. Cambridge: Cambridge University Press.

———. 1986. *The logic of writing and the organization of society*. Cambridge: Cambridge University Press.

———. 1987. *The interface between the written and the oral*. Cambridge: Cambridge University Press.

Haley, Andrew P. 2012. "The nation before taste: The challenges of American culinary history." *The Public Historian* 34 (2): 53–78.

Hanks, William F. 2010. *Translating words: Maya in the age of the cross*. Berkeley: University of California Press.

Hawkins, Rush C., and William J. Fanning. 1893. "The American hotel of today." *The North American Review* 157. https://archive.org/stream/northamreview157miscrich/northamreview157miscrich_djvu.txt.

Kaufman, Cathy K. 2002. "Structuring the meal: The revolution of *service à la Russe*." In The meal: Proceedings of the Oxford Symposium on Food and Cookery, edited by Harlan Walker, 123–33. Totnes, UK: Prospect Books.

Lambek, Michael. 1993. *Knowledge and practice in Mayotte: Local discourses of Islam, sorcery, and spirit possession*. Toronto: University of Toronto Press.

Latour, Bruno. 1986. "Visualization and cognition: Thinking with eyes and hands." *Knowledge and Society: Studies in the Sociology of Culture Past and Present* 6: 1–40.

Ledderose, Lothar. 2001. *Ten thousand things: Module and mass production in Chinese art*. Princeton, NJ: Princeton University Press.

Lévi-Strauss, Claude. (1958) 1963. "The effectiveness of symbols." In *Structural anthropology*. Translated by Claire Jacobson and Brooke Grundfest Schoepf, 181–201. New York: Basic Books.

MacDonogh, Giles. 1987. *A palate in revolution: Grimod de la Reynière and the Almanach des Gourmands*. London: Robin Clark.

McCawley, James D. 1984. *The eater's Guide to Chinese Characters*. Chicago: University of Chicago Press.

Pembroke, James. 2013. *Growing up in restaurants: The story of eating out in Britain from 55 BC to nowadays*. London: Quartet.

Rice, Jeff. 2011. "Menu literacy." Special issue, "Food theory," *PRE/TEXT: A Journal of Rhetorical Theory* 22 (1–4): 119–31.

Severi. Carlo. (2007) 2015. *The chimera principle: An anthropology of memory and imagination*. Translated by Janet Lloyd. Chicago: Hau Books.

Silverstein, Michael, and Greg Urban, eds. 1996. *Natural histories of discourse*. Chicago: University of Chicago Press.

Trillin, Calvin. 2004. *Feeding a yen: Savoring local specialties, from Kansas City to Cuzco*. New York: Random House.

CHAPTER SEVEN

All translation is radical translation

Bruce Mannheim

RADICAL TRANSLATION

In his influential *Word and object* (1960) and in related essays, the philosopher
W. V. O. Quine introduced the notion of *radical translation* through a parable:
Imagine a linguist in a forest making contact with an individual who speaks
only a language that the linguist does not; the linguist has no intermediaries, no
translation manuals such as bilingual dictionaries, and no interpreter. During
their interaction, a rabbit darts by, and the linguist's interlocutor points to it and
says "gavagai." The linguist makes a mental note of it as gavagai = rabbit. But,
Quine observers, the linguist's equivalence, gavagai = rabbit is not warranted
by the stimulus. For example, it might be a guess on the part of the linguist's
interlocutor, as rabbits had been seen in the area; it might be rather "animal," its
color, "rabbit flies," "it runs," and so forth. These can be tested by aligning the
linguist's "stimulus meanings" with the interlocutor's. But even were the linguist
to pin down precisely what objects are pointed to, it would not disambiguate
the reference as we cannot be certain that "gavagai" denotes "rabbit" rather than
"undetached rabbit parts." Here Quine suggests that the denotational treatment of "rabbit" as an integral whole is a product of the obligatory grammatical categories of English (in the Boasian sense; Jakobson 1959; Whorf 1945)

rather than something that is given a priori, and thus that a calibration of gavagai = rabbit depends on the prior translational calibration of grammatical categories such as definiteness, number, and person (see Silverstein 2003). Not only is reference indeterminate on the basis of individual stimuli; so too is ontology[1] indeterminate, made determinate only within the framework of grammar. In this case, Quine warns us "entification begins at arms length," projected through the obligatory grammatical categories of the language in question.

What makes translation *radical* for Quine, then, even in the relatively restricted domain of denotational equivalence (and the even more restricted domain of concretely denotational nouns) is the absence of shared scaffolding: no translation manuals, no interpreters, no common grammatical structures through which denotational equivalences can be calibrated. These normally provide language-to-language scaffolding of translation. In addition, because the ontological commitments of a speaker are grounded in her linguistic practices—especially in the grammatical system—denotational equivalences across languages cannot be grounded in a shared ontology.

I do not wish to leave you with the impression that Quine's thought experiment, now more than fifty years old, can serve as the foundation for a theory of translation today. Indeed, Quine's own students, especially Donald Davidson and Saul Kripke, saw to that. And while Quine restricted himself to a narrow

---

1. "Ontology" is currently a contested term in anthropology, used in multiple ways that bear only fleeting resemblance to each other. My own approach to ontology, essentially "what there is" in the world is grounded in analytic philosophy and strongly influenced by Quine's *Word and object.* There are three key pieces to it that I have found especially useful for discussing ontology in cultural terms: *ontological projection,* that what there is projected from and constituted by language and other social practices (my term, essentially an operationalization of Quine's slogan that "entification begins at arm's length"); *ontological* (or *ontic*) *commitment,* that engaging in talk and in other social practices entails that speakers commit tacitly to the world having a particular configuration; and *ontological relativity,* which follows from the first two principles. My own work largely concerns how ontological are produced by social practices or by social practices plus cognitive mechanisms, concentrating in four areas: properties of the world (for example the "river/rock" example discussed below; hierarchical social ontology (Mannheim, 2015a); spatial orientation and principles of semiotic interpretation (Mannheim 1995; 2015a: ch. 9; forthcoming b); agency (most discussions of ontology in social anthropology focusing on this area; Mannheim and Salas Carreño 2014); and causal structures (Gelman et al., forthcoming; Sánchez Tapia et al., forthcoming). My work on ontology is closest in spirit to Descola (2005) and Viveiros de Castro (1998), though with substantial methodological differences.

spectrum of language—denotation and grammatical categories—linguists and anthropologists today work with a far more expansive (and more complex) range of practices. Finally, Quine framed his argument in terms of a behaviorist psychology that was crumbling intellectually while he was writing. Consider though, three challenges to the Quinean model that bear more directly on the practices of social anthropologists and linguists: (1) "radical translation" does not characterize their practices in the field; (2) denotational meaning is only a narrow band of what is at stake in translation—particularly between two languages that are not closely related; and (3) there are ontological commitments built into cognitive processes that transcend linguistic and cultural differences without sacrificing Quine's austere ontology.

Rarely, if ever, do anthropologists or linguists find themselves in the circumstances of the linguist of Quine's parable, working without a history of prior contact that allows them to scaffold the encounter, be it in the form of translation manuals, grammars, or interpreters (euphemistically called "research assistants" even though they are not). Nor was the "monolingual elicitation exercise" made famous by the linguist Kenneth Pike—in which he sat across a table and elicited forms from a speaker of a language with which he had prior exposure—an instance of radical translation. The elicitation took place in an institutionally scaffolded environment, in which both the "informant" and the linguist had specific expectations as to the nature of the exercise, particularly that they would seek denotational and grammatical equivalences. Closer to radical translation was the first contact by Spanish invaders in South America. As legend goes, they encountered a fisherman who said "biru," though there is no way of knowing whether it meant "this is biru," "I am fishing," "Get the hell out of here," "Who are you?" or "undetached rabbit parts, this way." Regardless, "Biru" became the name of the river, and eventually of the country, Perú. The poor fisherman was captured and pressed into service as a "tongue," an interpreter; it was commonplace for Spaniards to travel with several interpreters, who would translate in a chain.

More common however (and perhaps routine for ethnographers) are pragmatic approximations of radical translation:

Speakers of Yanqa-simi move from place to place on rickety old blue and grey busses on which a child collects fares and acts as a conductor. As people are about to get on the bus the child yells "su-u-u-uwe-e-e-ee" and the bus stops. "Aha!" you surmise, "'su-u-u-uwe-e-e-ee' is the Yanqa-simi utterance 'stop.'" You repeatedly observe the child and others like him get buses to stop by yelling, "su-u-u-uwe-e-e-ee." One day the bus rides past your stop. Alarmed, you realize that there is only one thing to do. You shout, "su-u-u-uwe-e-e-ee." The bus grinds to a halt. You smile, thank the driver and get off the bus. You are pleased, because you have mastered the pragmatics of Yanqa-simi sufficiently well to get the bus to stop when you needed to do so. Everybody on the bus looks puzzled. There is nobody waiting to get on. Eventually you will learn from the many other utterances of Yanqa-simi you hear, speak, and speak about, that you should have yelled "baja" "getting off" and not "sube" "getting on." (Mannheim 1986: 47–48)

Alongside concretely denotational expressions and the structured grammatical systems that anchor them, qua Quine's argument—and that already challenge older and still traditional ideas of translation (Keane 2006)—are the relationships among concepts: lexical and textual; the pragmatic (see Severi, this volume); the indexical linkages that connect the expressions to verbal and behavioral contexts and imbue them with cultural and social value. Michael Silverstein (2003) coined the expression "transduction" for this on analogy to the transduction of energy from one physical system to another, "capturing . . . how both source expression and target expression point to appropriate contexts and create effective contexts in systems of use as verbally mediated social action" (2003: 85).

For example, without recognizing that for Quechua speakers, *mayu* "river" and *qaqa* "rock" have a semantically privative relationship,[2] and are consequently ontologically intertwined (rock flows like a river; Mannheim 1986: 63) it would be impossible to make sense of the iconics of living rock carved to resemble a water fall, of carved stone pathways for water, of the fluidity of rock itself among the (Quechua-speaking) Inkas (Cummins and Mannheim 2011). This relationship is not apparent in translating *mayu* and *qaqa* word-for-word, but requires an *analytic transduction* of both semantics and use of material form, the semantic relationship doubly entextualized in Quechua lyric and in the built environment. Moreover, to reduce them denotationally is to perform another kind of transduction, an *appropriative transduction*, one in which they are reintegrated into an alien configuration—ours—where they at best appear an exotic semiotic turn, at best appreciated through connoisseurship.[3]

---

2.   I discuss the conceptual semantics of nonobvious privative relationships such as that between *mayu* "river" and *qaqa* "rock" in Mannheim (1998).

3.   See Silverstein's related point that "we anthropologists seem easily to despair of the

Indeed, Silverstein (2003: 91) warns us that "in transduction, operating as we do in the domain of culture more frankly, there is always the possibility of transformation of the [en]textual[ized] source material contextualized in specific ways into configurations of cultural semiosis of a sort substantially or completely different from those one has started with." Transduction can encompass a translation more narrowly understood, evoking the contextualizations of one culture-and-language in another, or it can recontextualize it so thoroughly that it is no longer recognizable, but serves the social, political, or cultural interests of the other, in other words, an *appropriative transduction*. I return to the distinction between analytic and appropriative transduction in section 3, below.

COGNITION, CORE AND OTHERWISE

Quine admitted that an average field linguist would intuitively translate gavagai as "rabbit," rather than alternatives as "undetached rabbit parts": "The implicit maxim guiding his choice of 'rabbit'. . . is that an enduring and relatively homogenous object, moving as a whole against a contrasting background, is a likely referent for a short expression" (1969: 191). In the intervening half century, substantial experimental research by cognitive psychologists has moved many of the questions traditionally raised by philosophers onto an empirical plane. The individuation of objects such as rabbits is accomplished by mental structures that psychologist Susan Carey (2009, ch. 3) calls core cognition, "highly structured innate mechanisms designed to build representations with specific content," in the case of individuation identifiable in very young infants, younger than a year old, with converging evidence provided by numerous other researchers. Their reliance on spatio-temporal features to individuate objects effectively rules out translations such as "undetached rabbit parts" or "rabbit in a particular slice of time." But notice that core cognition constrains but does not specify a denotational set of ontological categories. Indeed, while Quine's gavagai example is absolutely falsified, there are features of the Quinean framework that are compatible with core cognition. Core cognition retains Quine's

---

transduction necessary to deal ethnographically with key labels for cultural concepts (2003: 88). Explications of "key concepts" cited in the original language without the corresponding (analytical) transduction amount to a reductionist appropriation of these concepts; they mystify rather than clarify.

a priori ontological austerity (the world does not contain a priori entities that are merely named); ontological projection ("entification begins at arm's length"), though grammatical categories do not have the exclusive (or perhaps any) role in projecting ontological categories; and within the limits of core cognition, ontological relativity.

The development of concepts for kinds (dogs, llamas, gold, chairs) produces a similar picture (Gelman and Coley 1991; S. Gelman 2003; Mannheim and Gelman 2013). In a traditional framework, the world was populated with entities, and concepts built up by observing similarities among the entities. In contrast, cognitive psychologists have adduced evidence that concepts emerge from more general and broad knowledge that people have about the world—that concepts are embedded in overarching theories (e.g., Gelman and Williams 1998; Gopnik and Wellman 1994; Keil 1991; Murphy and Medin 1985; Simons and Keil 1995; Wellman and Gelman 1998). These tacit theories establish ontologies, causal relationships, and unobservable entities specific to domains. From this point of view, the early acquisition of concepts is not strictly perceptual in origin but is related to broader ontological configurations (for example, a distinction between animate and inanimate entities) and expectations regarding the causal laws of which the concepts are part (for example, a dog is initially classified as a living being, an agent capable of autonomous movement). The tacit theories that scaffold concept formation are specific to domains (psychology, biology, physics, and so forth), and have domain-specific object-ontologies built into them, and these are in turn attributed to the kinds subsumed by them. (Kinds are routinely subsumed under multiple domains.) Yet there is crosslinguistic and crosscultural variability in the recruitment of concepts to domains (in Quechua, both mountains and rock are frequently treated as living kinds, whereas in English neither is) and in the causal structures assigned to domains. For both Quechua- and English-speaking adults, properties of artifacts are normally explained in terms of human-directed teleology; for living kinds however, Quechua adults commonly explain the properties of living kinds by appealing to an inevitable natural order to the animal world, whereas US adults had more of a "design" perspective on biological features, constructing explanations of animal features in an artifactualist mode (Sánchez Tapia et al., forthcoming).

Like core cognition, domain-specific theory constrains but does not specify concepts and ontology. (Indeed, as frameworks they may well be fully continuous.) Assignment of entities to domains can vary culturally, and the causal structures vary both culturally and developmentally. Key aspects of "radical translation" are retained in the two cognitive frameworks, particularly what I will call "ontological projection"—that is, that the objects of denotational relationships are not a priori but are projected from encompassing cognitive structures.

Whatever translation is for the anthropologist, then, it cannot be a mere matter of identifying denotational equivalences—that is, replacing one set of linguistic forms for a denotatum with another nor a reliance on translation manuals, which usually consist of sets of denotational equivalences. Rather, ethnographic translation would look like an updated version of Quine's "radical translation" grounded in evidence linguistic and cognitive, and embedded in the contexts of use and lexical and indexical relationships, in other words an analytic transduction.[4] The goal of this article is then, to recuperate Quine's notion of "radical translation" within a framework that is richer ethnographically, linguistically, and cognitively. So recuperated, "radical translation" is interchangeable with "analytic transduction."

I illustrate this with examples from Southern Peruvian Quechua, the Inka *lengua general* (Cerrón-Palomino 1987; Mannheim 1991; Durston 2014), still spoken in the six southeastern departments of Peru and by émigrés to the major Peruvian cities and beyond. The first Quechua translation manuals were produced in the middle to late sixteenth century, in religious settings (Durston 2007), and traditions for denotational equivalence established in the colonial era have persisted to the present day, where they are rendered in scores of bilingual dictionaries. But because these translation traditions (Collins 1983) were aligned to Spanish semantics and contexts of use (in other words were "appropriative transductions") they have distinct ontological projections from translations that are instead rooted in the practices of "radical translation" or "analytical transduction." An added complexity of the Quechua case is that the language has socially stratified registers, one of which—an elite register—is in fact semantically aligned with Spanish and has served as a template for establishing denotational equivalence with Spanish (and through Spanish with other world languages), much as has been the case for Tok Pisin vis-à-vis Ku Waru (Rumsey, this volume) and Maya Reducido vis-à-vis colloquial registers of Yucatecan Maya (Hanks 2010 and this volume). In the following two sections I lay out the social and historical settings of the elite register of Quechua and the

4.   Quine himself laid out a detailed procedure by which the linguist could ascertain the denotational translation of an expression, contextualized sentence by contextualized sentence, providing a rough, if utterly unmanageable methodology.

consequences for translation practices, and then work through some instances in which the semantics of the elite register—represented in the translation manuals—differs substantially from that of the colloquial registers. The takeaway lesson is that the common practice that ethnographers and archaeologists have of citing Quechua expressions accompanied by denotationally equivalent translations are misleading culturally and ontologically, and needs to be replaced by something closer to radical translation.

THE OVERLAY

The sociology of Quechua register stratification has a historical depth of almost five hundred years, first under Spanish rule (1532–1821), and under the Lima-centered republic. While their administrative and missionary structures were set in place in the first fifty years after the conquest, the settlement of Peru by Spaniards was uneven—Spaniards settled the coast and the newly-founded cities of the highlands (many of which subsumed prior indigenous settlements); in rural areas (for a primarily agrarian populace), in contrast, the presence of the Spanish empire was primarily administrative/legal and economic, the latter through estates owned by Spaniards or their American-born descendants or through fairly massive mining projects, without an appreciable settler population (Garrett 2005, ch. 2). Even those who lived in urban areas (such as Cuzco, Huamanga, Huanta, Arequipa, Cochabamba, and so forth) spoke Quechua as well as Spanish (and often to each other, a reflection of their regional allegiances). The pattern remained consistent until the middle of the twentieth century (Mannheim, forthcoming a).

Thus, it should not be surprising that the "interlanguage" that emerged was a special register (or variety) of Spanish-inflected Quechua, which developed primarily among provincial elites and traders (Itier 2000, on "Quechua general"), in tandem with a specifically religious register of Quechua (Durston 2007), both in urban settings such as Cochabamba, Puno, Ayacucho, and Cuzco, and among owners of rural estates (Lavallé 1987; Mannheim 1991: 71–74; 1992; Itier 1995; Cerrón-Palomino 1997). These registers brought Quechua lexical, morphological, and phonological forms into alignment with Spanish semantics and pragmatics. Indeed, for demographic reasons, Spanish-inflected local registers of Quechua were a much more common "intermediary" between the languages than were Quechua-inflected local varieties of Spanish, at least until the early part of the twentieth century.

There are three primary registers of Southern Quechua, distinguished by the linguistic histories of the speakers and indexed by the phonological systems of the register, particularly by the ways in which they use the supralaryngeal parts of their vocal tract. Register one (henceforth R1) speakers, the vast majority, are monolingual speakers of Quechua, perhaps with some Spanish, but with no accommodation to the Spanish phonological system. Register two (R2) is a smaller but substantial part of the Quechua-speaking population that speaks Spanish as a second language; R2 speakers have accommodated their phonological systems in Quechua to Spanish, but speak Spanish with a noticeable Quechua accent, particularly when it comes to the vowels of Spanish—they tend to have vowels that are more centralized than the corresponding vowels of first-language Spanish speakers. Register three (R3) speakers are a very small minority of Quechua speakers. R3 speakers are first language Spanish speakers who have learned Quechua, and speak their variety of Quechua quite fluently but have adapted the sound system of Quechua to Spanish. These include former owners and administrators of landed estates (haciendas), their older children, and people who have had major commercial or administrative business in the countryside, but also others who have official business in Quechua-speaking regions: professionals workers in nongovernmental organizations, and many people professionally engaged with the promotion and teaching of Quechua. The distinctions among registers of Quechua are indexed by a purely formal phonological process—which other than rhematizing differences among speakers has no semantic or ideological load of its own.[5]

From an articulatory point of view, the social differentiation of the vowel system revolves around the degree of opening—the aperture of the buccal cavity. First-language Quechua speakers (R1 and R2) use a relatively narrow aperture, first-language Spanish speakers (R3) use a relatively wide one. The fine muscle control involved in buccal aperture, as in other somatic aspects of behavior, such as gesture and gait, is habituated in early childhood, and though plastic, is relatively resistant to change. Buccal aperture is distinct among monolingual speakers of Quechua, speakers who are dominant in Quechua but also speak Spanish, and speakers who are dominant in Spanish but also speak Quechua. There are differences among the registers both with respect to the inventories of sounds

---

5.   My use of "register" here departs from more common uses in which it is possible for individual speakers to shift from one register to another (see Agha 2004). In this case, the registers are rigidly indexed to speakers.

they use and of the ways in which phonological processes work. (These are detailed in Pérez Silva, Acurio Palma, and Bendezú Arauja [2009] and Mannheim [forthcoming a].)

These differences are enregistered—recognized by Quechua speakers themselves, though not consciously, and used as the basis for making social judgments about each other, including social exclusion. Huayhua's study (reported in Huayhua, n.d.), carried out in a community just outside of Cusco, tested the distinction between R1 and R2 speakers (grouped together) and R3 speakers and found that speakers could identify the social origins of each guise with astonishing accuracy, regardless of the language being spoken, and evaluated the personal qualities of the speaker represented by the guise accordingly. The guises included two in Quechua and two in Spanish; for each language one guise was spoken with narrow aperture, and one with wide aperture. *All* of the first-language Quechua speakers and more than 90 percent of the first-language Spanish speakers identified the guises accurately and evaluated the guises socially according to aperture.

The differences in sound pattern are accompanied by enregistered differences in syntax, grammatical semantics, lexical meaning, and interactional routines. For example, along with a nominative-accusative agreement system (in which the agent of an action is the grammatical subject, as in English or Spanish), R1 has an ergative agreement system in subordinate clauses (in which the agent of a transitive verb is marked morphologically), and a semantic alignment system (in which the verb determines what or who is agentive), both of which greatly expand the options for expressing semantic agency (for a discussion and examples, see Mannheim and Salas Carreño 2014: 51–52). R3, in contrast, has its range of agreement possibilities limited to a Spanish-style nominative-accusative system. R1 treats possessive phrases as syntactic islands, closely binding an object to its possessor, with the object usually following immediately after the possessor; R3 does not. In R1, introducing oneself includes mention of the place one is from, almost always before one's name. In R3, in contrast, one introduces oneself (as in Spanish) by name only. In R1, the default form of narrative is conversational, requiring input, and at least assent from other participants in the speech event (Mannheim and Van Vleet 1998). In R3, it is monological. Such expressions as *"Allin p'unchay"* (Good day), *"añay"* (thank you), and *"allin kawsay"* (good life) are all innovations in R3, contrasting with *"Allillanchu/allillanmi"* (Is it good? / It's good), *"urpi sunqu"* (dove essence, focusing on the social relationship), and *"allin ñan"* (good road, usually wished to newlyweds), respectively. In short, R3 is regimented to Spanish-language linguistic and social practices, phonologically, syntactically, lexically, and pragmatically. Conversely, self-translations into Spanish by a speaker of R2 frequently reflect an underlying Quechua semantic, even as they are spoken with grammatically appropriate Spanish forms. A speaker of English or Spanish who asks directions of an R2 speaker in Spanish is likely to receive a reply that is grounded in the Quechua allocentric-intrinsic frame of reference, meaning that it will be a series of named landmarks, rather than a series of instructions that track the position of the person asking directions—and would find themselves lost.[6] In short, the division between R3 as opposed to R1 and R2 is not merely one of style; they live in different worlds with many of the same labels attached.

While the three registers look more-or-less equivalent on paper, in fact they are also vastly different demographically. Once one leaves the cities, young children speak Quechua monolingually and are exposed to Spanish only in the school system. The overwhelming majority of adults use R1, and a substantial minority R2. In rural areas, R3 is limited to a small minority of first-language Spanish speakers, though it is quite common in cities, creating the illusion that it is dominant.

The register hierarchy constrains the knowledge we have of Quechua language and culture (and so constrains the representation of Quechua language and culture in the Andean republics, in public media and in the schools), encapsulating the language and culture of speakers of R1 within R2 and R3. Scholars such as linguists and anthropologists are more likely to find their research intermediated by Spanish-inflected Quechua than by the Quechua of monolinguals, and to not recognize the fundamental differences between them. Pretenses to the intimacy of fieldwork notwithstanding, scholarly knowledge of the Andean languages and cultures is filtered through the overlay of R3, meaning that language structure and social practice are both rendered invisible, and that—insofar as it is grounded in denotational equivalence—translation is regimented conceptually to Spanish, the utterances of R1 and R2 speakers (appropriatively) transduced to fit a Spanish-language ontology. What we are facing is the flipside

---

6. In "allocentric" systems (like Quechua), the speech event and specific features of the physical environment is the frame of reference for activities important and mundane; in contrast, in "egocentric" systems (like English), the frame of reference is projected from the speaker. There is substantial comparative research (e.g., Levinson [2003]; Danziger [2010])—largely experimental—that shows variability among languages, constrained within narrow typological parameters.

of James Scott's (1998) notion of "legibility," through which populations that cannot easily be shoehorned into the rationality of a state-ordered society find that their language, culture, and social relations are literally rendered invisible in favor of proxies, the *overlay* (in linguistic terms, the Spanish-inflected Quechua that I described above).

What appears to be a native Quechua conceptual framework then, is frequently, the Spanish-inflected overlay. And conversely, because the R3 register projects a Spanish-based ontology, utterances by R1 and R2 speakers interpreted through the R3 ontology sometimes seem skewed: surreal, figurative, and opaque. For example the Quechua verb *rantiy* is usually translated in bilingual dictionaries as "comprar" (to buy), and its nominalization *rantina* as "species" (in the sense of currency). Nonetheless, the consensus view of Inka political economy was that it was based on a primary system of movement of labor (not of goods) with a secondary system of redistribution of surpluses, with an absence of internal markets (Murra 1956; D'Altroy and Earle 1985). A commonplace—and in my estimation not especially insightful—objection to this view was the existence of a verb meaning "to buy," the argument resting on the overlay, the R3 denotational equivalence. What does ranti mean in the vernacular?

Consider a baptism in which I participated, in which members of the family of the godchild spoke either only Quechua or Quechua with limited Spanish. In rural Peru, it is customary for the godparents to participate as a couple, and my wife was in the United States. After much discussion, it was decided that a ritual kinswoman of mine would participate as her *ranti*, which made my wife, not the ritual kinswoman, the godmother of the child. For the purpose of the baptism, the ritual kinswoman was the duplicate of my wife. The logic of duplication of a being (again, ranti) pervaded Inka political and ritual organization: the earliest chronicles identify multiple individuals as Inka, sent to the provinces with the powers of the Inka king (*Incap rantin*, Guaman Poma [1980/1615] 1987: 186), Similarly, the Inkas founded multiple versions of their capital city, Cuzco (*otro Cuzco*, Guaman Poma [1980/1615] 1987: 187). These were not merely administrative centers in the usual sense. Although like other Inka settlements, the landscapes of the "other Cuzcos" were attuned to their physical surroundings, the Inkas renamed the landscapes with the names of mountains and other places around the original Cuzco (Santillana 2012), rearticulating them as the ranti of their counterparts in Cuzco.

For *ranti*, denotational substitution ("to buy," "species"; R3) leads us into an analytical blind alley; radical translation challenges us to seek multiple, unexpected indexicalities and contexts of use and to build—transductively—a representation that accounts for the widest possible range of uses, contemporary and historical, and inter alia projects appropriately the ontological commitments of R1 and R2 speakers. Consider now some more complex cases of divergence in the ontological projections of translations-by-denotational-equivalence through translation manuals and radical translation (or "analytical transductions").

RADICAL TRANSLATION AS METHOD

Consider the Quechua verb *puriy*, which usually appears in translation manuals (R3) with the gloss "to travel." To be sure, there are circumstances in which this provides exactly the right translation, for example if I describe my travel from Peru to the United States or refer to someone as a traveler, a *puriq*. But in the following interview with a man (R1) from Checcacupe, a town in the Province of Canchis in Cuzco, we have a very different sense of *puriy*. He is describing what he calls "pukaras," a local term for mountain lords, and the interviewer is puzzled by the word.

The man explains:

> *Kukata huq yachayniyuqwan nawan k'intuchiyku chay pukarakunapaq purinanpaq.*
> We get someone who knows how to offer coca so that the pukaras *puriy*.

Interviewer: (overlaps) *Imataq chay pukarakuna sutin?*
And what are the names of the pukaras?

And the man continues:
> . . . *pukarakuna haqay* puri*nankupaqpuniyá.*
> . . . it's most certainly for the pukaras to *puriy*

And then answers the question:
> *Imayna . . . Chaypi Cheqakupipi ima urqukunaq, imacha sutin*
> How is it? There in Checcacupe, such-and-such mountains have such-and-such name.

In Quechua communities people are born into a relationship with the places
around them, particularly the mountains around them, and share an essence
with the places (and again, particularly with the mountains; see Salas Carreño,
forthcoming). The relationship is reinforced throughout the lifespan by regular
offerings of food and alcohol to the places, sometimes by the individuals themselves and sometimes through the mediation of a *paqu*, more "someone who
knows" how to perform the rite than a ritual specialist. The very last thing that
someone would do under such circumstances is make the offering in the expectation that the place or the mountain change location. Yet the man insisted
a second time that the offerings were made so that the mountains *puriy*. The
ethnographer now has a choice to make. He or she can decide that the speaker
really doesn't mean what he is saying or is speaking figuratively, though there
is no reason to suspect either one. (Recall Malinowski's [1935: 224] infamous
kluge, "the coefficient of weirdness.") Or he can give up the R3 denotational
equivalence *puriy* = "to travel."

If we reject the equation *puriy* = "to travel" we might take Quine's injunction
seriously to consider a broad range of contexts ("occasion sentences" in Quine's
formulation) or Silverstein's charge to attend to the indexical linkages that connect the expressions to verbal and behavioral contexts and imbue them with
cultural and social value. In the latter case there are lexical and entextualized
linkages to consider—*puriy* has a privative semantic relationship with another
verb, *tiyay* "to be in a single place," and these appear together in song texts
(Mannheim 1998). Here I sketch a range of contexts in which *puriy* is used,
some drawn from published materials. (The translations are mine.)

A description of a ritual offering by Alencastre and Dumézil (1953: 38–39)
is similar to the one I just discussed:

> *Wasiyuq runan sumaqta tiyarikun llapa ayllunkunawan; pay kikinmi paqumanta
> tiyaykun, hinaspataqmi pachamamaman awkikunaman platokunata haywan
> uywaq mirananta runaq allin* purin*anta mañaspa.*
>
> The householder sits himself beautifully with his house; he himself takes
> on the role of sorcerer; and so, plates [of food] are offered to pachamama
> (mother earth) while asking for fertility of the domestic animals and the
> well-being of the people.

Here I have translated *allin purinanta* as "well being."

Here are some other examples of *puriy*:

Imanaqtintaq hawa llaqta wachachakunari mana saq'apa simp'ayuqñachu pu-
rinku? (Cusihuamán Gutiérrez 1976: 79)

"And why don't young girls *go around* with braids anymore?"

Apuray puririy mana hinata tardiyasunchisri!

"Hurry up, get going so we don't become late!"

Allinta qhawarikuspa purinki. (Cusihuamán Gutiérrez 1976: 223)

"You should look carefully when you travel."

Allinchu reforma agraria purishan manachu?

"Is the Agrarian Reform going well or not?"

The R3 sense of *puriy*, codified in translation manuals is utterly unhelpful in understanding the range of uses of the word in even the small set of examples presented here. Conceptually (established in the privative relationship with *ti-yay*) and denotationally *puriy* has much broader range for R1 and R2 speakers than for R3 speakers, though the R3 sense is a proper subset of the range. There is no single-word or even phrasal equivalent in either Spanish or English that carries either the conceptual range of *puriy* or (ontologically) the action that it denotes.[7] We have no recourse other than to an analytic transduction of *puriy*, a context-by-context explication of its uses, and lexical and indexical relationships, in short, a fully ethnographic account.[8]

The problem of the overlay is multiplied by the historical path of the translation tradition. Consider the word *wak'a*, which is customarily translated as

---

7. See Harrison (1989: 159–61) for a comparable discussion of *puriy* in Ecuadorian Quichua.

8. Similarly, in discussing methodological criteria for semantic reconstruction in historical linguistics, Benveniste ([1954] 1971: 249) suggests that "the 'meaning' of a linguistic form is defined by the totality of its uses, by their distribution, and by the types of associations therefrom. In the presence of identical morphemes with different meanings, one must ask oneself whether there is some use in which the two meanings converge. The answer is never given in advance. It can only be found after a careful study of all the contexts in which the form may appear. One does not have the right to assume what the answer is, either positively or negatively on the basis of likelihood." Benveniste's goal was to establish a methodology for philologically oriented semantic reconstruction, but is every bit the methodological counterpart to "radical translation" and "analytic transduction."

(R3) "sacred object" or "shrine," with an emphasis on sacrality.[9] Like *puriy* the translation manuals are easy to falsify with respect to the "sacred object" translation of *wak'a*: Consider only the expression *siki wak'a*, "butt crack." While the R3 translation is a noun, in R1and R2, *wak'a* is ambivalent as to part of speech. Without further modification, it can be a noun, an adjective, and a verb (though not an adverb). As a verb, wak'a involves a change-of-state, from domestic to wild: *Chay michi wak'akushan* "That cat's gone wild"; or from a domestic species to a conceptually related species, such as a chicken turning into a condor a cat turning into an ocelot.[10] It can be used to denote a cleft, a fissure, a cavern, or a crevice, as in *riru wak'a*, "the crevices between the fingers," the aforementioned *siki wak'a* "butt crack," or in the phrase *makiyqa wak'ashanmi* to refer to the development of cracks in the skin of the hand (as, for example, occurs due to continual manipulation of nearly frozen water). It is ambivalent as to grammatical category; as a verb it can mean "to furrow," as one does when plowing. It also refers to deformities: a cleft-lipped or hare-lipped person or animal is *wak'a*, as is a person with six fingers. *Wak'a* is used to qualify places—such as rock formations, springs, pre-Hispanic cemeteries—as dangerous, risky, and associated with an evil agency toward humans. These places—many of which are difficult to get to—eat humans who dare to get close to them. In both the deformity and sacred senses of *wak'a*, it is an attribute. But it is important to recognize that in Quechua, unlike English, attributes are also ambivalent as to grammatical category, so *wak'a* can modify a noun but it can also be used in place of a noun. *Wak'a* alone would thus mean "a *wak'a* thing." And the ambivalence of *wak'a* as to grammatical category in R1 and R2—as an object, as an attribute, as an action, and as a change of state—means that the ontological projection of *wak'a* is radically different in the vernacular from the overlay. There are two key historical factors at play in shaping the overlay. First, colonial-era missionaries were obsessed with *wak'a*, as both concept and object. They brought with them a concern with non-Christian religious shrines, for which they initially used Arabic and Arawakan expressions before settling on *wak'a*. Their sermons modeled *wak'a*-as-shrine on the golden calf. And, following the grammatical categories of Spanish, they used the word *wak'a* as a "substantive"—that is, ambivalent between noun and adjective,

---

9. This discussion draws on a much more extensive account in Mannheim and Salas Carreño (2014).

10. For some speakers this is *waka*, with a plain rather than ejective stop.

with adjectival uses narrowed to "sacred." The second is as recent as the later nineteenth century, when *wak'a* was used in an even more restricted sense by Anglophone travelers and archaeologists to denote a "shrine"; in archaeology it has become a term of art, and has been back-borrowed into Spanish in that form. The Anglophone "tell" is that even in Spanish it is a noun, rather than a substantive.

As with *puriy*, the entries in translation manuals for *wak'a*—the R3 translational equivalences—conceal, rather than reveal, its semantic and ontological complexities. An ethnographer or a linguist who relies on translation manuals buys into a conceptual framework and a world that is utterly different from those inhabited by R1 and R2 speakers. Understanding *wak'a*, like understanding *puriy*, requires an ethnographically engaged radical translation, an analytic transduction. There is no single-word or even phrasal equivalent in either Spanish or English that carries either the conceptual range of *wak'a*.

Every translation requires the ethnographer to make substantive claims about Quechua ontological commitments, regardless of whether the ethnographer does so explicitly. Every translation requires an alignment to a specific, socially identifiable register of Quechua, again regardless of whether the ethnographer or linguist understands that they are doing so. Relying on translation manuals, as is the customary practice, entails an alignment to the overlay (R3), to its semantics regimented to Spanish, to its ontological commitments, to its pragmatics, and to its networks of cultural practices. To do so is to render the ethnography, linguistics, and history of (R1 and R2) speakers invisible. Only a reformulated radical translation—only an analytic transduction—will allow us to escape the limitations of the overlay.

Years ago, a now-well-known scholar of the Andes asked me rhetorically "What difference does it make if I look something up in Father Lira's dictionary (referring to a lexicographer of Quechua, R3) or ask a peasant (R1 or R2)?" Today my nonrhetorical answer is "It makes all the difference in the world." For an ethnographer, all translation is radical translation.

ACKNOWLEDGEMENTS

I am grateful to Susan A. Gelman for comments on an earlier draft.

REFERENCES

Agha, Asif. 2004. Registers of language. In *A companion to linguistic anthropology*, edited by Alessandro Duranti, 23–45. Cambridge: Cambridge University Press.

Alencastre, Andrés, and Georges Dumézil. 1953. "Fêtes et usages des indiens de Langui (province de Canas, Département du Cuzco)." *Journal de la Société des Américanistes* (n.s.) 42: 1–118.

Benveniste, Émile. (1954) 1971. *Problems in general linguistics.* Miami, FL: University of Miami Press.

Carey, Susan D. 2009. *The origin of concepts.* New York: Oxford University Press.

Cerrón-Palomino, Rodolfo. 1987. *Lingüística quechua.* Cuzco: Centro de Estudios Rurales Andinos "Bartolomé de las Casas."

———. 1997. "El diccionario quechua de los académicos." *Revista Andina* 15 (1): 151–205.

Collins, Jane. 1983. "Translation traditions and the organization of productive activity." In *Bilingualism: Social issues and policy implications*, edited by Andrew W. Miracle, 11–22. Athens: University of Georgia Press.

Cummins, Thomas, and Bruce Mannheim. 2011. "The river around us, The stream within us, the traces of the Sun and Inka kinetics." *Res* 59/60: 5–21.

Cusihuamán Gutiérrez, Antonio. 1976. *Gramática quechua: Cuzco-Collao.* Lima: Instituto de Estudios Peruanos.

D'Altroy, Terence N., and Timothy Earle. 1985. "Staple finance, wealth finance, and storage in the Inka political economy." *Current Anthropology* 26: 187–206.

Danziger, Eve. 2010. "Deixis, gesture and cognition in spatial frame of reference typology." *Studies in Language* 34 (1): 167–85.

Descola, Philippe. 2005. *Par: Delà nature et culture.* Paris: Gallimard.

Durston, Alan. 2007. *Pastoral quechua: The history of Christian translation in colonial Peru.* South Bend, IN: University of Notre Dame Press.

———. 2014. "Standard colonial quechua." In *Iberian Imperialism and Language Evolution in Latin America*, edited by Salikoko Mufwene, 225–43. Chicago: University of Chicago Press.

Garrett, David. 2005. *Shadows of empire: The Indian nobility of Cuzco, 1750–1825.* Cambridge: Cambridge University Press.

Gelman, Rochel, and Earl Williams. 1998. "Enabling constraints for cognitive development and learning: Domain specificity and epigenesis." In *Handbook of child psychology*, vol. 2 of *Cognition, perception and language*, 5th ed., edited by Deanna Kuhn and Robert S. Siegler, 575–630. New York: Wiley.

Gelman, Susan A. 2003. *The essential child.* New York: Oxford University Press.

Gelman, Susan A., and John D. Coley. 1991 "Language and categorization: The acquisition of natural kind terms." In *Perspectives on language and cognition: Interrelations in development,* edited by Susan A. Gelman and James P. Byrnes, 146–96. Cambridge: Cambridge University Press.

Gelman, Susan A., Bruce Mannheim, Carmen Escalante, and Ingrid Sánchez Tapia. forthcoming. Teleological talk in parent-child conversations in Quechua. *First Language.*

Gopnik, Alison, and Henry M. Wellman. 1994. "The theory theory." In *Mapping the mind: Domain specificity in cognition and culture,* edited by Lawrence A. Hirschfeld and Susan A. Gelman, 257–93. Cambridge: Cambridge University Press.

Guaman Poma de Ayala, Felipe. (1980/1615) 1987. *El primer nueva corónica y buen gobierno.* Edited by John V. Murra and Rolena Adorno with Quechua translations by Jorge L. Urioste. 3 vols. Madrid: Historia 16.

Hanks, William F. 2010. *Converting words: Maya in the age of the cross.* Berkeley: University of California Press.

Harrison, Regina. 1989. *Signs, songs, and memory in the Andes.* Austin: University of Texas Press.

Huayhua, Margarita. n.d. "Strangers in our own land: Social oppression in the southern Andes." Unpublished manuscript, University of Massachusetts, Dartmouth.

Itier, César. 1995. *El Teatro Quechua en el Cuzco.* Cuzco: Centro de Estudios Rurales Andinos "Bartolomé de las Casas."

———. 2000. "Lengua general y quechua cuzqueño en los siglos XVI y XVII." In *Desde afuera y desde adentro: ensayos de etnografía e historia del Cuzco y Apurímac,* edited by Luis Millones, Hiroyasu Tomoeda, and Tatsuhiko Fujii, 47–59. Osaka: National Museum of Ethnology.

Jakobson, Roman. 1959. "Boas' view of grammatical meaning." In "The anthropology of Franz Boas: Essays on the centennial of his birth," special issue, *Memoirs of the American Anthropological Association* 89: 139–45.

Keane, Webb. 2006. "Signs are not the garb of meaning: On the social analysis of material things." In *Materiality,* edited by Daniel Miller, 182–205. Durham, NC: Duke University Press.

Keil, Frank C. 1991. "Theories, concepts, and the acquisition of word meaning."
In *Perspectives on language and cognition: Interrelations in development,* edited
by Susan A. Gelman and J. P. Byrnes, 197–221. Cambridge: Cambridge
University Press.

Lavallé, Bernard. 1987. *Le marquis et la marchand, les luttes de pouvoir au Cuzco.
1700–1730.* Paris: Maison des Pays Ibériques, CNRS.

Levinson, Stephen C., ed. 2003. *Space in language and cognition,* Cambridge:
Cambridge University Press.

Malinowski, Bronisław. 1935. *Coral gardens and their magic,* vol. 2. New York:
American Book Company.

Mannheim, Bruce. 1986. "Popular song and popular grammar, poetry and metalanguage." *Word* 37 (1): 45–75.

———. 1991. *The language of the Inka since the European invasion.* Austin: University of Texas Press.

———. 1998. "'Time, not the syllables, must be counted': Quechua parallelism,
word meaning, and cultural analysis." *Michigan Discussions in Anthropology*
13: 245–87.

———. 2015a. "The social imaginary, unspoken in verbal art." In *The Routledge
handbook of linguistic anthropology,* edited by Nancy Bonvillain, 44–61. New
York: Routledge.

———. 2015b. "Allocentric person." Paper presented at the conference of the
Red Europeo de Estudios de Lingüística Latinoamericana, Leiden, September 2015.

———. Forthcoming a. "Xavier Albó's 'The future of the oppressed languages
of the Andes' in retrospect." In *History and Indigenous Languages in Latin
America,* edited by Alan Durston and Bruce Mannheim. Unpublished manuscript, York University.

———. Forthcoming b. *The horn of time,* chapter 9. Unpublished manuscript,
University of Michigan.

Mannheim, Bruce, and Susan A. Gelman. 2013. "El aprendizaje de los con-
ceptos genéricos entre niños quechua hablantes monolingües." *Bulletin de
l'Institut Français d'Études Andines* 42 (3): 353–68.

Mannheim, Bruce, and Guillermo Salas Carreño. 2014. "Wak'a: Entifications of
the Andean sacred." In *The archaeology of Wakas: Explorations of the sacred in
the pre-Columbian Andes,* edited by Tamara Bray, 46–72. Boulder: University
of Colorado Press.

Mannheim, Bruce, and Krista E. Van Vleet. 1998. "The dialogics of Quechua narrative. *American Anthropologist.*" 100 (2): 326–46.

Murphy, Gregory L., and Douglas L. Medin. 1985. "The role of theories in conceptual coherence." *Psychological Review* 92: 289–316.

Murra, John Victor. 1956. "The economic organization of the Inca state." PhD diss., University of Chicago.

Pérez Silva, Jorge Ivan, Jorge Acurio Palma, and Raúl Bendezú Arauja. 2009. *Contra el prejuicio lingüístico de la motosidad: Un estudio de las vocales del castellano andino desde la fonética acústica,* Lima: Instituto Riva Agüero, Pontificia Universidad Católica del Perú.

Quine, Willard van Orman. 1960. *Word and object.* Cambridge, MA: MIT press.

———. 1968. "Ontological relativity." *Journal of Philosophy* 45: 185–212.

Salas Carreño, Guillermo. forthcoming. "Places are kin." *Anthropological Quarterly.*

Sánchez Tapia, Ingrid, Susan A. Gelman, Michelle A. Hollander, Erika M. Manczak, Bruce Mannheim, and Carmen Escalante. forthcoming. "Development of teleological explanations in Peruvian Quechua-speaking and U.S. English-speaking preschoolers and adults." *Child Development.*

Santillana, Julian I. 2012. *Paisaje sagrado e ideología inca. Vilcas Huamán.* Lima: Fondo Editorial de la Pontificia Universidad Católica del Perú.

Scott, James C. 1998. *Seeing like a state.* New Haven, CT: Yale University Press.

Silverstein, Michael. 2003. "Translation, transduction, transformation: Skating glossando on thin semiotic ice." In *Translating cultures: Perspectives on translation and anthropology,* edited by Paula Rubel and Abraham Rosman, 75–105. Oxford: Berg.

Simons, D., and Frank C. Keil. 1995. "An abstract to concrete shift in the development of biological thought: The insides story." *Cognition* 56: 129–63.

Viveiros de Castro, Eduardo. 1998. "Cosmological deixis and Amerindian perspectivism." *Journal of the Royal Anthropological Institute* 4 (3): 469–88.

Wellman, Henry M., and Susan A. Gelman. 1998. "Knowledge acquisition in foundational domains." In *Handbook of child psychology,* vol. 2 of *Cognition, perception and language,* 5th ed., edited by Deanna Kuhn and Robert S. Siegler, 523–73, New York: Wiley.

Whorf, Benjamin Lee. 1945. "Grammatical categories." *Language* 21: 1–11.

CHAPTER EIGHT

Acting translation
Ritual and prophetism in twenty-first-century indigenous Amazonia

CARLOS FAUSTO and EMMANUEL DE VIENNE

"He said he was an Old Christian, born in the city of Silvis, in the reign of Algarve . . . and, confessing, he said that about six years ago, a gentile people from the hinterland emerged with a new sect named *Santidade* [Sanctity], one of them being called pope and a gentile woman Mary of God" (Furtado de Mendonça [1591–92] 1922: 35). And so confessed Fernão Cabral de Taíde before the Inquisitor Furtado de Mendonça during the First Visitation of the Holy Office in 1591. The slaveholder Cabral de Taíde had hosted the movement led by a certain Antonio, an Indian raised by Jesuits in the Tinharé mission in Bahia, who, according to other adepts of the movement, proclaimed himself pope—or God:

> The principal said he was God and Lord of the world, and there is another gentile among them whom they called Jesus and a gentile woman whom they called Holy Mary. (Confession of Cristovão de Bulhões, Furtado de Mendonça [1591–92] 1922: 137)

Known as *Santidade do Jaguaripe*, the movement brought together Indians, people of mixed blood, and some Whites, combining many different elements into its rites. The movement had a strong political connotation, as many confessions make clear:

> And they worshiped it [the idol] saying that their God would soon come to free them from the captivity they found themselves in, and would make them the masters of White people and the Whites would become their captives, and those who do not believe in that abomination they called Sanctity would become birds and other beasts of the forest. (Confession of Gonçalo Fernandes, Furtado de Mendonça [1591–92] 1922: 111)

Since the beginning of the colonization of the Americas, we find similar references to the emergence of indigenous charismatic leaders announcing a profound sociocosmic transformation, conceived both as the overcoming of the human condition and as the inversion of asymmetric relations between Amerindians and White people. In Lowland South America, references to such movements appear in the second half of the sixteenth century along the Brazilian Atlantic coast (Monteiro 1999: 1009–15)—as in the case of the *Santidade do Jaguaripe* (Vainfas 1995)—and accompany the history of indigenous peoples in the region until the present.[1]

These movements have been interpreted in a variety of ways—as messianic and millenarian, as resistance to colonialism, as political utopias, as syncretic cults resulting from the encounter of two cosmologies, or as structural

---

1. Famous cases discussed in the literature include, among others, the Guarani of Paraguay and Brazil from the late sixteenth to early twentieth centuries (Melià 1987; Nimuendajú 1987); the Arawakan peoples of Selva Central in Peru in the seventeenth century (Métraux 1942; Santos-Granero 1992; Varese 2006); the Upper Negro River Tukanoan and Arawakan peoples in the nineteenth century (Hugh-Jones 1994; Hill and Wright 1988); the Tikuna of the Solimões river in the twentieth century (Nimuendajú 1952; Oliveira Filho 1988; Goulard 2009); and the Ge-speaking Canela of Maranhão in the twentieth century (Melatti 1967; Carneiro da Cunha 1973). For the Guianas, Whitehead refers to an apocalyptic upheaval in Trinidad and the Orinoco region at the beginning of the seventeenth century, but also states that "no millennial tradition emerged until the nineteenth century, unlike in Peru or coastal Brazil" (1999: 897). From the mid-nineteenth century on, we witness the proliferation of the *Aleluia* prophetic movement among the region's Carib-speaking peoples (Butt Colson 1960, 1971, 1994/1996; Thomas 1976; Andrello 1993).

permutations of a mythic world facing new historical situations. Less attention has been given to the actual process of appropriating, translating, and creating a new cultural form, particularly in regard to the pragmatic dimensions and the interactive frames of this process. A more recent approach has come to see these events as providing a privileged entry for the investigation of ritual communication and cultural transmission in a broad sense. These studies focus particularly on the propagation of such movements through the analysis of their communicative dynamics, both within and outside the ritual setting.

Stemming from Boyer's analysis of the Fang epic genre (1988), which links the asymmetries of knowledge in public declamation with its repetition (and thus with its definition as a tradition), this line of inquiry has also drawn on certain developments in ritual theory (Humphrey and Laidlaw 1994; Houseman and Severi 1998). Severi, in particular, has contributed to the conceptualization of the kind of chimeric complexity that characterizes ritual enunciation in prophetic movements. Analyzing late-nineteenth-century Western Apache messianism, he shows how a pragmatic counterintuitivity was generated through the condensation of different and contradictory identities in the person of the "prophet" (Severi [2007] 2015). His earlier notion of a paradoxical enunciator (Severi 2004), in continuity with his analysis of Kuna shamanism, is also meant to explain how prophetic innovations "capture imagination" and rapidly spread beyond their original setting. From a more epidemological point of view, Pierre Déléage (2012, 2013) has investigated the ritual construal of a prophetic authority and the specific mediums employed for the spreading of the prophet's message.

Most anthropologists who have investigated such movements in South America have had to rely on historical data and secondhand accounts, making it difficult to produce a fine-grained analysis. Moreover, only successful movements at a certain stage of their development (when their choreographic, musical, and linguistic elements had more or less stabilized) appear in the written sources. The actual and initial process of invention is mostly absent in these studies. This article aims to fill this gap by peering into the microdynamics of an Amerindian prophetic movement. Here we examine a recent case that erupted in the Upper Xingu region, in Brazil, in 2006, when a man in his forties started curing people through radically new ritual techniques, claiming to have received his powers from a direct encounter with God-Sun. Self-designated "Master," this man also prophesied the end of witchcraft (i.e., the end of disease and death) and the end of the world.

We were not present during the movement's apogee, but we have at our disposal six hours of video recording of one of its climatic moments, and a number of later interviews.[2] This material makes possible a minute description of the ritual actions in all their dimensions: speech, gestures, bodily orientation, the gaze, the manipulation of objects, and so forth. It bears witness to the hesitations, uncertainties, misfires, and repetitions that characterize the birth of a new cosmology embedded in a new ritual form. Our case also has the advantage of being closer to failure than to success. The literature on prophetism and related phenomena has had no alternative other than to privilege the great movements that passed the test of history, and to dismiss the more discreet outbursts that remained unnoticed. The latter nevertheless deserve to be considered as minor variants of the former. While presenting a number of specific elements, our case pertains to the same family of phenomena commonly labeled "prophetism" in indigenous America, and it is directly relevant to its understanding. Although there is much discussion in the literature on how to characterize these movements (Brown 1991; Veber 2003; Fausto, Xavier, and Welper 2014), they all combine features of the colonizers' world (especially Christianity) and indigenous traditions in a particular way, generating a new propagating form. Here

---

2.   The filming was made by Takumã, Mahajugi, and Ahukaka, members of the Kuikuro Cinema Collective, who were trained by Fausto in filmmaking and have been close collaborators for the last ten years. The ethnographic data result from approximately two years of fieldwork among the Kuikuro (Fausto), and a year and a half among the Trumai (Vienne), both in the Upper Xingu. The Kalapalo and Kuikuro speak dialects of the same Southern Karib language (Meira and Franchetto 2005). Takumã Kuikuro and Yamaluí Mehinaku Kuikuro worked with us on the transcription and translation of the video recordings in Rio de Janeiro. Ahukaká Kuikuro collaborated on the transcription of the interviews made later with Manuá and his parents in the city of Canarana. Fausto has also interviewed two Kuikuro shamans who were protagonists of these episodes: Lümbu and Samuagü. However, in this text, we avoid using a posteriori discursive explanations of the episode in order to focus on actions. More apposite to our aim are the discussions we had with Takumã and Yamaluí on each of the main scenes recorded in the tapes, which gave us a firmer grasp of the actions and the backstage. (Takumã is not only the main filmmaker, but also Samuagü's first-born son and is half-Kalapalo.) Clearly, there was no stabilized exegesis at the time, and Takumã was also uncertain about some of Manuá's innovations. Further data were also collected through informal conversations with many Kuikuro and Trumai people in the following years. We also benefited from Cardoso, Guerreiro, and Novo's (2012) and Franco Neto's (2010) writings on Manuá, whose data were gathered among the Kalapalo. Marcela Coelho de Souza shared information about Manuá's visit to the Kinsêdjê village, where he treated Chief Kuiussi.

we propose to address the production of this new form as a special case of translation, one that is made of what we call *translating acts*.

TRANSLATING ACTS

We must first make clear the sense in which we take translation here. Let us proceed by means of a contrast: compare the sort of semantic-oriented translation intended by missionaries in the colonial space of the Reducciones (Hanks 2010) with the following iconic and ironic translation effected by a Guarani shaman at his village in the distant year of 1628. Named Ñeçu (possibly a corruption of Jesus), this shaman and chief had initially welcomed a few Jesuit missionaries into his people's lands, but then decided they should be killed. Montoya recounts what he did afterward:

> To show he was a priest, albeit a false one, he donned the liturgical paraphernalia of the priest and, thus attired, presented himself to the people. He summoned the children before him and proceeded to eradicate, through barbaric ceremonies, the indelible character which baptism had impressed upon their souls. (Montoya [1639] 1985: 201–2)

He scraped the tongues of the children who "had tasted the salt of the sapient spirit," as well as their backs and necks to "smudge the holy ointments," and reversed the ritual, washing the children from their feet up to their heads. This inverted baptism is an act of translation (and betrayal), which makes the Christian and indigenous imageries collide (and combine). A certain level of shared knowledge is required for people to engage in these actions. More than a conceptual operation, though, what is at stake here is the construction of a successful interactive and communicative context. Ñeçu undoubtedly mimics the priests, but he also transcreates their liturgy on the spot, counting on the engagement of his audience to make it work, and thus reinforce his own position. What kind of translation was he making?

As in our case, Ñeçu's translation does not involve questions of semantic or stylistic accuracy, nor the dilemma of privileging the target or the source language while trying to preserve meaning. It is, rather, a question of transference, of carrying across (as the etymology of the word makes clear), in order to produce a dynamic equivalence through which the translator establishes his/her authority. In this sense, it is closer to the notions of transcreation and transliteration characteristic of some strands of poetic translation theory (Campos 1981; Lages 2002), and also to notions of cultural translation as pragmatic situations involving what Pina-Cabral (1999) calls "equivocal compatibilities."[3] Specific to our case is the fact that there is someone—the Master—continuously producing these equivocal compatibilities in the act, and not two sides situated within different cultural traditions colliding. As we will see, our "prophet" transcreates his own experience of both worlds into a new form, striving to produce a commensurability between the indigenous and nonindigenous traditions.[4]

The expression "translating acts" also has a number of echoes and connotations. Firstly, in much the same way that speech act theory sees verbal utterances to be doing things and not only carrying meanings, we seek to explore how translating acts induce transformations in practical situations rather than only focusing on semantic and conceptual elements. These acts of translation are situated like any other social action, and subject to evaluation in terms of success or failure by the actors themselves in the course of their interaction. Secondly, "translating acts" is also to be understood as "translation made of actions," and not solely or mainly of utterances or texts. This widening of the scope

---

3. In his work on human trafficking in Macau, Pina-Cabral (1999, 2001) coined the expression "equivocal compatibility" to refer to the misunderstandings that emerge in intercultural situations, when each party defines the linguistic or material object that enables the relation using distinct criteria and conceptions. As Viegas points out, the interactions here are "pragmatically viable, that is, compatible, not only *despite*, but precisely *because* of the fact they are founded on equivocations" (2007: 237–38). In other words, the pragmatic translation here is based not on semantic accuracy, but on equivocal compatibilities. Viveiros de Castro (2004) applied this notion of equivocation to reconceptualize comparison in anthropology. He aims at the practice of anthropology as a form of translation, which must be controlled so that the source language (the "local," "native") subverts the target language ("anthropology"). Here we are looking at a process where a native person translates-subverts both the source and the target language by exploring equivocal compatibilities between Christianity and Xinguano mytho-ritual practices.

4. It would be interesting to compare the kind of "twisted commensuration" attained here with the one Hanks examines in the context of the colonial reduction of the Maya language, where the aim was to convert Christian doctrine into Maya utterances with minimal semantic distortion of the source language: "Cross-language commensuration is bidirectional, at least in principle . . . but in point of fact this reversibility is more a logical possibility than a historical actuality. The two languages were asymmetric . . . it was the Maya that was to be reformed according to the meaning patterns of Spanish, not the other way around" (2010: 159).

of translation in order to include multiple semiotic mediums implies giving as much attention to nonverbal as to verbal aspects of communication. Translation made of actions requires us to pay attention to choreographies, gestures, body transformations, the manipulation of artifacts, and so on. Speech is often not the main medium for translation, and semantic content is hardly ever the primary concern of participants in the course of translating acts. Finally, our concept also implies the idea of "translation in action." We wish to focus here on processes of transcreation unfolding in space-time, within certain interactive frames, and prior to the stabilization of any given translation. In sum, the expression "translating acts" contains three related ideas: "acts of translation," "translation made of actions," and "translation in action."

We are particularly interested in actions that produce a kind of working misunderstanding between two or more fields (call them "ontologies," "cosmologies," "cultures," or "religions" as you wish) by condensing them into certain ritual forms. Translating acts differ, for example, from a translation of the Bible negotiated between Amerindians and missionaries, in which equivalences between meanings are sought. Translating acts imply images coming together and colliding on the spot. They also have to create their own metacommunicational conditions in order to engage people in them. Their context is thus one of an interaction in which the felicity of each act of translation is calibrated within a complex set of relations, thus making them subject to correction and change over their course. Finally, translating acts imply uncertainty and experimentation, and work by triggering abductive reasoning.[5]

In order to ground our concept empirically, we shall describe and analyze a number of ritualized situations as they unfolded during the visit of the Kuikuro

---

5. As Boyer points out, abductive explanations are conjectural, and the process of inferring is triggered by the explanatory demands of particular situations (1994: 217–18). Taking his lead from Boyer, Fausto (2002) employed this notion to simultaneously account for the flexibility and resilience of magico-religious ideas among an Amazonian people, circumventing the problem of belief, and the distinction between practical action and religious ideas. Gell had recourse to abduction in order to formulate a radically nonlinguistic theory of art: "The usefulness of the concept of abduction is that it designates a class of semiotic inferences which are, by definition, wholly distinct from the semiotic inferences we bring to bear on the understanding of language, whose 'literal' understanding is a matter of observing semiotic conventions" (1998: 14–15). As is well known, it was Peirce ([1901] 1940) who introduced the concept of abduction in epistemology as a third term in-between induction and deduction.

people to the Kalapalo village of Tanguro, where the self-designated Master was prophesying and curing during the 2006 rainy season.

A CASE OF JESUS

The news about the miraculous cures performed by Manuá had begun to spread across the Upper Xingu.[6] The Kuikuro were the first to collectively engage in the movement, which until then had been limited to the Kalapalo people themselves. One day, the shaman Lümbu entered the Kuikuro village, running, swaying his head, and sighing as though in a trance. He said that Manuá had "made" (tüilü) him, and that he had become like him. He had adopted the Master's new curing technique: instead of smoking and extracting the spirit darts from the patient's body, he would strike the painful area. Some people immediately submitted themselves to the therapy, and paid for Lümbu's services in the appropriate way. At dusk, the men gathered in the middle of the village and summoned the shaman to tell his story.

Manuá had announced that the world would come to an end, and that those who did not go to his village would be taken away by Ogomügü, the anthropophagic double-headed vulture that holds up the sky. Having heard this prophecy, the men asked Lümbu: "When will the world end?" Not knowing our number system very well, he replied: "In thirty years." Since they were both in their sixties, Chief Afukaká and his brother-in-law Jakalu were relieved: "Let it go. By then we'll be well dead." Lümbu noticed his mistake and retracted himself: "No, it will happen in five years." Everyone was disappointed.

That night, Lümbu treated many people for free. Not all were convinced of his new powers. A man in his late twenties with a headache submitted to the

---

6. The Upper Xingu is a transitional zone between the savannah and the Amazonian rainforest, located to the north of the central Brazilian plateau and the southernmost limits of the Amazonian basin. It was first colonized by Arawak-speaking people as early as the ninth century AD, and received further migratory influxes after the Conquest. Carib-speaking people probably arrived in the region by the sixteenth or seventeenth century, Tupi-speaking in the eighteenth century, and the Trumai in the nineteenth century. Through a complex process of amalgamation and recreation, these peoples came to forge a single sociocultural constellation, known as the Upper Xingu society, which is plurilingual and multiethnic (Franchetto and Heckenberger 2001; Heckenberger 2005). In this text, we use the term "Xinguano" in reference to the people of this sociocultural constellation.

therapy, and after many ineffective blows to his head, decided to tell Lümbu he felt better just to avoid any more slaps. The next morning this man stayed home, but some thirty people—men, women, and children—decided to board the boat and depart for the village of Tanguro, under the guidance of Chief Afukaká.

With them went three Kuikuro videomakers, who started shooting halfway to Tanguro, when Manuá, having learned that the Kuikuro were arriving, went to their encounter. Over the next two days, the videomakers recorded all the ritual actions that took place at the village: the welcoming ceremony, the staging of the Master's illumination, the baptism rites, the healing sessions, and so on. The present article focuses on the first two moments only, starting, for analytic reasons, with the staging of the events that turned Manuá into a prophet.

In an interview recorded six months later, Manuá explained that everything began when, very ill, he went to defecate in the bush on the outskirts of the village and fainted.[7] On waking up, he saw Taugi, the Sun, donning a resplendent crown of yellow feathers.[8] The divinity said to him:

> I'm Taugi. To you, I reveal myself. I'm worried about you, you're almost dying. I've revived you and shall help you. You'll become a shaman, the most powerful shaman and all other shamans will be below you. (Manuá 2006—interview)

Taugi gave Manuá a new name: Master-King (*Mestre Rei*), which, as Taugi explained to him, was his own former name ("the one people used to call me"). Here Manuá conflates Taugi and God (*Deus*) with Jesus, who is commonly called "Master" or "Christ-King" (*Cristo Rei*) in Brazilian Christian churches. This conflation is made clear soon after in the interview when Manuá recounts

---

7. Takumã Kuikuro recorded this interview in July or August 2006, in the town of Canarana. Marina Cardoso obtained another version in Portuguese, which is very similar to our own, but contains additional data, particularly concerning Manuá's experience in the town, just prior to his "illumination" (see Cardoso, Guerreiro, and Novo,. 2012). Takumã also interviewed Manuá's parents, but we will not analyze these data here.

8. The typical Xinguano feather headdress is composed of four different layers: the frame woven from plant fibers, the diadem of toucan feathers (red, black, and yellow), the *Cacicus sp* tail-feather diadem (yellow), and the feathers of hawks and the red macaw. The Sun has a particularly bright version of this headdress, one he wears to obfuscate his enemies. Here there seems to be a conflation of this attire with Jesus' dazzling crown.

that Taugi presented his mother to him: "Her name is *Anhipe*, but I always call her Mary (*Maria*) to White people."[9]

Mary was beautifully adorned and painted: "Like a young girl leaving seclusion during a funerary ritual. Beautiful." And Manuá continues: "But she's old, from ancient times, she is his mother." Here he conveys a paradoxical image, insofar as Mary is presented both as a young woman at the height of her beauty and reproductive potential, and as Taugi's mother, the very one who nurses the dead. As we shall see, these paradoxical identifications are all acted out in the staged scene of Manuá's illumination. He relates it here directly to the pivotal Xinguano myth, at the same time as he inserts himself and the Christian deities within it.

Notably, six months after the events, the Master provided a stable oral version of his illumination, which contrasts with the improvisation and innovation that characterized the rituals we recorded. However, this story was stabilized much earlier, during the prophetic movement itself, and not afterward, as if Manuá needed a narrative framework to structure his own innovations. Here he draws directly on a striking feature of Xinguano rituals, in which myths function as a charter for ritual actions. This feature may have resulted from the historical process through which the Upper Xingu became a single multiethnic system. Rituals of different origins were appropriated and adopted by all the peoples forming this cultural constellation (Fausto, Franchetto, and Heckenberger 2008; Fausto 2011a). A mythical charter would have been a convenient tool for transmitting and making sense of complex ritual routines in the absence of prior shared knowledge.[10] And this was precisely the case for the recently arrived Kuikuro. It is not surprising, therefore, that the Master decided to put his own origin story on stage.

Manuá's followers had cleared a "plaza" (hugógo) for him—a circular space, carefully weeded, located at some distance from the village. It clearly pointed,

---

9.   *Anhipe* is the designation given to the women made from wood by Kuantüngü and sent to marry Jaguar. Two of them, made from a harder wood, arrived at Jaguar's village, and one of them, called Sangitsegü, gave birth to Taugi and Aulukumã, the twins Sun and Moon, the main figures in Xinguano mythology. Nowadays Sangitsegü puts the recently dead into seclusion and breastfeeds them, enabling them to rejuvenate.

10. It is difficult to say, however, which comes first: the learning of the ritual actions or the acquisition of the narrative charter. Moreover, these kinds of initiatory stories seem to be frequent in other Amerindian prophetic movements.

though, to another plaza: the village center, where the main chief, called the "master of the plaza" (*hugogó oto*), makes his formal speeches. The fact that this plaza was decentered in relation to the village meant not only that Manuá defied the chiefs from the periphery, but also that he wanted to distance himself from a specific setting in order to build a new physical context for his innovative communicative practices. He operated in space the kind of deictic "deanchoring" that one finds in myths. The new setting afforded him a considerable expansion in scope: Manuá's ambition being cosmopolitical, his plaza was a cosmic one, where indigenous and nonindigenous deities came together. His plaza synthesized all Xinguano plazas, and projected them onto a virtual space filled with the Sun's shining presence and Sangitsegü's eternal youth. From his plaza Manuá could hear everything, as he claimed in his interview: "Taugi improved my hearing. Tak! I could hear everyone, the whole world, as the Whites say."

STAGING THE ILLUMINATION[11]

The plaza is connected to the village by a large path. Manuá arrives totally naked, even though just shortly before, while still in the village, he had been fully adorned to formally welcome the Kuikuro. Now he is ill. He arrives talking. He says: "Look, here is my beginning," employing a term (*etihunte-*) that applies to origin narratives.[12] "My belly was hurting a lot, I went to defecate." He carries a little flute in his hands, the flute with which Whirlwind masks "talk" to ask for food.[13] He makes strange gestures, stretching his arms into the air and spinning around slowly. He enters the plaza, and addresses the people there: "My belly

---

11. From this point on, we shift to the present tense to describe the ritual events in question in order to convey the situation better. We call Manuá's revelation "illumination" in order to foreground the meanings associated with the Sun and his resplendent crown.

12. Origin myths are called X-*etihuntepügü* or X-*opogipügü*. These verbs (suffixed by a perfective aspect) connote the idea of "origin," and contain an explanation of how a certain feature of the world came into being.

13. Manuá told Cardoso that during his illness, a shaman had identified the Whirlwind as one of the agents causing his disease (Cardoso, Guerreiro, and Novo 2012: 14). Manuá did not mention this in his interview, but his father said that he had been ill for some time, "because his Atuguá was killing him," meaning that he had become an owner of this expensive mask, and thus a sort of double person: a human-whirlwind (on this mask, see Barcelos Neto 2008 and Fausto 2011b).

was really hurting. Do you like it when your bellies hurt?" They shout: "No!" Then he addresses Chief Afukaká, instructing him: "Go there, father, you will be Taugi." Manuá employs the correct kin term to address his classificatory father Afukaká, whereas previously, while still in the village during the welcoming ceremony, he would only call him *anetü* ("chief" or "noble"). Afukaká now dons a full feather diadem, similar to the one Manuá was wearing earlier.

Manuá turns to Afukaká's daughter, Auná, who is a high-ranking chief in her late thirties: "Maria, you stay there." The three characters—Taugi-Afukaká, Maria-Auná, and Manuá-Master-to-be—stand up in the middle of the circle formed by the men. "In no way am I lying. All of you, look! That's how it started." Manuá tells the audience how painful it was and how worried he was. He goes to the center of the circle, rests one knee on the ground, stretches up one of his arms, and addresses the Sun: "Taugi, look at me, my belly is hurting, what is doing that to me?" Then reporting Taugi's speech, he yells: "Manuá!" and falls down on the ground. After a brief moment, he raises his head slightly and talks to the audience, while pointing to Taugi-Afukaká: "Look behind me, is he haunting me?"[14] The audience respond in unison: "Yes!"

Manuá calls Maria-Auná to come and see what is happening to him. Entirely naked save for a shell necklace, Auná does not respond to the command. Manuá goes on talking: "Say: 'What am I going to do for my son, what are you going to do for him?'" Without moving from her place, Auná starts repeating her line. Afukaká murmurs: "Approach him." Manuá sits and talks to the audience: "Listen to me. I get it. It's still difficult for her, she hasn't absorbed it yet?" The audience applaud. Manuá tries once again, asking Afukaká to tell her what to do. But the chief is also puzzled. Manuá cuts it short, and asks Afukaká to come closer to him and play his part: "You are going to shout 'Manuá!' for them."

Standing up now in front of Manuá, who lies down on his back, Afukaká raises his arms and shouts very loudly. Manuá raises his head as though waking; the audience applaud. He gets onto his knees and, staring at Afukaká, asks: "Who are you?" The chief now replies without delay: "I'm Taugi." Manuá falls down again, this time facing the ground. He stays still for twenty seconds, and Afukaká becomes uneasy, not knowing what to do. He looks up at one of the Master's auxiliaries and makes a discreet inquiring gesture. He returns to his part again, raises his arms, and shouts once more: "Manuaaaaá!" Still lying on

---

14. He employs the verb *-ihintsi-*, which indicates an uncanny encounter, often portending a bad event.

the ground, Manuá suddenly turns over onto his back melodramatically. Fresh applause. He gets up again on his knees: "How are you going to cure me?" he asks Taugi-Afukaká, who answers: "I'm going to teach you." "What for?" replies Manuá. "To stop your belly pain."

The scene draws on the shaman–patient interview that precedes any cure in the Upper Xingu, but now recast in the manner of a Catholic revelation with the patient kneeling down and the divinity standing up. "What's inside my belly?" asks Manuá. Afukaká responds in a detached tone: "Who knows?" and Manuá murmurs: "Blood." Getting once more into the play, the chief repeats "blood" twice. Manuá whispers to him what to do next, and Afukaká takes some water from a huge aluminum pot and washes Manuá's head and back, while saying: "Get well, get well, get well." He then helps the sick man to stand on his feet. Manuá looks around, as if he had just gained consciousness. He then laughs in a bizarre way. Nobody talks, nobody applauds. He turns to Taugi-Afukaká and asks in a low voice: "Who is she?" "She's Maria," Taugi-Afukaká answers. "Oh, you came from inside her, didn't you?" "Yes." "Should I go to see her?" In this way, Manuá draws Auná back into the scene, but now with her own father identifying her as Maria. Manuá thus skillfully overcomes his initial failure to make her participate in the staging of his illumination.

He walks toward her, limping and tottering, and in a beseeching voice asks her to cure him. He repeatedly calls her name: "Maria, Maria." Auná hesitates, but finally capitulates and talks to him. She walks toward him, she stretches out her arm and almost touches him, but he falls down to the ground again. He stays there, waiting for her, but it is only after a while that she approaches him and yells: "Manuaaaaá!" With a brusque movement, he gets up on his knees and slowly stands up. Now he does everything gently, taking his time. He gets very close to Maria-Auná, facing her, but says nothing. He is a tall and sturdy man. Auna is visibly uncomfortable. After a brief pause she murmurs: "I'm going to teach you how to stop your belly pain." Manuá does not give any clue to the right answer now. She touches his belly lightly with the tip of her fingers, and he moves away, still limping, while one of his auxiliaries gestures for those present to applaud. They do so.

Manuá now addresses the audience directly, showing them the content of the aluminum pot: a reddish-brown liquid like permanganate water. He uses symmetric consanguine kinship terms ("my sisters," "my brothers") to address the Kalapalo, and refers to all the Kuikuro as "those who have arrived." He questions all of them: "Is this my blood?" and people respond in a somewhat shy and apathetic way: "Yes." This seems to have been an innovation even for the Kalapalo, who had already been taking part in Manuá's cures for some time. He keeps talking in a reflexive way, saying that they do not yet know how to answer his words, until he regains control of the situation, and reinstalls the frame of rhetorical questions and responses in unison.

GOD AS A HYPERSPIRIT

In order to gauge the innovations introduced by the Master, we need to provide a quick overview of shamanism and chieftaincy in the Upper Xingu. Shamans and chiefs are two prominent and distinct positions among the Kuikuro and the Kalapalo. They also both have different levels of power and legitimacy. In shamanism, the main difference resides in the modality of initiation. Some specialists are said to have been directly "made" (*tüilü*) by the spirits during a dramatic and recurrent illness, while others are said to have been made by other shamans only. The former are considered more powerful than the latter.

However, even shamans made by spirits must undergo a lengthy and expensive training process guided by another shaman, until he is ready to be initiated in a collective and secret ceremony. The first thing he must learn is how to smoke tobacco, which is the earmark of shamanism.[15] The crucial moment, though, is the transmission of a viscous substance (called *nguto* in Upper Xingu Carib languages) from initiator to initiate. This substance, which originally belonged to a spirit, allows the new therapist to remove the disease with his hands or mouth, or both, depending on where the substance is located in his body. This transmission establishes a substantial community between the spirit, initiator, and initiate.

Manuá short-circuits this institution by claiming to have been directly elected by Taugi-God, and refusing to submit himself to shamanic training. While his illumination can be interpreted as a form of shamanic election, his attitude implies a rupture: he tells all shamans to yield to his power, and even makes new shamans (or remakes old ones like Lümbu).[16] He also deprecates tobacco, and

---

15. Unlike the Arawakan and Tupian peoples in the Xingu, only shamans smoke among the Carib populations.

16. In a scene recorded inside his house, Manuá stands up on a stool and displays all his wealth (the shell belts and necklaces with which he was paid), while the kneeled shamans chant with their rattles.

claims that the substance he shares with Taugi is blood, which he exudes from his body. He does not cure by extracting pathogenic agents from the patients, but by hitting them and inflicting pain on them. Violence is indeed a recurrent therapeutic action, if not the main one. It expresses an obvious paradox: the injury is the remedy that relieves pain.

GOD AS A KING

Manuá's relation toward chieftainship is likewise complex, but overall more respectful than his relation toward shamanism. After all, he is a member of the Kalapalo elite, and had been a prestigious champion wrestler in his youth. Sportive wrestling competitions between hosts and guests are a central aspect of intertribal rituals in the Upper Xingu, and victory not only increases the prestige of a community, but also turns individuals into celebrities. Almost all the current executive chiefs in the region are former champions. Manuá was well placed, then, to acquire an eminent political position through traditional means, although perhaps not that of a "master of the plaza," which he certainly coveted (Franco Neto 2010: 252–53). According to Cardoso, Guerreiro, and Novo (2012: 26), from the very beginning of his prophetic movement, Manuá was haranguing people each morning in the village, something that only high-ranking chiefs would feel sufficiently legitimized to do.

Manuá's movement is full of resonances for Xinguano politics, including his cosmological conflation of Taugi-God and himself as Master-King. In the region's mythology, the Sun is the great transformer. Together with his twin brother Moon, he instituted the world in its contemporary form, including human mortality. It was also the twins' decision not to revive their mother Sangitsegü, but to commemorate her in a funerary rite by means of an artifact: a wooden effigy. Since then all dead chiefs have been celebrated in a ritual that depicts the substantial continuity existing between chiefs and demiurges: like Sangitsegü and her sons, chiefs are made of the noble wood that the Kuikuro and the Kalapalo call *uegühi*.[17]

---

17. This is also known as the "Sun's tree" (*kwaryp*) among the Tupi-speaking Kamayurá. This term (also *kwarup* or *quarup*) became the ritual's common designation in the anthropological literature.

As a chief, Afukaká is really the offspring of Tãugi and his mother. His eldest daughter Auná, who bears the name of his late mother, is also herself a chief. Not surprisingly, Manuá asks Auná to play the role of Mary, mother of Jesus, who is both young and old at the same time, while asking Afukaká to play Taugi's role, making him the son of his own daughter. In the Upper Xingu, names produce an infinite recursion between alternate generations, which leads back to the time of origins and forward to the future. And the future here is Manuá's.

Through his initiation by a hyperspirit (the cultural hero himself and his mother, alias the father and mother of White people), Manuá identifies himself with the very source of the power of both shamans and chiefs, approximating, as Cardoso, Guerreiro, and Novo (2012: 27) argue, a kind of authoritarian power that exceeds what local standards define as legitimate. The illumination scene has a clear political message, therefore: by attributing Tãugi's identity to an influential Xinguano chief, literally crowning him with shamanic, political, and Christian emblems in a context that emphasizes his own importance, Manuá actually dethrones both chiefs and shamans.

A PARADOXICAL I

In the illumination scene, Manuá inserts Christian imagery into the Xinguano mytho-ritual world, drawing on his fragmentary exposure to both Catholic and Evangelical church services in the city (Franco Neto 2010: 255). He makes simple identifications: Taugi is God (and Jesus), Sangitsegü is Maria. There is a theological simplification at work here too: the Christian Trinity is eclipsed, indigenous twinhood disappears. The Moon is never present, and the Sun, called by his personal name Taugi, is ever-present. Manuá's conflation of Christian and Xinguano deities thus presumes a prior de-complexification: each of them must appear as one in order to make the translation possible (Jesus, for instance, becomes one of God's names). Such simplifications, however, allow new condensations to occur and the creation of new complex figures. The reconfiguration of a plurality into a unity within each tradition seems to be a precondition for the production of a new plural and paradoxical person: the Master.

Severi's notion of a "paradoxical I," which he coined to describe Apache prophets in the nineteenth century, aptly captures this ritual configuration, and the ambivalent appropriation of the Conquering Other (Severi [2007] 2015: chapter 4). According to the author, the paradoxical character of Amerindian prophetism results not from the mapping of ontological concepts from one tradition onto the other, but from the production of a relational scheme where being "like the other" implies being simultaneously "different from (and above) the other."

During the night trip, Manuá boarded the Kuikuro boat and started to preach and cure. At a certain point, he stopped to recount that Taugi had told him that he would be higher than the pope, who cannot cure people: "I'm fed up with hearing my own speech from the Bible," God said to him. "That's why I'm teaching you, so that you can become the one who will spread my word." The Book does not cure; writing has no power or presence. It will befall the Master to talk and heal without mediation. Given the importance of writing in other prophetic movements in South America, such as the *Aleluia* in the Guianas, it is rather surprising that God-Taugi so clearly affirms the inefficacy of the written word.[18]

In contrast to Severi's study, the opposition to the Whites in our case is much less pronounced. The latter are not the main targets of the ritual communication. Yet the contradictory proposition "I am like you, thus I am different to you" is constantly mobilized in Manuá's interaction with Afukaká. In the illumination scene, Manuá plays himself as he was before becoming a Master: that is, as a sick person. At the same time, he duplicates himself, acting as both his former and present self. Here the "paradoxical I" is matched by a "paradoxical you," since Afukaká plays the role of Taugi-God, but he is also the sick patient asking to be cured. He is split between two simultaneous conditions, although a stable identity underlies the scene as a whole: he is undoubtedly the chief.

We have here a kind of pragmatic translation in which the focus is less on the equivalence between different entities (God = Taugi; Mary = Sangitsegü) and more on a translation of the ritual conditions under which these entities are normally mobilized. The Master activates different regimes of communication: the indigenous private shamanic communication with the spirits, the ecstatic collective communication with Jesus characteristic of some Evangelical cults, and the mediated communication of Catholicism where the mother of God plays a crucial role.

---

18. Among Carib-speaking peoples of the Guianas, by contrast, "books, including educational ones, gained a ritual use as soon as indigenous people put their hands on them. . . . Indeed, papers and books were often kept as true treasures" (Amaral 2014: 138). See also Abreu (2004) and Déléage's work (2013) on the role of writing in different prophetic and nonprophetic traditions.

While shamans converse with a variety of spirits, they never address the cultural heroes of indigenous mythology. Manuá, though, talks directly to the latter and reveals them to be the same as the White people's divinities. He puts himself in the position of an ultimate intermediary. At the same time, he establishes a communicational frame in which the indigenous collectivity directly addresses the deities by constantly calling them with their arms raised toward the sky: Taugi! Deus! Jesus! Maria! Sangitsegü! Manuá even makes his followers blow with hands clasped over their mouth and nose in order to unblock their ears and force them to listen to God's words.

Another essential aspect of Manuá's innovation is his use of "therapeutic violence." Shamanism in Amazonia does not ignore the link between suffering and healing. But suffering is a prerequisite to become a healer, not a solution in itself.[19] We can also find in shamanism an identification between the patient's present condition and the shaman's past (as a sick person) and future (as a healer). However, the whole system is based on the idea that personal communication with the spirits excludes normal communication with humans. The shaman is a double person, both a benevolent spirit (who extracts the pathogens instead of injecting them) and a visually perceptible human. People are left to watch over his shoulder while he interacts with his auxiliary spirits during the treatment (de Vienne 2011). True, the sound of the *maracá*, the smoke of the tobacco, and the dancing shaman do render the spirits present and material, but the patient must stand completely still, and never look at him. By importing the idea of a direct verbal encounter with the divinity, Manuá explodes this communicative context. If curing implies both speaking and listening to the gods on an open public stage, then the difference between healing and initiation disappears, and the suffering intrinsic to initiation now appears as the healing process itself.

IMPROVISATION AND THE MANAGEMENT OF UNCERTAINTY

The translation between two macro structures of communication with the supernatural is not the only remarkable feature of Manuá's ritual actions. We still have to account for how he manages to reenact his complex personhood

---

19. In this respect, see Davi Kopenawa's extraordinary account of his initiation and the pain the spirits inflicted on him (Kopenawa and Albert 2010: 140–42).

constantly and captivate his audience, how he can perform strange collective actions for hours on end, multiplying his translating acts ad nauseam, and how these are evaluated by the participants.

Any ritual innovation must face the problem of the paucity of shared knowledge about how to act in this or that situation. Translating acts are performed in a context of a profound asymmetry in knowledge. In the literature on ritual, such asymmetry is often considered the means, rather than the obstacle, to the efficacy of ritual interaction (Boyer 1988, 1990). In our case, however, a maximum discrepancy combines with other parameters: ritual knowledge is ultimately in the hands of a single individual who stands alone—except for his chosen assistants—before a crowd. Most of his actions are not only new, they also reveal themselves to be opposite to commonly accepted practices. In other words, the Master's stakes are quite high: the prophet can either convince people (i.e., convert patients into adepts) or end up being considered a fraud, a crook, or a sorcerer.

Presenting himself as the focus of attention and the main organizer of the collective action, he must continually switch from one interactive frame to another, invoking (or improvising) various aspects of context, sometimes in complex and potentially dissonant layers. According to the feedback received, he strives to control any misunderstandings that might jeopardize the fragile common ground achieved thus far. He thus acts not only as the main actor-translator in the scene, but also, at a meta level, as its director, incurring the risk of seeing the whole situation collapse. Becoming a "prophet" requires a communicative feat that we also need to explain.

While the work of translation mainly belongs to the prophet, the participants are not just mimicking actions or adhering to them out of a naïve belief. They are neither imitators nor believers, but interpreters, albeit not in a hermeneutical sense. The adhesion is practical and always subject to testing within what we could call "an abductive frame." This expression seeks to ground the cognitive notion of abductive inference, which Boyer takes from Peirce in order to explain magic-religious ideas. By replacing "inference" with "frame," we wish to convey the idea that abduction is a two-way relation: to captivate the participants, the prophet has to provide clues, which trigger abductive inferences, making it plausible that he is "a case of X." But more than just inferring, which supposes a kind of pure propositional operation, what seems to be at stake is the "capture of imagination" (Severi 2002). We could even say that the ritual frame is an "art-like" situation, in Gell's (1998) sense: at issue is the conflation of the prophet and his prototype (God-Sun), the power of this image, its "trapping quality," dependent on the success of a series of translating acts.

Let us now see how this was acted out during the welcoming ceremony held just before the illumination scene.

STABILIZING A CERTAIN COMMON GROUND[20]

Early morning, the hosts get ready to formally receive the visitors, as demanded by Upper Xingu etiquette. This time, though, the greeting ceremony is different from the one preceding or opening intertribal rituals. Kalapalo men and women gather inside Manuá's house, where the shamans are already sat on their stools, smoking. Manuá does not smoke, but sighs continuously as though in a pre- or posttrance state.

In front of the house, young men stretch out a sort of clothesline on which they suspend Xinguano luxury items (shell necklaces and cotton belts) as well as a ritual object (specifically the "face" of the Whirlwind mask). This line is similar to those strung up by a sick person's kin when shamans perform the soul retrieval ritual.[21] Luxury items are offered to the abducting spirits as a gift to persuade them to release the captured soul. The current setting is that of a superlative healing session that includes the whole village.[22]

---

20. Clark's concept of "common ground" refers to the mutual knowledge of participants in an interaction, which guides inferences about the contextual meaning of their utterances (Clark 1992, 1996). For Clark, common-groundness makes possible joint commitments, which are essential to all true joint activities. It is a basic condition of any cooperation, and therefore of human sociality in general (Clark 2006). Hanks (2006) applies this notion to the analyses of a Yucatec Maya shaman's divination session. In a situation where disparities in knowledge are very important at the beginning, the shaman progressively manages to build a common ground, in which the divination and therapeutic session becomes both true and effective, regardless of the semantic meaning of his utterances.

21. With one difference, though: no feather headdresses are hung on this occasion. The absence is due to the importance of its current use: as stated earlier, the crown of yellow feathers is the Sun's distinctive attire, and here it is worn by the main character in the staged events.

22. Most ritual events in the Upper Xingu originate in a healing process, in which the ex-patient is converted into the sponsor of a festival related to the spirits deemed to have caused the disease (Barcelos Neto 2008). These festivals are not, however, ritual healings on an amplified scale. The most public situation that maintains a similarity

Manuá organizes his people inside the house in a precise order. He gives a fine feather headdress to the young man leading the line, and asks the audience: "Is he now a shaman like me?" They all reply in unison: "Yes!" He claps his hands and everybody follows him. Well adorned, the Kalapalo exit the house and split into two parallel rows outside, men facing women, a formation that echoes both collective vaccination protocols and Evangelical baptism. Manuá shouts "Taugi! Deus! Jesus! Maria!" and says: "Extract the disease out of my shaman" (i.e., out of himself).[23] All the people raise their arms and shout in reply. Amid the shouting and applause, Manuá leaves the house held by his parents and parents-in-law, who are weeping. As he walks between the rows, he asks: "Did I cure you all?" and the audience respond: "Yes!" He then proceeds to ask: "Does your [some part of the body] hurt?" and the audience shout "No!" He arrives at the end of the rows and, pointing to his family, who are still crying, tells the people to listen to them weep. His family are unadorned and completely naked, as when people are ill or in mourning.

The whole scene conveys a paradoxical idea: although the Master has cured everyone, his kinfolk cry as if he were dead. Time-space collapses here: as we have seen, he did indeed die, only to be revived by God-Sun, becoming like him and starting to cure. At this stage of the ritual, however, his followers ask God-Sun to cure him, as though he were still dead, and his kin wail as though he were a corpse. He announces that he is about to leave them all, that he is going up to meet Taugi. "Am I going to take off?" he asks, and the people respond all at once: "No!" He ascertains the degree of adherence, admonishing the women: "If you do not cry enough, I shall take off." They cry louder.

He then approaches his wife and takes their little son from her arms, telling the participants that only the baby will become like himself: "You are not going to believe in him," he says, "that's why he is not looking at you. Call him Pope and he will look at you." The followers shout "Pope!" Manuá turns his baby to

---

with Manuá's collective healing sessions is called, among the Kuikuro, "the docking of the spirits." At the behest of the shamans, the community performs it during the therapeutic process, materializing a special relationship between a class of spirit and a patient that can later evolve into a future ritual cycle.

23. He says "*upagisü iküike*," the first word being formed by a possessive pronoun, plus the root *pagi* and a genitive suffix. The term specifically designates the shaman hired by the parents of a baby to provide care over its first two years. The parents make a single payment at the start of the contract, and can call the shaman whenever the baby needs (see Fausto 2014).

face the shouting audience and smiles as he says: "I told you." They keep repeating "Pope!" and the baby suddenly pees. Unperturbed, Manuá states that he has just urinated their illness. He then reproaches the women again for not shouting loudly enough. "Don't you want him to become the one who extracts illness from you?" and the women respond "Yes!" He tells them to applaud and thereby terminates this particular act.

Interval. People stop shouting, kin stop crying. Manuá reorganizes the setting, issuing mundane instructions. Next, his sister by his side and his parents and parents-in-law behind his back, he kneels down and stretches out one of his arms, showing a pigeon made of wood. He does not kneel as Christians do in a church, but as chiefs do when receiving visitors from other villages, with only one knee on the ground. He poses a new question: "Is he going to cure you with this pigeon?" Nobody answers. The Kalapalo do not understand the innovation. It is unclear what the pigeon is doing there. Xinguano people do confect wooden miniatures of birds, typically for the Pequi fruit festival, but not pigeons. Unaware of the Christian symbolism of the dove, the participants wait in silence until Manuá poses a more direct question: "Do you want it to become like me?" and the followers shout "Yes!" For a lapse of time he seems unsure what to propose next. He then asks: "Am I trembling?" People seem to already know the answer: "No!" "Who is trembling then?" and they immediately shout: "Maria!" Obviously his sister's association with Maria had been previously established, and Manuá regains control of the situation. He then hands the wooden pigeon to her and asks the people to applaud, quickly ending a frame in which people had failed to grasp part of his translations.

WILD TRANSLATIONS AND FAST SWITCHING

After staging this first ritual before his own people, thereby ensuring a certain level of shared knowledge, even if some innovations were lost in translation, Manuá tells his auxiliaries to fetch the guests. The Kuikuro enter the village in two lines divided according to sex. On the left, Chief Afukaká heads the male line; on the right, Auná leads the female one. In front of the two lines comes Lümbu, the Kuikuro shaman who had already learned how to cure in Manuá's style, and had gone to the Kuikuro village to persuade them to come to Tanguro.

The Kuikuro are completely naked, which, from the Xinguano point of view, evokes sickness, while the adorned bodies of the Kalapalo indicate that they are feasting, and therefore happy and healthy. This embodied distinction establishes a new frame: on the one side, we have the Master's followers, who have already been cured; on the other, the Kuikuro, who are collectively ill. It is from these distinctive conditions that Manuá will now try to establish a common ground with the visitors, who are unacquainted with any of his translations, except for the fact that he summons Taugi, Deus, Jesus, and Maria all the time.[24]

The visitors slowly enter the village circle, and stop at a distance to face the two rows formed by the Kalapalo. Chief Afukaká calls Manuá using a formal chiefly speech, addressing him as a consanguine of a younger generation, but then he adds: "Look, here are my followers. I brought them for you to cure them." Manuá walks with his sister (who still carries the wooden pigeon) to the end of the lines, raises one of his arms, and greets Afukaká in a nontraditional way: "If you were angry with me, I wouldn't cure you. It's really true, and you believe in me."[25]

His voice is slightly raised in pitch, the prosody flat and descending at the end of each sentence, like a whimper of pain, evocative of shamans as they moan while curing. While explicitly formulating a greeting, he is actually invoking another setting (Gumperz 1982): a shamanic séance. Pointing to the sky behind the Kuikuro, he then provides evidence of his power: "Look over there. Look what has come to cure you. Do you think that it is the rain you are seeing?" Bewildered, the Kuikuro turn and seek out the referent to his words. The Kalapalo applaud. Manuá continues: "Do you want your disease white or black?" No answer. He exhorts Afukaká to provide him with an answer: "Chief?" Afukaká

---

24. True, the previous night, while still on the boat, Manuá had performed a number of different "translating acts," but they were so wild that most of the time the Kuikuro were left completely baffled, and only the constant intervention of the shaman Lümbu ensured that they responded in the expected way.

25. Here Manuá employs the verb -ikeni-, meaning "to believe," the same term he had just used when chiding the women who seemed not to believe in his son, the peeing pope. In daily contexts, the verb -ikeni- is employed pretty much in the same way as we do. But here Manuá is also retranslating it from its use in religious contexts in the city. This retranslation impacts less on the semantics of the verb "to believe" than on the metalinguistic presuppositions about the possibility of saying the truth. The Sun is the greatest trickster. Our Kuikuro collaborators even interpret his name (Taugi) as an abbreviated form of the noun tauginhü ('liar'—the suffix -nhü is a nominalizer). Jehovah and Taugi stands thus in opposition in regard to truth and deceit. (On this topic, see Basso 1987.)

responds: "White." The Kalapalo applaud, making it clear that this was the right answer.

Without pausing, the Master now shows his people (and the still distant Kuikuro) a small measuring receptacle, a plastic cup used to administer drugs to patients. From this cup he drops a tiny white moth onto the palm of his hand, displaying it to those present, while saying: "Here it is, here it is, look at it! Is it?" The Kalapalo reply: "Yes!" And Manuá adds triumphantly: "He said it was white." One of his auxiliaries tells the people to applaud. Clapping hands.

Manuá now turns to face the Kuikuro, raises his hand, showing them the white moth, and tells them: "Look, you're no longer ill, here it is with me." The act of showing the pathogenic object extracted from the patient's body is an exaggerated and public version of what shamans normally do. Not only is its ostentatious and collective quality new, but also the fact that it is made at a distance, without any physical contact between specialist and patient—a technique that would later be adopted by some traditional shamans as a new form of curing among the Kuikuro.[26] The other innovation is to display the pathogenic agent inside a measuring cup, such as those that come with cough syrup or children's antibiotics. Instead of being an intaking device, the cup becomes, so to speak, an outtaking one. Here Manuá appropriates—and simultaneously inverts—the indigenous experience with Western medicines, which forms a central part of their relations with White people.

After the initial greeting, Manuá tells the visitor to approach. Chief Afukaká is the first to step forward. The Master takes out a soaked toucan-feather diadem from an aluminum pot full of water, places it on the chief's head upside-down, and makes a small gesture with his fingers, as though blessing him. Here he conflates an image of Christian baptism with an inverted Xinguano ritual attire. However, unlike the seventeenth-century Guarani shaman Ñeçu, he does not invert baptism, but the way Xinguanos don a feather diadem. Nude and perplexed, Chief Afukaká is overpowered by the Master, who presents himself as the Master of masters.

Still holding the white moth in his open hand, Manuá kneels down in the same posture used by a host chief to welcome a chiefly visitor. Instead of being

---

26. Gregor writes that in the 1970s the great Kamayurá shaman Takumã would extract pathogenic substances from his patients without any direct contact with them (1977: 348). After Manuá's debacle, however, some Kuikuro shamans started curing without even going to the patient's village. They would just send their spirits—particularly the "master of tobacco"—to do the job for them.

seated on a stool, however, Afukaká is standing up. Manuá starts with the classic opening of formal dialogues ("Chief, chief, chieeeeeeeef"), elongating the last vowel. Then he says something unexpected, retaining the correct prosody, but speaking in a louder voice: "I have been working while you were arriving." Chief Afukaká murmurs: "Do I have to respond to this?" "Yes," Manuá murmurs back, and Afukaká responds in the traditional chiefly way. Then, sighing again as shamans do, Manuá continues. Having grasped the dialogic structure of the scene, Afukaká now replies promptly. The dialogue revolves around the fact that the Kuikuro had all come to Tanguro in order to have their diseases extracted from their bodies.

Manuá is again clearly resorting to different, normally incompatible settings: ceremonial dialogue and precuring talk between the shaman and patient. He speaks in a louder voice, clearly addressing all participants, as well as Afukaká, who for his part answers in a lower voice, respecting normal usage, and thus considering the surrounding Kalapalo as mere "overhearers" (Goffman 1981). Manuá is already navigating between different frames of participation, splitting himself, so to speak, into two layers: Manuá the interlocutor of Afukaká, and Manuá who shows everyone that he is talking to Afukaká. This position as the publicist of the actions of others and himself is a defining trait of Manuá's translating role.

Next, while the Kalapalo audience clap, Manuá stands up, places the white moth in Afukaká's hand, and asks in a playful tone: "Did the dead thing open its eyes?" Staring at the perplexed Afukaká, Manuá smiles broadly and waits for a confirmation, which comes in the form of Afukaká's own shy smile in response. Manuá gives the signal for applause.

Now walking around the chief, he invokes a new setting, that of a humorous stage performance, as though on a TV show. This time the cue for the new "footing" is the amusing tone, as well the movement of his body.[27] He asks everybody: "Do we want it to fly? Say 'Yes'!" With the moth again held in his hand, he shouts at it: "Rise, rise!" He then throws it up into the air, but the little insect falls to the ground. This violation of what everyone was expecting fails to dent the Master's self-confidence. He analogically connects the moth's downward

---

27. Goffman defines footing as "the alignment we take up to ourselves and the others present as expressed in the way we manage the production and reception of an utterance" (1981:128).

flight to the disappearance of the disease for which it stands: "Your ex-disease is now on the ground!" he exclaims.

Sighing again, he scoops out some water from the aluminum pot with the little measuring cup and serves it to Afukaká, saying: "Drink the blood of Taugi." The chief drinks and is told to enter the house and sit on a stool. Next comes Afukaká's daughter, Auná. She also drinks, and is dispatched to join her father inside the house. But when she is about to walk between the Master and his sister, the former holds her and Lümbu tells her what to do: she has to pass to the left of the Master's sister rather than split them.

Here Manuá plays in two different keys. On the one hand, he produces an image-like association between dispensing medicines, Catholic communion, and the Sun, conflating in his own person the roles of priest and doctor, while he also convokes the main Xinguano mythological figure, with whom he identifies himself. The Eucharistic substance dispensed is not the bread-flesh but the wine-blood (here converted into Taugi's water-blood). However, in the local mythology, drinking blood is what distinguishes warlike Indians from pacific Xinguanos.[28] It is impossible to know how this cannibal translation reverberated in Afukaká's imagination. By any reckoning, though, Manuá was making a risky association here, one among many others that would eventually lead to him being accused of witchcraft.

On the other hand, the practical rectification of Auná's slight ritual mistake makes visible that there is a *correct* way of proceeding, one with which the Kuikuro are not yet acquainted, but which is central to the ritual's organization and success. Errors and corrections establish a differential in knowledge and give the impression that improvisation plays a minor part in the scene. This is played out at diverse levels of inclusion: the Master knows more than his auxiliaries, his auxiliaries know more than the Kalapalo, and the Kalapalo know more than the Kuikuro. This explains why Manuá stages a set of actions with his own people before letting the Kuikuro enter the village plaza. He has to establish different levels of shared knowledge.

Manuá continues to dispense Taugi's blood to the Kuikuro, who approach him in a hierarchical order. This is a basic structuring principle in Upper Xingu

---

28. In one famous narrative, the mythical character Ahinhuká offers a bowl of manioc porridge to the ancestor of the Xinguanos. The latter looks at the contents and sees only blood, refusing to drink it. The ancestor of "wild Indians" (*ngikogo*) drank the whole cup, however, confirming his predatory disposition.

rituals, but here it is reinforced both by Manuá's political ambitions and by the presence of one of the most important Xinguano chiefs. At a certain point, though, Kumãtsi, a Mehinaku man married to a Kuikuro woman and descendant of an ancient Kalapalo chief, presents himself, painted with red annatto dye and wearing a necklace and a belt, in stark contrast to the other visitors. Manuá interrogates him: "Who are you?" Kumãtsi responds in an Arawakan language: "I'm Mehinaku." "Who am I?" retorts Manuá. Without grasping the questioner's intent, Kumãtsi replies: "You are half Kalapalo, half Nahukwá."[29] Manuá accepts the answer, but then flips it over: "What did I become? I'm not Kalapalo anymore, I'm not Nahukwá anymore. What did I become?" he asks, raising his arms and pointing to the sky. Kumãtsi now says: "You have become God."

One would expect Manuá to call for applause at this point, but instead he continues to question the man: "How do you say God's name?" Kumãtsi once again fails to get his point, so Manuá gives him a clue: "The name I have now." Someone whispers to the baffled Kumãtsi: "The name you give to Taugi [in Arawak]." Kumãtsi still does not get it, and it is only after his wife whispers the correct term that he replies in a hesitant tone: "Kamü?" Clapping. Kumãtsi finally relaxes, while Manuá addresses the audience, saying that he had held his interlocutor's speech within his chest: "I hold 'Kamü' here."

This event shows how Manuá is able to reframe an interaction in order to regain control of the situation. Kumãtsi presents himself as a healthy visitor going to a traditional festival, not as someone ill expecting to be cured. Manuá presses him to give proper answers, without ever losing his magisterial grace, but always putting the visitor in an uneasy position. Manuá makes Kumãtsi mumble that he is God, but is not satisfied with the answer. He wants to make him say God in the Mehinaku language: he wants him to provide a new translation identifying Deus, Taugi, and Kamü, and, of course, himself, the Master.

IS THIS A RITUAL?

We cannot present the entire set of actions that ensued at the Kalapalo village of Tanguro on that damp day in 2006. We hope our description has shown how

---

29. There are four Carib-speaking peoples in the Upper Xingu: the Kalapalo, the Kuikuro, the Matipu, and the Nahukwá. They all speak mutually comprehensible languages (Meira and Franchetto 2005).

skillfully Manuá was able to switch from one footing to another. In his famous essay on footing, Goffman (1981) mentions that certain people in certain situations excel in acting like pivots, pursuing different courses of communication, with different persons, in different tonalities. While this ability may be constitutive of human communication in general, it also seems clear that Manuá takes it to a level of complexity rarely achieved in everyday communication. And he does so on many grounds.

The most obvious aspect is the extremely wide scope of the settings he invokes. These are often dissonant, sometimes contradictory: communion, baptism, dispensing medicines, shamanic treatment, chiefly reception, traditional formal speech, funerary wailing, witchcraft, TV shows, and Evangelical church services. He does so to a point where it seems futile to seek for a coherent preexisting metaphysical agenda. From the prophet's perspective, what is at stake is the invention of new settings in which different contexts and forms of communication become commensurate. To achieve this aim, he rapidly alters his tone, gestures, or addressees. For instance, he may be talking to a patient as a therapist and then suddenly address the audience, mobilizing a TV show setting, before immediately coming back to a kind of shamanic interview. He also combines different modalities simultaneously. When greeting Chief Afukaká, for example, his body posture invokes a ceremonial welcome, while his speech and prosody invoke shamanic healing. Finally, he also switches quickly from one context to the other, and employs a wide range of mechanisms to do so. By using different modalities in divergent ways, the Master not only juxtaposes settings, he also merges them.

Participation frames play an important role here in reducing this dazzling complexity. This is less explicit in the collective welcoming ceremony, but very clear during the curing therapies, where the communication between Manuá and the patient basically consists of straightforward instructions (stand up, lie down, drink), therapeutic gestures, and rhetorical questions. The communication between the Master and the audience corresponds largely to the dialogue established with the patient, which is closer to a monologue than a dialogue. The interactional pattern is similar to Evangelical testimony, where the pastor publicizes what the believer is saying by repeating, commenting on, and drawing circular conclusions from his or her words.

The Master is always controlling the flow of communication, and aligning different degrees of knowledge about each of his performative acts. He is indeed the universal translator he claims to be, someone able to hear and speak to everyone in an ever-changing context that he himself constantly recreates. At the same time, this communicative behavior risks trapping him in a vicious circle: the very moves he performs in order to construct a common ground or assure the participants' commitment invariably cast doubt on the ritual frame itself. Consider one of these frantic switches or combinations of footings. Most of the time they are meant to clarify the situation. Manuá explains to everyone what is going on, or to someone what he or she is supposed to do. Then he suddenly interprets a slight detail in the environment as a confirmation of his Taugi-quality, or as proof that Mary is indeed present (in the form of a blowing wind or a flying bird), and asks everyone to yell out their belief and faith in him. But these constant contextualizations loosen his grip on the audience, who forget what the main course of action is supposed to be. In addition, some states, like shamanic distress and pain, cannot be dismissed suddenly without arousing some suspicion about their sincerity.

Here two important reflexive actions are crucial: the applause and the Master's whimsical laughter.[30] Most of the time, his auxiliaries begin clapping as a way of forcing everyone to demonstrate their agreement on the situation publicly, as well as their active participation in it. But they clearly invoke staged situations, making it hard to decide what exactly is going on. Laughter, on the other hand, is almost entirely exclusive to Manuá and Manuá only. His laughs are often inserted at a juncture between two different actions, as a means to fill the gaps and, perhaps, to mask some slight embarrassment. They show that the Master knows what he is doing, even if no one else does. At the same time, no one is sure what exactly is supposed to be amusing, nor what sort of action he is reacting to or commenting upon. If his laughter applies to the highest order of context (i.e., to the whole ceremonial encounter), would that not imply that everything is just a (serious) play? We have already seen that there is a complex relation between acting and ritual in the illumination scene. One may wonder if this feature is not far more systematic, giving to the whole scene its predominant tone.

According to Bateson, any playful behavior implies metacommunication: "The actions in which we now engage do not denote what those actions *for which*

30. Applause is a nonindigenous form of expression which the Xinguanos incorporated in new activities in the villages (e.g., when someone scores a goal in a football match or after someone talks in a nontraditional political meeting). Applause is also quite common in TV shows and in Evangelical cults in Brazil.

they stand would denote" (1972: 180). A playful nip, for instance, does not denote aggression. Bateson also recognized a more complex form of play: "the game which is constructed not upon the premise 'This is play,' but rather around the question 'Is this play?'" (ibid.: 182). Following this insight, Houseman proposed to define hazing rituals in elite French preparatory schools as built upon this very question. While openly fictitious, the humiliations the new students suffer are decidedly too painful not to provoke real distress and anxiety. At the same time, the new students are "forced to pretend to pretend that this is so" (Houseman 2001: 4), that is, to maintain the fiction of the fictitious quality of hazing. Our case can be seen as an inversion of such a frame: while being submitted to what they believe to be a serious ceremony, the Master's patients constantly face the question "Is this really a ritual?" The whole event, therefore, oscillates between (fake) ritual and (serious) play, an oscillation that could partly account both for the Master's capacity to captivate, and for his later disqualification as a witch.

THE FALL

The Master effectively generated a new communicative context and established new ritual condensations. However, like the Red Queen in Alice in Wonderland, he had to run to remain in the same place, constantly innovate to continue to amaze. His task became ever more complex as he became famous and was asked to cure people in other indigenous villages and even White people in the city. He started asking for large sums of money, saying that his spirit Taugi no longer accepted traditional luxury goods. He had already hugely inflated the price of shamanic treatment in terms of luxury goods; now he was throwing the entire system of shamanic payments into disarray (Fausto 2014).

The Master's innovations were soon regarded with suspicion by a number of powerful shamans, who first suggested that he had to submit himself to formal training with another shaman, and later began spreading a counterinterpretation that attributed his powers to witchcraft. When other Kalapalo people, with a history of political dispute with Manuá's family, started to fall ill, many fingers pointed to the Master (Cardoso, Guerreiro, and Novo 2012: 28–29). As the accusations became ever stronger, the Master's fate was sealed, forcing him into exile under the threat of execution. His fall was as rapid as his rise.

The rise and fall of a prophet's empire is not exactly a question of belief and disbelief, at least not in a theological sense. The Master's translating acts were received within what we earlier called an "abductive frame." People took part in these actions as long as they could practically engage with the possibility of him really being a hypershaman, capable of putting an end to pain, sickness, and witchcraft (the only cause of death in the Upper Xingu).[31] For some he was actually managing to attain this condition and, to tell the readers the truth, a number of our acquaintances really were cured. But guess what? Most of them were not. Still, there is no consensual judgment about the Master today: Was he a fake? Had he been powerful but subsequently lost his power? Was sorcery the real source of his power?

After his downfall, traditional shamans adopted some of his innovations—like curing at a distance or via the radio—but most of them returned to business as usual. People just moved on, and so did the shamans. Even if the Kuikuro visitors were not entirely convinced, the event itself proved a success, communicated over an ample area through the grapevine and the radio. After the visit and some months before his fall, the Master went to the Kisedje (Suyá) people in order to cure their great chief Kuyusi, a therapy that cost a couple of thousand reais, paid by the municipality of the nearby town of Querência. This was probably the climax of Manuá's prophetic movement, which lasted approximately a year, spreading like wildfire, but containing within it the very sparks of its own failure.

CONCLUDING CLAIMS

Let us conclude with some straightforward general claims concerning the notion of "translating acts." We hope these claims will render more explicit the

---

31. As attested in the historical record, what became known as "prophets" in the literature on the indigenous peoples of South America were mostly hypershamans: that is, individuals who acquired a power similar to that of the cultural heroes. They were deemed capable of refounding the conditions in which humanity has lived since the end of mythic time by producing a state of continuous ritual effervescence. These movements were themselves sorts of hyperrituals intended to put the world in flux and remold it through unending ritual activity. The Tupi-Guarani who inhabited the Atlantic Coast in the sixteenth century had a category for incorporating this possibility: the term *karaiwa* or *karai* designated regional shamans, distinct from the more ordinary and local *payé*. In the early colonial period, this category was applied to both Europeans and leaders of "prophetic" movements (Clastres 1975). It is important to note, however, that hypershamans are more powerful than biblical prophets: they do not only announce the coming of a new time, but intend to ritually fabricate this new world themselves.

ideas that have guided our analysis of the ethnographic data. First of all, we claim that:

(1) translating acts are a modality of translation through actions, in which referential meaning plays a less important role than form, context, and expressive force.

From this privileging of pragmatics over semantics, we derive two main consequences: on the one hand, translating acts operate by using different modalities of communication and distinct semiotic modes; and, on the other, the failure or success of a translating act is not a matter of adjusting to the conceptual content of one or other of the languages/worlds in contact.

Our second major claim is that:

(2) ritual situations are a privileged experimental context for translating acts, especially those mediating between radical alterity, meaning that in different "cultural encounters" translation is less a matter of producing a lingua franca and more a question of generating a new ritual form.

Here we propose a shift in the way one understands such encounters: we address them as a way of creating new forms of communication (both with "spirits" and with people) rather than of producing a new syncretic cosmology. In this sense, the emerging rituals are a kind of experimental frame in which a certain number of communicative means are put to the test.

Rituals are not the only place for the production of new intercultural pragmatics (see Stasch, this volume), but they are remarkably rich in this respect. At the same time, they involve risk, since translating acts produce an abductive landscape of a special kind: one that involves both creating a new prototype (here Taugi-Sun) and convincing the audience that the main actor on the ritual stage is this very prototype (Master-King) and not a case of another, better-known person (a shaman, a crook, or even a sorcerer). Responding to this abductive landscape is a matter of practical engagement rather than belief.

As we have seen, the richness and riskiness of translating acts seem to presuppose a prior simplification of meaning and relations within each of the different worlds in contact. Simplification would be a precondition, then, for producing a new complex ritual configuration, meaning that in the process of translation, some elements must necessarily be eclipsed and others foregrounded.

Finally, there is a chronological and topological dimension to such prophetic movements, which involve the invention, selection, and transmission of new forms in space-time. They tend to speed up all the procedures involved. They rise as fast as they fall, they spread as far as they shrink back. But when some of the translating acts survive, and this is our last claim, then:

(3) the stabilization implies the begetting of a new tradition, a new original, which often implies the forgetting of the very process of translation that gave birth to the new form.

Memory effaces the acts of appropriation and translation, though traces of them remain registered in ritual form (Severi 1993; Fausto 2007; Santos-Granero 2007). Reading these acts back then only remains possible through a sort of indicial investigation (Ginzburg [1986] 1989). Here we have tried to present an ethnographic case in which these translating acts can be observed still unfolding before attaining any stabilization.

ACKNOWLEDGMENTS

The first version of this text was presented at Carlo Severi's seminar at the École des Hautes Études en Sciences Sociales in 2012, and a second one was prepared for the Fyssen Seminar 'Translating Worlds' held in Paris in 2014. We thank William Hanks and Carlo Severi for their kind invitation. We heartily thank Takumã, Mahajugi, and Ahukaka Kuikuro for making the tapes used to write this article available to us. Our gratitude also goes to the anonymous reviewers who helped us to improve the manuscript. David Rodgers revised our French–Brazilian English.

REFERENCES

Abreu, Stela Azevedo de. 2005. *Aleluia e o banco de luz: Messianismo indígena no norte Amazônica*. Centro de Memória da Unicamp, Campinas.

Amaral, Maria Virgínia Ramos do. 2014. "A caminho do mundo-luz celestial: O Areruya e os profetismos kapon e pemon." Master's dissertation, PPGAS, Museu Nacional, Universidade Federal do Rio de Janeiro.

Andrello, Geraldo. 1993. "Os Taurepáng: Memória e profetismo do século XX." Master's dissertation, Campinas, Unicamp.

Barcelos Neto, Aristóteles. 2008. *Apapaatai: Rituais de máscaras no Alto Xingu.* São Paulo: Edusp/Fapesp.

Basso, Ellen. 1987. *In favor of deceit: A study of tricksters in an Amazonian society.* Tucson: University of Arizona Press.

Bateson, Gregory. 1972. *Steps to an ecology of mind.* New York: Random House.

Boyer, Pascal. 1988. *Barricades mystérieuses et pièges à pensée: Introduction à l'analyse des épopées fang.* Paris: Société d'Ethnologie.

———. 1990. *Tradition as truth and communication: A cognitive description of traditional discourse.* Cambridge: Cambridge University Press.

———. 1994. *The naturalness of religious ideas.* Berkeley: University of California Press.

Brown, Michael. 1991. "Beyond resistance: A comparative study of utopian renewal in Amazonia." *Ethnohistory* 38 (4): 388–413.

Butt Colson, Audrey. 1960. 'The birth of a religion: The origins of a semi-Christian religion among the Akawaio." *Journal of the Royal Anthropological Institute* 90 (1): 66–106.

———. 1971. "Hallelujah among the Patamona Indians." *Antropologica* 28: 25–58.

———. 1994/1996. "'God's Folk': The evangelization of Amerindians in western Guiana and the Enthusiastic Movement of 1756." *Antropologica* 86: 3–111.

Campos, Haroldo de. 1981. "*Post-scriptum:* Transliteração mefistofáustica." In *Deus e o Diabo no Fausto de Goethe*, 179–209. São Paulo: Ed. Perspectiva.

Cardoso, Marina, Antonio Guerreiro, Jr., and Marina Pereira Novo. 2012. "As flechas de Maria: Xamanismo, poder político e feitiçaria no Alto Xingu." *Tellus* 23: 11–33.

Carneiro da Cunha, Manuela. 1973. "Logique du mythe et de l'action: Le mouvement messianique canela de 1963." *L'Homme* XIII (4): 5–37.

Clark, Herbert H. 1992. *Arenas of language use.* Chicago: University of Chicago Press

———. 1996. *Using language.* Cambridge: Cambridge University Press.

———. 2006. "Social actions, social commitments." In *Roots of human sociality: Culture, cognition and interaction*, edited by Nicholas J. Enfield and Stephen C. Levinson, 126–50. New York: Berg.

Clastres, Hélène. 1975. *La terre sans mal: Le prophétismo tupi-guarani.* Paris: Seuil.

Déléage, Pierre. 2012. "Transmission et stabilisation des chants rituels." *L'Homme* 203–4 : 103–37.

———. 2013. *Inventer l'écriture.* Paris: Graphê, Les Belles Lettres.

de Vienne, Emmanuel. 2011. "Traditions en souffrance: Maladie, chamanisme et rituel chez les Trumai du Haut Xingu, Matto Grosso." Doctoral thesis, Écoles des Hautes Études en Sciences Sociales.

Fausto, Carlos. 2002. "The bones affair: Knowledge practices in contact situations seen from an Amazonian case." *Journal of the Royal Anthropological Institute* 84 (4): 669–90.

———. 2007. "If God were a jaguar: Cannibalism and Christianity among the Guarani (16th–20th centuries)." In *Time and memory in indigenous Amazonia: Anthropological perspectives,* edited by Carlos Fausto and Michael J. Heckenberger, 74–105. Gainesville: University Press of Florida.

———. 2011a. "Mil años de transformación: La cultura kuikuro entre el pasado y el futuro." In *Por donde hay soplo: Estudios amazónicos en los países andinos,* edited by Jean-Pierre Chaumeil, Óscar Espinosa, and Manuel Cornejo, 185–216. Lima: IFEA-CAAP-PUCP.

———. 2011b. "Le masque de l'animiste: Chimères et poupées russes en Amérique Indigène." *Gradhiva: Revue d'Anthropologie et d'Histoire des Arts* 13: 48–67.

———. 2014. "How much for a song? The culture of calculation and the calculation of culture." In *Ownership and nurture: Studies in native Amazonian property relations,* edited by Marc Brightman, Carlos Fausto, and Vanessa Grotti. Unpublished manuscript.

Fausto, Carlos, Bruna Franchetto, and Michael J. Heckenberger. 2008. "Language, ritual and historical reconstruction: Towards a linguistic, ethnographical, and archaeological accout of Upper Xingu society." In *Lessons from documented endangered languages,* edited by K. David Harrison, David Rood, and Arienne Dwyer, 120–57. Amsterdam: John Benjamins.

Fausto, Carlos, Caco Xavier, and Elena Welper. 2014. "Can we speak of social reform in Indigenous Amazonia? Conflict, messianism and the ordinary utopia of living well." Unpublished manuscript.

Franco Neto, João Veridiano. 2010. "Xamanismo Kalapalo e assistência médica no Alto Xingu: Estudo etnográfico das práticas curativas." Master's dissertation, Campinas, Unicamp.

Franchetto, Bruna, and Michael J. Heckenberger. 2001. *Os povos do Alto Xingu: História e cultura.* Rio de Janeiro: Editora UFRJ.

Furtado de Mendonça, Heitor. (1591–92) 1922. *Primeira visitação do Santo Ofício as partes do Brasil: Confissões da Bahia (1591–92).* Edited by Capistrano de Abreu. São Paulo: Paulo Prado.

Gell, Alfred. 1998. *Art and agency: An anthropological theory.* Oxford: Clarendon Press.

Ginzburg, Carlo. (1986) 1989. *Clues, myths, and the historical method.* Translated by John and Anne C. Tedeschi. Baltimore, MD: Johns Hopkins University Press.

Goffman, Erving. 1981. *Forms of talk.* Philadelphia: University of Pennsylvania Press.

Goulard, Jean-Pierre. 2009 *Entre mortales e immortales El ser según los ticunas de la Amazonia.* Lima: Instituto Francés de Estudios Andinos.

Gregor, Thomas. 1977. *Mehinaku: The drama of daily life in a Brazilian Indian village.* Chicago: University of Chicago Press.

Gumperz, John J. 1982. *Discourse strategies.* Cambridge: Cambridge University Press.

Hanks, William. 2006. "Conviction and common ground in a ritual event." In *Roots of human sociality: Culture, cognition and interaction*, edited by Nicholas J. Enfield and Stephen C. Levinson, 299–328. New York: Berg.

———. 2010. *Converting words: Maya in the age of the cross.* Berkeley: University of California Press.

Heckenberger, Michael J. 2005. *The ecology of power: Culture, place, and personhood in the southern Amazon, AD. 1000–2000.* New York, Routledge.

Hill, Jonathan, and Robin Wright. 1988. "Time, narrative, and ritual: Historical interpretations from an Amazonian society." In *Rethinking history and Myth: Indigenous South American perspectives on the past*, edited by Jonathan Hill, 78–105. Urbana: University of Illinois Press.

Houseman, Michael. 2001. "Is this play? Hazing in French preparatory schools." *Focaal: European Journal of Anthropology* 37: 39–48.

Houseman, Michael, and Carlo Severi 1998. *Naven or the other self: A relational Approach to Ritual.* Leiden: Brill.

Hugh-Jones, Stephen. 1994. "Shamans, prophets, priests and pastors." In *Shamanism, history and the state*, edited by Nicholas Thomas and Caroline Humphrey, 32–75. Ann Arbor: University of Michigan Press.

Humphrey, Caroline, and James Laidlaw. 1994. *The archetypal actions of ritual: A theory of ritual illustrated by the Jain rite of worship.* Oxford: Clarendon Press.

Kopenawa, Davi, and Bruce Albert. 2010. *La chute du ciel: Paroles d'un chaman yanomami.* Paris: Plon.

Lages, Susana Kampff. 2002. *Walter Benjamin: Tradução e melancolia.* São Paulo: Edusp.

Meira, Sergio, and Bruna Franchetto. 2005. "The Southern Cariban languages and the Cariban family." *International Journal of American Linguistics* 71 (2): 127–90.

Melià, Bartomeu. 1987. "La tierra sin mal de los Guaraní: Economía y profecía." *Suplemento Antropologico* 22 (2): 81–97.

Melatti, Julio Cesar 1967. *O messianismo krahó.* São Paulo: Editora Herder/ Edusp.

Métraux, Alfred. 1942. "A Quechua messiah in eastern Peru." *American Anthropologist* 44 (4): 721–25.

Monteiro, John M. 1999. "The crisis and transformation of invaded societies: Coastal Brazil in the sixteenth century." In *Cambridge history of the native peoples of the Americas*, edited by Frank Salomon and Stuart Schwartz, Vol. III-1, 973–1023. Cambridge: Cambridge University Press.

Montoya, Antonio Ruiz de. (1639) 1985. *Conquista espiritual feita pelos religiosos da Companhia de Jesus nas províncias do Paraguai, Paraná, Uruguai e Tape.* Porto Alegre: Martins.

Nimuendajú, Curt. 1952. *The Tukuna.* Edited by Robert H. Lowie. Berkeley: University of California Press.

———. 1987. *As lendas da criação e destruição do mundo como fundamentos da religião dos Apapocúva-Guarani.* São Paulo: Hucitec.

Oliveira Filho, João Pacheco de. 1988. *O nosso governo: Os ticuna e o regime tutelar.* São Paulo: Editora Marco Zero/CNPq.

Peirce, Charles S. (1901) 1940. "Abduction and induction." In *The philosophy of Peirce: Selected writings*, edited by Justus Buchler, 150–56. London: Routledge.

Pina-Cabral, João de. 1999. "Trafic humain à Macao: Les compatibilités équivoques de la communication interculturelle." *Ethnologie Française* XXIX (2): 225–36.

———. 2001. *Between China and Europe: Person, culture, and emotion in Macao.* London: Continuum.

Santos-Granero, Fernando. 2007. "Time is disease, suffering, and oblivion: Yanesha historicity and the struggle against temporality." In *Time and memory in indigenous Amazonia: Anthropological perspectives*, edited by Carlos Fausto and Michael J. Heckenberger, 47–73. Gainesville: University Press of Florida.

Severi, Carlo. 1993. *La memoria rituale: Follia e immagine del Bianco in una tradizione sciamanica amerindiana*. Florence: La Nuova Italia.

———. 2002. "Memory, reflexivity and belief: Reflections on the ritual use of language." *Social Anthropology* 10 (1): 23–40.

———. 2004. "Capturing imagination: A cognitive approach to cultural complexity." *Journal of the Royal Anthropological Institute* (N.S.) 10 (4): 815–38.

———. (2007) 2015. *The chimera principle: An anthropology of memory and imagination*. Translated by Janet Lloyd. Chicago: HAU Books.

Thomas, David. 1976. "El movimiento religioso de San Miguel entre los Pemon." *Antropologica* 43: 3–52

Vainfas, Ronaldo. 1995. *A heresia dos índios: Catolicismo e rebeldia no Brasil colonial*. São Paulo: Companhia das Letras.

Varese, Stefano. 2006. *La sal de los cerros: Resistencia y utopía en la Amazonía peruana*. Lima: Fondo Editorial del Congreso del Perú.

Veber, Hanna. 2003. "Asháninka messianism: The production of a 'black hole' in Western Amazonian ethnography." *Current Anthropology* 44 (2): 183–211.

Viegas, Susana de Matos. 2007. *Terra calada: Os Tupinambá na mata atlântica do sul da Bahia*. Rio de Janeiro: 7Letras/Almedina.

Viveiros de Castro, Eduardo. 2004. "Perspectival anthropology and the method of controlled equivocation." *Tipití: Journal of the Association for the Anthropology of Lowland South America* 2 (1): 3–22.

Whitehead, Neil L. 1999. "The crisis and transformation of invaded societies: The Caribbean (1492–1580)." In *Cambridge history of the native peoples of the Americas*, edited by Frank Salomon and Stuart Schwartz, Vol. III-1, 864–903. Cambridge: Cambridge University Press.

CHAPTER NINE

Words and worlds
Ethnography and theories of translation

John Leavitt

Of the human sciences, only anthropology has consistently taken seriously the idea that beside or beyond the evident fact that all human beings live in the same world, there is a sense in which they live or have lived in different worlds. Since Boas, these have been called "cultures,"[1] and have recently returned as "ontologies." As it happens, the cultures that seem to be most different from the ones that have produced most anthropologists are those that have been colonized and transformed. Are we to think of an Australian or African tribal group as living in a different world, or rather as peripheral lumpen proletarians? How important is what is distinctive? As Bridget O'Laughlin wrote (1978: 103), what is distinctive about the zebra is its stripes, but stripes are hardly the most important aspect of a zebra's life.

---

1. Boas is the first to have used the word "culture" in the plural in English (Stocking 1968). The plural use in German (*Kulturen*) had been established in the late nineteenth century by Lazarus, Steinthal, and the school of *Völkerpsychologie* (Kalmar 1987).

Yet what is most important to people themselves depends in part on their historical situation and their expectations; these need not always be the same everywhere, at every time. Existing in a situation of starvation and disease is not the way any human being, or any organism, wishes to live. But once you can eat and feed and protect your children, then other factors come into play. These factors may be conscious or close to consciousness; or, as in the case of the language one speaks, they may be largely unconscious. And the record shows that these world-making factors can be extraordinarily diverse.

This means that human values, goals, and conceptualizations are themselves diverse, and maybe even incommensurable (Povinelli 2001): insofar as conceptions differ, lived worlds may be said to differ. Probably the most blatant diversity is that of human languages, this very diversity being one of the important language universals. This is a simple fact: the species speaks or has spoken thousands of different mutually unintelligible languages. How seriously should this diversity be taken? Some say not at all: according to Noam Chomsky, if a Martian arrived on Earth and observed how children learn language, he (in these parables it is always a male Martian) would say that there is only one human language with, in Steven Pinker's oxymoron, mutually unintelligible dialects (Pinker 1994: 240). On the other side, both George Steiner (1975) and Claude Hagège (1985) use the same parable to opposite effect: both say that if a Martian arrived on earth and observed human physical variation, he would assume that there were maybe a dozen human languages—instead of the five to ten thousand we actually find (for discussion of the Martian parable paradox, seeLeavitt 2011: 5–6). Diversity goes all the way up and down the levels of language structure, from sound to the dividing of experience in lexicon, to the directing of attention to one or another aspect of experience by pervasive grammatical categories, to genres of discourse, the kinds of things one is expected to say and hear in a given society. Both the music and the meanings of languages are organized differently for each one—and, again, there are thousands. This gives the continuing impression, through the generations, that different languages convey different worlds (Sapir 1921: 120–21; Friedrich 1986: 16).

The idea that ethnography is a kind of translation (Asad 1986; Rubel and Rosman 2003; and see the essays in this volume) has largely been treated metaphorically, as an implication of the broader movement to see cultures as texts to be interpreted (Geertz 1973; Ricoeur 1973). Now (Hanks and Severi, this volume), we are seeing an attempt to use the idea of translation as an alternative both to fixed cognitive universals and to an ontological pluralism of sealed worlds, implying instead a focus on the processes of exchange and transfer not only between societies ("cultures"), but also between different social classes, genders, caste groupings, within societies, which in fact define all social interaction.

There is, however, a risk here, as there is in any analogy. By extending the idea of translation out of language into culture more broadly, we weaken its force of surprise. Languages that are mutually unintelligible are absolutely so. To recap Roman Jakobson's functions of language (1960): when someone speaks, say, Turkish—one of the approximately 9,990. languages that I absolutely do not know,[2] I do not understand a single word. The referential function is missing, or rather was never there. A unilingual Turkish friend and I may be very phatic together over coffee, I may feel strong aspects of his expressivity, he can be effectively conative in getting me to jump out of the way of an oncoming bus, I may even sense some of the rhythm and alliteration if he recites a poem, but as long as he keeps speaking Turkish, there is no referential content, unless the two of us start working hard and for a long time on the metalinguistic function—which is to say that we start learning each other's languages.

Note how different this is from what is called translating culture. Since what we call culture includes virtually all aspects of life, as soon as I arrive in, again, say, Turkey, I think I recognize all kinds of things: houses, restaurants, markets, places of worship; men and women, children and adults, dressing somewhat differently from each other and occupying somewhat different roles. I can immediately begin to form impressions on what might someday become ethnographies of the economy, politics, social organization, religion. We can call these translations, and they share characteristics with interlingual translations. But there is a precious opacity to languages that other human practices do not share, or do not share so unavoidably. Staying close to actual linguistic translation practice offers ethnographers a salutary reminder of how much, in all aspects of a culture, they do not understand.

As against the model or metaphor of the text, an alternative tradition, of philology and ethnopoetics, has opted, rather, for what we might call the metonym of the text: texts exist in cultures and in particular linguistic media. In this view, texts are seen not as "fragments of culture" (Silverstein and Urban 1996: 1), but as cultural foci, incomprehensible outside of their cultural and social

---

2. I use the figure of ten thousand attested human languages. The figure ranges from five to ten thousand, depending on what is considered a language and what a dialect.

situations, and, above all, made of language, which is to say, always a particular distinct language.

The fact of linguistic difference involves every level of language, from the untranslatability of phonetics and phonology (Webster 2014) to that of the universe of presuppositions out of which the source text arises, with levels of lexicon and grammatical architecture in between. Moving from one language to another and trying to have coherent "normal" texts in both must necessarily mean suppressions and additions—what A. L. Becker (1995), following Ortega y Gasset, calls deficiencies and exuberances; what John McDowell (2000) calls muting and adding. Yet it seems to go without saying that modern Western translation, whether literary translation or the mass of "useful," that is, business, government, and other organizational translation, has as its central, often its only, goal to convey what are considered the necessary or useful aspects of the referential meaning of a text into another language.

But producing such a usable text, that is, a normal-sounding or normal-reading text in the target language (to use the rather frightening terminology of translation theory), requires alterations of what was there in the source text, even in its referential meanings, at every level of language. The original is thinned out (deficiency), or else one feels it has been thickened up with material that wasn't there in the original (exuberance). This situation is all the more acute if we hope to convey not only the referential sense, but also something of the style and poetics of the original, or its role in its own society (Silverstein 2003).

Sensitive or suspicious readers have long felt that this transmogrification involves loss or betrayal, as is conveyed in the many derogatory aphorisms about translation: *traduttore traditore*, "translator [=] traitor" (a classic bit of metapragmatics that illustrates itself in its patterned untranslatability); a translation is a "phantom limb" (Robinson 1996 [1997]); "a translation is like a stewed strawberry" (attributed to Harry de Forest Smith in Brower 1959: 173). This last simile conveys both the maintenance of *something* through translation and at the same time the loss of freshness, that is, of complexity, and also, evidently, of structure. But the converse, conveying all of the meanings carried in the source statement, and only those, requires creating a "monstrosity" (McDowell 2000) in the target language. In this theoretical sense, of full transference from one to another normal linguistic frame, translation is impossible. And yet in practice it is both possible and necessary. In Franz Rosenzweig's words, "Translating means serving two masters. It follows that no one can do it. But it follows also that it is, like everything that no one can do in theory, everyone's task in practice" (1926 [1994]: 47).[3]

Given this reality, "normal," ordinary translation, what Jakobson (1959a) calls interlingual translation or translation in the strict sense, already carries a huge conceptual and cultural load: any translation is a translation of cultures or worlds. If we take language diversity seriously at all, then translators are on the front line; they are pilots traversing a relativistic linguistic universe.

Here I will offer a brief run through some modern Western ideas about translation, highlighting what seem to me to be particularly acute formalizations, and propose a radical view of translation that seems particularly suited to anthropologists. Going over this material seems important for an anthropological audience: the history of translation theory in the West parallels that of anthropology as a history of attitudes toward other ways of saying and thinking.[4]

The following part of the paper will explore a single example drawn from a ritual performance carried out in the Central Himalayas of northern India.

RENAISSANCE DIVERSITY

From the sixteenth century, over a relatively short time, the Western European world, based on an agricultural economy, a fixed hierarchical social organization and concomitant ideology, and the cultural dominance of Latin, was transformed. The feudal economy and social order were being replaced by an expanding capitalism; nation-states were on the rise with the valorization of state vernacular languages against Latin; Western societies were conquering and colonizing whole sections of the globe, setting up a world political-economic system. New philosophical systems and experimental sciences were coming into being, and the great political-ideological structure of the church was being

---

3. "Übersetzen heißt zwei Herren dienen. Also kann es Niemand. Also ist es, wie alles, was theoretisch besehen niemand kann, praktisch jedermanns Aufgabe." Cf. Sapir's statements that two languages could be incommensurable, while it was clear that he never questioned the possibility of translation. To be incommensurable means to be operating with different coordinate systems. While ultimate and exact congruence cannot be achieved in this situation, one can find equivalences that will serve all practical purposes (Leavitt 2011: 136–38).

4. For histories from within translation studies, see Berman ([1984] 1992); Venuti (1995); Bassnett (2014).

challenged from within. For many scholars of the century, new worlds, in many senses of the word, were opening up. One focus of debate was the relative value of vernacular languages versus Latin and Greek; another was the accessibility of both scientific and biblical truth to the masses of people; and much of the discussion turned on questions of translation.

The dominant medieval view had been that the diversity of languages was a curse, God's punishment for the human pride manifested in the construction of the Tower of Babel. Both Protestant reformers in the center and north of Europe and Catholic language activists in France and Italy challenged this view and saw language diversity either as a positive good or as a problem that could be handled through translation. I will begin with the better-known Protestant theories, but devote more time to Italian views of diversity, since I presume that these are less familiar to anthropologists.

Translation, for some Reformation thinkers, such as John Calvin (1509–64), at least allowed some mitigation of the curse of Babel. What one could translate was the meaning, the sense of the text, and this could be conveyed in vernacular tongues as well as in classical ones. The question of whether and how to translate Holy Writ into vernacular languages became a central religious and political debate, one of the central issues of the Reformation. With the Bible translations of the sixteenth century, translation itself came to be an essential part of a double goal: to reveal the referential meaning of Holy Writ to anyone who could read the vernacular, thus dispossessing the clergy of their monopoly on sacred texts; and at the same time to valorize the vernacular itself as a national tongue, since a part of the Protestant argument was for national churches headed in each case by the secular head of the country, not by the pope.

In Protestant translation practice, what is important is not the particular form of the language, but that the referential meaning be conveyed in a colloquial vernacular that Everyman can understand. This view was expressed clearly by Luther: the goal is "to produce clear language, comprehensible to everyone, with an undistorted sense and meaning" ("Preface to the Book of Job," cited in Rosenzweig [1926] 1994: 48); "in speech the meaning and subject matter must be considered, not the grammar, for the grammar shall not rule over the meaning" ("Translator's letter," 1530, cited in Bassnett 2014: 59). This view has continued to inspire Protestant translation theory up to this day, notably that of the Summer Institute of Linguistics: true conversion requires that God's Word be accessible in the speaker's own language (see, e.g., Handman 2007).

In Italy, parallel issues arose around the *Questione della lingua*: what language should serve as the cultural cement for Italy, now thought of as at least a potential national entity in spite of its political fragmentation. Here the basic argument was that the multiplicity of vernaculars was an aspect of the diversity of the world, in itself a good thing, an expression of God's infinite creative power. As Claude-Gilbert Dubois puts it about this period in Italy and in a France heavily influenced by Italian thinking, we "witness a kind of ennobling of the multiple.... Multiplication is not corruption, but fecundity" (1970: 119).

This is an enormous shift from the medieval view of an ordered hierarchy: it is no longer easy to tell what is superior and what is inferior. In the words of the Florentine humanist Benedetto Varchi (1503–65), "In the universe there must exist . . . all the things that can exist; and nothing is so small or so ugly (*tanto picciola nè così laida*) that it does not contribute and add to the perfection of the universe" (cited in Stankiewicz 1981: 181). If even the smallest and ugliest thing adds to the perfection of the universe, this implies a fundamental incommensurability: instead of a clear hierarchy, perfection is an infinite scatter. And this refusal of hierarchy applies to languages as well: one cannot assert the superiority of some languages over others. In his *Dialogo delle lingue* ([1542] 2009: 35), the Paduan humanist Sperone Speroni (1500–1588) has his mouthpiece assert: "I hold it certain that the languages of every country, such as the Arabic and the Indian, like the Roman and the Athenian, are of equal value."

The implication of this argument is, then, to challenge the Babel story and say that the multiplicity and diversity of languages is neither a curse nor a mere *felix culpa*, but a positive good, a gift from God. This was said explicitly by the Sienese humanist Claudio Tolomei (1492–1556): "Fecund nature (*la feconda natura*) did not accept that there should be a single form of speech in this great and varied edifice of the world" (1531, cited in Stankiewicz 1981: 180). Varchi, for his part, concludes: "I say that nature could not, and indeed perhaps should not, have made a single language for the whole world" (cited in Demonet 1992: 513).

Edward Stankiewicz sums up the views of this period: "One of the central notions in this program is the recognition that each of the individual, living languages has a place in the overall scheme of things, and that each of them is endowed with linguistic properties which make up its distinctive character, or 'genius'" (1981: 180).

The second part of this statement raises the notion of the distinctiveness of each language. Languages are not only valuable, but their value lies in their differing specifics, the distinctive character or genius of each one. Dubois (1970: 119) makes an explicit link between the diversity of words and the new idea of an infinite plurality of distinct worlds proposed by Giordano Bruno later in the century: "The plurality of languages, like the plurality of worlds invented by Giordano Bruno during the same period, demonstrates the immense richness of the spirit."

But the evocation of Bruno (1548–1600) raises a different point. We have seen that for Luther, and for Reformation Bible translators generally, what mattered was a clear conveyance of referential meaning—precisely not the exploitation of the specific riches of each language. Bruno's own defense of translation was based on a similar view of philosophical and what we would call scientific discourse. Bruno said that it was perfectly all right to read Aristotle in an Italian translation rather than the original Greek, in that either of these permitted the reader to test Aristotle's theories empirically and so recognize Aristotle's errors. Scientific knowledge was based not on the "pedantry" of knowing Greek and Latin, not on the word, but on knowledge of the world.

Unlike the Bible translators, the Italian theorists went on to justify a different side of language use from that of either Scripture or science: in literary and poetic discourse, the unique genius of each language comes into fruition as a form of social play. The Florentine shoemaker-sage Giovan Battista Gelli (1498–1563) writes that "every language has its particularities and its caprices (*capresterie*)" ([1551] 1976: 201–2); Varchi writes that Florentine has a "certain peculiar or special or particular property, as do all other languages" and boasts of "certain qualities and capricious turns (*certe proprietà e capestrerie*) in which the Florentine language abounds." And these turns are particularly apparent in everyday popular discourse (cited in Stankiewicz 1981: 182–83). Language cannot be encompassed in a definite set of rules, according to Varchi, because the rational faculty is incapable of capturing the expressive power of language in everyday speech. "Reason should prevail and win in all matters, except in language, where if reason is contrary to usage, or usage to reason, it is usage, not reason, which must always take precedence" (cited in ibid.: 183).

The most famous phrasing of this distinctive quality was in Joachim du Bellay's 1549 *Deffense et illustration de la langue françoyse*. Most of this text is a translation from Speroni's *Dialogo*, but it is du Bellay who specifies that each language possesses a certain *je ne scais quoy propre*—and he makes this point as part of a discussion of the difficulties of translation, as indeed do a number of Italian authors. Each language has its own force and beauty (*forze e bellezza*) which cannot be carried over into another tongue. Gelli ([1551] 1976: 201) writes: "They say that discourses (*cose*) that are translated from one language into another never have the same force or beauty that they had in their own. . . . To say things in one language in the style of another has no grace at all."

Repeatedly, the discussion of the distinctiveness of each language is part of the discussion of the difficulties of translation. The examples used are usually literary ones: Homer, Virgil, and Dante or Petrarch—and notably not Aristotle—none of whose work can be translated without losing its most important quality: the distinctive beauty of each. We find the example in the *De subtilitate* (1550) of the peripatetic mathematician-physician Girolamo Cardano (1501–76):

> The utility of the diversity of languages is that they can thereby express all the affects of the soul. The proof is that one cannot express Homer's sentences in Latin or in our mother tongue, nor Virgil in Greek or in our mother tongue, and even less the poems of Francesco Petrarch in Latin or Greek. (Cited in Dubois 1970: 118)

Implicit in the discussion is a distinction between two goals of discourse, that of conveying information and that of projecting the force and beauty of a language—to use anachronistic terms, between the referential and poetic functions of language. Translations from any language into any language can convey what we could call referential meaning but fail to convey play, *capresterie*, the force and beauty deriving from specific circumstances of social life. The distinction is central for Bruno, and Gelli writes, "I know that translation is done for the sake of sciences, and not to display the power and beauty of languages" ([1551] 1976: 202, cited in Stankiewicz 1981: 182). The formal distinction of the two modes was made by Sir Francis Bacon (1561–1626) between literary grammar, which deals with languages and which cannot really render the *je ne scai quoy* of each language in translation; and philosophical grammar, which deals with "the analogy between words and things, or reason" (Hüllen 2001: 213) and is in fact adequate for the advancement of learning.

Already, then, different goals of translation were being distinguished in the seventeenth century. For Protestants, the Sacred Scripture plays the role of science for Gelli or Bruno: in both cases, the goal is to convey clear meanings that are of immediate spiritual or secular use. But both presume the possibility of another attitude, one that fully recognizes the genius of each language. This possibility is developed above all by the Italians, with their recognition that linguistic worlds are constructed by bringing out the possibilities of each language in social interaction and in play.

"LES BELLES INFIDÈLES"

By the early 1600s, the French language and French style were dominating Europe. Already in the previous century, French discussion of translation had tended to be nationalistic and, notably, contrasted the "direct order" of the French sentence (Subject–Verb–Object, with adjectives coming for the most part after the noun) with the horrid mixup of Latin word order. With the rise of Cartesian rationalism, the assumption came to be strongly reinforced that all human beings think in the same way, languages being a mere means of external formulation and communication. When Descartes himself was challenged (by Hobbes) as to whether what he called reason could really be merely a local way of linking words, he replied: "Who doubts that a Frenchman and a German can have the same thoughts or reasonings about the same things, despite the fact that the words they think of are completely different?" (Descartes 1984: II, 125–26). In 1669, Descartes' follower Louis Le Laboureur claimed that since everyone in the world thought in the direct order of French, the Romans too must have conceived their sentences in French, then added a step to scramble the syntax before speaking or writing.

This basic position, as well as a strong sense of cultural self-sufficiency, motivated French translation theory. The argument was that the translator should reproduce not just the words of the text, but also the effect it had on its original readers. Since the text was not exotic or strange-sounding for its intended public, we should translate it in a way that is not disturbing for our public. If this requires changing meanings, so be it: such changes will in fact often be an improvement on what are sometimes needlessly repetitive, longwinded, incoherent, or indelicate originals. And this applies equally to scientific, religious, and literary works. In the words of the great translator of the century, Nicolas Perrot d'Ablancourt (1606–64),

> It would be a Judaic superstition to attach oneself to the words and abandon the design for which they were used. . . . It is only rendering half of an Author if one cuts off his eloquence. As he was agreeable in his own language, he should be so

in ours as well, and insofar as the beauties and graces of the two are different, we should not hesitate to give him those of our own country, since we are removing his. Otherwise we would be making an ugly (*meschante*) copy of an admirable original. (1638, cited in Horguelin 1996: 76)

When Perrot's translation of Tacitus—in which he says he sought "to look not so much to what [the author] said, as to what he should say " (cited in ibid.: 78)—came out during the 1640s, the general opinion was that it was a great improvement on the original. But a more extreme statement accompanies his 1654 translation of the quite scatological Greek satirist Lucian of Samosata. Plainly there is plenty in Lucian that would shock seventeenth-century French sensibilities.

It was . . . necessary to change all this, to make something agreeable; otherwise, it would not have been Lucian. . . . For this reason I do not always attach myself to the words or the ideas of this Author; and, maintaining his goal, I arrange things to our air and our style. Different times require not only different words, but different thoughts; and it is the custom of Ambassadors to dress in the fashion of the land to which they have been sent, for fear of appearing ridiculous to those they aim to please. It is true that this is not, strictly speaking, Translation; but it is better than Translation. (Cited in Horguelin 1996: 80)

Indeed, Perrot would write that his translation of Thucydides had brought his author back from the dead in the form of a modern Frenchman; this is something for which Thucydides might well have been grateful. On the contrary, failing to change the original sufficiently, writes Perrot, produces a "monstrous body" (*corps monstreux*; cited in Venuti 1995: 47).

Not everyone's arguments were as intelligently put as Perrot's. Pierre Perrin (c. 1620–75), the so-called Abbé Perrin, claimed that his 1648 translation of Virgil brought Aeneas back as a French cavalier, "dressed up with pomp and plume and bangles" (cited in Ladborough 1938: 86).

There were a few detractors of this method, mainly among philologists and what were called the *traducteurs scrupuleux* (as opposed to Perrot and the *traducteurs libres*). Among these, Gilles Ménage (1613–92) is reported to have said that Perrot's translations were like a lady he had once known in Tours: she had been *belle*, but *infidèle*. Since then the whole movement of elegant domesticating translation has been known as "Les Belles Infidèles."

MANY WORLDS

Unlike the French, who saw French as the closest linguistic approximation to universal values of reason and art, seventeenth-century German scholars valorized German for its very particularity and distinctiveness, its German-ness. Justus Georg Schottel (1612–76) devotes a section of his *Extensive work on the German language* (1663) to "How one should en-German (*verteutschen*)"—this is, characteristically, an alternative German word for übersetzen, "translate":

> To achieve this [the improvement of German] the arts, the sciences, history, and other *realia* should be dressed and become known in truly natural German, so that our language . . . will not smell of un-German Spanish pride, or Italian splendour gone stale, or French pronunciation and circumlocutions that are neither here nor there, or of other things, but it will have its own short and euphonious German nature, rich in meaning and sense. (Cited in Lefevere 1977: 11)

Leibniz's writings on German go in the same direction, arguing, for instance, that it would be a pity if German ended up denatured like English (Leibniz [1697] 1916: 30).

The reaction against French models, and against all universal abstract standards, was part of a wider movement to create a cultural Germany even in the absence of a political one. These tendencies reached their fulfillment in the work of Johann Gottfried Herder (1744–1803) and the following generation of Romantics (see Berman [1984] 1992). Herder's view of human history was one of clear celebration of diversity. In explicit rejection of French translation models, he insists on fidelity (*Treue*) to the distinctiveness of the source language and the source text, and, in an echo of Renaissance theorists, writes:

> I certainly do not believe that there exists any language in the world that can convey the words of another language with the same force and equivalent words. . . . The richest and the most useful language is one that best lends itself to word-for-word translations, translations that follow the original step by step. (Cited in Sdun 1967: 21)

Herder goes so far as to propose that the best thing for a language's unique development might be to keep it pure of all translations, all influence from other languages, "like a young virgin" (cited in ibid.: 26). These apparent contradictions grow out of a single problematic. To argue for foreignizing translations that make other languages and cultures accessible to us, each in its unique character, or to argue that we should stay clear of other languages and cultures so as to preserve our own unique character, are conclusions from a single set of premises: that there are a multitude of distinct and unique language-cultures, each one valuable. This is very different from the assumptions behind "Les Belles Infidèles."

In the early nineteenth century, the Romantics mounted a full-scale defense of "faithful" translation. A. W. von Schlegel criticizes what he calls French translation for making the foreign visitor "dress and behave according to [French] customs" (cited in Lefevere 1992: 79), and, in the period's translation manifesto (1813), Friedrich Schleiermacher (1768–1834) says that to translate a foreigner as he would have written had he *not* been foreign is like painting a portrait of a man not as he actually looks, but as he would have looked if he had had a different father. And it was Schleiermacher who posed the great dichotomy in a formulation that has been cited in most of the major statements on translation since then:

> The true translator, who really wants to bring together these two entirely separate (*ganz getrennten*) persons, his author and his reader, and to assist the latter in obtaining the most correct and complete understanding and enjoyment possible of the former without, however, forcing him out of the circle of his mother tongue—what paths are open to the translator for this purpose? In my opinion, there are only two. Either the translator leaves the author in peace as much as possible and moves the reader toward him, or he leaves the reader in peace as much as possible and moves the author toward *him*. ([1813] 1992: 41–42, translation modified)

Typically Romantic is the insistence here on the separateness and uniqueness of persons, and by implication of their worlds.

Schleiermacher presents his division as balanced, but his sympathies are with translation that moves the reader toward the author. Where the reverse type offers the reader no surprises, this has the potential of opening up his or her sensibilities, and with it that of his or her culture and language. After all, Schleiermacher was also the founder of hermeneutics as a discipline. German Romantic foreignizing challenged French hegemony and called for making Germany a center of intercultural ferment at the heart of Europe:

Our nation may be destined, because of its respect for what is foreign and its mediating nature, to carry all the treasures of foreign arts and scholarship, together with its own, in its language, to unite them into a great historical whole, so to speak, which would be preserved in the centre and heart of Europe, so that with the help of our language, whatever beauty the most different times have brought forth can be enjoyed by all people, as purely and perfectly as possible for a foreigner. (Schleiermacher cited in Venuti 1995: 110)

So Germany's openness to others sets it up to be the center and arbiter of world culture.

Since the positing of clear positions in the seventeenth through the early nineteenth centuries, translation practice in the West has wavered between that of the treacherous but lovely "Belles Infidèles" and that of the faithful Romantics; these tendencies have been called domesticating and foreignizing (e.g., Bassnett 2014), remarkably untranslatable terms that correspond, for instance, to the equally ugly French *cibliste* and *sourciste*.

BOAS AND TRANSLATION

When he came to America from Germany, Franz Boas (1858–1942), the founder of modern North American anthropology and linguistics, brought the German assumption of diversity with him, but in a more radical form. Given his practice of doing research by actually living with "primitive" people, and his goals of attending to the history of all peoples (Bunzl 2004) and treating all verbal traditions with the philological respect usually given to Greek and Latin (Boas 1906), Boas shared neither the nationalist agenda nor the hierarchization of peoples and languages that marked most Euro-American thinking about language and culture. Instead, his own political agenda, like that of his students, was largely contestatory, seeing exposure to alternative ways of living and constructing the world through language as inherently challenging the prevailing assumptions of the Euro-American societies of his time.

From his paper "On alternating sounds" (1889) through the Introduction to the *Handbook of American Indian languages* (1911) and into his later writings, Boas focused on examples of misunderstandings between languages and cultures (discussion in Leavitt 2011: 130–32). His is an anatomy of misreadings—of

sounds, of the meanings of and relationships among words, of grammatical patterns. In every case, the speaker of a given language expects to find familiar
patterns when confronting a new one, and the speaker's errors can be shown
to result not from the inferiority of the other language, its lack of structure
or vagueness or excessive fussiness, as several generations of evolutionists had
claimed marked primitive languages, but from the mutual interference of different coherent systems. We—that is, all speakers—mishear sounds, misattribute
meanings, and misconstrue grammatical forms in a different language because
of our own legitimately acquired prejudices as speakers of our own language;
and speakers of the other language will make exactly the same kinds of mistakes—not the same mistakes, but the same kinds of mistakes—when they try
to handle ours.

This means that the site of illumination is on the edge, on the frontiers
between systems: foreseeable misunderstandings are evidence for the existence
of distinct systems. There is a theory of translation inherent in this approach,
although Boas did not formulate it as such. Once differences have been established, the researcher should seek to grasp the forms of the new language as
they are actually used, not replace them with familiar forms. This is the method
propounded by Wilhelm von Humboldt (1767–1835), as, for instance, when he
attacked Jesuit manuals of Japanese for using largely inapplicable Latin parts of
speech (Humboldt [1825] 1906). Boas (1900) similarly criticizes a missionary
grammar of Kwak'wala for drawing parts of speech from English and forcing
pieces of Kwak'wala into this structure.

Such a view of languages as coherent and different systems means that the
analyst must not be satisfied with translation equivalents, nor take the possibility of glossing as proving that languages are "really" the same. The fact that an
English sentence involving tense might be the best, in the sense of the most
normal-English, gloss of a Hopi sentence without tense does not prove that
Hopi has "tacit tense." A. L. Becker has put this point elegantly in a book with
the significant title *Beyond translation*:

> Our general tendency is to "read into" our experience of a distant language the
> familiar things that are missing, all the silences, and then we claim that these
> things are "understood," "implied," or "part of the underlying logical structure" of
> these languages. . . . It takes a while to learn that things like tenses, and articles,
> and the copula, are not "understood" in Burmese, Javanese, or Malay. . . . In Bur-
> mese these things aren't implied; they just aren't there. (1995: 7–8)

If required, Burmese is perfectly capable of conveying the information carried in tenses, articles, and the copula by using its own methods. As Boas insisted, one can speak of any subject in any language—at the limit, one might have to add some vocabulary. This means that referential content can be translated, if only sometimes via elaborate paraphrases: the fact of translatability of referential content is indeed universal.

Boas further elaborated Humboldt's recognition of the importance of obligatory grammatical categories, which oblige the speaker to choose alternatives within a given realm of experience. In English, for instance, most nouns require a choice of singular or plural forms; finite verb forms require a specification of person and tense, that is, relationship between the time of speaking and the time of the event spoken about. While it is possible to specify this information when speaking any language, plenty of languages do not *require* their constant specification. And other obligatory categories may exist: you may be required to specify how you know what you are talking about (evidentiality); or every noun may be classified by its shape (Jakobson 1959a, 1959b; Friedrich 1969). This immediately raises a question of translation: How much does one translate obligatory grammatical categories? Should they be suppressed *because* they are obligatory and therefore "invisible"? How does one judge that they are coming into "visibility"?

This is the central question of Jakobson's often-quoted paper on translation (1959a). He gives the example of French gender. We are told in our high-school French classes that gender is a purely formal part of French grammar: you just have to memorize that it's *la table* and *le mur*, but there is no sense in which a table is really thought of as feminine and a wall as masculine (this position is stated in Brown and Lenneberg 1954). Against this, Jakobson shows that in some circumstances gender does play a role in ideation and certainly in connotation.[5]

If we accept this, then gender-meaning is there, hovering, potentially marking every noun. Should we be translating *la table* as "the table (it's a girl)"? Paul Friedrich tried something like this in his treatment of the tale of Uncle Peanut and Aunt Onion (1969: 30; 1979: 485) from Purépacha (earlier called Tarascan by outsiders), a Mexican language that has fourteen obligatory markers of

5.   Going farther in this direction, some psychologists (e.g., Konishi 1993) have started to find clear sex-based connotations for differing grammatical genders. Most recently, Lera Boroditsky has run experiments on native speakers of German and Spanish that show that gender connotation remains even when they are speaking in English (Boroditsky, Schmidt, and Phillips 2003).

shape. Friedrich's English translation adds little tags indicating the shape of activities. The English of this text is odd indeed, and in fact requires a paragraph of grammatical annotation for each paragraph of translation. It would be hard to tell this story as a story in Friedrich's rendering—but, on the other hand, his treatment does tell you an enormous amount about the Purépacha language and, I dare say, the Purépacha world.

Many of the central arguments in the writings of Boas' students Edward Sapir (1884–1939) and Benjamin Lee Whorf (1897–1941) deal with obligatory grammatical categories, using the same kind of treatment of examples that Boas does. In fact, this whole Boasian literature on language differences, given that it is taking place in English, can be read a series of reflections on translation.

The "Sapir–Whorf hypothesis," first proposed in the 1950s well after the deaths of both Sapir and Whorf, is often taken to claim that each language is a closed and sealed system unto itself. This is utterly different from the Boas–Sapir–Whorf practice of operating on the borders of systems with the understanding that passage between worlds is always possible but requires work. The reading of Sapir and Whorf as linguistic determinists led to easy refutations: first, that Whorf contradicted himself by seeking to describe Hopi concepts in English; second, that the very fact that translation is possible proves that all languages are carrying the same content (Black [1959] 1962; Davidson 1974). This last view should be contrasted with the reverse one, maintained by German linguists who did believe that one could never really escape the horizon of one's native language: for them, the fact that there are any difficulties in translation proves that languages are profoundly different (Bynon 1966: 472).

MISERY AND SPLENDOR

During the same decades that Boas and his students were active, Saussure-inspired linguists and philosophers on the Continent were developing their own theories of the systematicity of languages, whether through Prague School linguistics or a developing French structural linguistics represented in the work of Émile Benveniste (1902–76). Here, as in other fields, the recognition of multiple systems typical of structuralism parallels the views of the Boasians (see, e.g., Jakobson 1959b).

Within translation, one statement of the radical differences among languages is found in the dialogue "The misery and splendor of translation" ([1937] 2000) by the Spanish philosopher José Ortega y Gasset (1883–1955), another of the most anthologized pieces in the translation canon. Here is how the case is put in the last part of the dialogue, "El esplendor":

> "The simple fact [is] that the translation is not the work, but a path (*un camino*) toward the work. If it is a poetic work, the translation is not one, but rather an apparatus, a technical artifice that brings us closer to the work without ever trying to repeat or replace it. . . . I imagine, then, a form of translation that is ugly (*que sea fea*), as science has always been, that does not claim to wear literary garb; that is not easy to read but is very clear indeed, although this clarity may demand copious footnotes. The reader must know beforehand that when he reads a translation he will not be reading a literarily beautiful book, but rather will be using a fairly boring apparatus (*un aparato bastante enojoso*); one, however, that will truly help him transmigrate within the poor man Plato (*transmigrar dentre del pobre hombre Platón*)." (Ortega y Gasset [1937] 2000: 61, 62, translation modified)

I put this quote within quotes because in his dialogue Ortega is not, in fact, putting these words into his own mouth—which he could well have done, since he presents himself as one of the speakers, and he has himself talk quite a lot. The scene takes place in Paris, apparently in 1937, during Ortega's exile from the Spanish Civil War. It happens at the Collège de France and is said to involve professors and students of the Collège. This section of the text is provoked by Ortega's asking one of his interlocutors, described as "a brilliant scholar of linguistics of the new generation," to give his own views on translation. If there is any historical reality to this setting, the only person this could possibly have been was Benveniste, who was elected to the Collège that very year at the age of thirty-five. If we take this attribution seriously—as far as I know, Benveniste never laid claim to it—then the real source of these ideas is the other great structural linguist of Jakobson's generation: this ringing repudiation of "Les Belles Infidèles" in favor of ugly translation and respect for the otherness of the source text—and the source world—comes not out of Spanish existentialism, but French structuralism. The Spanish philosopher is the channel and, of all things, the translator of Benveniste's views on translation.

REFERENCE AND STYLE

We have seen that Reformation and Renaissance traditions distinguished between translating for what we would call referential meaning, which is held to be appropriate for sacred and philosophical texts, and the much less evident, perhaps impossible, process of seeking to capture the full exploitation of the resources of a language as exemplified in literary texts; and we have seen Ortega/Benveniste propose a radically scientific approach to the otherness of poetic language. Scholars of the Boasian tradition, for their part, focused almost exclusively on referential meaning, which, as they maintained, can always be translated, if you are willing to use enough circumlocutions.

The exception within this tradition was in the work of Edward Sapir. Sapir, unlike Boas and Whorf a student of literature and a poet himself, felt he recognized an implicit poetic character in the very structure of a given language: a music in phonetics, resonances of suggestion in the choice of words and how words are put together, and figures implicit in grammatical categories. For Sapir, once again, the ideal position is on the edge, on the front line between linguistic worlds:

> Since every language has its distinctive peculiarities, the innate formal limitations—and possibilities—of one literature are never quite the same as those of another. The literature fashioned out of the form and substance of a language has the color and the texture of its matrix. The literary artist may never be conscious of how he is hindered or helped or otherwise guided by the matrix, but when it is a question of translating his work into another language, the nature of the original matrix manifests itself at once. All his effects have been calculated, or intuitively felt, with reference to the formal "genius" of his own language; they cannot be carried over without loss or modification. (Sapir 1921: 227)

Sapir distinguishes different literary styles, more or less dependent on the specifics of their linguistic material versus their referential content and so more or less satisfactorily transferrable between languages. This of course recalls the distinction made in the Renaissance and Reformation, except that these earlier authors reified the problem as one of different kinds of texts, rather than different functions of language, as suggested by Sapir and made explicit by Jakobson (1960).

The development of a North American school of ethnopoetics in the 1960s and 1970s, a cooperative enterprise among anthropologists, linguists, and poets, was predicated on recognizing the Boasian failure to grasp the poetic dimensions of the texts being recorded (e.g., Hymes 1999 on Boas). The ethnopoetic work of Dell Hymes, Dennis Tedlock, and their colleagues, the effort to rediscover or re-present poetic form from non-Western texts, can be seen as an attempt to add new dimensions to translation, bringing the reader closer to the singer or teller of tales. The great arguments in ethnopoetics (e.g., Hymes 1981; Tedlock 1983; cf. Mason 2008) have been about how to translate and how to present a translated text. From the side of the poets, the inspiration for ethnopoetics was exemplified in Jerome Rothenberg's experiments in what he called "total translation," seeking, again, to add contextual and interpretive dimensions to his English renderings of Seneca ritual texts (see Rothenberg 1968).

Sapir's idea of a poetry implicit in the grammar of a language was developed by Paul Friedrich (e.g., 1986) in ways that had direct implications for translation, and particularly for the dichotomy between the poetic and the supposedly purely referential. If a given grammar lends itself to certain connections, metaphors, metonyms, rather than to others, then a translator is dealing with an underlying poetics that is there in the very weave out of which any text is made, however referential it may look.

In his work on the necessarily situated nature of any enunciation, Michael Silverstein has shown how reference is only one dimension of what are necessarily far more complex communicative acts. In particular, he has drawn attention to aspects of language that are cross-culturally more or less available to the metalinguistic awareness of speakers themselves (Silverstein [1981] 2001), thus granting a greater role to the effect of language ideologies on languages themselves than had been allowed in the pure Boasian model. Silverstein's work on translation (2003) distinguishes among translation proper, that is, transfer of referential meaning including grammatical meaning; what he calls transduction, the attempt to transfer stylistic and indexical qualities of usage; and transformation, a shift in semiotic modality to try to render some aspect of the situational meaning of the source event.[6] Silverstein is led to call for a necessary role for ethnography in going as far as transduction:

---

6.   While it is justified with an analogy to energy transducers, the choice of the word "transduction" is translationally problematic, since some version of it is already the standard word for translation in Romance languages (e.g., *tradução, traducción, traduction, traduzione*).

How does one capture the "tone," i.e., indexical penumbra, of a word or expression in a source text by one in a target language used in a highly distinct culture? Clearly, something on the order of a cultural analysis of both systems of usage is a prerequisite to finding a route of transduction, in analytic terms that reveal both the similarities and the differences, so as to be able to navigate a proper transduction from the source to the target. (2003: 89)

TRANSLATION STUDIES AND REALITY

What is usually referred to as translation theory or translation studies has come into being since the 1970s as an interdisciplinary field. Two developments mark it off from earlier debates, which, as we have seen, focus primarily on *how* one should translate. One is the recognition that translation is always carried out *within* what has been called the target culture, for reasons peculiar to the target society. Since this is the case whatever strategy of translation one adopts, foreignizing translation serves purposes that are defined by the target society as much as does domesticating translation, or else it would not be taken on.

Another of the developments of recent translation studies has been to recognize the hard reality of translation practice. Instead of simply asking how one should translate, these theorists are also asking what a society chooses to translate and why. While contemporary translation *theory* tends to come down in favor of foreignizing translations, which respect the original and seek to transform the reader (Venuti 1995; Bassnett 2014), normal translation *practice* continues to be very much like "Les Belles Infidèles"—after all, translation is a business, and most translations are made to sell. It is clear (Venuti 1995; Bellos 2011) that the mass of translation going on in the world is from English to other languages, with a much smaller percentage going in the other direction, and this primarily from a very small number of tongues. In translations into English, domestication dominates. In other words, what actually gets translated, in substance and style, tends to reinforce the hegemony of Anglo-American and, to a lesser degree, Western European culture.

The question, then, is what we want to translate and why. Anthropologists are in a particularly strong position to bring little-considered texts into the current world tradition, and to do so in a way that allows serious consideration both of the implications of language structure and of the anchoring of the text in particular values and particular interpersonal situations.

TWILIGHT SWINGING

Traditionally, anthropologists have worked in societies that fall outside the main concerns of Western academic history. Many of these societies have only recently adopted systems of writing and still function to a large degree in oral media. For linguistic anthropologists working with oral texts, the question of translation involves yet another layer of complexity. It requires an imagined *parcours* from performance and reception to recording of one kind or another to written fixation in one or more text-artifacts to interpretation and translation (cf. Silverstein and Urban 1996). These problems have emerged for me in the most telling way in working on texts emerging out of oral performance traditions of the Central Himalayan region of Kumaon in what is now the state of Uttarakhand in northern India. These are largely performed by professional—that is, remunerated—drummer-singer-poets who are masters of a large number of named genres, some narrative, some ludic, many highly ritualized. Some of the ritual genres are performatively effective in bringing gods to be present and to manifest themselves in human bodies in what the Western tradition calls possession.

In Kumaon, the language spoken by the bulk of the population in their homes is one or another dialect of Kumaoni, a member of the Pahari branch of the Indo-Aryan language family, itself a member of the Indo-European family. Government, education, and commerce are carried out primarily in Hindi, the official language of the state. Most Kumaonis are Hindus who interact with a host of regional divinities as well as with the great Hindu gods. The regional divinities manifest themselves "in person" in nocturnal possession rituals called *jāgar* or "waking"; their appearance is provoked and controlled by the professional drummer-poet (Gaborieau 1975; Leavitt 1997). All ritual devoted to these regional gods is carried out in the Kumaoni language.

In what follows, I raise some of the questions that have come up in considering a small part of one of the early sections of a *jāgar* performance I recorded in 1982 in the northern part of District Nainital. Here the drummer-poet was Sri Kamal Rām Ārya, one of the area's better-known performers in a number of oral-poetic genres. The utterances come from the poet's opening invocation to the gods and to the coming night, called *sandhyā*, "twilight" or "evening." As is usually the case in this tradition, this is an oral performance; until recently, most of the poets were illiterate, and while Kamal Rām knows how to read and write, as far as I can see writing plays no part in his art. For the would-be

translator this means that there is a series of steps, each one riddled with potential pitfalls, which must be crossed over before one has a "source" text(-artifact)
with which to work—and such an artifact is never the only possible one. In the
case of the utterances presented here, there was a recording in situ; there was
an initial transcription of the recording by Sri Indar Singh Negi, an inhabit-
ant of a neighboring village and native speaker of the language, who had gone
through some months working with me and so had an idea of what transcription involved. Then transcriber and translator—and this, of course, meant that
the translator already had done the basic work of phonological and grammatical
analysis of the language—read over the transcription together while listening
to the recording, making corrections and asking for explanations. In some cases,
we returned to the poet for explanations, but these were rarely forthcoming: for
the poet himself, his performative skill was never considered as separate from its
exegesis (as is the case, for instance, of Yugoslav bards: Lord 1960; cf. Tedlock
1983: 3). After various iterations and revisions, we had a text-artifact in "the"
Kumaoni language: "the" is in quotes because our transcription represented only
the dialect and distinctive diction of this singer, and to some degree only on this
occasion.

Note one of the crucial differences between this kind of ethnographic pre-
translation, involving the creation of a text-artifact, and standard text translation: the former involves living performers and living interpreters, and so must
necessarily be collaborative in nature (cf. McDowell 2000). How collaborative it
is, in what direction the questions and answers go, depends on the situation; but
it has the potential to shake up the usual flows of information.

The initial questions are thus those which center not on how to translate
from code to code (i.e., from Kumaoni to English), but on how, in Jakobson's
terms, to operate an intersemiotic transfer (i.e., from speech to writing). Can we
present the *transcribed* text in a way that preserves some of the qualities of a performance that has rhythmic, dynamic, and melodic dimensions? Even if a "total"
transcription is impossible, Dennis Tedlock (1983) has shown that experiment-
ing with transcription can allow the indication of elements of a performance
which are lost in a standard prose or verse transcription.

Here is an initial transcription of some verses, with interlinear treatment of
the first, including indications of grammatical marking.[7] Kumaoni nouns have

---

7.   The following abbreviations are used here for grammatical terms: N = noun, A =
adjective, P = pronoun, V = verb, pp = postposition, ppl = present participle, m =

three cases, direct, oblique, and vocative—which are only overtly distinguished
in some nouns—two genders, and two numbers. Like other modern Indo-Aryan languages, Kumaoni makes constant use of compound verbs, in which the
first element carries the referential meaning while the second modifies or orients the way of being or doing and carries the grammatical information.

jhulani	sandhyā	mē	kyā	kām	hai	rī,
swing	twilight	in	what	work	be, become	remain
V.ppl.f.s.ob.	N.f.s.ob.	pp.	A.m.p.dir.	N.m.p.dir.	V.conj.	V.past.3p.
swinging	twilight-in	what	works		have become?	

In the swinging twilight what works have been done,

isvar	mero	bābā,	sandhyā	kā	bakhat	mē,
Lord	my	father	twilight	- of	time	- in
N.m.s.voc.	A.m.s.voc.	N.m.s.voc.	N.f.s.ob.	pp.m.ob.	N.m.s.ob.	pp.
Lord	my	father of	twilight	at the	time	

Lord, my father, at twilight time,

isvar mero bābā, gāi	bachan	kā	bādan	lāgī,
cow	calf	- of	tying	lay, put
N.f.s.ob.	N.m.p.ob.	pp.m.p.dir	N.m.p.dir.	V.past.3p.
of cow	of calves		tyings	have been put on

Lord my father, the cow and calves have been tied up,

*ghōl ki cari jo cha ghōl mē lhai gai cha, isvar mero bābā, sandhyā kā bakhat mē
bāṭi baṭauv ko ḍyār jo cha, isvar mero bābā, bāṭai bādi go, isvar mero bābā,
sandhyā kā bakhat mē godi ko bālak jo cha god mē sukālo hai go, isvar mero bābā,
sandhyā kā bakhat mē tumāro nām lhinū, isvar mero bābā.*

The little bird of the nest has gone into the nest, Lord my father, at twilight
time, the traveler on the road, Lord my father, has tied his camp on the road,
Lord my father, at twilight time the child of the lap has become happy in
the lap, Lord my father, at twilight time we take your name, Lord my father.

---

masculine, f = feminine, s = singular, p = plural, dir. = direct, obl. = oblique, voc. =
vocative, conj. = conjunctive verb form, pres. = present, past = past; numbers indicate
first, second, or third person.

What we have offered is a fairly straightforward transfer of the referential meaning of this fragment of a text-artifact. But even here a great deal has been added and a great deal supressed. Kumaoni, like other North Indian languages, has masculine and feminine gender, and feminizing a word is often used as a diminutive: here the "little bird" is my pragmatic reading of what in fact is "female bird." I have suppressed the repeated use of *jo cha*, "who is," which seems to me to be a nonsemantic filler in Kumaoni bardic performance. How to handle the semantic penumbras of *isvar*, borrowed from Sanskrit Īśvara, a title of God associated with certain schools of Hinduism but not others and which I have simply given as "Lord," or *bābā*, both the vocative of *bāp*, "father" and the word for a guru or spiritual "father"? Kumaoni having no determinative article, I have put in "the" where it seemed appropriate, although the translation could as well read "a little bird has gone into a nest."

This is a series of utterances that have only been heard, never written down except by Sri Indra Singh Negi by hand in prose presentation on sheets of lined paper. Basing myself on the poet's apparent phrasing rather than his pauses, I could as well transcribe it:

ghōl ki caṛi jo cha
ghōl mē lhai gai cha,
isvar mero bābā,
sandhyā kā bakhat mē

and so forth, rendering it something like:

as twilight swings
what works are worked
Lord my father
at twilight time
Lord my father
cows, calves have been tied up
nest's little bird
in the nest has gone
Lord my father
at twilight time

The basic syntax of the Kumaoni sentence, as we have seen, is Subject–Object–Verb. This means that in unmarked discourse, the verb acts as a sealant of sentences or clauses, which appear as packages with the complements tucked in between the subject and the verb. In Kumaoni narrative poetry, this structure is nice and tight: each line is a clause, usually a sentence, ending unambiguously with the verb. In the *sandhyā*, too, which is emphatically nonnarrative, many clauses do end with verbs, again helping to mark each one off as clearly as the stress on the first syllable marks off half-clauses; but syntactic ambiguity comes in when we try to find a place to put nonsentence clauses like "Lord my father" which must be connected to what precedes or what follows but give us no hint as to which option is to be preferred.

Thus the first transcription and tentative translation, in paragraph-like blocks, does convey something of the text's weird syntagmatic structure, a string of clauses that can be connected up in several ways, making it impossible to tell where one sentence ends and the next begins. Like the relentless repetitions, the ambiguous clausal pattern of this opening recitative—a pattern that is completely different from that of narrative parts of the ritual—serves to hook in and focus the attention of the listeners, whether divine or human. What in more standard discourse would be clearly distinguished sentences here overlap to form much longer units, along which the listener is pulled. This quality is conveyed better, I think, in blocks rather than, say, in breath-lines (Olson [1950] 1997), or in a transcription strictly based on timing. The poet seems to be at pains to push the line of language through his breaths to create somewhat longer units, themselves divided by periods of his voice's silence and the continuing beating of the drum.

But already this choice of transcription, using clauses separated by commas rather than, say, imposing a standard sentence-structure, involves a preliminary analysis of the relations among the participants in the ritual: that the singer is singing to gods and ancient gurus, that the audience is there as privileged overhearers. In the ritual world, the point of this section is to invite and pull in the gods, into what we may call the empirical world, that available to immediate observation: the most evident thing about the performance of the *sandhyā* is the way it seems to trap the attention of the assembled people, who as it begins are chatting away, but are silent and attentive five minutes later, when the chant has taken over. The point of this part of the ritual is to capture and hold the attention of all these interlocutors, divine and human. The choice of how to present a transcription and a translation, in other words, already presupposes what Silverstein calls a transductional analysis.

Looking at other levels of language adds to the complexity of the task. Phonetics and phonology represent the most evidently untranslatable level. The Kumaoni text is full of alliteration: this short passage is extremely heavy with initial *b*s and *g*s, both unaspirated and aspirated. Other parts of this section rely heavily on rhyming, which will either be lost in translation or, to be maintained, will require suppressions of and additions to elements of the referential sense.

Rhythm and stress are also lost in translation. Kumaoni has a stress accent on the first syllable of most words. In this text there is a steady beat of hyper-stressed syllables at the beginning of each half-clause (*gāi bachan kā / bādan lāgī*), maintaining a pattern that allows varying numbers of relatively unstressed syllables to be inserted between the stresses. A translation, even into another word-stress language such as English, loses the accent that here metricalizes half-clauses; this might be indicated by adding boldface to the translation, as I have added it to the transcription above, or, if in an oral rendition, by reading aloud with the right stresses. But here other problems, this time from the "target" language, impose themselves: to present something like normal English, determiners are unavoidable, adjectives precede nouns, and word order is Subject–Verb–Object rather than the Subject–Object–Verb order of Kumaoni and almost all other South Asian languages. If we stress the first syllable of each half-clause in English, different words are accentuated than in the Kumaoni, and these turn out to be words that don't "deserve" the stress: "**The** cow and the calf / **have** been tied up, // **the** little bird of the nest / **has** gone into the nest." If we stress the words corresponding semantically to those stressed in the Kumaoni, we lose the distinction among half-clauses: "The **cow** and the calf / have been **tied** up, // the little bird of the **nest** / has gone into the **nest**." And if we force the English words into a Kumaoni order, we have a monstrosity, but one that maintains something like the rhythm: "**Cow** calf's / **tying** have-done, // **nest's** birdie / **nest**-in has gone." This is the only way to give the reader an idea of what is going on. It hardly can stand by itself, but requires explanation with reference to the transcription-artifact, to which the reader must have access. It is a case of going "beyond translation."

Word choice, too, is always problematic: we can find English glosses for the important words in the Kumaoni text, but to understand what they are doing there, they must be explained or annotated. An exegetical paratext must surround the text. The oft-repeated word *sandhyā*, which is also the name given to this section of the ritual, means far more than simply twilight or evening: in orthoprax Hinduism, it is the word used for both of the junctures between day and night, which are holiest moments of the daily cycle, and for the prayer said at dawn and dusk. Its phonology also marks it as a borrowing from Sanskrit, the sacred language, rather than an inherited Kumaoni word: the Kumaoni word for evening, which has undergone the expected transformations from Sanskrit, is *sås*. Thus the word *sandhyā* has religious connotations that the English word twilight (or alternatives: dusk, evening) does not. This choice of the word ties the immediate perceptible scene into a cosmic scene, which is exactly what this section of the ritual is seeking to do.

Kumaoni oral poetry is not memorized, but composed in performance by combining fixed formulas (see the ideal model in Lord 1960).[8] Giving that this is a living tradition, other poets from the same tradition are available to be listened to, and are being listened to, by thousands of people today. The performance of any given poet can change from twilight to twilight: while Kamal Rām's *sandhyā*s show great stability in style and wording, they too are longer or shorter depending on the occasion. And each poet has his own style or styles (they are mainly men), each drawing on a treasury of formulas that are largely shared across the region. The intertextuality is extraordinarily dense: this rendition of the *sandhyā* by this poet on this night echoes others at many degrees of distance. The reality of this variation could certainly be called to the reader's attention, which means that the translated text is no longer the sole text, but becomes one element in a potential multitext of variations (as now exemplified for Homer: see the Homer Multitext website). In the single recording we possess of one of his *jāgars*, the most famous Kumaoni oral poet of recent generations, Gopi Das of Kausani (c. 1900–75),[9] begins his *sandhyā*:

dhārā ḍuba dinā, devo, / gāṛō paṛi chāyā
hari jagadīsā, o devo, / gāṛō paṛi chāyā
The day has sunk down on the mountain crests, gods, / in the valleys shadow has fallen
Oh Lord, oh gods, / in the valleys shadow has fallen

---

8. This is not always the case with oral poetry. The Veda, Inuit poetry, and Somali poetry (Finnegan 1977) were or are orally composed, then memorized word for word.

9. Gopi Das was recorded in 1970 by Marc Gaborieau, to whom I am grateful for granting me access to the audiotape. An epic sung by Gopi Das, and a long interview with the singer, can be found in Meissner (1985).

And he too uses the trope of birds returning to the nest at twilight time:

cārā oṛo kā panchī lai / cārā oṛo bāso lhai cha
ghōlā ko panchī lai / ghōlō mē bāso lhai cha
Birds of the four directions / have settled in the four directions.
Birds of the nest / have settled in the nest.

The poet Jay Rām, whom I was able to record in a village close to that of Kamal Rām the previous year, chanted:

ghōl ki caṛi ghōl mē baiṭh rai cha, gāy bāchō kā badaṇ bāndhi jānī, nau lākh tārā
khul jānī, jaṅgal kā ghasyāri ai jānī, pāṇi kā panār ai jānī.
The little bird of the nest is sitting in the nest, the cow and the calves have been tied up, the nine hundred thousand stars have opened up, the grass-cutting girl has come from the forest, the drawers of water have come from the water.

And each of these singers had his own rhythm, his own melody for the *sandhyā* quite different from those of the others.

At the same time, an oral text like this is only *realized* in a unique situation: ethnographic information about it and around it are a necessary part of the philology of the text. This is a song sung at (and about) nightfall, a sacred time when rural families do in fact come back together from the day in the fields, in the forests, or at a job, just as birds go back to their nests, just as the grazing cows come back to be tied up in the cow-basement. In this song of crepuscular invitation, the gods are being asked to enter this human house at this moment of daily reuniting. The text is, in fact, the part of the ritual that indexically centers this spot, where the ritual is taking place, in a transformed landscape, now to be identified with the gods of regional mythology. The different realizations of this theme are capitalizing on this lived fact of Kumaoni rural life, and perhaps on a fantasy of idealized hill life; they are conveying it in beautiful rhythmic language; and they are doing so to specific transformative effect.

In a case like this, a verbal object, a text, illuminates aspects of wider life; at the same time, there is no way to understand what the text itself is doing in its world without an ethnographic exposition of broader aspects of that world. To what extent is this true of any translation?

CONCLUSION

Unlike translators and publishers, who have to make a living proposing palatable equivalences, anthropologists have their own agenda. In the North American tradition, at least, this has involved the attempt to understand nonmodern, non-Western ways of living and speaking in a way that usually constitutes at least an implicit critique of the idea of the universality, naturalness, and correctness of our own. In terms of translation, anthropologists—those who are prepared to treat texts not as a model for, but as anchoring points in the movement of life we label society and culture—could offer a radically sourcist, radically contextualizing, and collaborative translation practice which seeks to open up a text and its world to the reader, rather than replacing it with an easy-to-assimilate rendering of what some intermediary decides is its relevant referential content (cf. Leavitt 2005).

Such revelation recalls the methods of the old philology: it requires going into the text in its specificity, but also into the specificity of its language and its generic tradition; it demands a contextualization of the text in its world—a world the existence which you become aware of because you sense its boundary effects on your own. Anthropologists are uniquely suited for working on the edges of languages and worlds, making the differences manifest, keeping the paradoxes sharp and alive. As Dell Hymes (1981) called for an anthropological philology, perhaps this would be a philological anthropology. For such a text-focused practice, translation would also be exegesis; exegesis requires ethnography, and ethnography requires collaboration.

Professional translators, it is clear, have to avoid monstrosities and "unreadable" renditions. But anthropologists need not fear monsters; they are uniquely positioned to respond to Ortega/Benveniste's call for ugly translations. They are free to experiment with forms of "experience-close" transcription, so as to include aspects of orality and the particular circumstances of a performance, and translation, to try to bring worlds together. If this means having to deal with "English monstrosities" (McDowell 2000: 225), then so be it: we should seek not only "to acquire a sense of how natives hear their poetry" (ibid.: 229), but also to change ourselves and our readers so that what at first sight is a linguistic monstrosity can come to sound like poetry. This means a violation of the literary, and to a degree of the social, canons we have all internalized.

And this would not take place in a social void: there is a small but real public in today's societies, if made up only of anthropologists' students and colleagues—but it certainly goes beyond them—for trying to understand other worlds.

ACKNOWLEDGMENTS

I am grateful to the organizers of and other participants in the "Translating Worlds" colloquium for their invitation and comments, and to the anonymous readers for *Hau* for their very helpful suggestions. Special thanks to Luke Fleming for his close reading and perspicacious advice. This paper is dedicated to the memory of Alton L. Becker (1932–2011). When not marked or cited from published translated works, translations are my own.

REFERENCES

Asad, Talal. 1986. "The concept of cultural translation in British social anthropology." In *Writing culture: The politics and poetics of ethnography*, edited by James Clifford and George E. Marcus, 141–64. Berkeley: University of California Press.

Bassnett, Susan. 2014. *Translation studies*. Fourth edition. London: Routledge.

Becker, A. L. 1995. *Beyond translation: Essays toward a modern philology*. Ann Arbor: University of Michigan Press.

Bellos, David. 2011. *Is that a fish in your ear?* London: Allen Lane.

Berman, Antoine. (1984) 1992. *The experience of the foreign: Culture and translation in Romantic Germany*. Translated by S. Heyvaert. Albany, NY: SUNY Press.

Black, Max. (1959) 1962. "Linguistic relativity: The views of Benjamin Lee Whorf." In *Models and metaphors*, 244–57. Ithaca, NY: Cornell University Press.

Boas, Franz. 1889. "On alternating sounds." *American Anthropologist* 2: 47–53.

———. 1900. "Sketch of the Kwakiutl language." *American Anthropologist* (N.S.) 2: 708–21.

———. 1906. "Some philological aspects of anthropological research." *Science* 23: 641–45.

———. 1911. "Introduction." In *Handbook of American Indian languages*, edited by Franz Boas, 1–83. Washington, DC: Government Printing Office.

Boroditsky, Lera, Lauren A. Schmidt, and Webb Phillips. 2003. "Sex, syntax, and semantics." In *Language in mind*, edited by Dedre Gentner and Susan Goldin-Meadow, 61–79. Cambridge, MA: MIT Press.

Brower, Reuben A. 1959. "Seven Agamemnons." In *On translation*, edited by Reuben A. Brower, 173–95. Cambridge, MA: Harvard University Press.

Brown, Roger, and Eric H. Lenneberg. 1954. "A study in language and cognition." *Journal of Abnormal and Social Psychology* 49: 454–62.

Bunzl, Matti. 2004. "Boas, Foucault, and the 'native anthropologist': Notes toward a Neo-Boasian anthropology." *American Anthropologist* 106: 435–42.

Bynon, Theodora. 1966. "Leo Weisgerber's four stages in linguistic analysis." *Man* (N.S.) 1: 468–83.

Davidson, Donald. 1974. "On the very idea of a conceptual scheme." *Proceedings and Addresses of the American Philosophical Association* 47: 5–20.

Demonet, Marie-Luce. 1992. *Les voix du signe: Nature et origine du langage à la Renaissance (1480–1580)*. Paris: Honoré Champion.

Descartes, René. 1984. *The philosophical writings*. Translated by John Cottingham, Robert Stoothoff, and Dugald Murdoch. Cambridge: Cambridge University Press.

Dubois, Claude-Gilbert. 1970. *Mythe et langage au seizième siècle*. Bordeaux: Ducros.

Finnegan, Ruth. 1977. *Oral poetry*. Cambridge: Cambridge University Press.

Friedrich, Paul. 1969. "On the meaning of the Tarascan suffixes of space." *International Journal of American Linguistics*, Memoir 23.

———. 1979. "Poetic language and the imagination." In *Language, context, and the imagination*, 441–517. Stanford: Stanford University Press

———. 1986. *The language parallax*. Austin: University of Texas Press.

Gaborieau, Marc. 1975. "La transe rituelle dans l'Himalaya central: folie, avatar, méditation." *Purushartha* 2: 147–72.

Geertz, Clifford. 1973. *The interpretation of cultures*. New York: Basic Books.

Gelli, Giovan Battista. (1551) 1976. "I caprici del Bottaio." In *Opere*. Edited by Delmo Maestri. Third edition, 125–288. Turin: Union Tipografico-Editrice Torinese.

Hagège, Claude. 1985. *L'homme de paroles*. Paris: Fayard.

Handman, Courtney. 2007. "Access to the soul: Native language and authenticity in Papua New Guinea Bible translation." In *Consequences of contact: Language ideologies and sociocultural transformations in Pacific societies*, edited by Miki Makihara and Bambi B. Schieffelin, 166–88. Oxford: Oxford University Press.

Horguelin, Paul A. 1996. *Traducteurs français des XVIe et XVIIe siècles*. Montreal: Linguatech.

Hüllen, Werner. 2001. "Reflections on language in the Renaissance." In *Language typology and language universals*, Vol. I, edited by Martin Haspelmath, Ekkehard König, Wulf Oesterreicher, and Wolfgang Raible, 210–21. Berlin: Walter de Gruyter.

Humboldt, Wilhelm von. (1825) 1906. "Notice sur une grammaire japonaise imprimée à Mexico." In *Gesammelte Schriften*, V. Edited by Albert Leitzmann, 237–47. Berlin: B. Behr.

Hymes, Dell. 1981. *"In vain I tried to tell you": Essays in Native American ethnopoetics*. Philadelphia: University of Pennsylvania Press.

———. 1999. "Boas on the threshold of ethnopoetics." In *Theorizing the Americanist tradition*, edited by Lisa Philips Valentine and Regna Darnell, 84–107. Toronto: University of Toronto Press.

Jakobson, Roman. 1959a. "Linguistic aspects of translation." In *On translation*, edited by Reuben A. Brower, 232–38. Cambridge, MA: Harvard University Press.

———. 1959b. "Boas' view of grammatical meaning." In *The anthropology of Franz Boas*, edited by Walter Goldschmidt, 139–45. Washington, DC: American Anthropological Association.

———. 1960. "Linguistics and poetics." In *Style in language*, edited by Thomas E. Sebeok, 350–77. Cambridge, MA: MIT Press.

Kalmar, Ivan. 1987. "The *Völkerpsychologie* of Lazarus and Steinthal and the modern concept of culture." *Journal of the History of Ideas* 48: 671–90.

Konishi, Toshi. 1993. "The semantics of grammatical gender: A cross-cultural study." *Journal of Psycholinguistic Research* 22: 519–34.

Ladborough, R. W. 1938. "Translations from the Ancients in seventeenth-century France." *Journal of the Warburg Institute* 2 (2): 85–104.

Leavitt, John. 1997. "The language of the gods: Craft and inspiration in Central Himalayan ritual discourse." In *Poetry and prophecy*, edited by John Leavitt, 129–68. Ann Arbor: University of Michigan Press.

———. 2005. "Thick translation: Three soundings." In *Language, culture, and the individual: A tribute to Paul Friedrich*, edited by Catherine O'Neil, Mary Scoggin, and Paul Tuite, 79–108. Munich: LINCOM.

————. 2011. *Linguistic relativities: Language diversity and modern thought.* Cambridge: Cambridge University Press.

Lefevere, André. 1977. *Translating literature: The German tradition from Luther to Rosenzweig.* Assen: Van Gorcum.

Leibniz, Gottfried Wilhelm. (1697) 1916. "Unvorgreifliche Gedanken betreffend die Ausübung und Verbesserung der deutschen Sprache." In *Deutsche Schriften*, I, edited by Walther Schmied-Kowarzik, 25–54. Leipzig: Felix Meiner.

Lord, Albert Bates. 1960. *The singer of tales.* Cambridge, MA: Harvard University Press.

Mason, Catharine. 2008. "Ethnographie de la poétique de la performance." *Cahiers de Littérature Orale* 63–64: 261–94.

McDowell, John H. 2000. "Collaborative ethnopoetics: A view from the Sibundoy Valley." In *Translating Native Latin American verbal art*, edited by Kay Sammons and Joel Sherzer, 211–32. Washington, DC: Smithsonian Institution Press.

Meissner, Konrad. 1985. *Mālushāhī and Rājulā: A ballad from Kumāūn (India) as sung by Gopī Dās.* Wiesbaden: Otto Harrassowitz.

O'Laughlin, Bridget. 1978. Review of Marshall Sahlins, *Culture and practical reason. Dialectical Anthropology* 3: 97–104.

Olson, Charles. (1950) 1997. "Projective verse." In *Collected prose*, 239–49. Berkeley: University of California Press.

Ortega y Gasset, José. (1937) 2000. "The misery and splendor of translation." Translated by Elizabeth Gamble Miller. In *The translation studies reader*, edited by Lawrence Venuti, 49–63. London: Routledge.

Pinker, Steven. 1994. *The language instinct.* New York: William Morrow.

Povinelli, Elizabeth. 2001. "Radical worlds: The anthropology of incommensurability and inconceivability." *Annual Review of Anthropology* 30: 319–34.

Ricoeur, Paul. 1973. "The model of the text: Meaningful action considered as a text." *New Literary History* 5: 91–117.

Robinson, Doug. (1996) 1997. "Translation as phantom limb." In *What is translation?*, 113–31. Kent, OH: Kent State University Press.

Rosenzweig, Franz. (1926) 1994. "Scripture and Luther." In *Scripture and translation*, Martin Buber and Franz Rosenzweig. Translated by Lawrence Rosenwald and Everett Fox, 47–69. Bloomington: Indiana University Press.

Rothenberg, Jerome, ed. 1968. *Technicians of the sacred.* New York: Doubleday.

Rubel, Paula G., and Abraham Rosman, eds. 2003. *Translating cultures*. Oxford: Berg.

Sapir, Edward. 1921. *Language*. Boston: Houghton Mifflin.

Schleiermacher, Friedrich. (1813) 1992. "On the different methods of translating." Translated by Waltraud Bartscht. In *Theories of translation*, edited by Rainer Schulte and John Biguenet, 36–54. Chicago: University of Chicago Press.

Sdun, Winfried. 1967. *Probleme und Theorien des Übersetzens in Deutschland*. Munich: Hueber.

Silverstein, Michael. (1981) 2001. "The limits of awareness." In *Linguistic anthropology: A reader*, edited by Alessandro Duranti, 382–402. Malden, MA: Blackwell.

———. 2003. "Translation, transduction, transformation: Skating 'glossando' on thin semiotic ice." In *Translating cultures*, edited by Paula G. Rubel and Abraham Rosman, 75–108. Oxford: Berg.

Silverstein, Michael, and Greg Urban. 1996. "The natural history of discourse." In *The natural history of discourse*, edited by Michael Silverstein and Greg Urban, 1–17. Chicago: University of Chicago Press.

Speroni, Sperone. (1542) 2009. *Dialogo delle lingue/Dialogue des langues*. Translated by Gérard Genot and Paul Larivaille. Paris: Les Belles Lettres.

Stankiewicz, Edward. 1981. "The 'genius' of language in sixteenth-century linguistics." In *Logos semantikos*, Vol. I, edited by Jürgen Trabant, 177–89. Madrid: Gredos.

Steiner, George. 1975. *After Babel*. London: Oxford University Press.

Tedlock, Dennis. 1983. *The spoken word and the work of interpretation*. Philadelphia: University of Pennsylvania Press.

Stocking, George W., Jr. 1968. *Race, culture, and evolution: Essays in the history of anthropology*. New York: Free Press.

Venuti, Lawrence. 1995. *The translator's invisibility*. London: Routledge.

Webster, Anthony K. 2014. "In favor of sound: Linguistic relativity and Navajo poetry." Paper presented to the Symposium about Language and Society—Austin (SALSA) XXII, Austin, Texas.

CHAPTER TEN

On the very possibility of mutual intelligibility

G. E. R. Lloyd

Like the ethnographer, the student of ancient societies is faced with a recurrent problem of translation, and in one important respect suffers from an obvious considerable disadvantage. Modern ethnographers can question members of the groups they study to get some reaction to the question of whether or how well they have understood them, though the quality of the response will reflect the relationship the ethnographer has been able to build up. He or she may be told, simply out of politeness, how brilliantly he or she has grasped the meaning of their words and of their actions. The ancient historian is just confronted by documents and texts, those that have survived the vagaries of transmission and are mostly now buried beneath a pile of previous interpretations.

In both cases we have to be realistic about the level of understanding that can be achieved. But we have also to be realistic about the level of understanding attainable even when the conditions are optimal, when we are dealing with someone who shares with us the same natural language, maybe also the same upbringing and environment. The particular problems of trying to grasp the meaning of some ancient text in a foreign language, or the work of an author as a whole, are mirrored, even if less severely, in our efforts to understand some writing in English. What is it to say that we have grasped the meaning of *King Lear*, let alone of Shakespeare as a whole, or, to come down to today, of Salman

Rushdie or A. S. Byatt? To state the obvious, it is never the question of "the" meaning, just the one, but always of multiple meanings. The point is familiar from religious hermeneutics, and although in that context we may sometimes suspect deliberate mystification, the lesson that readings are open-ended is surely obvious across the board. Not even scientific communications are immune to multiple interpretations.

But if being realistic means we have to acknowledge difficulties, it also means that we should not be unduly pessimistic, which is certainly part of the message Hanks and Severi have insisted upon. One important point about translation and about understanding in general is that, although always difficult and always imperfect, it is seldom (they would say never) the case that we have to admit to complete and utter defeat. That is true even with terms that are admitted to have no exact single equivalent in any but the natural language in which they occur, like German *Gemütlichkeit*, Welsh *hwyl*, Russian *toska*, or Ifaluk *fago*, where we can get at least some inkling of what they cover.[1] No ethnographer returns from the field to say that he or she understood nothing of the society that was the subject of investigation. No student of ancient Greek philosophy admits to understanding Plato not at all. It is only if we have no grasp whatsoever of a particular language that we must admit to total incomprehension, of the words at least, and even then the body language of our interlocutors may leave us in little doubt about some of their feelings.

What the first line of the *Daodejing* means, *dao ke dao fei chang dao*, has been the subject of countless commentaries down the ages in many different languages.[2] But if you have some classical Chinese, you will know, for instance, that *dao* can mean not just "way," but also "guide," that is, show as the way. So while the first *dao* is "the Way," with all its multiple associations, the second *dao* can be taken as "shown as a *dao*," so that the whole says, very roughly, "the Way that can be spoken of as a way is not the constant way." The constant (*chang*) Way is thereby contrasted with others that fail the requirement of constancy, *because* they can be spoken of. That illustrates what an approximate translation can be like, with the added bonus, perhaps, of the substantive message to do with (in) expressibility that this particular famous line conveys.

---

1.   The opacity of those last three terms was discussed in Lloyd (2007: ch. 4).

2.   I discussed the interpretation of this first line of the *Daodejing* in Lloyd (2002: ch. 5).

We can study the range of usage of *dao* and that of *chang*. At that point some might attempt to cordon off "literal" from "metaphorical" or "figurative" uses. But that is one of the dichotomies that cannot be taken for granted. I have rehearsed my reasons for challenging it on other occasions.[3] My preferred alternative is to make use of the notion of "semantic stretch," which has the advantage that it allows that all terms have some stretch. *Dao* may be exceptional: there is a *dao* of butchery and even one of robbery, though it is the *dao* of the Sages to which one aspires. Yet it is as well to make allowance for stretch in every term in any communicative exchange, and that is even before we factor in further complex points from the pragmatics of the situation. When a live conversation is in question, there is the body language of the speakers to consider and the relationships between them, of friendliness or hostility, cooperativeness or competitiveness, superiority or deference.

That may seem to open up an infinite number of options for interpretation, far beyond anything that Wittgenstein contemplated when discussing "family resemblances" in his famous discussion of the concept of "game" (not forgetting his own notion of "language games," e.g., Wittgenstein 1963: paras. 66–71, 83, 86). Yet semantic stretch, so far from precluding progress in understanding, may even be a necessary condition for it. The possibilities in interpretation are not limitless, even when we are faced with the *Daodejing*, but they are liable to be prematurely circumscribed if we start from the assumption that there is just the one, correct, understanding to be secured by homing in on a single "literal" meaning. We must acknowledge that much always escapes us; but that does not mean that we are always in a state of complete bafflement. Reminding ourselves that we may not have got it right is always salutary, but should encourage us not simply to give up in despair, but to renew our efforts. This is of course what we naturally do, at least when we are not inhibited by some sense that we must be able to resolve the philosophical issues before we can even start.

Texts look as if they ought to say something that we shall have some opportunity to construe in other terms, even if that may involve heavy paraphrasing. But what about pieces of music, works of art, ritual performances? We should not say that they do not signify anything, even when, as often, they do not refer.

---

3.   I analyzed the historical background to the introduction of the literal/metaphorical dichotomy in Lloyd (1990: ch. 1), and proposed "semantic stretch" as an alternative in Lloyd (2002: ch. 5). I introduced "multidimensionality" in my sense in Lloyd (2004: ch. 7).

But to begin to put into words what we believe them to signify is always difficult, often seemingly impossible. What Beethoven's Fifth Symphony meant for the different members of the audience whom E. M. Forster described as listening to it in *Howards End* is expressed, in that novel, in what now seem rather jejune terms. But in any case what a piece of music means for one person on one occasion is never going to be precisely what it means for another on that occasion, or even for the same person on a different occasion. Again the hermeneutic temptation is to elide all that diversity to get at some essential, core, understanding, but to do so is always going to be reductionist, always to miss the opportunity to explore other possible resonances and associations.

Warnings as to the difficulty and imperfection of understanding are always needed, but it is amazing how much we *can* understand, including across different languages and dealing with unfamiliar subject-matter. We should never underestimate the capacity of humans to learn and to adapt, even in the face of pressures that urge us to stay with the views and practices of our elders and betters. Sure, we sometimes delude ourselves that we are on the right track. Sure, we are sometimes the victim of deliberate deception on the part of our interlocutors. But that would not be possible if there was *always* deception. Our default assumption is that we are not being deliberately misled by our partners in conversation. Obscurantism, in turn, is only recognizable by contrast with the relatively plain and clear. The very fact that, with the help of an interlocutor, or just on our own, we can improve our grasp of what is being communicated, and correct some of our misunderstandings, should encourage us to continue our efforts, including even in the face of an insistence, on the part of those interlocutors or the apparent message of a text, that what we are dealing with is the inexpressible. *Dao ke dao fei chang dao* takes away with one hand, but gives us something with the other.

It is true that some aspects of modern philosophical discussion of the problems have not helped as much as they might. Quine's inscrutability of reference (Quine 1960) and Kuhn's incommensurable paradigms (Kuhn [1962] 1970) certainly underline the difficulties. But we can concede that ultimately reference is inscrutable without conceding that it is arbitrary. Even if there is always an element of indeterminacy, we can narrow down the possibilities by a process we may compare to bracketing—in particular by excluding what lies outside the brackets. There was no ostrich on the scene when our friend announced "gavagai," while there was indeed a rabbit, so it is less likely that "gavagai" has to do with an ostrich or even temporal ostrich slices than with something to do with rabbits, even though it may not be the creature in mind, but rather the event, or again it may be neither. Even when a rabbit event occurs, there are always plenty of other items and occurrences in the scene that may have occasioned the comment. Faced with the first exclamation "gavagai," the outsider will be baffled: sufficient repetition of the word should get the process of bracketing under way. Similarly I learnt to recognize *hwyl* (roughly, inspired speech) by being exposed to it on many occasions and registering that people acknowledged it in some speakers, but not in others, in some performances, but not in others.

As for Kuhn's incommensurabilities, they do not preclude, but may even presuppose, the possibility of comparison, where at least we can make a start. There is no common measure for the side and the diagonal of a square. But we can certainly say that the diagonal is longer than the side. It is only if both are recognized as lengths that we can say they are incommensurable. We do not bother to remark that there is no common measure between a length and a color, for that involves a straightforward category mistake. Paradigm shifts always pose tough problems of interpretation, especially when the same term, say "force", or "weight," or "mass," comes to be used with quite new senses and referents. But in the stock historical instances used to illustrate such shifts, we should not say there was total lack of comprehension between the parties. Copernicus certainly had a fair grasp of Ptolemy's astronomical system, Galileo of Aristotle's idea of natural motion, Einstein of Newton's classical dynamics, even when the definitions of key terms were being transformed and new ones had to be coined to convey the new understanding.

But while the ideas of Quine and Kuhn have often been construed as threatening to undermine mutual intelligibility, conversely other attempts to come to its defense likewise may suffer from shortcomings. Faced with such famous but much-abused examples as the Nuer belief that twins are birds (Evans-Pritchard 1956) or the Dorze's that the leopard is a Christian animal (Sperber [1974] 1975), some adopt Davidson's hermeneutic principle of charity in interpretation (Davidson 2001), which recommends that whatever statements are reported should be construed, so far as possible, as making sense in our terms.[4] Maybe we can find points of similarity between twins and birds and again between leopard behavior and Christian behavior to see how the reported belief can be made to make sense, without our having to follow those interpreters who have recourse

---

4.   For a recent review of the different ways in which the principle of charity has been taken, see Delpla (2001).

to the idea that the statements were not meant "literally" but only "metaphorically." Trying to decide between those alternatives regularly led to an impasse,
the problem being compounded by the fact that the actors themselves, the Nuer
and the Dorze, had no such explicit categories.

On the one hand, the supposition that those holding what seem to us counterintuitive beliefs are just foolish or irrational obviously will not do as a general
methodological principle. There are fools in every society, not excluding our
own, but attempting to diagnose wholesale folly in whole communities is not
just racist, but hardly compatible with their evident ability to survive, often in
difficult circumstances, including many where the average urbanized citizens
of "advanced" industrial societies would simply perish. Yet that of course is not
to say that every custom and belief that is maintained in any human group is
well adapted to the aims of survival or of flourishing. That would be straightfor-
wardly to commit the functionalist fallacy.

But on the other hand the translation of Nuer or Dorze beliefs into terms
that make sense according to our given categories presupposes that those categories are already up to the job, and there is no reason a priori to go along with
that. Evans-Pritchard was a great ethnographer, but, truth to tell, some of his
interpretations now reek of some of his own preoccupations, theological ones,
perhaps, especially. Faced with those counterintuitive statements, whether in
ethnography or in ancient texts, we may need to revise our own categories and
understandings, quite substantially perhaps, on such matters as the notion of
a person, for instance, or of agency and causation.[5] It cannot be assumed that
our existing concepts will be adequate, and to do so is to miss the opportunities
for learning that ethnography and the study of ancient societies both present. I
believe my exposure to ancient Greek and Chinese ideas has taught me a thing
or two. I shall give an example—nature—shortly.

Such general points are particularly germane to the recent ontological turn
in anthropology, to explorations of radically different ontologies in Descola or

---

5.   Thus the concept of a person, which was already problematized by Mauss (1938),
     has in recent years become even more of a field for contending interpretations (see,
     e.g., Carrithers, Collins, and Lukes 1985). We have been introduced to the notion
     of "fractal persons" and to the view that persons are not individuals but, in the phrase
     made famous by Marilyn Strathern, "dividuals," divisible into multiple components
     formed from relations with others and subject to constant disequilibrium (e.g.,
     Strathern 1988, 1999, 2005; Wagner 1991; Mosko 2010; Viḷaça 2011).

of perspectivism in Viveiros de Castro.[6] In the perspectivism of Viveiros de Castro it is not nature that is universal while cultures differ. Rather, all beings share culture while their natures differ, so this is monoculturalism and multinaturalism as opposed to multiculturalism and mononaturalism. Moreover, the key categories that we might suppose to be given in nature, "animal" and "human" among them, turn out to be inherently relational. For while humans see themselves as human, and animals as animals, and even spirits (if they see them) as spirits, animals see themselves as human and humans as animals whether as predators or as prey (Viveiros de Castro 1998: 470–71; contested, however, by Turner 2009).

Descola ([2005] 2013) invokes some of the same ethnographic data in defining what he calls "animism," but that for him is only one of four different ontological regimes, varying according to the continuity or discontinuity they assume with regard to interiority and physicality. He uses those two differentiae to give him his fourfold schema, animism, totemism, analogism, and naturalism, which he uses to investigate practices of giving, taking, exchange, producing, protecting, and transmitting. While Descola calls these "ontologies," Severi has pointed out that they differ from the philosophical usage of that term in being much looser and less explicit. "What is particularly interesting about them is precisely their unsystematic character, the fact that they always leave a space open for different strategies of thought" (Severi 2013: 195). This was a point he made to drive a wedge between some of my ancient ontologies (Lloyd 2012) and Descola's regimes (ideal types, as Anne-Christine Taylor [2013] has insisted).

The implications of both Descola's and Viveiros de Castro's views for translation and understanding are momentous. From the jaguar's perspective the blood of his prey (as we see it) is manioc beer. This controlled equivocation, as Viveiros de Castro calls it, might appear to a naturalist completely to undermine mutual understanding, to the point where the only thing we can understand is that the jaguar's perception is indeed radically different from "ours," though that is not to say anything about *his* understanding, except that it appears that

---

6. Latour's ([2012] 2013) monograph, stimulated in part by his reflections on the impasse of modernity, introduces further considerable possibilities for the exploration of multiple ontologies. The recent literature on the ontological turn comprises notable contributions, including some revisions of previously held views, by Pedersen (2011, 2012), Heywood (2012), Holbraad (2012), Laidlaw (2012), Laidlaw and Heywood (2012), and Holbraad, Pedersen, and Viveiros de Castro (2014).

jaguars, like us, enjoy drinking "beer." Yet that is to miss the whole point of perspectivism, which is that both the senses and the referents of terms (including "beer") shift across the languages of different kinds of creatures, being relative to the creatures in question, in particular being determined by the bodies they have. Translation is, then, a matter not of finding equivalent words to convey information about a single world, but of identifying different worlds to which the same words apply.

But how is the jaguar's perspective to be accessed? It is only shamans who are in a position confidently to pronounce on that, for they alone can cross species boundaries, which in turn means that what is taken for a jaguar may be a shaman in disguise, or vice versa. It is certainly not easy to know where you are. But that is precisely the fundamental message. Rather than conclude that this difficulty, for us, of accessing others' perspectives undermines the whole enterprise, we should reflect on what we can learn from considering what it would be for persons and substances to be relational, where we can start from, and use as a model, our familiar—banal—acceptance that the same individual can be both father (of one person), brother (of another), and son (of yet another), though in the perspectivist process "the same individual" gets to be radically reinterpreted. The Achuar and the Araweté and many other groups, not limited to Amazonia, of course, hold that other beings besides themselves are defined by the culture, rituals, rules of exchange, and so on, that constitute their way of being in the world. But what each kind of being apprehends depends on the bodies they have.

The same applies, these people would say, to the Whites who come to study them, for they (we) have the customs they (we) have because their (our) bodies are as they are. It is clear that the Achuar and the Araweté themselves puzzle over the Whites studying them. Indeed they can be said to do anthropology on the Whites, as much as the Whites do anthropology on them, as Viveiros de Castro suggested in his *Cannibal metaphysics* ([2009] 2015).[7] But their anthropology does not presuppose the same commonalities and divergences as ours does, for, as I noted, their commonalities relate to culture, their divergences to nature.

---

7.   The trope of indigenous peoples doing anthropology on anthropologists goes back to Rivers (1912), and was taken up by Hocart (1915) in his criticisms of Marett (1912). Cf. Stocking (1996: 236) and Schaffer (2010: 286–87).

Now I must recognize my own limitations in the face of the ethnographic aspects of the issues of translation raised by the "ontological turn." But I do not think it is impossible to bring to bear some historical points from the study of ancient ontologies. At least my investigations of those ontologies prompt me to propose a different way of bypassing the treacherous dichotomy between nature and culture, which was of course what Descola's book set out to transcend and was radically revised by Viveiros de Castro. My historical analysis of how the concepts of nature, *natura*, Greek *phusis*, originate in the West yields what may be a crucial point, that they were very much the product of a particular polemical situation, for which we have direct evidence in Greece.[8]

Those who went into battle, there, under the banner of *phusis* were dubbed the *phusikoi* or natural philosophers (they begin to be prominent in the fifth and fourth centuries BCE), and they claimed "nature" as the domain over which they were to be the acknowledged experts. Where traditionally in Greece such phenomena as earthquakes, thunder and lightning, eclipses, and diseases had generally been assumed to be the work of the gods (they were not *natural* phenomena then), the *phusikoi* argued that that was a category mistake. It was to ignore that those phenomena had regular causes, natures, in fact, that could be investigated; and they, the natural philosophers, could supply the correct theories and explanations (though most of those they proposed were quite fantastical). Where the traditionalists faced with lightning saw Zeus at work, the naturalists spoke of clashing clouds or whatever. Where the traditionalists saw eclipses as omens, the naturalists said they were regular and predictable. And note that in this instance it would be hard to apply the point that these different perceptions were due to differences in the bodies of the actors concerned. We move into a different mode of discourse, one that depends heavily, most would say, on literacy and a certain level of complexity of social organization.

Yet reference to other ancient societies shows that literacy by itself cannot be the whole answer. Ancient China had no single concept that covered what *phusis* covered in Greek or *natura* in Latin, and the same applies to every other ancient society with which I am familiar—Mesopotamia, Egypt, India, though I know far less about them. The Chinese recognized the spontaneous as the spontaneous, heaven and earth as heaven and earth, the different characteristics that different

---

8.   My original proposal that "nature" was invented (not discovered) by the ancient Greeks was first published in my *Methods and problems in Greek science* (Lloyd 1991: ch. 18), though in earlier work (Lloyd 1970) I had indeed talked of a discovery.

creatures (including humans) are born with as those characteristics, and so on. But they were not tempted to suppose that they were dealing with the *same problem* in all those instances. Nor were they tempted to read off value judgments from "nature" as such, even though they certainly debated moral questions and took different views on whether humans are inherently good, bad, or indifferent.[9]

Nature, I conclude, is not natural at all, but a cultural artifact,[10] as much as a political regime or a set of religious beliefs and practices is. And that should release us from any assumption that whatever people thought they were dealing with in the physical world has to correspond to "nature," has to be shoehorned into our category in other words. Of course some idea of the *regularities* in the phenomena *is* universal: we rely on that when we plant crops or light a fire. But *which* phenomena they are, and how exceptions are to be accounted for, are *questions* where we cannot just assume that an explicit concept of nature will provide the answers.

So when I claim that nature is an invention, I am sometimes understood to mean that just the understanding of nature is. But in fact I make a much stronger claim, that our notion of nature is not fit for purpose, but a trap. If we hold that nature is out there waiting to be discovered, we have simply not been critical enough of our own pet assumptions. That is a conclusion that the ontological turn in anthropology partly agrees with, but maybe for different reasons.

So the way I recognize the pluralism in ontologies proceeds rather differently from Descola's or Viveiros de Castro's approach. I agree with them in rejecting the assumed privileged status of a naturalist ontology. But my brand of ontological pluralism is a matter of what I call the multidimensionality of the phenomena or, alternatively, the multidimensionality of reality. It may seem shocking to consider those two formulations interchangeable. But the appearance/reality dichotomy is another one that needs to be pensioned off. In many contexts what is real is what appears, and conversely, though, to be sure, appearances may deceive. But then reality too may hide. The more important point, in both cases, is the possible, indeed the likely, multidimensionality.[11]

---

9. There is a hard-hitting debate between Mencius, Gaozi, and Xunzi on precisely that issue in the fourth and third centuries BCE (see Graham 1989: 117–23, 244–51).

10. Others tackling the problems from other perspectives might agree with this conclusion, though without depending, as I do, on a historical argument.

11. See Viveiros de Castro (2010), where he explored the "multidimensionality of incommensurability."

Let me cite one of my favorite examples, color, to illustrate that multidimensionality.[12] In that case, the three dimensions of hue, luminosity, and saturation provide three different sets of differentiations, although that point is not always taken into account, particularly by those on the hunt for cross-cultural universals. There is no one correct way to talk about color. We should not privilege one of the three ways and exclude the other two. All three are valid, and it is a mistake to think we have to choose between them. That does not mean that this introduces ambiguities that preclude generalization. It is true that a multidimensional phenomenon cannot be given a *per genus et differentiam* definition. But it can and should be given a disjunctive definition, where each of the disjuncts (in the color case, hue, luminosity, and saturation) can be identified unambiguously, though each has its considerable semantic stretch.

But if thus far my position is "relativist," it is not at all relativist insofar as I recognize that in each case there are more or less correct ways of doing the differentiations. Color talk is certainly not merely arbitrary: it is not the case there (or anywhere else) that just anything goes, whatever Feyerabend may have claimed. Nor is it impossible to allow communication between different modes of color talk, even though the particular vocabulary for the particular differentiations in view may be distinctive for that particular mode. Multidimensionality does not rule out mutual intelligibility. In this case it may even be a necessary condition for it.

The consequences for translation and understanding go like this. A vocabulary that simply differentiates hues will not by itself be up to the task of capturing the other two modes of differentiation. Thus far translation is not possible if we stick to that single vocabulary. But why should we have to? What we need is complementary modes of discourse to do justice to all three dimensions of differentiation, yielding a more comprehensive understanding of the subject-matter. But then there is nothing to prevent our conveying the complementary character of the phenomena in different natural languages, with more or less adequate translations between them. In some cases neologisms will be needed. In many cases the idiosyncratic range of particular color terms in one language will need a gloss or a paraphrase in another: the French "brun" is an odd-ball from an Anglo-Saxon point of view, and so too is "blond" used of tobacco and of beer. But of course the phenomenon is not confined to French: ancient

12. Lloyd (2007: ch. 1) discusses the problem with some background information concerning earlier and ongoing controversies.

Greek *xanthon* and *chlōron* (conventionally inadequately rendered as "yellow" and "green") are other examples. *Chlōron*, for instance, denotes what is fresh, unripe, full of sap.

In many cases what may be represented as color terms may come to be seen as not color terms at all, but rather terms to pick out the living from the dead, or the succulent from the dry.[13] Within a single natural language, there will be shifts between one register and another, and other possible sources of ambiguity. But at least we shall not be driven, as the former British prime minister William Gladstone thought he was driven, from the observation that ancient Greek focused especially on luminosity to conclude that they were all color blind and could not distinguish hues (Gladstone 1877). He never read, or if he read, he ignored, Aristotle on the rainbow.

Where, I may now ask more generally, do my suggestions leave the epistemology of anthropology or of ancient history? Does the ontological turn in anthropology spell the demise of its epistemology (as some have thought), leaving us perhaps with the conclusion that epistemologies are relative to the distinctive ontologies in play? Once again that gestures toward a conclusion of mutual unintelligibility. But once again that may be resisted.

It is true that the traditional dichotomies or dualisms within epistemology, between reason and perception, or between the a priori and the empirical, once again exhibit their limitations if considered as alternatives. But the correct response is not to abandon both sides of each pair, nor to plump for one to the exclusion of the other, but to combine them. That corresponds to my own practice here, for on the one hand I have been discussing what understanding is possible on the basis of an abstract analysis, but on the other I do that with as much attention as I can manage to empirical case histories which can act as a check on where the analysis needs correcting and complexifying. Epistemology, on this view, is not the bogey man it has been represented as being by those who suspect that it is merely a covert way of denying others' claims to know. The multidimensionality of what is there to be known cannot help but generate a multidimensionality of ways of knowing.

But several possibly fundamental objections to my use of those notions of multidimensionality and of semantic stretch must now be met in conclusion. First it might be argued that I am still trapped in my own particular conceptual framework, even that everyone always is. Is it not the case that others' categories

---

13. This was a point that I argued against Berlin and Kay (1969) in Lloyd (2007: ch. 1).

either will be reduced to mine, or will forever remain beyond reach? Of course my particular conceptual resources are whatever they are at any moment in time (though I can see they have changed over time, as I said). But my answer to that first question would be to reject the alternative. Provided I am indeed allowed the point that conceptual frameworks (like languages themselves) are revisable, reductionism can be avoided.

Then a second objection might be that I am somehow presupposing some transcendent metalanguage into which all others can be parsed, which surely savors of Western hegemonic pretensions: give me a place to stand and I can move the world. Again I would resist, for I would claim both that I allow a voice to each pluralist rendering of multidimensionality, and that I recognize the revisability, indeed the imperfections, of my own understanding. A single metalanguage, let alone one that imposes a rule of strict univocity, is a chimera; rather, we can and should exploit the full resources of every understanding to which we can have access, and that will include those expressed in actions rather than words.[14]

I am reminded of a Chinese story in *Zhuangzi* (13: see Graham 1989: 187) about carpenter Bian. He had the cheek to reprimand his employer, Duke Huan, for reading old books. The Duke protests: "What business is it of a carpenter to criticize what I read? If you can explain yourself, well and good, but if not, you die." Whereupon Bian refers to his own work as a carpenter. When he makes a wheel, if he chips at it too slowly, the chisel slips and does not grip; but if he is too fast, the chisel jams and catches in the wood. The right way to do it is something he feels in his hands but he cannot put it into words. That is how one becomes an expert carpenter, and the books of the past are just "dregs." In such a case the feeling is the understanding.

However, even if we reject the notion of a metalanguage, the problem does not go away, indeed it might be thought aggravated by that rejection. How, I asked, is any translation *across* ontologies to be achieved? It is all very well, some will say, to insist that reality is multidimensional and that every term exhibits some degree of semantic stretch, but how does that bridge the gulf between divergent perspectives? If we reject the realist option, according to which only one ontology is correct, and the others must be dismissed as mistaken, are we

---

14. Again this point was emphatically made by Wittgenstein (1963) and has been taken up by many others, notably by Ingold (2000) and the contributors to Henare, Holbraad and Wastell (2007).

not forced to the relativist view, according to which not only should we say all are correct, but also that there is no neutral way of judging them?

Once again that dichotomy obstructs a resolution. The multidimensional move would have it first that each ontology deals with a particular manner of ordering reality, including the key considerations of interiority and physicality. Secondly each may do so in a more or less satisfactory, and certainly not arbitrary, way. But more or less satisfactory to whom? In the first instance, of course, to the actors themselves, to the Achuar and the Araweté and to all those others whose cosmologies have been explored by the ethnographers, allowing, as before, that some are more explicit and comprehensive than others. But it is up to observers, to us, to see what we can learn from the exercise of investigating their ways of being in the world. That means suspending disbelief and being prepared to revise just about everything we normally take for granted about those key concepts of person, agency, causation, space, time and, yes, certainly, nature. Clearly we must abandon the assumption that reality is a given, to which unmediated access is possible. Yet neither actors nor observers will settle for "anything goes."

But then does that not amount to some wishy-washy politically correct liberal relativism? Not if we can still provide for the possibility of diagnosing error in ourselves and others, allowing that both of those are tricky—for different reasons, for we may be insufficiently self-critical in the first case and overcritical in the second. But evidently we are not infallible, no more was any given ancient Greek or Chinese thinker, no more are present-day Achuar or Araweté. But before we conclude that we or they have made a mistake, we have first to consider the complexities of interpretation that I have been talking about, and there may always be an element of doubt about how thorough that exploration has been. In many cases we may say it can never be complete. But in some simple ones it is certainly possible to draw a line and to reassure ourselves that the job has been adequately done at least for the occasion in question. We have to get on with our everyday transactions, and indeed we do so.

Of course it is up to other researchers, not just ethnographers and ancient historians, but also linguists, cognitive scientists, evolutionary psychologists, to react to these proposals. I attempt no general theory of translation, of course, let alone a general formula for how understanding is possible. But I offer these thoughts as suggestions about what can reasonably be expected and about how one can go about the job. The very open-endedness of translation may look to be a menace to mutual intelligibility; but that is only so if we hanker after definitive results. Abandoning that will of the wisp, we can rather welcome that open-endedness as a positive resource for increasing understanding.

REFERENCES

Berlin, Brent, and Paul Kay. 1969. *Basic color terms: Their universality and evolution*. Berkeley: University of California Press.

Carrithers, Michael, Steven Collins, and Steven Lukes, eds. 1985. *The category of the person*. Cambridge: Cambridge University Press.

Davidson, Donald. 2001. *Essays on actions and events*. Second edition. Oxford: Clarendon Press.

Delpla, Isabelle. 2001. *Quine, Davidson: Le principe de charité*. Paris: Presses Universitaires de France.

Descola, Philippe. (2005) 2013. *Beyond nature and culture*. Translated by Janet Lloyd. Chicago: University of Chicago Press.

Evans-Pritchard, Edward E. 1956. *Nuer religion*. Oxford: Clarendon Press.

Gladstone, William E. 1877. "The colour sense." *The Nineteenth Century* 2: 360–88.

Graham, Angus C. 1989. *Disputers of the Tao*. La Salle, IL: Open Court.

Henare, Amiria, Martin Holbraad, and Sari Wastell, eds. 2007. *Thinking through things: Theorizing artefacts ethnographically*. London: Routledge.

Heywood, Paolo. 2012. "Anthropology and what there is: Reflections on 'ontology.'" *Cambridge Anthropology* 30: 143–51.

Hocart, Arthur M. 1915. "Psychology and ethnology." *Folk-Lore* 26: 115–37.

Holbraad, Martin. 2012. *Truth in motion*. Chicago: University of Chicago Press.

Holbraad, Martin, Morten Axel Pedersen, and Eduardo Viveiros de Castro. 2014. "The politics of ontology: Anthropological positions." *Fieldsights—Theorizing the Contemporary, Cultural Anthropology Online*. January 13. http://culanth. org./ fieldsights/ 462-the-politics-of-ontology-anthropological-positions.

Ingold, Tim. 2000. *The perception of the environment*. London: Routledge.

Kuhn, Thomas S. (1962) 1970. *The structure of scientific revolutions*. Revised edition. Chicago: University of Chicago Press.

Laidlaw, James. 2012. "Ontologically challenged." *Anthropology of This Century* 4. http://aotcpress.com/articles/ontologically-challenged.

Laidlaw, James, and Paolo Heywood. 2012. "One more turn and you're there." *Anthropology of This Century* 5. http://aotcpress.com/articles/turn.

Latour, Bruno. (2012) 2013. *An inquiry into modes of existence.* Translated by Catherine Porter. Cambridge, MA: Harvard University Press.

Lloyd, Geoffrey E. R. 1970. *Early Greek science: Thales to Aristotle.* London: Chatto & Windus.

———. 1990. *Demystifying mentalities.* Cambridge: Cambridge University Press.

———. 1991. *Methods and problems in Greek science.* Cambridge: Cambridge University Press.

———. 2002. *The ambitions of curiosity.* Cambridge: Cambridge University Press.

———. 2004. *Ancient worlds, modern reflections.* Oxford: Clarendon Press.

———. 2007. *Cognitive variations.* Oxford: Oxford University Press.

———. 2012. *Being, humanity, and understanding.* Oxford: Oxford University Press.

Marett, Robert R. 1912. "The study of magico-religious facts." In *Notes and queries on anthropology,* edited by Barbara W. Freire-Marreco and John L. Myres, 251–60. Fourth edition. London: Royal Anthropological Institute.

Mauss, Marcel. 1938. "Une catégorie de l'esprit humain: La notion de personne, celle de 'moi.' Un plan de travail." *Journal of the Royal Anthropological Institute* 68: 263–81.

Mosko, Mark. 2010. "Partible penitents: Dividual personhood and Christian practice in Melanesia and the West." *Journal of the Royal Anthropological Institute* (N.S.) 16: 215–40.

Pedersen, Morten A. 2011. *Not quite shamans: Spirit worlds and political lives in northern Mongolia.* Ithaca, NY: Cornell University Press.

———. 2012. "Common nonsense: A review of certain recent reviews of the 'ontological turn.'" *Anthropology of This Century* 5. http://aotcpress.com/articles/common_nonsense.

Quine, Willard van Orman. 1960. *Word and object.* Cambridge, MA: MIT Press.

Rivers, William H. R. 1912. "The primitive conception of death." *Hibbert Journal* 10: 393–407.

Schaffer, Simon. 2010. "Opposition is true friendship." *Interdisciplinary Science Reviews* 35: 277–90.

Severi, Carlo. 2013. "Philosophies without ontology." *HAU: Journal of Ethnographic Theory* 3: 192–96.

Sperber, Dan. (1974) 1975. *Rethinking symbolism.* Translated by Alice L. Morton. Cambridge: Cambridge University Press.

Stocking, George W. 1996. *After Tylor: British social anthropology 1888–1951.* London: Athlone.

Strathern, Marilyn. 1988. *The gender of the gift.* Berkeley: University of California Press.

———. 1999. *Property, substance and effect: Anthropological essays on persons and things.* London: Athlone.

———. 2005. *Kinship, law and the unexpected.* Cambridge: Cambridge University Press.

Taylor, Anne-Christine. 2013. "Distinguishing ontologies." *HAU: Journal of Ethnographic Theory* 3: 201–4.

Turner, Terence S. 2009. "The crisis of late structuralism. Perspectivism and animism: Rethinking culture, nature, spirit and bodiliness." *Tipití: Journal of the Society for the Anthropology of Lowland South America* 7: 1–42.

Vilaça, Aparecida. 2011. "Dividuality in Amazonia: God, the Devil and the constitution of personhood in Wari' Christianity." *Journal of the Royal Anthropological Institute* (N.S.) 17: 243–62.

Viveiros de Castro, Eduardo. 1998. "Cosmological deixis and Amerindian perspectivism." *Journal of the Royal Anthropological Institute* (N.S.) 4: 469–88.

———. (2009) 2015. *Cannibal metaphysics.* Translated by Peter Skafish. Minneapolis: Univocal.

———. 2010. "In some sense." *Interdisciplinary Science Reviews* 3–4: 318–33.

Wagner, Roy. 1991. "The fractal person." In *Big men and great men*, edited by Maurice Godelier and Marilyn Strathern, 159–73. Cambridge: Cambridge University Press.

Wittgenstein, Ludwig. 1963. *Philosophical investigations.* Translated by G. E. M. Anscombe. Reprinted second edition. Oxford: Blackwell.

Index

HAU Books is committed to publishing the most distinguished texts in classic and advanced anthropological theory. The titles aim to situate ethnography as the prime heuristic of anthropology, and return it to the forefront of conceptual developments in the discipline. HAU Books is sponsored by some of the world's most distinguished anthropology departments and research institutions, and releases its titles in both print editions and open-access formats.

www.haubooks.com